Communications in Computer and Information Science   **2256**

Series Editors

Gang Li , *School of Information Technology, Deakin University, Burwood, VIC, Australia*
Joaquim Filipe, *Polytechnic Institute of Setúbal, Setúbal, Portugal*
Zhiwei Xu, *Chinese Academy of Sciences, Beijing, China*

AF173479

Rationale

The CCIS series is devoted to the publication of proceedings of computer science conferences. Its aim is to efficiently disseminate original research results in informatics in printed and electronic form. While the focus is on publication of peer-reviewed full papers presenting mature work, inclusion of reviewed short papers reporting on work in progress is welcome, too. Besides globally relevant meetings with internationally representative program committees guaranteeing a strict peer-reviewing and paper selection process, conferences run by societies or of high regional or national relevance are also considered for publication.

Topics

The topical scope of CCIS spans the entire spectrum of informatics ranging from foundational topics in the theory of computing to information and communications science and technology and a broad variety of interdisciplinary application fields.

Information for Volume Editors and Authors

Publication in CCIS is free of charge. No royalties are paid, however, we offer registered conference participants temporary free access to the online version of the conference proceedings on SpringerLink (http://link.springer.com) by means of an http referrer from the conference website and/or a number of complimentary printed copies, as specified in the official acceptance email of the event.

CCIS proceedings can be published in time for distribution at conferences or as post-proceedings, and delivered in the form of printed books and/or electronically as USBs and/or e-content licenses for accessing proceedings at SpringerLink. Furthermore, CCIS proceedings are included in the CCIS electronic book series hosted in the SpringerLink digital library at http://link.springer.com/bookseries/7899. Conferences publishing in CCIS are allowed to use Online Conference Service (OCS) for managing the whole proceedings lifecycle (from submission and reviewing to preparing for publication) free of charge.

Publication process

The language of publication is exclusively English. Authors publishing in CCIS have to sign the Springer CCIS copyright transfer form, however, they are free to use their material published in CCIS for substantially changed, more elaborate subsequent publications elsewhere. For the preparation of the camera-ready papers/files, authors have to strictly adhere to the Springer CCIS Authors' Instructions and are strongly encouraged to use the CCIS LaTeX style files or templates.

Abstracting/Indexing

CCIS is abstracted/indexed in DBLP, Google Scholar, EI-Compendex, Mathematical Reviews, SCImago, Scopus. CCIS volumes are also submitted for the inclusion in ISI Proceedings.

How to start

To start the evaluation of your proposal for inclusion in the CCIS series, please send an e-mail to ccis@springer.com

Hamid R. Arabnia · Masami Takata ·
Leonidas Deligiannidis · Pablo Rivas ·
Masahito Ohue · Nobuaki Yasuo
Editors

Parallel and Distributed Processing Techniques

30th International Conference, PDPTA 2024, Held as Part
of the World Congress in Computer Science, Computer
Engineering and Applied Computing, CSCE 2024
Las Vegas, NV, USA, July 22–25, 2024, Revised Selected Papers

Springer

Editors
Hamid R. Arabnia (ID)
The University of Georgia
Athens, GA, USA

Masami Takata (ID)
Nara Women's University
Nara, Japan

Leonidas Deligiannidis (ID)
Wentworth Institute of Technology
Boston, MA, USA

Pablo Rivas (ID)
Baylor University
Waco, TX, USA

Masahito Ohue (ID)
Tokyo Institute of Technology
Meguro City, Japan

Nobuaki Yasuo (ID)
Tokyo Institute of Technology
Meguro City, Japan

ISSN 1865-0929   ISSN 1865-0937 (electronic)
Communications in Computer and Information Science
ISBN 978-3-031-85637-2   ISBN 978-3-031-85638-9 (eBook)
https://doi.org/10.1007/978-3-031-85638-9

© The Editor(s) (if applicable) and The Author(s), under exclusive license
to Springer Nature Switzerland AG 2025

This work is subject to copyright. All rights are solely and exclusively licensed by the Publisher, whether the whole or part of the material is concerned, specifically the rights of translation, reprinting, reuse of illustrations, recitation, broadcasting, reproduction on microfilms or in any other physical way, and transmission or information storage and retrieval, electronic adaptation, computer software, or by similar or dissimilar methodology now known or hereafter developed.
The use of general descriptive names, registered names, trademarks, service marks, etc. in this publication does not imply, even in the absence of a specific statement, that such names are exempt from the relevant protective laws and regulations and therefore free for general use.
The publisher, the authors and the editors are safe to assume that the advice and information in this book are believed to be true and accurate at the date of publication. Neither the publisher nor the authors or the editors give a warranty, expressed or implied, with respect to the material contained herein or for any errors or omissions that may have been made. The publisher remains neutral with regard to jurisdictional claims in published maps and institutional affiliations.

This Springer imprint is published by the registered company Springer Nature Switzerland AG
The registered company address is: Gewerbestrasse 11, 6330 Cham, Switzerland

If disposing of this product, please recycle the paper.

Preface

It is our great pleasure to introduce this collection of selected papers presented at the 30th International Conference on Parallel & Distributed Processing Techniques & Applications (PDPTA 2024). The conference was held as part of the federated 2024 Congress on Computer Science, Computer Engineering, and Applied Computing (CSCE 2024), which took place from July 22 to July 25, 2024, in Las Vegas, Nevada, USA.

The CSCE 2024 Congress brought together papers from a diverse array of communities, including researchers from universities, corporations, and government agencies. Accepted papers are published by Springer Nature, and the proceedings showcase solutions to key challenges in various critical areas of Computer Science, Computer Engineering, and Applied Computing.

Computer Science (CS) is the study of computational systems, data processing, information management, and automation. Many applications in CS focus on solving problems that would be impossible or extremely difficult to address without the use of computers. It serves as a bridge between computational science and other scientific fields. The interdisciplinary nature of CS involves leveraging computers to understand and solve complex challenges, making it the science of using computers to advance scientific discovery. Computer Engineering (CE), on the other hand, integrates aspects of computer science, electronic engineering, and electrical engineering. It encompasses the design and production of computer hardware, such as chips, servers, supercomputers, embedded systems, and communication systems, among others.

Considering the above broad outline, the CSCE 2024 Congress was composed of the following focused conferences:

Applied Cognitive Computing (ACC); Bioinformatics & Computational Biology (BIOCOMP); Biomedical Engineering (BIOENG); Scientific Computing (CSC); e-Learning, e-Business, Enterprise Information Systems, & e-Government (EEE); Embedded Systems, Cyber-physical Systems, & Applications (ESCS); Foundations of Computer Science (FCS); Frontiers in Education (FECS); Grid, Cloud, & Cluster Computing (GCC); Health Informatics (HIMS); Artificial Intelligence (ICAI); Data Science (ICDATA); Emergent Quantum Technologies (ICEQT); Internet Computing & IoT (ICOMP); Wireless Networks (ICWN); Information & Knowledge Engineering (IKE); Image Processing, Computer Vision, & Pattern Recognition (IPCV); Modeling, Simulation & Visualization Methods (MSV); Parallel & Distributed Processing Techniques & Applications (PDPTA); Security & Management (SAM); and Software Engineering Research & Practice (SERP). The scope of each track can be found at: https://www.american-cse.org/csce2024/conferences

The primary objective of the CSCE Congress and its associated conferences is to foster opportunities for cross-fertilization between the fields of Computer Science (CS) and Computer Engineering (CE). The CSCE Congress is deeply committed to promoting diversity and eliminating discrimination, both in its role as a conference organizer and as a service provider. Our goal is to create an inclusive culture that respects and values differences, promotes dignity, equality, and diversity, and encourages individuals to reach their full potential. We are also dedicated, wherever possible, to organizing a conference that represents the global community. We sincerely hope that we have succeeded in achieving these important objectives.

The Steering Committee and the Program Committees would like to extend their gratitude to all the authors who submitted papers for consideration. This year's conferences received submissions from 52 countries, with approximately 50% of them coming from outside the USA. Each submitted paper underwent a rigorous peer-review process, with at least two experts (an average of 2.3 referees per paper) evaluating the submissions based on originality, significance, clarity, impact, and soundness. In cases where reviewers' recommendations were contradictory, a program committee member was tasked with making the final decision, often consulting additional referees for further guidance. The Congress followed the guidelines of COPE (Committee on Publication Ethics):

- Typical submissions underwent a single-blind peer review process, in which the authors remained unaware of the identities of the reviewers, while the reviewers were informed of the authors' identities.
- Papers authored by one or more members of the program committee, including co-chairs, were subjected to a double-blind peer review process, ensuring that neither the authors nor the reviewers were aware of each other's identities or affiliations.

The PDPTA 2024 Conference received 143 submissions, of which 24 full and 4 short papers were accepted, resulting in a paper acceptance rate of 19.6%.

We are deeply grateful to the many colleagues who contributed their time and effort to organizing the Congress. In particular, we extend our thanks to the members of the Program Committees, the Steering Committee, the referees, and the Chairs and organizers of individual sessions and conferences. We would also like to express our appreciation to the primary sponsor of the conference, the American Council on Science & Education. The list of members of the Program Committee for each track can be found at: https://www.american-cse.org/csce2024/committees

We extend our heartfelt gratitude to all the speakers and authors for their valuable contributions. We would also like to thank the following individuals and organizations for their support: the staff at the Luxor Hotel, the staff of Springer Nature Soheyla Amirian (Pace University), Farzan Shenavarmasouleh (Medialab Inc., USA), and Farid Ghareh Mohammadi (Mayo Clinic, USA) for their assistance in various aspects of the event.

We are pleased to present a curated selection of papers from PDPTA 2024. This book represents a collection of outstanding research contributions that reflect the diversity and depth of work in core areas of HPC, Parallel and Distributed Processing, Algorithms, Computational Science, and Applications.

Hamid R. Arabnia
Masami Takata
Leonidas Deligiannidis
Pablo Rivas
Masahito Ohue
Nobuaki Yasuo

Organization

Steering Committee – Co-chairs (CSCE 2024)

Hamid R. Arabnia	University of Georgia, USA
Leonidas Deligiannidis	Wentworth Institute of Technology, USA
Fernando G. Tinetti	Universidad Nacional de La Plata, Argentina
Quoc-Nam Tran	Southeastern Louisiana University, USA

Co-Editors of PDPTA 2024, GCC 2024, ICEQT 2024, and MSV 2024 Proceedings – Publication Co-chairs

Hamid R. Arabnia (Co-chair, PDPTA 2024, GCC 2024, MSV 2024)	University of Georgia, USA
Masami Takata (Co-chair, PDPTA 2024)	Nara Women's University, Japan
Leonidas Deligiannidis (Co-chair, PDPTA 2024, ICEQT 2024, MSV 2024)	Wentworth Institute of Technology, USA
Pablo Rivas (Chair, ICEQT 2024)	Baylor University, USA
Masahito Ohue (Co-chair, PDPTA 2024)	Tokyo Institute of Technology, Japan
Nobuaki Yasuo (Co-chair, PDPTA 2024)	Tokyo Institute of Technology, Japan

Members of Steering Committee (CSCE 2024)

Babak Akhgar	Sheffield Hallam University, UK
Abbas M. Al-Bakry	University of IT & Communications, Iraq
Emeritus Nizar Al-Holou	University of Detroit Mercy, USA
Hamid R. Arabnia	University of Georgia, USA
Rajab Challoo	Texas A&M University-Kingsville, USA
Chien-Fu Cheng	Tamkang University, Taiwan
Hyunseung Choo	Sungkyunkwan University, South Korea
Kevin Daimi	University of Detroit Mercy, USA
Leonidas Deligiannidis	Wentworth Institute of Technology, USA

Eman M. El-Sheikh	University of West Florida, USA
Mary Mehrnoosh Eshaghian-Wilner	University of California Los Angeles, USA
David L. Foster	Kettering University, USA
Henry Hexmoor	Southern Illinois University at Carbondale, USA
Ching-Hsien (Robert) Hsu	Chung Hua University, Taiwan; and Tianjin University of Technology, China
James J. (Jong Hyuk) Park	SeoulTech, South Korea
Mohammad S. Obaidat	University of Jordan, Jordan
Marwan Omar	Illinois Institute of Technology, USA
Shahram Rahimi	Mississippi State University, USA
Gerald Schaefer	Loughborough University, UK
Fernando G. Tinetti	Universidad Nacional de La Plata, Argentina
Quoc-Nam Tran	Southeastern Louisiana University, USA
Shiuh-Jeng Wang	Central Police University, Taiwan
Layne T. Watson	Virginia Polytechnic Institute & State University, USA
Chao-Tung Yang	Tunghai University, Taiwan
Mary Yang	University of Arkansas, USA

Research Tracks – Co-chairs (CSCE 2024)

Abeer Alsadoon (Co-chair, Health Informatics)	Charles Sturt University, Australia
Soheyla Amirian (Co-chair, Computer Vision & AI)	Pace University, USA
Hamid R. Arabnia (Co-chair, HPC)	University of Georgia, USA
Kevin Daimi (Co-chair, Security)	University of Detroit Mercy, USA
Leonidas Deligiannidis (Co-chair, Imaging Science, AI)	Wentworth Institute of Technology, USA
Richard Dill (Co-chair, Military and Defense Modeling)	US Air Force Institute of Technology, USA
Ken Ferens (Co-chair, Cognitive Computing & AI)	University of Manitoba, Canada
David de la Fuente (Co-chair, Information Management)	University of Oviedo, Spain
Farid Ghareh Mohammadi (Co-chair, Computer Vision & AI)	Mayo Clinic, USA

Michael R. Grimaila (Co-chair, Military and Defense Modeling)	US Air Force Institute of Technology, USA
Douglas D. Hodson (Co-chair, Military and Defense Modeling)	US Air Force Institute of Technology, USA
Masahito Ohue (Co-chair, Mathematical Modeling)	Tokyo Institute of Technology, Japan
Jose A. Olivas (Co-chair, Information Management)	University of Castilla - La Mancha, Spain
Javier Ordus (Co-chair, Quantum Computing & AI)	Baylor University, USA
Pablo Rivas (Chair, Quantum Computing & AI)	Baylor University, USA
Farzan Shenavarmasouleh (Co-chair, Computer Vision & AI)	MediaLab Inc., USA
Robert Stahlbock (Co-chair, Data Mining)	Universität Hamburg, Germany
Masami Takata (Co-chair, Mathematical Modeling)	Nara Women's University, Japan
Quoc-Nam Tran (Co-chair, Education & Bioinformatics)	Southeastern Louisiana University, USA
Nobuaki Yasuo (Co-chair, Mathematical Modeling)	Tokyo Institute of Technology, Japan

PDPTA 2024 Program Committee – Parallel and Distributed Processing Techniques and Applications

Hamid R. Arabnia	University of Georgia, USA
Juan-Vicente Capella-Hernandez	Universitat Politècnica de València, Spain
Juan Jose Martinez Castillo	Universidad Nacional Abierta, Venezuela
Kevin Daimi	University of Detroit Mercy, USA
Leonidas Deligiannidis	Wentworth Institute of Technology, USA
Richard Dill (Co-chair, Military and Defense Modeling)	US Air Force Institute of Technology, USA
Mary Mehrnoosh Eshaghian-Wilner	University of Southern California, California, USA; and University of California Los Angeles, USA
Michael R. Grimaila (Co-chair, Military and Defense Modeling)	US Air Force Institute of Technology, USA

Houcine Hassan	Universitat Politècnica de València, Spain
Douglas D. Hodson (Co-chair, Military and Defense Modeling)	US Air Force Institute of Technology, USA
Hiroshi Ishii	Tokai University, Japan
Makoto Iwata	Kochi University of Technology, Japan
George Jandieri	Georgian Technical University, Georgia
Kazuki Joe	Nara Women's University, Japan
Byung-Gyu Kim	Sun Moon University, South Korea
Tai-hoon Kim	University of Tasmania, Australia
Guoming Lai	Sun Yat-sen University, China
Hyo Jong Lee	Chonbuk National University, South Korea
Andrew Marsh	HoIP Telecom Ltd, UK
Salahuddin Mohammad Masum	Southwest Tennessee Community College, USA
Ali Mostafaeipour	California State University, Fullerton, USA
Hiroaki Nishikawa	University of Tsukuba, Japan
Robert Ehimen Okonigene	Ambrose Alli University, Nigeria
Masahito Ohue	Tokyo Institute of Technology, Japan
Javier Ordus (Co-chair, Quantum Computing & AI)	Baylor University, USA
James J. (Jong Hyuk) Park	SeoulTech, South Korea
Pablo Rivas (Co-Chair, Quantum Computing & AI)	Baylor University, USA
Masakazu Sekijima	Tokyo Institute of Technology, Japan
Manik Sharma	DAV University, India
Hayaru Shouno	University of Electro-Communications, Japan
Ashu M. G. Solo (Publicity)	Maverick Technologies America Inc., USA
Masami Takata (Co-chair, Mathematical Modeling)	Nara Women's University, Japan
Fernando G. Tinetti	Universidad Nacional de La Plata, Argentina
Hahanov Vladimir	Kharkiv National University of Radio Electronics, Ukraine
Haoxiang Harry Wang	Cornell University, USA; and GoPerception Laboratory, USA
Shiuh-Jeng Wang	Central Police University, Taiwan
Layne T. Watson	Virginia Polytechnic Institute & State University, USA
Heng (Fred) Wu	West Virginia State University, USA
Nobuaki Yasuo	Tokyo Institute of Technology, Japan
Jane You	Hong Kong Polytechnic University, China

GCC 2024 Program Committee – Grid, Cloud, and Cluster Computing

Emeritus Nizar Al-Holou	University of Detroit Mercy, USA
Hamid R. Arabnia	University of Georgia, USA
Juan-Vicente Capella-Hernandez	Universitat Politècnica de València, Spain
Kevin Daimi	University of Detroit Mercy, USA
Leonidas Deligiannidis	Wentworth Institute of Technology, USA
Mary Mehrnoosh Eshaghian-Wilner	University of Southern California; and University of California Los Angeles, Los Angeles, USA
Hyo Jong Lee	Chonbuk National University, South Korea
Houssem Eddine Nouri	Institut Supérieur de Gestion de Tunis, University of Tunis, Tunisia
Robert Ehimen Okonigene	Ambrose Alli University, Nigeria
Ashu M. G. Solo (Publicity)	Maverick Technologies America Inc., USA
Fernando G. Tinetti	Universidad Nacional de La Plata, Argentina
Layne T. Watson	Virginia Polytechnic Institute & State University, USA
Jane You	Hong Kong Polytechnic University, China
Farhana H. Zulkernine	Queen's University, Canada

ICEQT 2024 Program/Organizing Committee – Emergent Quantum Technologies

Hamid R. Arabnia	University of Georgia, USA
Leonidas Deligiannidis	Wentworth Institute of Technology, USA
Bikram Khanal (Co-chair)	Baylor University, USA
Javier Ordus	Baylor University, USA
Pablo Rivas (Chair)	Baylor University, USA

MSV 2024 Program Committee – Modeling, Simulation and Visualization Methods

Nizar Al-Holou	University of Detroit Mercy, USA
Hamid R. Arabnia	University of Georgia, USA
Kevin Daimi	University of Detroit Mercy, USA
Leonidas Deligiannidis	Wentworth Institute of Technology, USA
Richard Dill (Co-chair, Military and Defense Modeling)	US Air Force Institute of Technology, USA

Michael R. Grimaila (Co-chair, Military and Defense Modeling)	US Air Force Institute of Technology, USA
Douglas D. Hodson (Co-chair, Military and Defense Modeling)	US Air Force Institute of Technology, USA
Byung-Gyu Kim	Sun Moon University, South Korea
Hyo Jong Lee	Chonbuk National University, South Korea
Muhammad Naufal Bin Mansor	Universiti Malaysia Perlis, Malaysia
Aree Ali Mohammed	University of Sulaimani, Iraq
James J. (Jong Hyuk) Park	SeoulTech, South Korea
Xuewei Qi	University of California, Riverside, USA
Ashu M. G. Solo (Publicity)	Maverick Technologies America Inc., USA
Masami Takata (Co-chair, Mathematical Modeling)	Nara Women's University, Japan
Fernando G. Tinetti	Universidad Nacional de La Plata, Argentina
Haoxiang Harry Wang	Cornell University, USA; and GoPerception Laboratory, USA
Shiuh-Jeng Wang	Central Police University, Taiwan
Layne T. Watson	Virginia Polytechnic Institute & State University, USA
Heng (Fred) Wu	West Virginia State University, USA
Jane You	Hong Kong Polytechnic University, China

Contents

Workshop on Mathematical Modeling and Problem Solving (MPS)

Parallel and Distributed Processing Techniques and Applications + HPC (PDPTA)

A Methodical Approach to Parallel IO Analysis in Distributed Deep Learning Applications

Edixon Parraga[1]([✉]) [iD], Betzabeth Leon[1] [iD], Sandra Mendez[2] [iD],
Dolores Rexachs[1] [iD], Remo Suppi[1] [iD], and Emilio Luque[1] [iD]

[1] Computer Architecture and Operating Systems Department, Universitat
Autònoma de Barcelona (UAB), Bellaterra, Barcelona, Spain
{edixon.parraga,betzabeth.leon,dolores.rexachs,
remo.suppi,emilio.luque}@uab.es
[2] Computer Sciences Department, Barcelona Supercomputing Center (BSC),
Barcelona, Spain
sandra.mendez@bsc.es

Abstract. Deep learning applications have become crucially important
for the analysis and prediction of massive volumes of data. However, these
applications impose substantial input/output (I/O) loads on computing
systems. Specifically, when running on distributed memory systems, they
manage large amounts of data that must be accessed from parallel file
systems during the training stage using the available I/O software stack.
These accesses are inherently intensive and highly concurrent, which can
saturate systems and adversely impact application performance. Consequently, the challenge lies in efficiently utilizing the I/O system to allow
these applications to scale. When the volume of data increases, access can
generate high training latency and add overhead significantly when data
exceeds the main memory capacity. Therefore, it is essential to analyze
the behavior of the I/O patterns generated during the training stage
by reading the data set to analyze the behavior when the application
scales and what amount of resources it will need. The paper presents a
methodology to analyze parallel I/O patterns in Deep Learning applications in this context. Our methodological approach mainly aims at
providing users with complete and accurate information. This involves
a thorough understanding of how the application, the dataset, and the
system parameters can significantly influence the parallel I/O of their
deep learning application. We seek to empower users to make informed
decisions through a structured methodology that allows them to identify
and modify configurable elements effectively.

This research has been supported by the Agencia Estatal de Investigación (AEI), Spain,
and the Fondo Europeo de Desarrollo Regional (FEDER) UE, under contract PID2020-
112496GB-I00 and partially funded by the Fundacion Escuelas Universitarias Gimber-
nat (EUG).
The authors thankfully acknowledge RES resources provided by CESGA in FinisTerrae
III to RES-DATA-2022-1-0014.

© The Author(s), under exclusive license to Springer Nature Switzerland AG 2025
H. R. Arabnia et al. (Eds.): CSCE 2024, CCIS 2256, pp. 3–19, 2025.
https://doi.org/10.1007/978-3-031-85638-9_1

Keywords: Distributed Deep Learning · Parallel I/O · I/O Analysis · HPC cluster · I/O behavior patterns

1   Introduction

Deploying DL applications on High-Performance Computing (HPC) systems introduces substantial Input/Output (I/O) loads during the training phase, characterized by prolonged file access, high concurrency, and persistence. The significant data required to train DL models necessitates HPC systems grappling with sizable data loads and novel I/O patterns. The effective utilization of the I/O system by data-intensive DL applications becomes a formidable challenge, potentially resulting in heightened training latency and added overhead, particularly when datasets exceed the capacity of main memory. Although more processes can be created or more nodes can be used to have more memory, they would be processes limited by memory and not by computation. There is a possibility that the execution is not viable due to restrictions imposed by the HPC system.

The training phase, particularly for distributed DL applications, demands intensive use of the I/O system, which does not only consist of a sequential loading of the data at the beginning of training, but also a final writing of results. The data is accessed using different access patterns, depending on the data, application checkpoints can be made, in different epoch numbers. File data management in DL applications necessitates a distinct approach tailored to the inherent characteristics of DL I/O patterns, encompassing variability, randomness, frequency, and repetitive use. Efficient configuration of I/O system parameters relies on various factors, including the application's I/O pattern, storage hardware, problem size, and degree of parallelism. Unlike the traditional HPC I/O subsystem, the I/O software stack and patterns diverge from classical software and tools for scientific applications.

To facilitate this analysis, we propose a methodology to identify significant patterns that may influence application performance and I/O efficiency. This information serves as a valuable guide to users about the parameters involved in the I/O behavior of a DL application. Our methodological approach provides users with a complete and detailed understanding of how parameters at the application, the size and type of data, the format of the dataset can all impact the parallel I/O of deep learning applications. We strive to provide useful, complete and accurate information, allowing users to understand how specific system configurations and application settings can significantly influence overall system efficiency. By delving into these details, we aim to empower users, providing them with the necessary knowledge to make informed and strategic decisions.

The paper unfolds as follows: Sect. 2 refers to a collection of articles relevant to our research, positioning our work in the context of I/O and deep learning research. Section 3 describes the methodology applied to identify different patterns generated by the application during the training stage, extracting fundamental values for the behavior description and selecting significant parameters validated with the DLIO benchmark. Section 4 presents the experimental results of the methodology in the Deep Galaxy application, and the final section presents the conclusions.

2   Related Work

In the related literature, some studies describe the different techniques that deep learning distributed systems use. Our work is based on the training phase; the characterization in [7] of different systems offers a compact overview of the resources used. In [1], dealing with the behavior of the I/O, the authors propose techniques and methods used in various classes of generated I/O. In [5], the authors analyze the bottleneck generated by the I/O in the training phase of machine learning. This analysis includes access patterns and a performance model for an overview of storage strategies and their influence on I/O. In addition, in [10], the authors experimented with machine learning techniques and hyperparameters. Other authors have focused on the analysis of access patterns [6,9,11], where it is stated that storage subsystems are complex and the I/O operations of DL applications have more irregular patterns than scientific applications.

Our research distinguishes itself from previous work by focusing on a detailed analysis of parallel data input and output in DL applications within HPC environments. The main objective of this methodological approach that we have adopted is to provide the user with exhaustive, useful and accurate information about how a series of parameters of the application, dataset, and system can significantly affect the performance of their Deep Learning application. By understanding how system configuration and application-specific settings influence system efficiency, we aim to empower users to make informed decisions and achieve optimal performance in their DL applications in HPC environments.

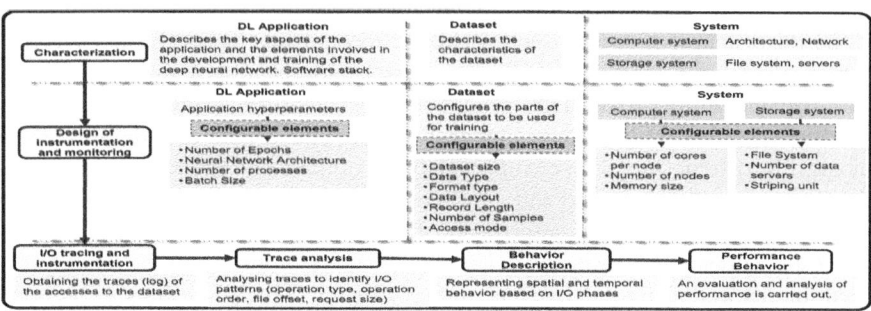

Fig. 1. Methodology for the Analysis of I/O Patterns of DL Applications

3   Methodology for the Analysis of I/O Patterns of Deep Learning Applications

Our methodology allows us to analyze the parallel I/O pattern based on the spatial and temporal I/O behavior of dataset access patterns in the training stage of DL applications executed in HPC systems to detect significant patterns or phases (behavior description) and analyze which aspects impact performance (Performance Behavior). Figure 1 presents the methodology, which is composed of six steps: 1) Characterization, 2) Design of instrumentation and monitoring, 3) I/O tracing and instrumentation, 4) Trace analysis, 5) Behavior Description, and 6) Performance Behavior.

To show our methodology for specific data sets and exemplify each of the steps, we use Input/Output for Deep Learning (DLIO). DLIO [4] is a representative benchmark which is built based on the I/O profiling of selected workloads. It can accurately emulate the I/O behavior of modern deep-learning scientific applications. This benchmark allows the execution of various input/output operations, such as read, write, random, and sequential access. Its purpose is to evaluate storage performance. It also uses a set of parameters that allow the configuration of scenarios for Deep Learning (DL) applications, simulating various storage workloads. DLIO plays HDF5, NPZ, and TFRecord file formats, among others. We describe each phase of the methodology below:

3.1   Characterization

The characterization phase consists of identifying the significant elements for the description of the behavior (functional and performance) of the application, the data set, the computer system and the storage system.

Application: Characterizing a deep learning application encompasses delineating its pivotal facets. Initially, this involves elucidating the tasks undertaken by the deep neural network, such as image recognition, natural language processing, and object detection. Following this, the determination of the software stack becomes imperative. This process entails identifying and describing the constituent software components integral to the application's foundational technological infrastructure. These components encompass the framework, programming language, libraries, and software modules.

Furthermore, in the characterization process, vital elements like the framework type (TensorFlow, Keras, or Horovod), the number of epochs, checkpoint execution, as well as frequency come under scrutiny. This stage aims to pinpoint the software requisites and parameters essential for configuring the application's execution, influencing its input/output dynamics.

Applying the application characterization using the DLIO. In order to perform this process, a specific software stack is required, including Horovod [tensorflow] $\geq$ 0.19.5, tensorflow $\geq$ 2.2.0, numpy $\geq$ 1.19.1, h5py $\geq$ 2.10.0, pandas $\geq$ 1.1.3 and mpi4py $\geq$ 3.1.3.

Dataset: In the case of image datasets, characterization involves understanding and describing specific aspects related to the images and how they relate to the machine learning or computer vision tasks intended to be performed. These aspects are previously defined by the DL application's user or designer. Therefore, much of the information related to the characterization of the dataset can be found directly with the source that designed the DL application, such as image dimensions, color depth, format of the images, and distribution of the images among different categories or classes, among others. In the case of DLIO, as it is a benchmark that can emulate datasets of various file formats, three datasets will be generated in formats such as HDF5 (Hierarchical Data Format version 5), NPZ (NumPy Zip File), and TFRecord (TensorFlow Record).

System: Describing the system involves providing detailed and accurate information about the environment in which the DL application will run. The computer system (number of nodes, amount of memory, type of processor, type of network), the storage system (storage capacity, file system, number of data/ metadata servers).

The experiments were run on an HPC computing system with 256 compute nodes (16,384 cores), based on 2x Intel Xeon Ice Lake 8352Y processors with 32 cores each (64 cores per node), 256GB of RAM (247GB for real use), 960GB SSD NVMe of local storage, and interconnected via Infiniband HDR 100 connection, LUSTRE File System (formed by a set of 12 I/O servers (OSSs) and Object Storage Target (OST) disks).

3.2   Design of Instrumentation and Monitoring

In this stage, the elements that will be monitored during the execution of the application are identified.

Application: Refers to the application's input hyperparameters for execution. The hyperparameter settings of the deep learning application are the values chosen before model training and affect the model training process. Some hyperparameters are the number of epochs, the neural network architecture, and the number of processes. The number of epochs refers to how many times the machine learning model will see the entire training data set during the training process. The choice of neural network architecture can significantly impact the complexity of the model, the computational resources required, the preprocessing strategies, and the way data flows through the network during training, all of which can affect the I/O of the deep learning model's training process. This can affect the data needed for training and, therefore, influence the I/O, as larger networks may require more extensive datasets for effective training. In the case of DLIO, a single epoch was used to apply the methodology.

Dataset: This refers to the dataset used to train the deep neural network, including the data's size, quality, and diversity. Describing the characteristics of a dataset involves identifying and providing detailed information about the different aspects of the dataset. Among these are:

- *Dataset size:* The size of a dataset refers to the amount (GiB) of data or samples it contains.
- *Data Type:* This refers to the type of data found in the dataset, for example, numeric, categorical, text, image, video, audio, etc.
- *Format type:* This refers to the structure and organization of the information stored in a file or data storage system; for example: HDF5, NPZ, TFRecord, JPG, PNG, etc.
- *Data Layout:* This refers to how the data is laid out, for example, whether it is separated into subdirectories or all together.
- *Record Length:* The size of a record/image within the dataset expressed in Bytes.
- *Number of Samples:* The number of samples per file refers to the total number of records/images within the dataset.
- *Batch Size:* This refers to the number of data samples used in an iteration during a model's training.
- *Access Mode:* This refers to the methods by which processes can interact with a file on a storage system. Among the access modes are the following:
  - *Multi-access:* In this mode, each process has its copy of the input data and operates independently.
  - *Shared Access:* In this mode, processes work together to read or write to a shared file in parallel. Each process accesses the same file, and each input/output operation is coordinated between processes to avoid conflicts.

In applying the characterization of the dataset using the DLIO benchmark to create a synthetic dataset for our experiments, we have identified the configurable elements for generating the dataset in a LUSTRE file system, such as the number of samples and the sample size. In addition, we have considered aspects of the application and system, such as the number of processes and nodes, which influence the number of files by the access mode to the dataset according to its format. Several parameters have been selected to generate the datasets (Table 1). Additionally, to generate the dataset with the TFRecord format, the transfer size was configured at 256 KiB in all cases.

For the generation of files and adjusting the DLIO configuration parameters, the workload that each process would handle according to the type of access to the file was considered. For example, in the case of HDF5, whose access mode is shared, each process accesses a part of the same file; therefore, a single file is generated regardless of the number of processes. With NPZ and TFRecord having a multi-access mode (independent), in which each process accesses its file, the DLIO parameters were set to the number of images each process would handle to equalize the size of each file per process with file size handled in HDF5.

To maintain the same workload per process in the NPZ and TFRecord experiments concerning the HDF5 experiments, for NPZ and TFRecord, the number of Samples was divided by the number of processes (Eq. 1).

$$Workload\,per\,process = \frac{Number\,of\,Samples}{Processes} \tag{1}$$

System. Configuring the system consists of selecting the type of file system to be used, the amount of memory needed to run the application, the number of processes, and the number of nodes. If a parallel file system is being used, the size of the data blocks written on each disk (striping unit (stripe size) refers to the size of the data blocks written to each disk [8].) and the number of data servers (stripe count) are configured.

Applying this phase in DLIO, the system configuration involves selecting the type of file system, which in this case is LUSTRE, and specifying the amount of memory necessary to run the application; in this case, 16GiB and 32GiB were used. Additionally, the configuration includes the number of processes, ranging from 4 to 48, and the number of nodes, ranging from 1 to 12. When using the LUSTRE parallel file system, the stripe size is set to 1 MiB, and the stripe count can be set to 1, 2, 4, 8, or 12. The striping unit = 1048576 bytes, number of data servers (OST) = 1 per node.

Table 1. HDF5, NPZ, TFRecord Formats. Dataset Design Parameters DLIO

File format	Configurable parameters			Dataset size	Sizes per file (GiB)	Record length (bytes)	Number of samples	Batch size
	Proc.	Nodes	Processes per node					
HDF5	4	1	4	48	48	131072	786432	64
	8	2						
	16	4						
	32	8						
	48	12						
NPZ, TFRecord	4	1	4	96	24	131072	196608	64
	8	2			12		98304	
	16	4			6		49152	
	32	8			3		24576	
	48	12			2		16384	

3.3 I/O Tracing and Instrumentation

Once the application, dataset, and system have been configured, it must be decided at which layer of the I/O software stack we will trace and monitor, after which we must find the appropriate tools for this purpose. In this paper, we have selected the `Darshan` tool version 3.4.3 [3] to track I/O operations at the application level and the `seff` tool to monitor system resource usage. Therefore, this phase of the methodology consists of executing and monitoring the application to obtain the trace of process events.

3.4 Trace Analysis

To understand and describe I/O behavior, we selected as main factors the file access type (sequential, strided, random), the open file mode (read, write, write/read), the file access mode file (shared or multi-access), file format (HDF5, TFRecord, NPZ, etc.), request size(fixed/variable, small/medium/large), repetitions, as well as time intervals (fixed, variable). In this way, the trace analysis is carried out in this phase, identifying the I/O patterns to obtain the necessary elements to describe the I/O behavior based on the main selected I/O factors. We track the type of operation, order of operation, file offset, request size, and I/O processes for each file opened during training. The spatial pattern is represented using the number of I/O processes, the file offset, and the request size. The temporal pattern is also represented, considering the file, the request size, the I/O processes, the order of operation, and the repetitions.

3.5 Behavior Description

Based on the pattern of I/O operations accessing the dataset, the spatial and temporal behavior is described to search for significant phases due to the following two factors: - Spatial behavior: volume of data accessed. - Temporal behavior: the number of repetitions of a pattern or consecutive patterns. In this stage, the global I/O behavior is represented, where significant patterns will be identified and grouped into I/O phases. An I/O phase is defined as a set of similar I/O operations where similarity is defined by operation type, request size, and offset. The offset can be sequential, strided, or random. We use the Eq. 2 to identify the sequential case.

$$file\_Offset_i = file\_Offset_{i-1} + Request\_Size_{i-1} \qquad (2)$$

where $file\_Offset_i$ is equal to the previous file offset plus the request size, therefore, spatial and temporal behavior is modeled at this stage based on the I/O patterns. The spatial pattern indicates the size of the operation (Request_Size), and how the file is accessed at each file offset for each I/O process. The temporal pattern shows the order of I/O operations performed for each process and the number of repetitions of similar patterns or similar operations. In both patterns, the repetitions, the size and the number of I/O processes are essential to assess the weight of each I/O phase. To validate the methodology, we have applied it to the DLIO benchmark, which can generate various patterns simulating real applications. In this way, we can validate how we detect the generated pattern. Furthermore, the impact of changing configuration parameters on performance is analyzed, specifically the impact of the file access type, the file format, the number of processes and nodes, the number of data servers, and the transfer size.

Illustrative Case: HDF5, NPZ, and TFRecord File Formats. This section explores the temporal and spatial I/O behaviors during the training stage, utilizing the dataset generated in the previous section. Figures 2 and 3 depict the temporal patterns associated with three different file formats. The x-axis represents the range of processes, the y-axis indicates the order of operations, the z-axis shows file offsets, and the color highlights the size of the operations. We illustrate the spatial and temporal I/O patterns for these formats to demonstrate their specific behaviors:

DLIO - HDF5 (Shared Access Type). In the case of the HDF5 file format, a single shared file was read where all processes accessed the same file. Figure 2 shows the temporal and spatial pattern of the I/O accesses, which are repeated periodically. Figure 2(a) shows the behavior with 8 processes, each reading 6 GiB, resulting in a total file size of 48 GiB. In this case, 1552 read operations were performed for each process, totaling 12416 operations. On the other hand, Fig. 2(b) shows the behavior with 48 processes, each one reading 1Gib, also for a total file size of 48Gib. In this case, 272 read operations were performed for each process, totaling 13056 operations.

The spatial pattern was sequential and the size of the operations, represented in blue, remained constant in all cases, being 4 MiB. In addition, small operations were observed at the beginning, represented in green, which constitute the access or reading of the file's metadata. Therefore we see two differentiated phases: access to metadata and access to data, the data access phase is considered significant due to the number of repetitions.

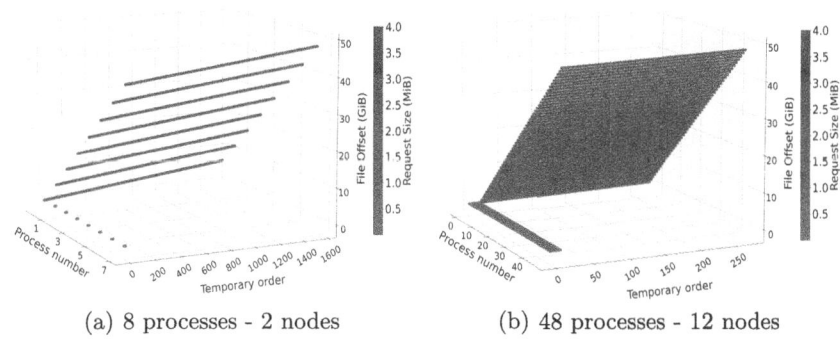

(a) 8 processes - 2 nodes   (b) 48 processes - 12 nodes

Fig. 2. DLIO temporal and spatial pattern (HDF5 format). All processes access a single shared file at a different file offset. 4 processes per compute node.

DLIO - NPZ and TFRecord (Multi-access Type): Figure 3(a) shows the spatial and temporal I/O pattern of NPZ format, where each process reads the entire file independently. With 48 processes, 519 reads of 4 MiB each were performed, resulting in a cumulative total of 24,912 read operations. Each file has a size of 2 GiB, making the total 96 GiB. The spatial pattern for NPZ was

sequential, and in all cases, five short reads were consistently performed at the
beginning of the file, corresponding to the metadata.

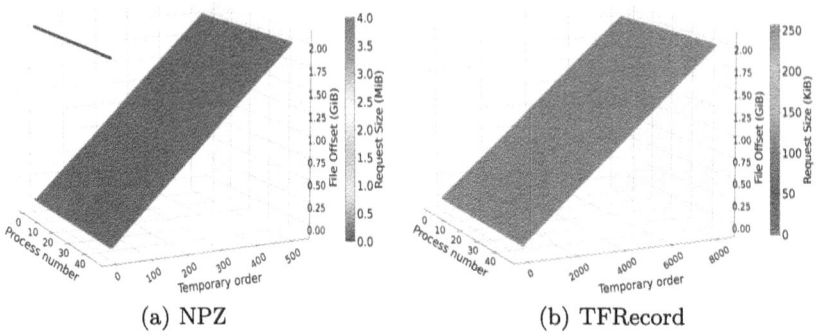

(a) NPZ   (b) TFRecord

Fig. 3. DLIO temporal and spatial pattern (NPZ and TFRecord format). Each process
accesses its own file. 48 processes - 12 nodes. 4 processes per compute node.

For TFRecord format, Fig. 3(b) illustrates the temporal and spatial I/O
pattern when using 48 processes. The behavior is repetitive, with each process accessing its respective file. The transfer size was set to 256 KiB. With 48
processes, 8,197 operations were conducted, each with a size of 256 KiB. Consequently, each process performed a total read of 2 GiB, resulting in a combined
read of 96 GiB for all processes. The total number of operations for the 48 processes amounted to 393,456 operations. Experiments were also conducted for
TFRecord with a transfer size of 1 MiB, resulting in 100,374 read operations.
Therefore, it is evident that both the number of processes and the transfer size
impact the number of reads.

Concerning the spatial pattern, access was sequential, and the read size
matched the configured transfer size (256 KiB and 1 MiB). All processes independently read their respective files, and the offset increased with the size of
each read operation.

3.6 Performance Behavior

Following the earlier phases, the final phase of our methodology focuses on the
evaluation and analysis of performance. The performance metrics for the dataset
in HDF5 format-such as data transfer rate, execution time, and I/O time-are
illustrated in Fig. 4.

As the number of processes, nodes, and data servers increases, the data
transfer rate also increases. This expected behavior results from allocating more
resources to manage the growing I/O workload. Conversely, both I/O time and
execution time decrease as additional processes are incorporated into training
the dataset. This improvement is attributed to the availability of more processing units and consequently, more resources, facilitating faster data handling and
processing.

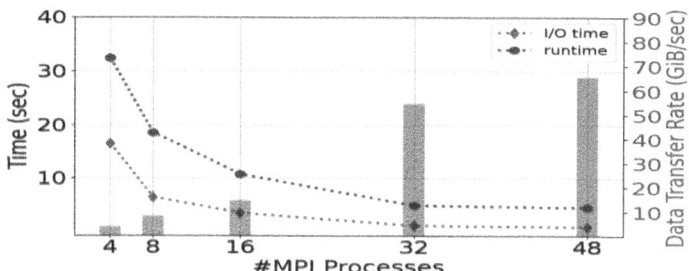

Fig. 4. Performance Behavior, I/O Pattern Impact, HDF5 (Shared access mode)

The worst-case scenario was observed when using four processes on a single node with only one OST, which resulted in longer execution times and lower data transfer rate. On the other hand, the best-case scenario was observed with 48 processes distributed across 12 nodes and with 12 OSTs, resulting in higher data transfer rate and lower execution times. The I/O time remained relatively constant between 32 and 48 processes but became more significant in runtime as the number of resources increased.

Figure 5(a) and 5(b) shows how NPZ and TFRecord scale with increased processes, nodes, and data servers (OST). data transfer rate increases and runtime decreases as resources increase. In Fig. 5(a), for NPZ format, it can be seen that for 4 processes run in 1 compute node and reading from 1 data server, the gap between runtime and I/O time is more significant than for 48 processes that were run using 12 nodes and reading from 12 data servers, the gap decreases, making I/O time important.

Figure 5(b) for TFRecord format shows that the data transfer rate increased as the number of processes increased; Processes 4, 8, 16, and 32 had a similar behavior for 256 KiB and 1 MiB. In contrast, for 48 processes with a transfer size of 1 MiB, the data transfer rate was much larger than 256 KiB. Overall, these findings suggest that transfer size optimization can significantly impact system performance, particularly in the context of the TFRecord format.

4 Case Study: Deep Galaxy Application

In this section, we will apply the methodology in a real application, such as Deep Galaxy. To achieve this, the methodological procedure will be presented in detail and step by step.

4.1 Characterization

DeepGalaxy [2] is a general-purpose galaxy image processing framework. This dataset consists of 35,784 images from 36 N-body simulations with different initial conditions. It is divided into 80% training data and 20% validation data. The simulations' snapshots use cameras from 14 different positions, generating

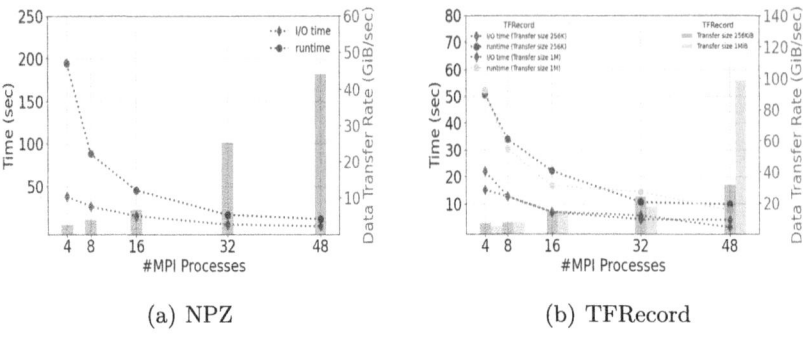

(a) NPZ   (b) TFRecord

Fig. 5. Performance Behavior, I/O Pattern Impact, NPZ and TFRecord (Multi-access mode)

14 2D images stored in a compressed HDF5 dataset with a resolution of (512, 512) pixels.

The configurable parameters are: number of epochs, CNN architecture (EfficientNetB4, EfficientNetB7, ResNet50), batch-size, number of cameras, and datasets used (all or part of the datasets). The organization of the dataset every -m epoch is as follows: m = −1: each process loads the entire dataset; m = 0: data is divided between processes and loaded only once, so a process will never see the data of other processes; m > 0: data is divided between processes, and data loading triggers every -m epoch, allowing a process to access data from other nodes/workers.

4.2 Design of Instrumentation and Monitoring

In the case of the Deep Galaxy application, we have selected the parameters to use different data loading modes and evaluate their impact on latency and data transfer rate.

DL Application: The CNN Architecture = EfficientNetB4 was used by default in the application. A single epoch was used since the specific objective was to observe the I/O pattern. This allowed us to capture the initial behavior of the I/O pattern at the beginning of model training. This was useful in identifying trends and initial characteristics in the data flow.

Dataset: The images are stored in a compressed HDF5 dataset. The image resolutions used were 512x512 pixels, with a size of 2 GiB. The file structure of HDF5 has 36 datasets (groups), each one composed of 2 * 14 datasets that correspond to cameras from 14, with 71 images in each of the camera positions, and the batch size is 4. The dataset access type is $m = 0$ and $m > 0$ (Data Loading Model). If "m" is set to 0, the training/test data is split between nodes/workers and loaded only once during the code initialization phase, and a compute node will never be able to see data from other nodes. If "m" is set to an integer greater than 0, the training/test data is also split between nodes/workers, but the data loading pipeline will be triggered every -m epoch, allowing one node to access previous data in other nodes.

System: The number of processes are 4, 8, 16, 32, 48, and 64. The number of nodes are 1, 2, 4, 8, 12, and 16. Two file systems NFS and LUSTRE were used, for which experiments were carried out with 1 and 4 OSTs.

4.3   I/O Tracing and Instrumentation

The Darshan tool has been used as the instrumentation tool. It is a tool that captures information about each file the application opens. However, instead of tracking all operating parameters, Darshan captures key features that can be processed and stored in a compact format. The Darshan instruments POSIX, MPI-IO, Parallel netCDF, and HDF5 all function to collect a variety of information. In this way, Darshan reports were selected for analyzing I/O patterns.

4.4   Trace Analysis

In the trace analysis phase, we extract key metrics to evaluate the performance of I/O operations within the Deep Galaxy application. These metrics include:

- **Operation Type:** Categorizes operations into reads and writes to identify access patterns.
- **Operation Order:** Examines the sequence of I/O operations to understand data access over time.
- **Offset:** Analyzes how I/O operations are distributed across the file or dataset.
- **Request Size:** Indicates the granularity of I/O operations, crucial for optimizing block size.
- **Execution Time and I/O Time:** Measures efficiency and overall performance.

We represent the I/O patterns both temporally and spatially, providing insights into the application's interaction with the file system and the impact of configuration parameters on efficiency. This graphical analysis (Fig. 6) helps identify bottlenecks, such as non-sequential data accesses that can degrade performance. The goal is to establish a basis for optimizing the application's I/O operations.

4.5   Behavior Description

After performing the instrumentation and trace analysis, the description of the I/O behavior of the application is carried out. Figure 6 exhibits spatial and temporal patterns corresponding to a Deep Galaxy run using 48 processes. The process number is represented on the "X" axis, the order of operations is shown on the "Y" axis, and the offset is indicated on the "Z" axis. The colored vertical bar on the graph represents the size of the request in bytes, reflecting the size of each read operation.

The access mode was defined as m = 0, which implies that each process accesses a different section of the file, excluding other processes, except in specific cases such as reading metadata, where all processes access the same offset. Each process accessed a different file offset in the rest of the operations. The total number of readings was 627726 operations. Figure 6(a) exhibits variability in sizes represented by different colors, showing readings of very small, medium and large dimensions. A closer look at some sequences with a single process was performed in Fig. 6(b) to offer a more detailed visualization of this behavior.

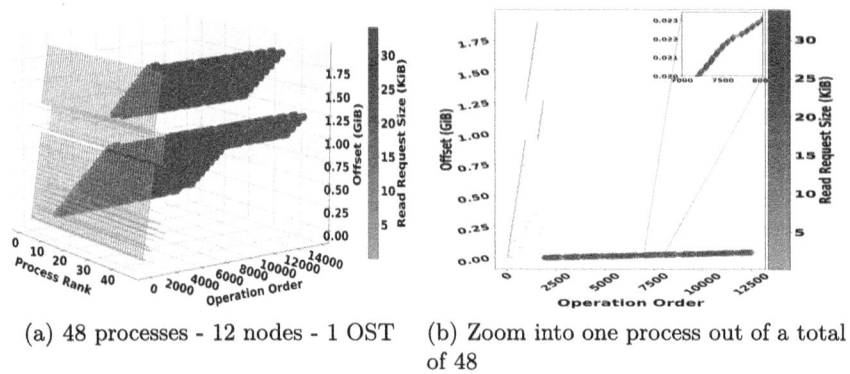

(a) 48 processes - 12 nodes - 1 OST   (b) Zoom into one process out of a total of 48

Fig. 6. Deep Galaxy Spatial and Temporal I/O Pattern

This analysis revealed a pattern in the sizes of the reads and the order in which the file has been read. The pattern begins with very small read operations (green), followed by medium (red) and large (blue) reads, alternating between them. Additionally, separations between operations can be identified, indicating times with low frequency in input/output (I/O) activities. This suggests that processes request reads at a slower rate, possibly due to concurrent execution of calculations that could affect the observed I/O time.

4.6   Performance Behavior

Figure 7 present the performance observed in the Deep Galaxy application on two file systems: LUSTRE and NFS. A key aspect of the comparison focuses on the access mode or data loading model for a data set in HDF5 format with a size of 2 GiB, distinguishing between scenarios when m = 0 (data loading model shared) and m > 0 (data loading model shared with reload+shuffle). Additionally, configurations with 1 OST and 4 OST were used in the case of the LUSTRE file system. All runs were carried out using 4, 8, 16, 32, 48 and 64 processes, distributed over 1, 2, 4, 8, 12 and 16 nodes, with 4 processes per node. Within the access mode, we will analyze the data loading model that significantly influences I/O time. When m = 0 indicates that each process reads a different part of the file without accessing what is read by other processes, the time remains consistently lower compared to the situation when m > 0. In the latter case, processes can read their assigned section of the file and reread areas already processed by others, which causes a notable increase in I/O time in all cases, due to the possibility of repeated reads between processes.

Therefore, with m > 0, the I/O time becomes more significant within the total execution time. The data transfer rate was higher in the scenarios with m > 0 due to increased data transfer compared to m = 0. Consequently, the system scales and does not saturate because the data transfer rate scales as we increase the number of processors, not taking advantage of the LUSTRE file system when configured with 4 OSTs.

Employing this methodological approach, we glean insights into I/O behavior and overall performance trends, enabling an evaluation of how the application responds to modifying particular parameters. From such analysis, it becomes apparent that for this specific case, the LUSTRE file system with a single OST suffices, negating the need for enhanced parallelism offered by a 4 OST setup. It is also discerned that the inflection point for optimal resource allocation to execute the application lies between 16 and 32 processes.

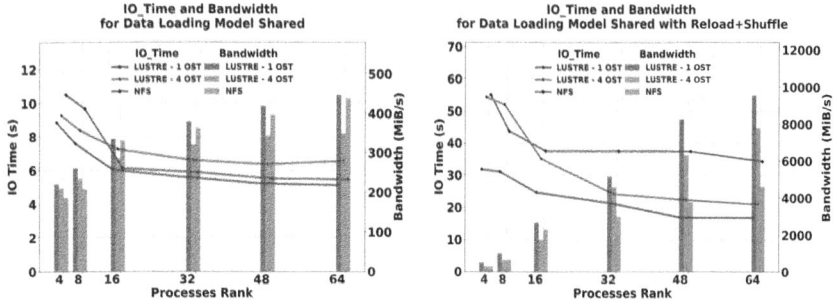

(a) I/O time with data loading model shared

(b) I/O time with data loading model shared with reload+shuffle

Fig. 7. Deep Galaxy Performance Behavior

5   Conclusions

This study has implemented a methodology to analyze input/output behavior in deep learning applications. It uses the DLIO Benchmark to illustrate the methodology and the Deep Galaxy application as a concrete case study. Through this approach, we manipulated various configuration parameters in the application, dataset, and system, allowing us to observe how these changes impact I/O patterns and performance directly.

During the research, it was observed that the performance of both Deep Galaxy and DLIO applications scaled efficiently as the number of processes increased from 4 to 48, keeping other critical parameters such as the number of epochs and neural network architecture constant. Additionally, changes in the access mode and dataset format type significantly impacted performance. For example, shared access optimized space usage and reduced reading time, whereas independent access increased the required storage space and reading time.

Regarding the data loading model in Deep Galaxy, access type $m = 0$, where data is divided among processes and loaded only once without cross-access between processes, was the most efficient. System configurations, such as the LUSTRE and NFS file systems, stripe size, and OST settings, also significantly improved performance. As the number of processes and OSTs increased, execution time and I/O time decreased while data transfer rate increased.

These findings provide valuable insights for future configurations of deep learning applications and offer practical implications. They highlight how specific adjustments to configuration parameters can significantly optimize performance, making this research directly applicable in real-world deep learning environments.

Future work will focus on analyzing how variations in system and application parameters, such as stripe size and stripe count in the LUSTRE file system, influence I/O performance. Additionally, new optimization techniques for I/O operations in deep learning applications will be developed and tested, with a particular emphasis on improvements at the I/O library level within the deep learning software stack, including strategies similar to those used in HDF5 for managing complex access patterns. Finally, the methodology will be applied to a broader range of deep learning applications to validate the results and refine the approach for effectiveness across diverse contexts.

References

1. Betke, E., Kunkel, J.: Footprinting parallel I/O–machine learning to classify application's I/O behavior. In: International Conference on High Performance Computing, pp. 214–226. Springer (2019)
2. Cai, M.X., et al.: Deepgalaxy: deducing the properties of galaxy mergers from images using deep neural networks. In: 2020 IEEE/ACM Fourth Workshop on Deep Learning on Supercomputers (DLS), pp. 56–62 (2020). https://doi.org/10.1109/DLS51937.2020.00012
3. Carns, P., et al.: Understanding and improving computational science storage access through continuous characterization. Trans. Storage **7**(3), 8:1–8:26 (2011). https://doi.org/10.1145/2027066.2027068. http://doi.acm.org/10.1145/2027066.2027068
4. Devarajan, H., Zheng, H., Kougkas, A., Sun, X.H., Vishwanath, V.: Dlio: a data-centric benchmark for scientific deep learning applications. In: 2021 IEEE/ACM 21st International Symposium on Cluster, Cloud and Internet Computing (CCGrid), pp. 81–91 (2021). https://doi.org/10.1109/CCGrid51090.2021.00018

5. Dryden, N., Böhringer, R., Ben-Nun, T., Hoefler, T.: Clairvoyant prefetching for distributed machine learning I/O. In: Proceedings of the International Conference for High Performance Computing, Networking, Storage and Analysis, pp. 1–15 (2021)
6. Farhangi, A., Bian, J., Wang, J., Guo, Z.: Work-in-progress: a deep learning strategy for I/O scheduling in storage systems. In: 2019 IEEE Real-Time Systems Symposium (RTSS), pp. 568–571. IEEE (2019)
7. Langer, M., He, Z., Rahayu, W., Xue, Y.: Distributed training of deep learning models: a taxonomic perspective. IEEE Trans. Parallel Distrib. Syst. **31**(12), 2802–2818 (2020)
8. OpenSFS, EOFS: About the lustre® file system (2023). https://www.lustre.org/
9. Wan, L., et al.: I/O performance characterization and prediction through machine learning on HPC systems. In: CUG2020 Proceedings (2020)
10. Zacarias, F.V., Petrucci, V., Nishtala, R., Carpenter, P., Mossé, D.: Intelligent colocation of HPC workloads. J. Parallel Distrib. Comput. **151**, 125–137 (2021)
11. Zhu, Y., Yu, W., Jiao, B., Mohror, K., Moody, A., Chowdhury, F.: Efficient user-level storage disaggregation for deep learning. In: 2019 IEEE International Conference on Cluster Computing (CLUSTER), pp. 1–12. IEEE (2019)

Parallel N-Body Performance Comparison: Julia, Rust, and More

Mark C. Lewis[1]([✉]) [iD], Clarissa Garcia[1], Audrey Tollett[1], Seven Aguirre[1], Henry Hafner[1], John McMahon[1], and Amanda A. Sickafoose[2] [iD]

[1] Trinity University, San Antonio, TX 78212, USA
enckegappan@gmail.com
[2] Planetary Science Institute, Tucson, AZ 85719, USA
https://www.trinity.edu , https://psi.edu

Abstract. This paper explores parallelism performance for C, C++, Go, Java, Julia, and Rust on N-body simulations. We begin with a basic $O(N^2)$ simulation for each language based on the n-body benchmark in the Benchmark Game. The original benchmark is adjusted to include a larger number of particles and run in parallel. We also add parallelism to the force calculations using a kD-tree. This work builds on previous work by including parallelism and adding the Julia programming language to our survey. We find that for straight number-crunching, all of these languages provide similar performance, and all have sufficient support for parallelism that runtimes scale well with thread counts. On the other hand, when a spatial data structure, such as the kD-tree, is introduced, the runtimes vary dramatically between languages. In that situation, Julia's performance looks more like Python, taking over 100 times as long as Rust/C/C++ to finish. Rust comes out on top with an impressive 50% lead over C and C++.

Keywords: N-body · simulation · performance · Rust · Julia

1 Introduction

This work builds on our previous work [15] comparing language performance for N-body simulations using a variety of programming languages. Part of the goal of that paper was to see if Rust was a suitable alternative to C/C++ for larger N-body simulations that use a spatial tree to provide $O(N \log N)$ performance. In this paper, we are interested to see how well various languages work with the inclusion of shared-memory parallelism. We also add Julia to the mix of languages we consider.

We look at two separate benchmarks. The first is a basic $O(N^2)$ approach used in the n-body benchmark in the Computer Language Benchmark Game [2]. We submitted the original versions of that benchmark to the site roughly 20 years ago. They maintain a suite of benchmarks across multiple languages. They are all based on small programs, but they stress the computer in various

© The Author(s), under exclusive license to Springer Nature Switzerland AG 2025
H. R. Arabnia et al. (Eds.): CSCE 2024, CCIS 2256, pp. 20–31, 2025.
https://doi.org/10.1007/978-3-031-85638-9_2

ways and highlight the strengths and weaknesses of different languages. In recent years, the Benchmark Game has been used as the foundation for energy efficiency studies as well [6,10,11].

This paper includes a second set of benchmarks using the kD-tree implementations from [15] and parallelizing the force calculations. The $O(N^2)$ code is effectively a test of raw number crunching. Particles are stored in flat arrays, and no interesting data structures are used. These simulations are also limited in how many particles can be considered because of the scaling. This leads to a smaller memory footprint in all languages. The kD-tree tests the languages in different ways. There is still a large amount of number crunching, but the building and navigation of the tree is a different type of workload. In addition, better scaling means that the simulations can be extended to over a million particles, significantly increasing the memory footprint.

For both of these styles of simulation, once the code has been adjusted properly, the actual calculation of the forces is an embarrassingly parallel problem. This makes it easy to add parallelism to the force calculations in many languages. Note that the construction of the kD-tree in parallel is non-trivial. We do not undertake that task here.

1.1   Language Selection

We began with the same set of languages used in [15]: Rust, C, C++, Java, Golang, TypeScript, and Python. For this study, we decided to replace JavaScript/TypeScript and Python with Julia. The decision to drop the JavaScript environment and Python was mainly because of the focus on parallelism. While Node.js does have support for worker threads, it is not a strength of the platform. The GIL in Python means multithreading generally provides no performance boost for CPU-bound workloads. We replaced them with Julia [3], a scripting language that is aimed in many ways at replacing Python, R, and Matlab for numerical computations. Unlike Python, R, and Matlab, Julia was designed with performance in mind, especially numerical performance. In the n-body benchmark testing [4], Julia is only topped by Chapel and Rust. That implies that Julia can beat the fastest safe implementations in C and C++ for that particular benchmark. Julia also has built-in support for parallel processing, making it an ideal candidate for this work.

As many readers might be unfamiliar with Julia, we'll provide a bit more information on it here. As was mentioned, Julia is a scripting language that aims to provide a programming interface similar to Python or R, but with a focus on performance. Julia has a fully functional REPL, and scripts can be written with low syntactic overhead. The language itself isn't object-oriented. It uses `structs` that hold data, but they don't have methods attached. The language can be written as a dynamically typed language, but its real power is achieved when the user specifies types, which enables Julia's most unique language feature: multiple dispatch. Multiple dispatch can be reasonably well described as function overloading with dynamic binding on all the arguments. Function overloading only makes sense when the types of arguments are specified to differentiate the overloaded versions. In our own testing, we also found that specifying types also allows Julia's JIT to produce faster code. For example, if Julia knows that it has an array of doubles, it will generate faster code to sort that array than if given an array of an unspecified type.

The motivation for having a fast scripting language is given in [7] and [12], where they describe the two language problem in scientific computing. This is when algorithms are implemented first in a language like Python where people feel they can construct them more quickly[1], but then they have to be translated into other languages when they are used on full-scale problems that require more speed. Several papers, such as [17], look at Julia's performance in different scenarios. This work aims to add to that list.

2   O(N^2) Approach

The benchmark that is part of [2] is a test of raw number crunching. It uses a first-order, symplectic integrator to integrate the orbits of the four giant planets around the Sun. This is a standard test of the accuracy of an integrator for planetary science, as the orbits should evolve in predictable ways over long timescales [13]. Unfortunately, that form of the benchmark does not work well for testing parallelism as there are only five bodies, and each time step must be calculated sequentially. To get around this, we use a setup that resembles a variable number of asteroids in order around a star.

The approach for performing the integrations also had to be updated slightly. The algorithm runs through all pairs of particles, calculates the force of gravity between the pair, and then adds that force to either an aggregate acceleration or the velocities of the particles. When done sequentially, this is done with an outer loop that runs through all the particles and an inner loop that goes through all the particles after the first one. The distance is calculated once for each pair, and that distance is used to calculate the force on each particle.

This approach minimizes the number of distance calculations, but if run in parallel, it will introduce race conditions as different iterations of the outer loop will mutate the same aggregators in the inner loop. To make the code work better in parallel, the inner loop also runs through all the particles, skipping the one the outer loop is on, and it only updates the aggregator for the outer loop particle. This results in twice as many distance calculations, but each iteration through the outer loop mutates separate memory, so there are no race conditions if the outer loop is turned into a parallel loop.

For these tests, we started with versions of the code copied directly from the Benchmark Game site. We picked the fastest version from each language that was amenable to parallelization. We then changed the loop structure, as described above, and changed the outer loop to execute in parallel. The details

---

[1] The authors of this paper don't necessarily agree with this analysis. In our experience, creating correct/working software in dynamically typed scripting languages often takes longer than in statically typed languages because of the lack of static syntax/type checking.

of how the outer loop was parallelized varied by language, as each language supports different parallelization mechanisms.

The code in the Benchmark Game also includes energy calculations. In that context, they are primarily used to verify that the algorithm works. These calculations are also O(N^2), but with only five particles, the computational cost is minimal. As we are boosting the number of particles and taking fewer time steps, the relative cost of the energy calculation grows. This calculation can also be done in parallel with a map-reduce operation. Unfortunately, Julia and Golang do not have good support for parallel map-reduce, so the energy calculations were removed for the timing results to keep the comparisons even.

2.1 Implementations

The full version of all the O(N^2) implementations can be found at https://github.com/MarkCLewis/ParallelNBodyPerformance. This also includes the scripts used to run and collect data from the benchmarks. Table 1 summarizes the languages, what version of the code from the Benchmark Game was used to build our solution, and what approach/library was used to add the parallelism.

Table 1. Implementation Details

Language	Benchmark Game	Parallelism
C (GCC 9.4.0/clang 10.0.0)	#6	OpenMP
C++ (GCC 9.4.0/clang 10.0.0)	#9	OpenMP
Go (1.22.3)	#3	go-parallel
Java (GraalVM-java17-22.2.0)	#5	Parallel Streams
Julia (1.10.3)	#4 and #8	Thread macro
Rust (1.77.0-nightly)	#3	Rayon

OpenMP is the standard for multithreaded HPC work in C, C++, and Fortran. Java's parallel streams were added in Java 8 and provide a simple mechanism for both parallel loops and doing functional transformations in parallel. Julia has built-in support for multithreading in the form of the @Threads macro. This macro provides parallel loops but doesn't include strong support for much else. While Rust doesn't currently have support for parallel loops or other similar operations in the standard library, the Rayon library has gained significant traction, and it seems to be the de facto standard for this type of work in Rust. Lastly, while multithreading and parallelism are part of the selling points of the Go programming language, this support comes in the form of goroutines and channels. The language does not have built-in support for parallel loops. Unlike Rust, there doesn't seem to be a clear leader in this space for Go. We chose to use [8].

The fastest version of n-body in both Julia and Rust wasn't an acceptable starting point as it uses an approach that stores all the distance pairs. There are only 10 of these when there are only five bodies, but we want to consider simulations with 10,000 and 100,000 bodies, which makes this approach unacceptably memory intensive. It also doesn't lend itself well to parallelization.

We did draw some inspiration from the fastest version of the Julia code. That code uses immutable `structs`. We wanted to see if the immutability allowed the Julia JIT to do extra optimizations, so we implemented two versions of this code in Julia, one with mutable `structs` and one with immutable `structs`. While these two versions had a very different structure to the code, their benchmark results were equal within the error bars. Therefore, we only present the timing results of the mutable version. Both versions can be found in the GitHub repository.

One other element worth noting is that while the safety features of Rust can make it a little more challenging to create working code, they do truly help with preventing errors. There was a period of time when we had created race conditions in the implementations in a few languages by merging the loop that updates positions into the loop that aggregates accelerations. This can cause some forces to be calculated with new positions instead of old ones. This creates a subtle bug as the differences between positions before and after a time step are generally small. But it breaks the symplectic nature of the integrator and would cause the system's overall energy to drift for long integrations. Attempting to create this bug in Rust leads to an error message from the borrow checker, as it requires having an immutable borrow simultaneously as a mutable one [9].

2.2   Results

The benchmarks were run on a Linux workstation with two Intel(R) Xeon(R) CPU E5-2680 v3 @ 2.50GHz processors and 64 GB of RAM. To get consistent timing values across all the languages involved, we used the Linux `time` command instead of timing commands built into any of the languages. This potentially provides a small penalty to Java and Julia as they use a JIT instead of compiling to a native machine executable. This penalty would be most obvious in the shortest-running benchmarks.

We ran simulations with 10,000 and 100,000 particles for ten time steps. This was done seven times for each language using 2, 4, 6, 8, 12, 24, and 48 threads. We present the mean and the standard deviation of those seven runs. The timing results are shown in Fig. 1.

For both the smaller and larger simulations, the performance scales very close to linearly up to 12 threads for all the languages. This makes sense, given that the machine used has two 12-core processors. Going from 12 to 24 threads, performance gains were still shown. These gains were close to linear for the larger simulations but distinctly sub-linear for the smaller ones. That jump moves the simulation off of a single processor, making the cache locality worse. That impact is more negative when there isn't as much data. One interesting result is that all the languages see performance gains going from 24 to 48 threads.

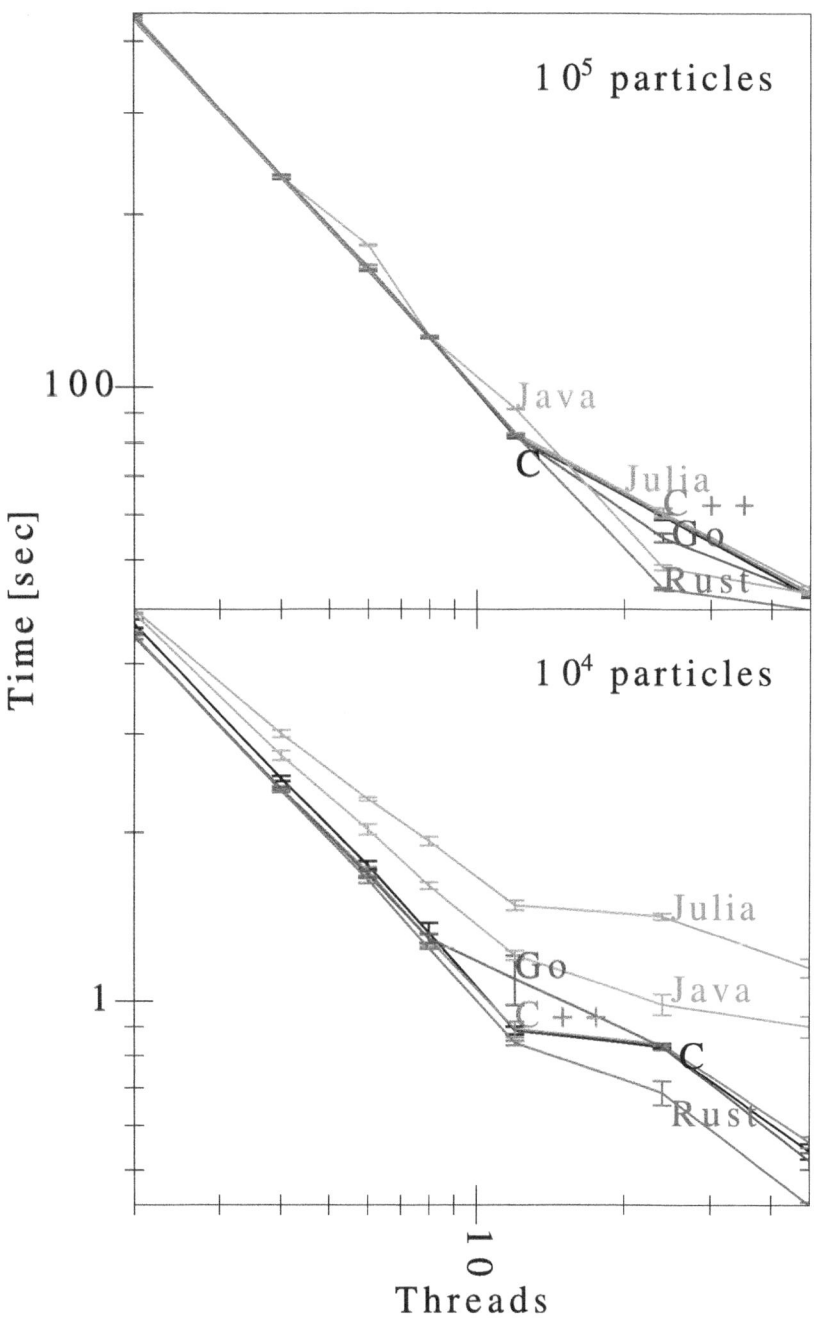

Fig. 1. Run times for ten time steps using the $O(N^2)$ approach. One standard deviation error bars are shown.

This is surprising as "hyperthreading" often doesn't provide speed benefits for numerically intensive applications.

When comparing languages, a few patterns jump out. One is that Rust is the performance winner across the board, especially at the higher thread counts, where it matters most for actual research work. In the smaller simulations, it is somewhat surprising that Julia is the slowest by a fair margin. From there, the trends are more what one might expect. Julia is followed by Java, with Go, C, and C++ having similar performance and Rust being the fastest. The slow performance for Java and Julia at high thread counts could be largely the result of the short total times and the fact that they have JITs that give them longer startup times. However, the patterns are far less clear for the larger simulations, where startup time will matter less. Two main things stand out in the timing results of the larger simulations. First, the difference between the performance of the languages is remarkably small at every thread count except 24 threads. Second, the JVM/Java performance is erratic. It is the slowest language at 6 and 12 threads but the second fastest at 24.

The key takeaway from the results is that for raw number crunching across multiple threads, all these languages have remarkably similar performance as long as there is enough work to be done, enough memory being used, and the JIT startup time isn't a significant fraction of the workload. While Rust is the fastest, it is generally by less than 10%, even compared to Java and Julia with 10^5 particles.

3   kD-Tree Approach

Most research simulations need significantly more than 100,000 particles. The first approach's $O(N^2)$ scaling makes that infeasible, even with the introduction of parallelism. This motivated using a kD-tree in [15]. Tree-based structures have a long history in numerical simulations going back to Barnes and Hut [5]. The original work used an octree. The idea is that gravitational interactions with distant groups of particles can be modeled as a force from the collection of particles instead of having to calculate the forces from each of the individual particles. This gives $O(N \log N)$ scaling behavior. This approach has been applied generally to astrophysical simulations ranging from cosmology [18,19] to planetary rings [14,16] and allows for simulations involving many millions to even billions of particles.

The kD-tree approach is also more interesting with the inclusion of Julia. The Benchmark Game doesn't include a kD-tree or any other spatial data structures used for number-crunching benchmarks. However, the kD-tree is, in many ways, a fancy binary tree, and the Benchmark Game does include a binary tree benchmark [1]. It is worth noting that Julia does quite poorly in this benchmark. While Julia is one of the fastest languages in the n-body benchmark, it is more than 14 times slower than the top languages in the binary-tree benchmark. Note that Python is more than 34 times slower than the fastest languages in the binary-tree benchmarks, so Julia still does much better than Python, but the best Java implementation is only 2.5 times slower than C++ and Rust, so Julia looks more like a slow, scripting language here. This begs the question of whether a kD-tree integrator will perform more like the pure number crunching code or the data structure code.

3.1   Implementations

The C, C++, Go, Java, and Rust implementations began with the versions used in [15]. The Rust version was slightly updated to use an **enum** for the tree nodes. Then, all the loops over the particles in the main function were updated to work in parallel. The parallelization techniques were the same as described in Sect. 2.1.

The Julia version of the code was built as a conversion from the Java version with a few modifications. The tree nodes in Julia were implemented as an abstract type with two subtypes for the leaves and the internal nodes. The functions to traverse the tree use Julia's multiple dispatch. As described above, we have seen that Julia is able to provide more optimization when it knows more about the types. Hence, we annotated all functions with types for both inputs and outputs.

Section 1 mentioned that thanks to the borrow checker, the Rust implementation of multithreading could catch bugs accidentally added in other languages. Unfortunately, something of the opposite is true in Julia. The creators of Julia decided to follow in the footsteps of Fortran instead of C and use 1-indexed arrays. While there are certain arguments that this makes sense for a language aimed at scientists and others who aren't professional programmers, it also leads to subtle bugs when converting code from languages that are 0-indexed, which is the case for all the other languages we looked at.

As was mentioned earlier, the code to construct the kD-tree was not parallelized. This is another $O(N \log N)$ operation that happens once each time step and is completely sequential in the current implementations. The full implementations for all the languages can be found at https://github.com/MarkCLewis/MultiLanguageKDTree in the **Parallel** subdirectory.

3.2   Results

These benchmarks used the same machine as described above. The same thread counts were used, but the particle counts were bumped up by a factor of 10 to 100,000 and 1,000,000 particles for the two simulation sizes. The timing results are shown in Fig. 2. Note that the results for Julia are not complete for 1 million particles.

Unsurprisingly, these results roughly mirror what we found with the sequential kD-trees in [15] for the languages that had been part of the original study. As before, we see roughly linear scaling up to 12 threads. Performance continues to improve all the way up to 48 threads, though it is distinctly sub-linear. We see that Rust is the fastest, with C and C++ tied and taking nearly 50% longer than Rust. Go is slightly faster than Java, with both taking nearly twice as long as Rust to complete the simulations.

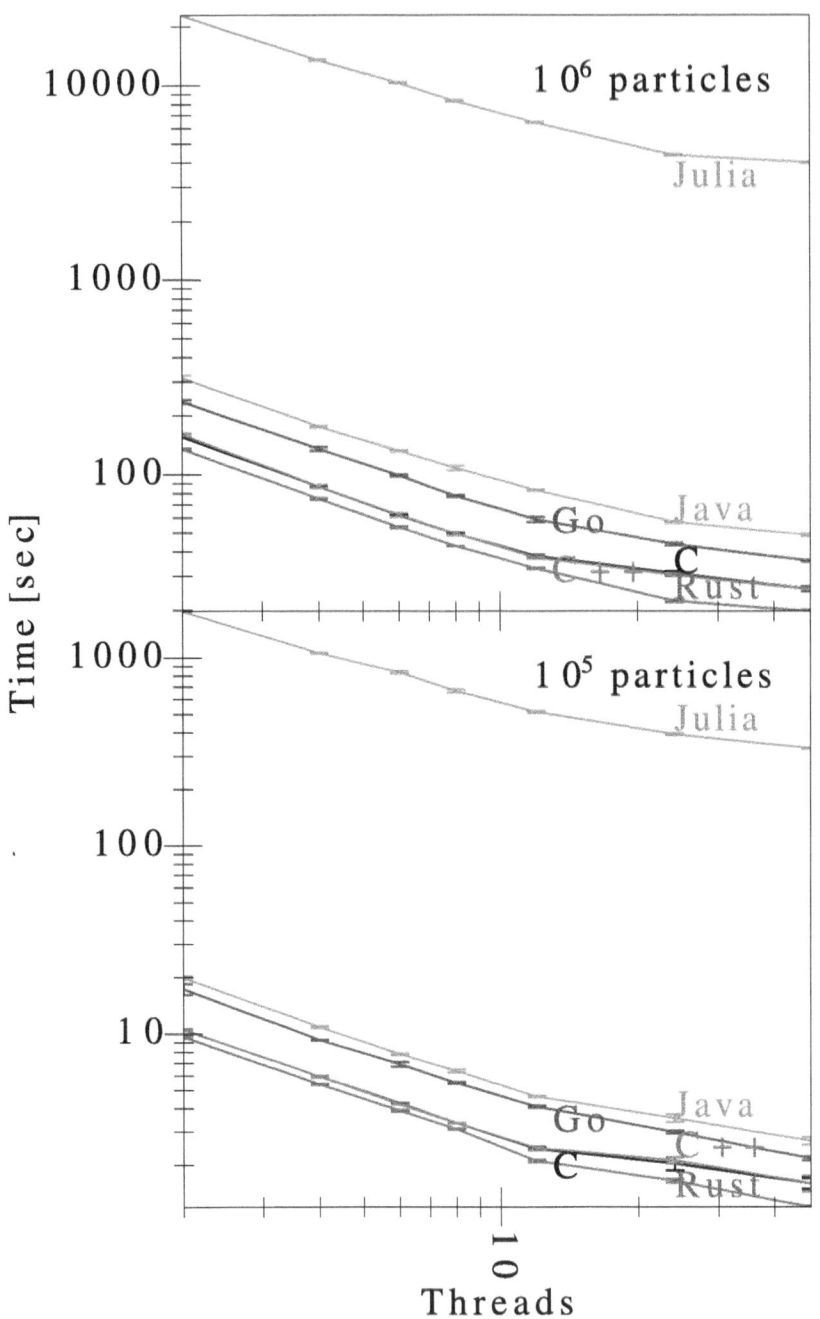

Fig. 2. Run times for ten time steps using the kD-tree versions. One standard deviation error bars are shown.

The surprising result here is Julia's remarkably poor performance. In these tests, Julia is as far behind the Rust implementation as Python was in the sequential testing. Indeed, Julia is so slow we did additional testing to ensure there wasn't a bug. We added code to the Julia and Java versions to count how many times various operations were performed. The counts between the two matched. So, the Julia code does the same number of gravity calculations as the other versions. It is simply much slower at doing them.

Another factor that could be playing a role is that the multithreading in Julia appears to have issues with load balancing in this code. Watching the load bar on the machine as the benchmarks are running, we see it go up and down many times during a time step. Depending on the implementation details, each time step has two or three parallel loops. With the other languages, the load bar is observed to jump to roughly the number of threads used in that run and stay close to that level until the end of the time step when it hits a period of sequential processing for the tree construction.

This also shows up in the output of `time`, which includes lines for `real` and `user`. The `@Threads` macro in Julia is not doing as good a job of evenly distributing the work across threads as other implementations.

A second surprising result is how well Rust with Rayon performs compared to C and C++ with OpenMP. OpenMP is a well-established standard used across industry and in most HPC workloads. Despite this, Rust opens its biggest performance lead over C and C++ when the thread count is high. This trend holds for both simulation sizes we considered.

The main message from these results is somewhat different from that of the first round of benchmarks. When we include a data structure and the number of particles scales up, the choice of language becomes much more significant. Instead of having results within 10% of each other, here we see a solid factor of two difference in the performance between languages. Even the difference between Rust and C/C++ is large enough it should make people consider using Rust for large, expensive workloads.

4   Conclusions and Future Work

If all you are doing is large amounts of double arithmetic, with little to no data structures required, all of the languages looked at in this paper provide similar performance, and they all scale well with the addition of more threads. However, if your work involves more complicated data structures, there are clear benefits to using systems languages.

In particular, Rust stands out as the best overall choice for performance in these benchmarks, even compared to C and C++. This isn't too unexpected, but what is truly impressive is that Rust, with Rayon, can beat out C and C++ using OpenMP. Indeed, Rayon seems to scale slightly better when the thread count on our machine is maxed out.

The most disappointing result is how poorly Julia performs when we are using a kD-tree. While Julia is highly competitive with the other languages for pure number crunching on larger systems, its performance with the kD-tree was so slow that it would be on par with Python. At least with Julia, some performance can be gained by multithreading, which would provide no benefit in current versions of Python. However, even running with 48 threads, the Julia version with the kD-tree was still slower than Java would be with a single thread.

The main element missing from this work, which remains a task for future work, is to parallelize the building of the kD-tree. The force calculations were low-hanging fruit as they are embarrassingly parallel. However, parallelizing the kD-tree construction is much more challenging. It is a recursive process. In the lower parts of the tree, the parallelization can be done by distributing each subtree to a different thread. However, each tree level requires $O(N)$ work to partition the particles, so multithreading the upper levels is just as important as multithreading the lower levels. We are still working on finding efficient ways to do this, especially with mechanisms that don't have significant memory overhead and that work well across multiple languages.

Acknowledgment. This work has been supported by NSF Award ID 2206306, "Unraveling the mysteries of small-body ring systems through numerical modeling". We'd like to thank Zachary Taylor for suggesting including Julia in this work.

References

1. Anon: binary-trees - which programs are fastest (benchmarks game) (2024). https://benchmarksgame-team.pages.debian.net/benchmarksgame/performance/binarytrees.html
2. Anon: The computer language 24.04 benchmarks game (2024). https://benchmarksgame-team.pages.debian.net/benchmarksgame/index.html
3. Anon: The julia programming language (2024). https://julialang.org/
4. Anon: n-body - which programs are fastest (benchmarks game) (2024). https://benchmarksgame-team.pages.debian.net/benchmarksgame/performance/nbody.html
5. Barnes, J., Hut, P.: A hierarchical o (n log n) force-calculation algorithm. Nature **324**(6096), 446–449 (1986)
6. Couto, M., Pereira, R., Ribeiro, F., Rua, R., Saraiva, J.: Towards a green ranking for programming languages. In: Proceedings of the 21st Brazilian Symposium on Programming Languages, pp. 1–8 (2017)
7. Engheim, E.: Julia as a second language: general purpose programming with a taste of data science. Simon and Schuster (2023)
8. Graves, D.: dgracesq/go-parallel - go parallel construct inspired by openmp (2022). https://github.com/dgravesa/go-parallel
9. Matthews, B.: Code Like a Pro in Rust. Simon and Schuster (2024)
10. Pereira, R., et al.: Energy efficiency across programming languages: how do energy, time, and memory relate? In: Proceedings of the 10th ACM SIGPLAN International Conference on Software Language Engineering, pp. 256–267 (2017)
11. Pereira, R., et al.: Ranking programming languages by energy efficiency. Sci. Comput. Program. **205**, 102609 (2021)

12. Perkel, J.M., et al.: Julia: come for the syntax, stay for the speed. Nature **572**(7767), 141–142 (2019)
13. Perminov, A., Kuznetsov, E.: The orbital evolution of the sun-jupiter-saturn-uranus-neptune system on long time scales. Astrophys. Space Sci. **365**, 1–21 (2020)
14. Richardson, D.C., Quinn, T., Stadel, J., Lake, G.: Direct large-scale n-body simulations of planetesimal dynamics. Icarus **143**(1), 45–59 (2000)
15. Rotter, J., Lewis, M.C.: N-body performance with a KD-tree: comparing rust to other languages. In: 2022 International Conference on Computational Science and Computational Intelligence, pp. 458–463 (2022). https://american-cse.org/csci2022-ieee/pdfs/CSCI2022-2lPzsUSRQukMlxf8K2x89I
16. Salo, H., Ohtsuki, K., Lewis, M.C.: Planetary Ring Systems, chap. Computer simulations of planetary rings, pp. 434–493. Cambridge University Press (2018)
17. Sells, R.: Julia programming language benchmark using a flight simulation. In: 2020 IEEE Aerospace Conference, pp. 1–8. IEEE (2020)
18. Stadel, J., Wadsley, J., Richardson, D.C.: High performance computational astrophysics with pkdgrav/gasoline. In: High Performance Computing Systems and Applications, pp. 501–523. Springer (2002)
19. Stadel, J.G.: Cosmological N-body simulations and their analysis. University of Washington (2001)

REFT: Resource-Efficient Federated Training Framework for Heterogeneous and Resource-Constrained Environments

Humaid Ahmed Desai[1]([✉])(iD), Amr Hilal[1,2](iD), and Hoda Eldardiry[1](iD)

[1] Virginia Tech, Blacksburg, VA, USA
{humaiddesai,ahilal,hdardiry}@vt.edu, ahilal@tntech.edu
[2] Tennessee Tech, Cookeville, TN, USA

Abstract. Federated Learning (FL) is vital in distributed systems, especially for ensuring data privacy, particularly in IoT and edge-based setups. However, existing research mainly focuses on data heterogeneity, leaving gaps in addressing varying device capabilities and communication efficiency. To bridge this, we propose the "Resource-Efficient Federated Training Framework for Heterogeneous and Resource-Constrained Environments (REFT)". REFT leverages Variable Pruning to adapt pruning strategies to client computational capabilities, enhancing resource utilization. Additionally, our approach employs knowledge distillation to reduce bidirectional client-server communication, reducing bandwidth usage. Experimentation in image classification tasks demonstrates the effectiveness of REFT in resource-limited environments. Our method preserves data privacy and performance standards while accommodating diverse client devices, offering a minimal bandwidth solution for FL-based systems.

Keywords: Federated Learning · Variable pruning · Distributed systems · Efficient communication · Bandwidth · Data privacy · IoT

1 Introduction

Recent advancements in deep learning have yielded significant progress across diverse domains, including, but not limited to, image classification and natural language processing. Nevertheless, the training of complex Deep Neural Network (DNN) models necessitates the availability of massive amounts of data. Training models with substantial data volumes work well in centralized scenarios where the model has access to all of the data. However, in most cases, particularly within distributed systems involving Internet-of-Things (IoT) and edge devices, data resources are inherently decentralized. This decentralized data distribution presents challenges for collaborative training, primarily stemming from technical

---

A. Hilal—Affiliated to both Virginia Tech and Tennessee Tech during the development of this paper.

© The Author(s), under exclusive license to Springer Nature Switzerland AG 2025
H. R. Arabnia et al. (Eds.): CSCE 2024, CCIS 2256, pp. 32–50, 2025.
https://doi.org/10.1007/978-3-031-85638-9_3

intricacies, privacy concerns, and the intricacies of data ownership. In response to these challenges, Federated Learning (FL) has emerged as a promising solution, enabling distributed model training through decentralized data while maintaining data privacy.

FL techniques facilitate collaborative training by iteratively sharing model parameters, or gradients, during the training process. This communication takes place between client devices connected to the Internet, encompassing IoT and edge devices, and a central server located remotely in the cloud, thus forming an FL-based system. Typically, this exchange is carried out via widely adopted protocols such as TCP or UDP [35], or alternative application layer protocols [1]. After each round of training on local data, a client transmits its model parameters to the central server, which then aggregates these parameters from all clients using traditional data aggregation methods. However, this iterative process necessitates a significant number of back-and-forth client-server communications, leading to increased bandwidth consumption and reduced communication efficiency. This challenge poses significant hurdles in the establishment of efficient FL-based systems, particularly in resource-constrained environments, such as smart home setups involving IoT and edge devices with limited hardware resources and simplified web infrastructure. Effectively harnessing FL in such applications while giving equal importance to data privacy is challenging. To alleviate communication bottlenecks in such FL scenarios, certain research initiatives [1, 35] have been dedicated to streamlining communication time and minimizing packet loss by optimizing application layer protocols. Specifically, they explore Message Queue Telemetry Transport (MQTT), Advanced Message Queuing Protocol (AMQP), and ZeroMQ Message Transport Protocol (ZMTP) to enhance the efficiency of data exchange.

Despite these advancements, challenges persist in FL-based systems, including the substantial number of bidirectional communication rounds, the size of each model update, and concerns related to data privacy. This leads us to the following questions: How can we execute FL with the fewest communication rounds, minimizing bandwidth consumption in each exchange and optimizing overall network traffic, all while preserving FL's fundamental principle of data privacy? Furthermore, client devices in FL, such as IoT and edge devices, are often significantly more constrained resources compared to data center servers, with limitations in processing power, memory, and storage. This prompts the subsequent question: How can we efficiently execute FL as IoT and edge devices become increasingly prevalent while optimizing resource usage on each client and accommodating a wide array of diverse client devices, particularly when working with complex DNN models?

To address these challenges, we propose "Resource-Efficient Federated Training (REFT)", a framework that combines variable pruning and knowledge distillation techniques. Variable pruning reduces model parameters based on the client's computational capacity, while knowledge distillation enhances communication efficiency and data privacy. Our method is inspired by FedKD [4], which employs a public dataset to mitigate privacy concerns. Unlike existing methods, we perform asynchronous updates and leverage public data, reducing communication and privacy risks. Our experiments demonstrate significant reductions in parameters, FLOPs, and bandwidth consumption while maintaining accuracy levels comparable to existing FL techniques. We summarize our key contributions as follows:

- We introduce **variable pruning**, a framework for applying model pruning techniques that adjust the pruning level for individual clients based on their available computational resources. By performing one-shot structured pruning on the initial model weights at the server, we customize the pruning level for each client. This approach utilizes client resources efficiently and reduces both computational and communication overhead (or keeps them at an acceptable level), making the model more suitable for training on resource-constrained devices.
- We employ a one-way, one-shot client-to-server knowledge distillation approach using unlabeled, non-sensitive public data. This technique further enhances communication efficiency in federated learning by optimizing the transfer of knowledge from clients to the server. We also accommodate clients with heterogeneous model architectures, which are obtained after structured pruning, enabling their active participation in the training process.

Overall, our proposed approach combines variable model pruning and one-shot knowledge distillation to improve the efficiency and effectiveness of federated learning, making it more feasible for resource-constrained devices, resulting in better resource utilization on the client side, and accommodating diverse client architectures.

2   Related Works

2.1   Efficient Federated Learning

The foundational concept of Federated Learning by McMahan et al. [23] addresses decentralized training while safeguarding data privacy. Their approach, Federated Averaging (FedAvg), calculates local gradients on client data in each round, followed by parameter averaging via a server until convergence. Various FedAvg derivatives have emerged to address aspects like non-IID data [20,26] and to introduce novel aggregation techniques [13,36]. However, high training costs persist as a challenge.

Recent efforts focus on curbing communication costs [14,28,30,38,39]. While some [15] target client-to-server communication expenses, they overlook downlink (server-to-client) communication costs. Approaches like [38] emphasize bit reduction during training through quantization and pruning, while also minimizing server communication for model updates. However, communication frequency with the server remains unchanged, limiting efficiency gains. Our REFT excels in communication and computation efficiency via pruning alone, surpassing [38], which combines quantization, pruning, and selective updates. The incorporation of knowledge distillation further enhances the efficiency of our approach.

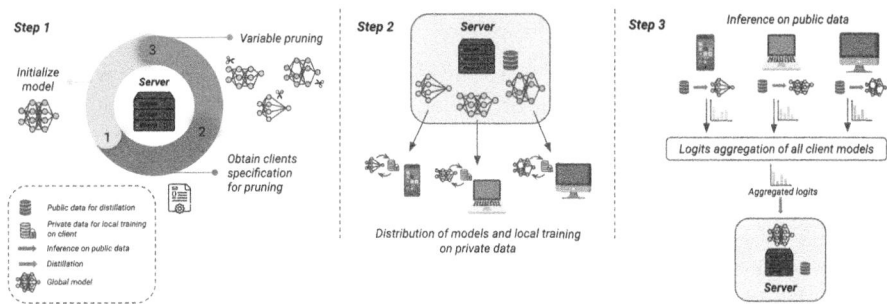

Fig. 1. Overview of *REFT*

2.2 Model Compression

Neural network pruning optimizes large networks by removing redundant or irrelevant connections. Early attempts used second-order Taylor expansion [10,17], but the impractical computation of the Hessian matrix led to alternative strategies. Han et al.'s work [8,9] popularized magnitude-based pruning, where small-magnitude parameters are pruned. [14,38] have leveraged pruning in federated learning to reduce communication and computation overhead. [14] adopts a two-stage approach, initially unstructured pruning on a selected client and then "adaptively" pruning the model during learning, i.e., reconfiguring the model by removing and adding back parameters. However, unstructured pruning leads to irregularly sparse weight matrices and relies on weights to be stored in a compressed format. Consequently, such matrices are less compatible with data-parallel architectures in GPUs and multicore CPUs, necessitating specialized hardware and software support [37].

In contrast, [38] employs structured pruning based on the L1 norm, combined with quantization and selective updates. Unlike unstructured pruning, structured pruning produces hardware-friendly weight matrices. However, for effective pruning benefits, it's crucial to reshape the weight matrices, reducing inference latency and model size. While [14,38] rely on simulations to assess pruned model performance, creating weight masks to estimate potential reductions in model or parameter size, these approaches may not guarantee actual reductions. Our approach compresses models by reshaping input and output tensors using generated masks, aiming to reduce model complexity and enhance inference latency. Notably, [14,38] concentrate solely on uniformly distributed data scenarios (for CIFAR10) which might not represent real-world FL settings characterized by non-IID data distribution. Such situations pose optimization challenges [19]. In contrast, our method is tailored to remain robust against data and model heterogeneity, ensuring convergence with superior or comparable performance.

2.3   Knowledge Distillation

Knowledge distillation, initially introduced by Hinton et al. [11], has witnessed significant progress in the realm of model ensemble, with a particular emphasis on the student-teacher learning paradigm, where the student model seeks to approximate the output logits of the teacher model [29,34,41]. Existing works either aim to average the logits from an ensemble of teacher models or extract knowledge at the feature level. The majority of these approaches utilize existing training data for the distillation process. Some works [24,27] have explored distillation through pseudo-data generation from the weights of the teacher model or through a generator adversarially trained with the student model, particularly when real data are unavailable for training. FedDF [22], on the other hand, utilizes an unlabeled dataset for ensemble distillation, which is generated from a pre-trained GAN [6].

Guha et al. [7] proposed a one-shot federated learning approach, wherein the server learns a global model of devices in the federated network in a single communication round. However, unlike their approach, which employs unlabeled public data collected from the same domain, we adopt the approach used by Gong et al. [3–5], which aggregates local predictions on unlabeled public data from different domains for enhanced privacy guarantee. Unlike Gong et al., whose primary focus is on preserving privacy, our approach is oriented towards increasing communication efficiency and resource utilization while maintaining privacy.

3   Preliminaries

A typical Federated Learning system consists of a central server S and a group of participating clients C. Each client in the network possesses its own labeled private dataset D_C, which it uses to train a local model M_C. The server S then combines these local updates using an aggregation method to obtain an updated global model, M_G. This iterative process continues until a stopping condition is met. The widely used FL algorithm, FedAvg [23], initially defines a training task, including setting hyperparameters, and selects a fraction of clients for training. The initial global model, M_G^0 is then broadcast. In each round R, clients C perform a local computation on their respective data and update their model parameters W_C^R. The primary objective is to minimize the global loss, which is a weighted average of the individual client's loss function.

$$L(w) = \sum_{c=1}^{C} \frac{k_c}{k} \ell_c(w), \qquad (1)$$

$$\text{where } \ell_c(w) = \frac{1}{k_c} \sum_{i \in D_c} f_i(w)$$

Here, k_c represents the number of data samples in the client's dataset D_c, k denotes the total number of samples, and ℓ_c is the loss function of client c.

Ensuring constant communication with the server is essential to achieving the objective in Eq. 1. However, in the context of IoT and edge devices, these devices are often resource-constrained, which significantly limits communication and computation resources. Training DNNs on such devices becomes time-consuming, and multiple rounds of communication with the server result in substantial bandwidth consumption, making this approach inefficient for FL-based systems.

4   Proposed Framework: *REFT*

Our aim is to lower communication and computation overheads within the FL process, with a specific focus on resource-constrained devices. These devices, which often fall within the IoT or edge-device paradigm, play a pivotal role in generating valuable data for the FL process. However, existing pruning methods such as [14,38] adopt a one-size-fits-all approach to pruning models without considering individual clients' hardware capabilities. This results in inefficient resource utilization among participating clients. To tackle these issues, we introduce the *REFT* framework. It features a three-stage pipeline designed to decrease the training cost of complex DNNs, enhance client training's resource utilization, and optimize communication efficiency. This is achieved by minimizing redundant communications between clients and the server while maintaining data privacy.

In the first stage, we estimate the computational capacity of each client device by obtaining their FLOPS (Floating Point Operations Per Second) values and subsequently prune the model to a level suitable for training on that client. This approach presents two advantages: it reduces the model's complexity, thereby decreasing its computational demands, and it minimizes bandwidth usage during the initial model transfer.

The second stage encompasses the distribution of the global model, followed by individual client model training on their respective private datasets. To maintain privacy, the server is restricted to accessing only public data. Notably, the server maintains its own public dataset, which we presume is universally available to all clients as an independent dataset. Consequently, for the purpose of bandwidth calculation, we omit the inclusion of this server-side public dataset, focusing solely bandwidth cost of server-client communication during FL training. This exclusion aligns with the established practices in existing works, as exemplified in [4,22], wherein public datasets have been utilized. However, these studies have typically disregarded the associated communication costs of public datasets in their analyses.

In the final stage, we employ knowledge distillation. This method curbs the need for frequent and large model updates between clients and the server, significantly cutting communication costs. Additionally, this distillation-based approach enhances the framework's versatility, allowing clients to possess distinct architectures aligned with their local data distribution and computational capabilities.

The details of the 3-stage REFT training process are depicted in Fig. 1 and are further described below:

- *Variable model pruning*: In the initial round (round 0), the server S initializes the global model parameters W_G and prunes them according to client specifications. The pruned global model, $M_{G_P}^0$, is then sent to clients. Pruning is done just once using a one-shot approach, with pruning percentage P ($100\% > P \geq 0\%$) varying based on client computational power. This method supports heterogeneous model architectures, allowing different clients to have distinct versions of $M_{G_P}^0$.
- *Model distribution and local training*: After pruning, the pruned model $M_{G_P}^0$ is broadcast along with the public dataset D_P. Each client C then trains the model on its private labeled dataset $D_c = \{(x_c^i, y_c^i)\}$ where $i = 1, 2, 3, ..., |D_c|$, and initializes the received global model $M_{G_P}^0$ with parameters W_c. It is important to note that the model architecture for each client may differ due to variable pruning or each client having its own custom model architecture.
- *Knowledge distillation*: To ensure privacy, the private datasets of clients are isolated. The public dataset D_P on the server is employed for client-to-server knowledge distillation. An ensemble of local models M_C and the global model M_{G_P} forms a teacher-student arrangement. This maintains privacy while transferring knowledge from clients to the server.

4.1   Variable Pruning

Training complex DNNs on resource-limited devices is often impractical due to their intricacy. Pruning, as explained in Sect. 2.2, provides a means to accelerate training and reduce computational demands. However, the inherent diversity of devices in federated learning adds complexity. Clients possess varying computational power, introducing challenges for traditional static pruning techniques. These methods, aimed at minimizing communication costs, employ uniform pruning strategies, irrespective of the diverse capacities of individual clients. Consequently, this approach underutilizes the potential of more capable clients by tailoring pruning to the least powerful client, failing to harness their potential for an efficient model training.

Our approach addresses these limitations via variable-structured model pruning, tailored to individual client computational abilities. Unlike static pruning, which underestimates more potent clients, our strategy optimizes both computation and communication overheads. By assessing a client's computing capacity and estimating the necessary FLOPs for effective model training, we customize the pruning process. This results in models that are finely tuned for each client, enhancing the overall efficiency of the FL process. Given the significance of FLOPs in hardware assessment for DNN training [32,33], we prioritize FLOPS as the primary metric for computation assessment and pruning degree determination. FLOPS provides a reasonable and hardware-independent measure for assessing the feasibility of neural network training. As memory capacity and other client hardware parameters can also offer valuable insights, we complement this assessment with an analysis of memory requirements (RAM) and GPU utilization for the DNNs discussed in the following sections. We adopt L1 norm-based pruning, a straightforward method to gauge weight importance in DNNs [18], and apply it to both convolutional and fully connected layers. This approach is justified as convolutional layers typically contribute significantly to computational overhead, while fully connected layers primarily impact the model size [18,31].

To effectively reduce the model's size and improve both training and inference speed, we employ the NNI toolkit. This toolkit allows us to perform pruning not only based on performance metrics like the L1 norm associated with each output channel but also to take into account the broader network architecture and its topology. Specifically, we harness the toolkit's dependency-aware pruning technique [25] to identify and prune output channels shared by layers that exhibit channel dependencies. This ensures that the pruning process is carried out in a manner that preserves these critical inter-layer dependencies. The pruner (L1 norm algorithm) initiates the model pruning process, generating a weight mask. This mask is then subsequently utilized by the ModelSpeedup module to reconfigure the weight tensors, ensuring a meaningful reduction in both model size and inference speed. The overall variable pruning procedure is described in Algorithm 1.

4.2   Knowledge Distillation

In the knowledge distillation phase, we initiate local model training M_c with the private labeled dataset D_c at each client. Post-local training, the server dispatches an unlabeled public dataset $D_p = (x_p^i)$, with $i = 1, 2, 3, ..., |D_p|$, to every client for knowledge distillation. Referring to [4], the private dataset $D_c = (x_c^i, y_c^i)$, $i = 1, 2, 3, ..., |D_c|$ (with $c \in C$), entails existing classes $T_c \subset 1, 2, ..., T$ (T as total classes across clients). The local model's output on the public data sample x_p^i for class $t \in T_c$ is $z_{tc}^i = f(x_p^i, w_c, t)$, with w representing model parameters. In high-data heterogeneity settings, traditional aggregation methods averaging all teachers' logits lack suitability, as the client's dataset may not share identical target classes. To address this, we introduce the importance weight I for each client, reflecting local private data distribution. The weight is computed as the ratio of samples in local client c belonging to class t to total samples across clients:

$$I_c^t = \frac{N_c^t}{\sum_{c \in C} N_c^t}, \tag{2}$$

where N_c^t is the sample count in local client c for class t. It is important to note that this distillation holds true as long as the target class t of public data sample x_p^i matches the target class T_c of the client's private dataset.

Kullback-Leibler divergence is utilized for teachers' soft label aggregation. Loss function L is the cross-entropy sum between teacher and student model predicted probabilities. Here, p_t and q_t are probabilities of a sample belonging to class t by teacher and student models:

$$L = \sum_t p_t \log \frac{p_t}{q_t} \qquad (3)$$

The central model's output logits $\tilde{z}_t = f(x_p, w_s, t)$ form student knowledge, and aggregated logits $\hat{z}_t$ are teacher knowledge. Probabilities p_t and q_t are computed using softmax on logits with a temperature parameter τ. As indicated in [11], minimizing the loss with high-temperature parameter τ equates to minimizing the L2 norm between teacher and student network logits, simplifying loss to $L = ||\tilde{z} - \hat{z}||$.

REFT employs a one-shot offline distillation, predicting with each public data sample once, iteratively training the central model. This boosts privacy, reduces queries to local models, and limits local knowledge exposure. Moreover, synchronous updates and repetitive communication are eliminated, enhancing communication efficiency and flexibility.

5 Variable Pruning vs. Static Pruning for Resource Utilization

In the context of federated learning with n clients $(c_1, c_2, ..., c_n)$, each client (c_i) possesses unique hardware capability h_{c_i} and computation capacity F_{c_i} in FLOP. Our analysis centers on variable pruning versus static pruning's efficiency in harnessing resources. The pruning level P_{c_i} for a client depends on its hardware, with $NP_{c_i} = N \times (1 - P_{c_i})$ total pruned model parameters, where N is the total number of parameters in the unpruned model. We assume uniform pruning across layers and connections and a uniform distribution of FLOPs across pruned and unpruned parameters.

By reducing the number of parameters, we can reduce the training overhead and communication load. We define the FLOP reduction factor for client c_i as $FP_{c_i} = F \times (1 - P_{c_i})$. The accuracy for training the pruned model is denoted as AP_{c_i}. It is worth noting that typically $A_{c_i} \geq AP_{c_i}$, where A_{c_i} is unpruned model accuracy.

Static pruning (P_{static}) uses $P_{\min}$ based on least capable hardware $(h_{\min} = \min(h_1, h_2, ..., h_n))$. All clients, including those with higher hardware capabilities, are then pruned at the level $P_{\text{static}} = P_{\min}$, resulting in $NP_{\text{static}} = N \times (1 - P_{\text{static}})$ total number of parameters. Thus, higher-capability clients with $F_{c_i} > F_{\text{static}}$ might be underutilized, leading to reduced training performance. This underutilization results in the following inequality: $A_{c_i} \geq AP_{c_i} \geq AP_{\text{static}}$, where $1 \geq P_{\text{static}} \geq P_{c_i} \geq 0$ We can define the utilization factor for client c_i as $U_{c_i} = \frac{F_{\text{static}}}{F_{c_i}}$, indicating the ratio of the least performing client's hardware capacity to the client c_i's hardware capacity. Our variable pruning strategy overcomes this underutilization by identifying a link between pruning level and FLOP reduction, which can be expressed as:

$$P_{c_i} = 1 - \frac{F_{c_i}}{F_\lambda} \tag{4}$$

Here, F_{c_i} signifies client c_i's computational capability (FLOPS), and F_λ is a trade-off coefficient between communication efficiency and accuracy. The choice of F_λ allows the administrator (or orchestrator of FL) to prioritize either more efficient communication or better accuracy/performance. Note that if $F_{c_i} \geq F_\lambda$, no pruning will be performed for client c_i.

For instance, consider 5 clients with FLOP capacities of 10, 20, 40, 60, and 100 GFLOPS (GigaFLOPS). By setting F_λ to 100 GFLOPS, pruning percentages are: $P_{c_1} = 90\%$, $P_{c_2} = 80\%$, $P_{c_3} = 60\%$, $P_{c_4} = 40\%$, and $P_{c_5} = 0\%$ (no pruning). This choice reflects the administrator's preference for communication efficiency over performance. Alternatively, opting for $F_\lambda = 50$ GFLOPS, clients c_1, c_2, and c_3 are pruned to 80%, 60%, and 20% respectively, while clients c_4 and c_5 remain unpruned. This choice reflects the administrator's emphasis on accuracy or performance over communication costs.

Algorithm 1. Variable Pruning

Require: n clients, each client $c_i \in C$ has computation capacity of F_{c_i} FLOPS where $i = 1, .., n$, trade-off coefficient F_λ, client model M_{c_i}
    for each client c_i in C **do**
        $F_{c_i} \leftarrow$ Request client's estimated FLOPS
        Calculate pruning ratio:
        $P_{c_i} \leftarrow 1 - \frac{F_{c_i}}{F_\lambda}$ ▷ Eq. 4
        Apply L1 Norm pruning and create weight mask:
        $m_{c_i} \leftarrow L1NormPruner(M_{c_i}, P_{c_i})$
        $ModelSpeedup(M_{c_i}, m_{c_i})$ ▷ Model reconfiguration
    end for

---

6 Experiments

Our experiments aimed to assess our proposed approach's performance in image classification using the CIFAR10 and CIFAR100 datasets [16]. Private datasets for local training were created using a Dirichlet distribution, generating heterogeneous data splits [12,40]. The α parameter controlled dataset non-IID-ness, with higher values promoting similar data distributions across clients.

We employed simulations to emulate the training of diverse clients on HPC clusters. To accomplish this, we gathered estimated FLOPS values for various potential client devices and integrated these values into our simulation framework. For instance, devices in the category of Raspberry Pi models 3 and 4, and similar counterparts, were categorized as weak clients due to their FLOPS capabilities falling within the range of 8 to 40 GFLOPS. In a similar context, wearable devices, including high-end smartwatches and mobile phones, were classified as

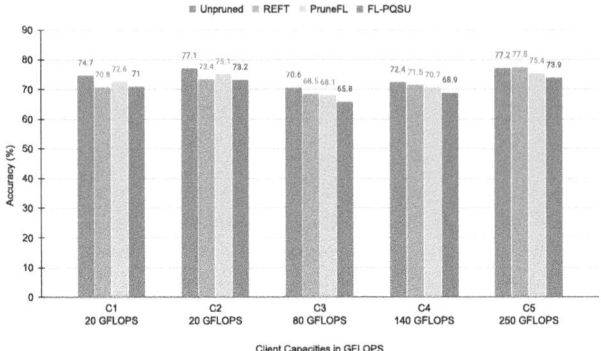

Fig. 2. Comparing client accuracies: static pruning (FL-PQSU and PruneFL) vs. REFT on the VGG-16 model.

moderate to good clients, exhibiting FLOPS capacities below 150 GFLOPS. Conversely, devices equipped with high-performance computing units, such as laptops and desktops featuring dedicated GPUs, were designated as strong clients. It is noteworthy that our hardware configuration encompassed two 12 GB NVIDIA GRID P40-12Q GPUs and an Intel (R) Xeon (R) CPU E5-2640 v4 clocked at 2.40GHz.

6.1   Datasets and Models

For consistency and meaningful comparison, our experimental setup adhered to FedKD [4]. CIFAR10 was the private dataset, and CIFAR100 served as the public distillation dataset. While our experiments were exclusively conducted on these datasets, it is worth noting that our approach exhibits versatility and can potentially be adapted to accommodate different datasets, including but not limited to large-scale datasets like ImageNet, provided that the prerequisites outlined in Sect. 4.2 regarding the private and public dataset conditions are met. We evaluated the test accuracy of our framework and compared it with the baselines. For our experiments, we employed ResNet-8 and VGG-16 model architectures, as described in the respective prior works [4,38]. To demonstrate the robustness of our approach, we performed experiments on non-IID data and created disjoint training sets for each client with the value of α set to 1.0.

6.2   Baselines

Our focus lies in enhancing resource utilization while maintaining performance and minimal communication. Thus, we compared against FedAvg [23], PruneFL [14], FedKD [4], and FL-PQSU [38]. Personalized FL methods (Per-FedAvg [2], q-FedAvg [21]) were excluded, as they prioritize adapting to individual client's data distribution.

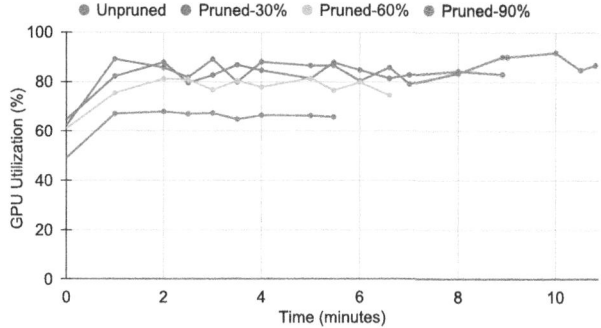

Fig. 3. Effect of pruning on GPU utilization and training time of VGG-16.

6.3   Metrics

Our experiments focus on evaluating model performance in terms of test accuracy and comparing it with baseline approaches. Our main goal is to showcase resource-efficient training, achieving significant reductions in model size, parameter count, and FLOPs while maintaining minimal accuracy loss. We also delve into communication bandwidth analysis, a critical factor in federated learning that affects time and cost. For non-distillation training, communication bandwidth is computed based on parameters such as parameter size (W), the number of participating clients (C), communication rounds (R), and the number of bits (B) used for representing parameters and logits. This calculation is expressed as:

$$\text{Bandwidth} = C \times R \times W \times B \tag{5}$$

We analyze both downstream (server-to-client) and upstream (client-to-server) communication per client per round. For response-based knowledge distillation, where W isn't transferred, we adapt the equation as $Bandwidth = L \times S \times B$, with L as logits and S as distillation steps.

6.4   Implementation Details

For ResNet-8, we used SGD optimizer with momentum of 0.9, weight decay of 3×10^{-4}, and Cosine Annealing scheduler (learning rate, lr, decreased from 0.0025 to 0.001) over 500 epochs with a batch size of 16. VGG-16 employed a lr of 0.1 without weight decay and a batch size of 128. Optimizer, momentum, and epochs matched ResNet-8. Distillation employed a constant lr of 10^{-3} and batch size of 512 with Adam optimizer.

For a fair comparison, we aligned with FedKD's hyperparameters for client model training. It utilized the SGD optimizer (momentum 0.9, weight decay 3×10^{-4}) with the Cosine Annealing scheduler over 500 epochs and batch size 16. Distillation used a constant lr of 10^{-3} and batch size of 512 with Adam Optimizer.

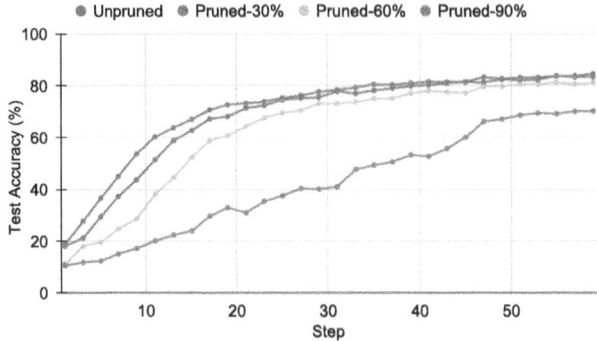

Fig. 4. Effect of pruning on test accuracy of VGG-16.

7 Results

7.1 Resource Utilization

To demonstrate the effectiveness of our variable pruning strategy in optimizing hardware resource utilization, we compared accuracies per client across different pruning strategies (Fig. 2). This experiment involved five clients with varying hardware capabilities. Clients c_1 and c_2 had limited computational capacity, necessitating a high pruning level (90%) to accommodate the model. Pruning levels were determined using Eq. (4), with F_λ set to 200 GFLOPS ($10^9 \times$ FLOPS). Clients c_3 and c_4 possessed better hardware capabilities and required 60% and 30% pruning, respectively, for model training. Client c_5 had ample hardware resources and required no pruning.

For comparison, our proposed REFT employs three pruning levels: 30%, 60%, and 90%, based on client device FLOPs. As seen in Fig. 3, increasing pruning lowers GPU utilization from around 84% to about 65%. Figure 4 shows accuracy variations with increased pruning. Pruning VGG-16 to 90% accelerates training by approximately 48%, reducing training time. In Fig. 6, pruning to 90% decreases inference time by roughly 30%. This accelerates both training and inference, enhancing FL efficiency. Since REFT utilizes structured pruning, specifically based on the L1 norm (discussed in Sect. 4.1), to reduce model complexity, it's noteworthy that the structured pruning approach may result in a minor decline in accuracy, as illustrated in Fig. 4. To retain performance, our approach avoids pruning clients capable of training unpruned models. In contrast, approaches like FL-PQSU prune all clients to the least capable hardware level, not considering individual capacities and incurring performance loss.

In Fig. 2, the FL-PQSU method prunes the model for all clients using a level best suited for clients c_1 and c_2. While clients c_1 and c_2 achieve satisfactory model training, the hardware resources of $c_3, c_4,$ and c_5 are underutilized, resulting in a decline in accuracy. This reduction in accuracy stems from the model being pruned to a higher level than what is ideally suited for their hardware, thereby leading to suboptimal overall performance. As a result, we observe that clients

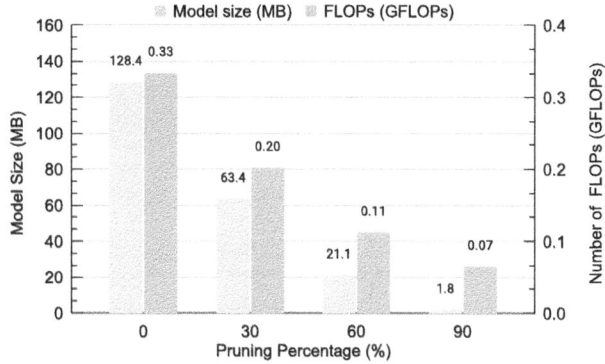

Fig. 5. Reduction in model size and FLOPs of VGG-16 by REFT.

c_3, c_4, and c_5 exhibit higher accuracy when our variable pruning strategy is employed compared to the static pruning methods. This observation underscores the effectiveness of our approach in tailoring the pruning level to match the specific hardware capabilities of each client. By leveraging the benefits of variable pruning, we achieve higher accuracy rates and overall improved performance.

In addition to the observed improvements in resource utilization and performance, we observed RAM utilization during our experiments. We found that RAM usage ranged from 3 to 3.3 GB across different client models. This indicates that the optimal execution of our approach aligns with industry standards, as even a relatively weak client device like the Raspberry Pi 4, which features up to 8 GB of RAM, comfortably meets the minimum memory requirement, highlighting the practicality and accessibility of our proposed approach across a range of hardware configurations.

7.2   Model Size, Computation, and Inference Time

In this set of experiments (Figs. 5 and 6), we show that REFT achieves a substantial reduction in model size, FLOPs, and inference time as a result of the pruning performed while incurring negligible loss in final accuracy. We don't include FL-PQSU and PruneFL in the computation and inference time comparison because their pruning results in sparse matrices, which require special hardware and software for computing actual computation and inference time, as discussed in Sect. 2.2. Furthermore, PruneFL prunes the model iteratively while training until the training converges, making it unsuitable for direct comparison with specific pruning levels. To assess the impact of REFT on model size and computation, we measured the number of model parameters and FLOPs of VGG-16 across different pruning levels. Figure 5 illustrates the significant reduction achieved by REFT, compressing the size of the model from 128.4 MB to 1.8 MB, resulting in a 98.5% reduction. Similarly, the FLOPs are reduced from 0.33 GFLOPs to 0.07 GFLOPs.

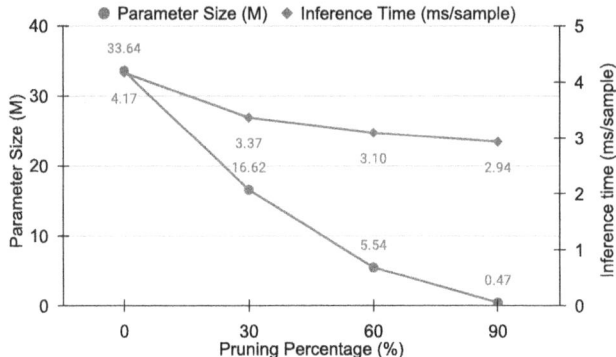

Fig. 6. Parameter size and inference time reduction with an increase in pruning of VGG-16 by REFT.

Table 1. Comparison of accuracy (central) and communication efficiency on RestNet-8 and VGG-16 models with 20 clients ($C = 20$). The table presents the downstream and upstream communication costs per client for each round, excluding FedKD and REFT. The total column represents the total bandwidth cost for a client to complete the federated learning training.

Model	Method	Pruning Ratio (%)	Accuracy (%)	Bandwidth		
				Downstream	Upstream	Total
ResNet-8	FedAvg	-	74.7	37.6 MB	37.6 MB	73.5 GB
	FL-PQSU	30%	73.7	37.6 MB	**4.7 MB**	41.3 GB
		60%	71.9	37.6 MB	**4.7 MB**	41.3 GB
		90%	70.3	37.6 MB	**4.7 MB**	41.3 GB
	PruneFL	Adaptive (~60%)	76.2	~20.8 MB	~20.8 MB	~36.6 GB
	FedKD	-	81.5	37.6 MB	4.9 MB	42.5 MB
	REFT	Variable (30-90%)	80.8–**81.7**	**3.65–25.74 MB**	7.8 MB	**11.46–33.5 MB**
VGG-16	FedAvg	-	73.6	256.6 MB	256.6 MB	200 GB
	FL-PQSU	30%	74.5	256.6 MB	32 MB	140.1 GB
		60%	73.1	256.6 MB	32 MB	140.1 GB
		90%	71.3	256.6 MB	32 MB	140.1 GB
	PruneFL	Adaptive (~60%)	78.9	~102 MB	~102 MB	~93.6 GB
	FedKD	-	79.3	256.6 MB	**4.9 MB**	261.5 MB
	REFT	Variable (30–90%)	77.6–**80.8**	**3.6–126.8 MB**	7.81 MB	**11.4–134.6 MB**

As pruning also improves the model speedups by reducing the inference time, we visualize the improvements in inference time in Fig. 6 along with the parameter size reduction. Our pruning reduces the parameter size of VGG-16 from 33.6 M to 0.47 M parameters, achieving about 98.3% reduction. Similarly, the inference time is reduced from 4.17 ms/sample to 2.94 ms/sample for 1000 samples.

7.3 Communication Efficiency

We evaluated REFT's communication efficiency against baselines using ResNet-8 and VGG-16 models. Table 1 summarizes the outcomes in terms of total communication bandwidth and test accuracy. Notably, REFT achieves the lowest total communication bandwidth with comparable or superior accuracy compared to baselines. Due to variable pruning in REFT, accuracy and bandwidth are presented as a range to reflect pruned clients and ratios. The range accommodates various scenarios, from highly constrained clients (90% pruning) to less constrained ones (30% pruning). This captures REFT's trade-off between accuracy and bandwidth efficiency.

For FedKD and REFT, the knowledge distillation process required minimal communication cost, as only 200 distillation steps were performed. In contrast, FedAvg, FL-PQSU, and PruneFL required significantly more communication rounds (900 to 1000 for ResNet-8 and about 500 for VGG-16) to complete the federated learning training. Moreover, given the dataset that we are using, the cost associated with transferring logits is considerably less than that associated with transferring model weights. Therefore, the total bandwidth of REFT and FedKD is far less than the other baselines. Given that PruneFL performs iterative pruning and reconfiguration at fixed intervals, we simplify the analysis by considering its final pruning ratio. Consequently, we provide approximate values for the bandwidth to maintain clarity and simplicity in the comparison.

FL-PQSU stands out in terms of upstream cost reduction among weight-sharing methods like FedAvg and PruneFL. This advantage can be attributed to its utilization of INT8 quantization during client-server communication. As elaborated in Sect. 2.2, FL-PQSU maintains consistent total bandwidth usage across various pruning levels, primarily because it avoids the need for post-pruning model weight reconfiguration. Consequently, this approach leads to the emergence of sparse weight tensors and a model architecture that remains unaltered. As a result, the actual model size and computational requirements experienced no meaningful change.

Table 1 highlights our method's superior downstream communication efficiency for both ResNet-8 and VGG-16 models, outperforming other pruning-based techniques like FL-PQSU and PruneFL. These methods anticipate sparse matrix support in future hardware and software developments, but such resources are not yet available. As a result, they encounter practical constraints, particularly PruneFL, which relies heavily on sparse matrices. In contrast, REFT adopts structured pruning, yielding hardware-friendly weight matrices that undergo size reduction through shape reconfiguration. This strategy significantly reduces parameter size and enhances latency. Furthermore, REFT and FedKD exhibit lower bandwidth needs than other baselines, leveraging one-shot distillation. Remarkably, FedKD employs quantization before transmitting logits to the server, further curbing upstream communication costs.

8   Conclusion and Future Work

In this study, we introduced REFT, a framework that improves resource utilization in federated learning. Through variable pruning and knowledge distillation, we enhanced resource utilization, training time, and bandwidth consumption. Our experiments showcased REFT's efficiency compared to baselines while sustaining performance. The adaptation of variable pruning enabled diverse clients to contribute effectively in resource-constrained scenarios, thereby enhancing resource utilization. Furthermore, employing one-shot knowledge distillation on public data minimizes repetitive communication, ensures privacy, and boosts efficiency. Our future work entails exploring the synergistic effect of quantization with REFT to further reduce upstream bandwidth communication, thereby enhancing overall communication efficiency.

References

1. Cleland, G., Wu, D., Ullah, R., Varghese, B.: FedComm: Understanding Communication Protocols for Edge-based Federated Learning. arXiv:2208.08764 (2022)
2. Fallah, A., Mokhtari, A., Ozdaglar, A.E.: Personalized Federated Learning: A Meta-Learning Approach. CoRR abs/2002.07948 (2020). arXiv:2002.07948. https://arxiv.org/abs/2002.07948
3. Gong, X., et al.: Ensemble attention distillation for privacy-preserving federated learning. In: 2021 IEEE/CVF International Conference on Computer Vision (ICCV), pp. 15056–15066 (2021). https://doi.org/10.1109/ICCV48922.2021.01480
4. Gong, X., et al.: Preserving privacy in federated learning with ensemble cross-domain knowledge distillation. In: Thirty-Sixth AAAI Conference on Artificial Intelligence, AAAI 2022, Thirty-Fourth Conference on Innovative Applications of Artificial Intelligence, IAAI 2022, The Twelveth Symposium on Educational Advances in Artificial Intelligence, EAAI 2022 Virtual Event, 22 February–1 March 2022, pp. 11891–11899. AAAI Press (2022). https://ojs.aaai.org/index.php/AAAI/article/view/21446
5. Gong, X., et al.: Federated Learning with Privacy-Preserving Ensemble Attention Distillation. arXiv:2210.08464 (2022)
6. Goodfellow, I.J., et al.: Generative Adversarial Networks. CoRR abs/1406.2661 (2014). arXiv:1406.2661. http://arxiv.org/abs/1406.2661
7. Guha, N., Talwalkar, A., Smith, V.: One-Shot Federated Learning. CoRR abs/1902.11175 (2019). arXiv:1902.11175. http://arxiv.org/abs/1902.11175
8. Han, S., Mao, H., Dally, W.J.: Deep compression: compressing deep neural network with pruning, trained quantization and huffman coding. In: Bengio, Y., LeCun, Y. (eds.) 4th International Conference on Learning Representations, ICLR 2016, San Juan, Puerto Rico, 2–4 May 2016, Conference Track Proceedings (2016). http://arxiv.org/abs/1510.00149
9. Han, S., Pool, J., Tran, J., Dally, W.: Learning both weights and connections for efficient neural network. In: Cortes, C., Lawrence, N., Lee, D., Sugiyama, M., Garnett, R. (eds.) Advances in Neural Information Processing Systems, vol. 28. Curran Associates, Inc. (2015). https://proceedings.neurips.cc/paper_files/paper/2015/file/ae0eb3eed39d2bcef4622b2499a05fe6-Paper.pdf

10. Hassibi, B., Stork, D., Wolff, G.: Optimal brain surgeon: extensions and performance comparisons. In: Cowan, J., Tesauro, G., Alspector, J. (eds.) Advances in Neural Information Processing Systems, vol. 6. Morgan-Kaufmann (1993). https://proceedings.neurips.cc/paper_files/paper/1993/file/b056eb1587586b71e2da9acfe4fbd19e-Paper.pdf

11. Hinton, G., Vinyals, O., Dean, J.: Distilling the Knowledge in a Neural Network. arXiv:1503.02531 (2015)

12. Hsu, T.-M.H., Qi, H., Brown, M.: Measuring the Effects of Non-Identical Data Distribution for Federated Visual Classification. CoRR abs/1909.06335 (2019). arXiv:1909.06335. http://arxiv.org/abs/1909.06335

13. Hsu, T.-M.H., Qi, H., Brown, M.: Federated Visual Classification with Real-World Data Distribution. CoRR abs/2003.08082 (2020). arXiv:2003.08082. https://arxiv.org/abs/2003.08082

14. Jiang, Y., Wang, S., Ko, B.J., Lee, W.-H., Tassiulas, L.: Model Pruning Enables Efficient Federated Learning on Edge Devices. CoRR abs/1909.12326 (2019). arXiv:1909.12326. http://arxiv.org/abs/1909.12326

15. Konečný, J., McMahan, H.B., Yu, F.X., Richtárik, P., Suresh, A.T., Bacon, D.: Federated Learning: Strategies for Improving Communication Efficiency. CoRR abs/1610.05492 (2016). arXiv:1610.05492. http://arxiv.org/abs/1610.05492

16. Krizhevsky, A.: Learning Multiple Layers of Features from Tiny Images, pp. 32–33 (2009). https://www.cs.toronto.edu/~kriz/learning-features-2009-TR.pdf

17. Lecun, Y., Denker, J.S., Solla, S.A., Howard, R.E., Jackel, L.D.: Optimal brain damage. In: Denver, C.O., Touretzky, D. (ed.) Advances in Neural Information Processing Systems (NIPS 1989), vol. 2. Morgan Kaufmann (1990)

18. Li, H., Kadav, A., Durdanovic, I., Samet, H., Graf, H.P.: Pruning Filters for Efficient ConvNets. In: International Conference on Learning Representations (2017). https://openreview.net/forum?id=rJqFGTslg

19. Li, T., Sahu, A.K., Talwalkar, A., Smith, V.: Federated Learning: Challenges, Methods, and Future Directions. CoRR abs/1908.07873 (2019). arXiv:1908.07873. http://arxiv.org/abs/1908.07873

20. Li, T., Sanjabi, M., Beirami, A., Smith, V.: Fair Resource Allocation in Federated Learning. arXiv:1905.10497 (2020)

21. Li, T., Sanjabi, M., Smith, V.: Fair Resource Allocation in Federated Learning. CoRR abs/1905.10497 (2019). arXiv:1905.10497. http://arxiv.org/abs/1905.10497

22. Lin, T., Kong, L., Stich, S.U., Jaggi, M.: Ensemble distillation for robust model fusion in federated learning. In: Larochelle, H., Ranzato, M., Hadsell, R., Balcan, M.-F., Lin, H.-T. (eds.) Advances in Neural Information Processing Systems 33: Annual Conference on Neural Information Processing Systems 2020, NeurIPS 2020, 6–12 December 2020, virtual (2020). https://proceedings.neurips.cc/paper/2020/hash/18df51b97ccd68128e994804f3eccc87-Abstract.html

23. McMahan, H.B., Moore, E., Ramage, D., Hampson, S., y Arcas, B.A.: Communication-Efficient Learning of Deep Networks from Decentralized Data. arXiv:1602.05629 (2023)

24. Micaelli, P., Storkey, A.J.: Zero-shot knowledge transfer via adversarial belief matching. In: Wallach, H.M., Larochelle, H., Beygelzimer, A., d'Alché-Buc, F., Fox, E.B., Garnett, R. (eds.) Advances in Neural Information Processing Systems 32: Annual Conference on Neural Information Processing Systems 2019, NeurIPS 2019, 8–14 December 2019, Vancouver, BC, Canada, pp. 9547–9557 (2019). https://proceedings.neurips.cc/paper/2019/hash/fe663a72b27bdc613873fbbb512f6f67-Abstract.html

25. Microsoft NNI Contributors. Overview of NNI Model Pruning; Neural Network Intelligence - nni.readthedocs.io (2023). https://nni.readthedocs.io/en/v2.10/compression/pruning.html#dependency-awaremode-for-output-channel-pruning. Accessed 20 Aug 2024

26. Mohri, M., Sivek, G., Suresh, A.T.: Agnostic Federated Learning. arXiv:1902.00146 (2019)

27. Nayak, G.K., Mopuri, K.R., Shaj, V., Radhakrishnan, V.B., Chakraborty, A.: Zero-Shot Knowledge Distillation in Deep Networks. CoRR abs/1905.08114 (2019). arXiv:1905.08114. http://arxiv.org/abs/1905.08114

28. Reisizadeh, A., Mokhtari, A., Hassani, H., Jadbabaie, A., Pedarsani, R.: FedPAQ: a communication-efficient federated learning method with periodic averaging and quantization. In: Chiappa, S., Calandra, R. (eds.) Proceedings of the Twenty Third International Conference on Artificial Intelligence and Statistics (Proceedings of Machine Learning Research, vol. 108), pp. 2021–2031. PMLR (2020). https://proceedings.mlr.press/v108/reisizadeh20a.html

29. Romero, A., Ballas, N., Kahou, S.E., Chassang, A., Gatta, C., Bengio, Y.: FitNets: Hints for Thin Deep Nets. arXiv:1412.6550 (2015)

30. Sattler, F., Wiedemann, S., Müller, K.R., Samek, W.: Robust and communication-efficient federated learning from non-i.i.d. data. IEEE Trans. Neural Netw. Learn. Syst. 31(9), 3400–3413 (2020). https://doi.org/10.1109/TNNLS.2019.2944481

31. Singh, P., Verma, V.K., Rai, P., Namboodiri, V.P.: Play and Prune: Adaptive Filter Pruning for Deep Model Compression. CoRR abs/1905.04446 (2019). arXiv:1905.04446. http://arxiv.org/abs/1905.04446

32. Tang, R., Adhikari, A., Lin, J.: FLOPs as a Direct Optimization Objective for Learning Sparse Neural Networks. CoRR abs/1811.03060 (2018). arXiv:1811.03060. http://arxiv.org/abs/1811.03060

33. Tang, R., Wang, W., Tu, Z., Lin, J.: An Experimental Analysis of the Power Consumption of Convolutional Neural Networks for Keyword Spotting. CoRR abs/1711.00333 (2017). arXiv:1711.00333. http://arxiv.org/abs/1711.00333

34. Tung, F., Mori, G.: Similarity-preserving knowledge distillation. In: Proceedings of the IEEE/CVF International Conference on Computer Vision (ICCV) (2019)

35. Vineeth, S.: Federated learning over WiFi: Should we use TCP or UDP? (2021). https://doi.org/10.31219/osf.io/tuz6c

36. Wang, H., Yurochkin, M., Sun, Y., Papailiopoulos, D., Khazaeni, Y.: Federated Learning with Matched Averaging. arXiv:2002.06440 (2020)

37. Wang, Y., et al.: Non-structured DNN Weight Pruning Considered Harmful. CoRR abs/1907.02124 (2019). arXiv:1907.02124. http://arxiv.org/abs/1907.02124

38. Wenyuan, X., Fang, W., Ding, Y., Zou, M., Xiong, N.: Accelerating federated learning for IoT in big data analytics with pruning, quantization and selective updating. IEEE Access 9(2021), 38457–38466 (2021). https://doi.org/10.1109/ACCESS.2021.3063291

39. Yang, Z., Chen, M., Saad, W., Hong, C.S., Shikh-Bahaei, M.: Energy efficient federated learning over wireless communication networks. IEEE Trans. Wirel. Commun. 20(3), 1935–1949 (2021). https://doi.org/10.1109/TWC.2020.3037554

40. Yurochkin, M., Agarwal, M., Ghosh, S., Greenewald, K., Hoang, N., Khazaeni, Y.: Bayesian Nonparametric Federated Learning of Neural Networks. arXiv:1905.12022 (2019)

41. Zagoruyko, S., Komodakis, N.: Paying More Attention to Attention: Improving the Performance of Convolutional Neural Networks via Attention Transfer. CoRR abs/1612.03928 (2016). arXiv:1612.03928. http://arxiv.org/abs/1612.03928

An Efficient Data Provenance Collection Framework for HPC I/O Workloads

Md Kamal Hossain Chowdhury$^{(\boxtimes)}$ and Purushotham V. Bangalore

Department of Computer Science, College of Engineering, University of Alabama, Tuscaloosa, USA
mhchowdhury@crimson.ua.edu, pvbangalore@ua.edu

Abstract. Scientific data is essential for research and development in many fields, and its provenance and lineage are crucial for ensuring the validity of these findings. However, traditional data management methods fall short of transparency and accountability, leading to data manipulation and falsification of research findings. By offering a transparent and impermeable mechanism for logging and verifying data integrity, tracking the provenance, and viewing the lineage of scientific data, blockchain technology provides a promising solution to address these issues. Metadata, verifiable research data, and configuration changes can be stored transparently and reliably using private blockchain technology. This paper proposes a framework to support secure scientific data provenance with minimum overhead on application performance while requiring minimal user intervention.

Keywords: Data provenance · I/O tracing · Blockchain · smart contract

1 Introduction

Provenance [9] is typically defined as the origin or source of an object, and it is also applied to electronic data, providing insight into how documents were created, simulations were performed, or analyses were conducted. For scientists, data provenance can reveal how results were obtained, which parameters influenced the outcome, and which datasets were used. Ultimately, data provenance is essential for reproducibility, a critical component of the scientific method.

Provenance is essential to establish scientific research quality, relevance, and trust. However, tracking provenance information attributes through complex transformations is very arduous. Moreover, provenance is necessary to describe one's experiment to others for better understanding or future reuse. It also helps to provide evidence supporting scientific claims as actual findings. Moreover, distributed data provenance is necessary for petascale and exascale computing to ensure large-volume data I/O operation tracking [23].

Moreover, data provenance addresses the challenge of insufficiently tracked experiments [17]. Provenance collects metadata detailing the lineage of data

© The Author(s), under exclusive license to Springer Nature Switzerland AG 2025
H. R. Arabnia et al. (Eds.): CSCE 2024, CCIS 2256, pp. 51–64, 2025.
https://doi.org/10.1007/978-3-031-85638-9_4

entities [5], typically containing scripts and datasets. These entities' characteristics may include version details, while their interconnections delineate dependencies or causality. While data provenance addresses the technical hurdles in
reproducibility by documenting the absent components necessary for experiment
replication, it lacks in aiding users' comprehension of the reproduced pipeline [3].

For scientific reproducibility, users may need to know what datasets and types
of analyses with what parameters were used. The hardware architecture, environment variables, and library version details information may be necessary to
reproduce results. By examining task execution, runtime distribution and other
factors must be collected as provenance data for scientific reproducibility [10].
The collection of provenance data can help us to build reproducible experiments.

Besides, "open science" is useful for overcoming scientific research credibility
and reproducibility through data sharing. Collaboration, transparency, accessibility, and inclusiveness are the key features of open science research [14,21].
Beyond aiding reproduction and audits, sharing fosters reuse in different contexts, enhancing efficiency by preventing redundant research spending and
enabling previously unattainable research avenues [22]. The trustworthiness
of findings becomes questionable, hindering replication and verification when
research data isn't shared. Enabling secure, independently verifiable data reuse
is vital for advancing research.

Maintaining the provenance of scientific application is a crucial challenge. To
ensure the provenance of scientific research, we need to consider the following
research questions:

- Can we ensure data integrity and provenance among research groups sharing
  and working on the same datasets?
- Can we detect if the shared dataset is corrupted due to hardware failure or
  unintentional errors?
- Is it possible to enable quick verification of the exact datasets used for a
  particular published research?

This paper explores the above research questions and makes the following
contributions:

- We propose a new framework for secure and reliable data provenance on
  High-Performance Computing (HPC) systems to collect the metadata transparently and securely without user intervention.
- We evaluate our proposed framework, which shows a minimal overhead to
  overall application performance based on different file sizes, operations, and
  processes.

This paper focuses on data provenance in HPC systems. First, we introduce
data provenance in the HPC system. Second, we discuss scientific data provenance, how it can be collected for analysis in blockchain, and its use in data
provenance for datasets. After that, we propose a framework for provenance
collection. Finally, we discuss, compare, and contrast the results and draw conclusions.

2 Background

There are several ways to collect the provenance data for scientific experiments. One might choose Merkel tree-based [18], Git-based [11], and blockchain-based provenance collection methods. We picked the blockchain-based provenance system for our experiment. Moreover, in the HPC system, user activity is restricted. One cannot have kernel-level access to the HPC system. We want to use eBPF to check the viability of our experiment.

The relationship between data provenance and reproducibility in scientific computing is self-evident. Data provenance is crucial for reproducibility, as it provides a history of data creation and which actions create which data. Secure provenance is essential for data forensics, accountability, and building trust in HPC systems. Similarly, reproducibility is critical for scientific research, yet concerns have been raised about the ability to reproduce computational work. To ensure the reproducibility of the scientific data, we propose a framework based on blockchain, which contains metadata from the granularity level. Here, we will discuss the background of provenance, eBPF, and blockchain for better understanding.

2.1 Provenance

The provenance data provides a history of the origins of all changes to a data object, a list of components that have forwarded or processed the object, a list of users who have viewed (read) and/or modified (write) the object, specifically files, and enhanced assurance requirements [12]. Data provenance is metadata of an object that records the history of the creation and operations on the object. Metadata of the process, user, and entity are helpful to determine data accountability, privacy, provenance, forensic investigation, and malicious activity identification [12,16].

Moreover, lineage and provenance are metadata terms describing a piece of data's past. It shows the connections between every component-data sources, processing steps, background knowledge, and dependencies-that goes into creating a piece of data [8]. The provenance of the output files should be traced by who, when, and what. The files provenance is traced by tracing the job submission in the HPC system [7].

Besides, data provenance pertains to the historical lineage of data originating from its initial sources. For fine-grained data provenance, the value-level details should be focused on, which involves uncovering how a specific data point was generated and manipulated. Fine-grained data provenance is similar to the NoWorkflow technique, a data tracing technique used to check data provenance [15]. This fine-grained approach assists scientists in retracing the roots of individual values within the input data sources. In contrast, coarse-grained or workflow provenance operates at a higher level of granularity.

2.2   Extended Berkeley Packet Filter (eBPF)

Extended Berkeley Packet Filter (eBPF) is a powerful, universal networking and systems programming technology. eBPF allows small programs that can run within the kernel, providing a secure and efficient way to the observability of the system. Moreover, eBPF is a revolutionary technology in the Linux Kernel that can run sandboxed programs. The kernel's capabilities can be extended by eBPF safely and efficiently without changing the kernel source code. Using eBPF, anyone can trace any I/O operation from the kernel level. Simple eBPF programs can provide kernel-level data to detect anomalies with minimal overhead [6].

Moreover, any I/O operation should go through the kernel. So, tracking user activities from the kernel level can provide us with the provenance of the scientific data. Insights from the system level can help to introspect user activities and trace data changes. eBPF programs can be written in the C programming language and attached to the system to track user activities.

2.3   Blockchain

Blockchain, a distributed ledger technology, provides a secure and cryptographically protected record of transactions known as blocks [24]. In addition to transaction details, each entry in the ledger typically includes a unique cryptographic signature, a transaction timestamp, and the previous block's hash. The blockchain's "append only" structure ensures that previously entered data cannot be altered or deleted. This immutability and verifiability of data within the blockchain ledger are vital for auditing and providing reproducibility.

Al-Mamun et al. [1] proposed a provenance service based on blockchain. Their proposed SciChain utilizes blockchains to provide immutable and autonomous data provenance services, establishing trust in scientific discoveries. It is the first practical blockchain system designed explicitly for provenance services on HPC. However, SciChain could not handle parallel processes in the HPC infrastructure. It is incompatible with MPI and fault tolerance mechanism [13].

To enable scientific data sharing and ensure data provenance for further research, Sivagnanam et al. [19] introduced the Open Science Chain (OSC), utilizing blockchain technologies to securely store metadata and verification information about research data while tracking any changes made to the data transparently and securely. The OSC's primary aim is to efficiently share, verify, and validate the scientific data while preserving the provenance data. However, OSC has no details of the provenance data collection process. If provenance data is altered before being stored in the blockchain, it cannot be verifiable to be used for reuse and reproducibility.

Different frameworks work for scientific data provenance; none is a silver bullet solution. As discussed, SciChain cannot work on the HPC system and MPI compatible [13]. Similarly, Open Science Chain (OSC) is not concerned about the provenance of data collection. So, a framework to produce the provenance of scientific data is an urgent need. Our primary focus in this research is to collect provenance data to ensure data integrity.

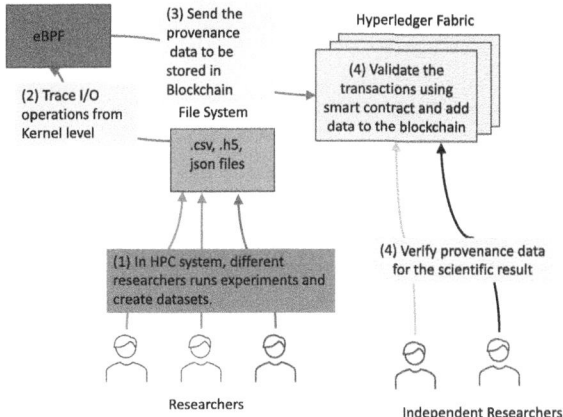

Fig. 1. Overview of our framework

3 Proposed Framework

Our framework can work on the data provenance, store it, and verify it without user intervention. We can collect provenance data from the experimental test bed. The system administrators can set up our framework and enable data storage in the blockchain. They need to manage the user's credentials to allow them blockchain access. Users with credentials can store the provenance data and validate and verify provenance data from the blockchain for future needs. Moreover, blockchains can be distributed on the system, and existing networks can be used for the security and isolation of the blockchains.

Our framework mainly collects I/O-based provenance data, collected through an eBPF and stored in the private blockchain called $Hyperledger Fabric$. eBPF is a helpful tool for kernel-level observability and can trace user-level I/O operations without user concern. Users do not need to do any extra work in their application. The system administrator can set up eBPF and $Hyperledger Fabric$ and provide appropriate privileges to the users. $Hyperledger Fabric$ can use other nodes except the computation node for the blockchain consensus and ordering. Since blockchain peers are stored in different nodes rather than computation nodes, it does not hamper the performance of HPC systems. Moreover, we use the HDF5 for the experiment because HDF5 is the most widely used high-level I/O library for scientific applications [20].

Figure 1 provides the overview of our framework. It shows that in the HPC system, different researchers run experiments and create datasets. Kernel-level eBPF traces I/O operations for provenance and sends the collected provenance data to the blockchain to be stored. $Hyperledger Fabric$ validates the transactions using smart contracts and, after validations, adds the transaction to the blockchain. In the end, independent researchers can verify and validate scientific results based on their individual needs.

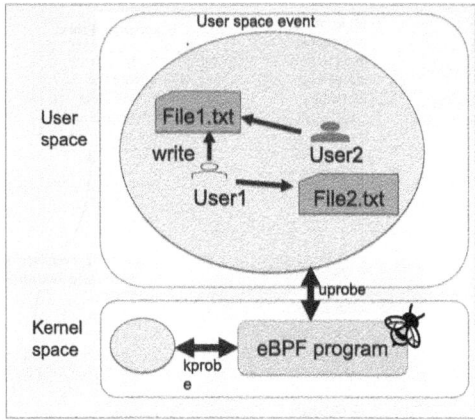

Fig. 2. Tracking user-level data access using eBPF program

4   Implementation

In this section, we will discuss the implementation and experimental setup. We need to implement eBPF, blockchain, and set up the experiment. To evaluate the result we perform read, write, and append operations on different file sizes with provenance and without provenance. After collecting the data, we determine the overhead of provenance collection.

4.1   eBPF Implementation

We use the eBPF program to trace the provenance data in this experiment. For that, a Python program needs to be written with eBPF programs to trace the I/O operations for our experiment. This program collects the I/O events on specific files or folders. The eBPF program is written in the user space to trace I/O events and trigger kernel spaces. Figure 2 shows that user1 and user2 write file1.txt file whereas user2 reads file2.txt. These events are traced by the user probe (*uprobe*), and those trigger the kernel probe (*kprobe*) program for the I/O trace. The eBPF program is written to maintain the communication between the user and kernel spaces [2].

We have developed an eBPF script and efficient algorithm that detects Read and Write operations from individual users using eBPF tracing, which can track any I/O operation as shown in Algorithm 1 below. The algorithm works on the eBPF traces. At the beginning of the trace operation, eBPF scans through the system call to trace any read-and-write (I/O) operation. We need to provide the list of files or folder names as input to collect the I/O operations. The algorithm will result in trace records of the I/O operations. At the very beginning of the algorithm, the *pre_mode* and *Mod_diction* are defined as empty [Line 1–2]. If the system call detects any read/write operation, it checks if the same operation is in the same file [Line 3]; if not, it creates an

---

Algorithm 1: File tracing using eBPF

Data: List of files, collection mode of system call
Result: Trace Read/Write operation on file

1 *pre_mode*=None
2 *Mod_dictionary*={}
3 **if** *syscall_mode!=pre_mode* **then**
4   *operation_list*={filename:{$'username'$:*username*, $'pid'$:*process_id*, $'program_name'$:*program_name*, $'CPU'$:*CPU_id*}}
5   **if** *syscall_mode==read* **then**
6   *read_transaction=operation_list+timestamp*
7   pre_mode=read
8   **if** *operation_list is NOT in Mod_dictionary* **then**
9   Update *Mod_dictionary* with *operation_list*
10   Send the *read_transaction* to the Blockchain.
11   **end**
12   **end**
13   **if** *syscall_mode==write* **then**
14   *write_transaction=operation_list+timestamp*
15   *pre_mode*=write
16   **if** *operation_listis NOT in Mod_dictionary* **then**
17   Update *Mod_dictionary* with *operation_list*
18   Send the *write_transaction* to the Blockchain.
19   **end**
20   **end**
21 **end**

---

operation list [Line 4]. The *operation_list* will contain a dictionary where the filename is the key, and all other attributes such as *username, process_id, program_name*, and *CPU_id* are marked as values. If the system call mode is read, the *read_transaction* is created with the *operation_list* and the timestamp [Line 6], and *pre_mode* is assigned as read [Line 7]. If the *operation_list* is not in the same mode dictionary, the mode dictionary will be updated with the operation list, and *read_transaction* will be sent to the blockchain [Line 9-10]. Similarly, if the system call is in the write mode, the *write_transaction* is created with the *operation_list* and the timestamp [Line 14], and *pre_mode* is assigned as write [Line 15]. If *operation_list* is not in the *Mod_dictionary*, it updates the *Mod_dictionary* with the *operation_list* and sends the *write_transaction* to the blockchain [Line 17–18].

Since eBPF traces every I/O operation, the program will provide read/write events for every chunk of data, which will cause a huge number of read/write events. Since we only want to trace the specified users' reading and writing to specified datasets, we trace every read/write by every process and every user. Suppose the program has a file write operation of four processes in a single file, eBPF will trigger four write operations and send the data to the blockchain.

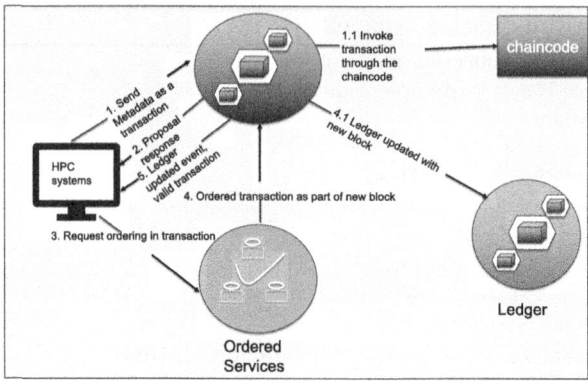

Fig. 3. Provenance data in the blockchain

4.2 Blockchain Implementation

A private blockchain, like *Hyperledger Fabric* [4], works on different peers, *ordered* services, and operates based on a smart contract called *Chaincode*. *Chaincode* is a self-executing contract based on the terms written into the code. Different peer nodes build the blockchain and host the ledgers and smart contracts, *Chaincode*. Transactions are stored in the ledger after invoking *Chaincode*, and ordered nodes form an ordering service. Since fabric relies on deterministic consensus algorithms, after any block, validation by the peer is guaranteed to be correct and final. In HPC systems, gRPC client is installed to send the collected provenance data to another server where the gRPC server is installed to collect data. In the gRPC server, *Hyperledger Fabric* is installed to store the provenance data. While the computing node is busy with I/O operations, eBPF scripts collect the provenance data and send them to another server for storage in the blockchain. Figure 3 shows how user activities are collected as provenance data and sent to the peers (Step 1). Peers send the transaction to chaincode for invocation (Step 1.1). If correct, it sends a response as a proposal (Step 2). An ordering request has been sent to the ordered services (Step 3). The ordered service sends ordered transactions as a new block to the peers (Step 4), a new block in the ledger with valid transactions (Step 4.1), and peers then update the ledger (Step 5).

5 Evaluation

5.1 Experimental Setup

The performance of our proposed framework is evaluated based on synthetic data for different I/O operations by imitating scientific applications. The experiments are conducted on the OpenStack-based cloud computing service Exosphere, provided by ACCESS allocation (advanced cyberinfrastructure and associated support systems) through Indiana University. Exosphere uses an AMD EPYC-Milan

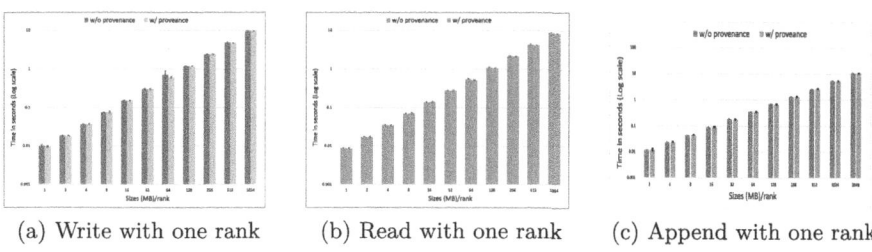

(a) Write with one rank   (b) Read with one rank   (c) Append with one rank

Fig. 4. Comparing different operations with single rank. "w/o provenance" means vanilla operations, and "w/ provenance" means using provenance data tracing in HDF5 file.

Processor, and the system is OpenStack Nova. It has 64 CPUs and 6 GiB of system memory. It uses mountable block storage called Volumes that are attached to the Exosphere. The data storage for the experiment is the NFS file system.

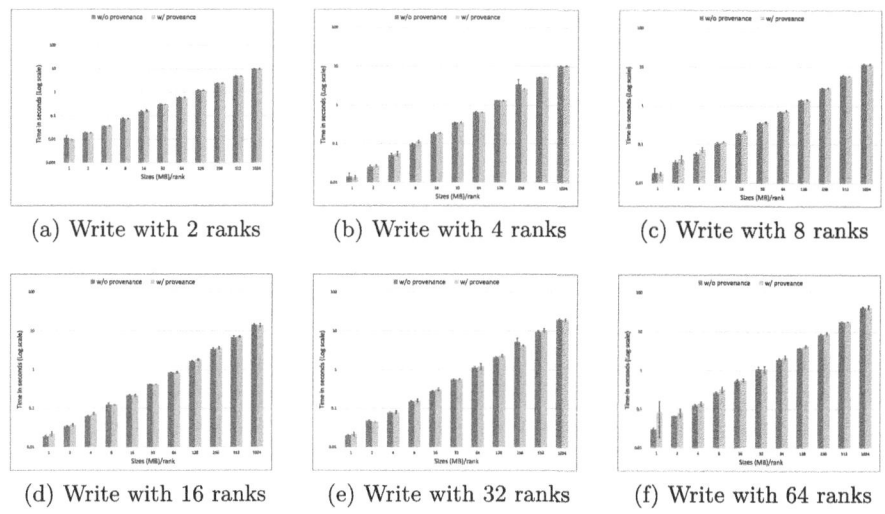

(a) Write with 2 ranks   (b) Write with 4 ranks   (c) Write with 8 ranks

(d) Write with 16 ranks   (e) Write with 32 ranks   (f) Write with 64 ranks

Fig. 5. Comparing write time on different data sizes with different numbers of ranks. "w/o provenance" means vanilla write operations, and "w/ provenance" means using provenance data tracing in write operations.

To show the effectiveness of our proposed framework, we collected the provenance data using the eBPF data, which was sent to the blockchain through the gRPC protocol. We performed extensive benchmark evaluation in three modes: read, write, and append to different file sizes. We compared the performance of the blockchain-enabled provenance I/O operations and vanilla I/O operations on HDF5 file systems. Since our goal is to measure the overhead of I/O performance with provenance, we did not include any compute time between any operations,

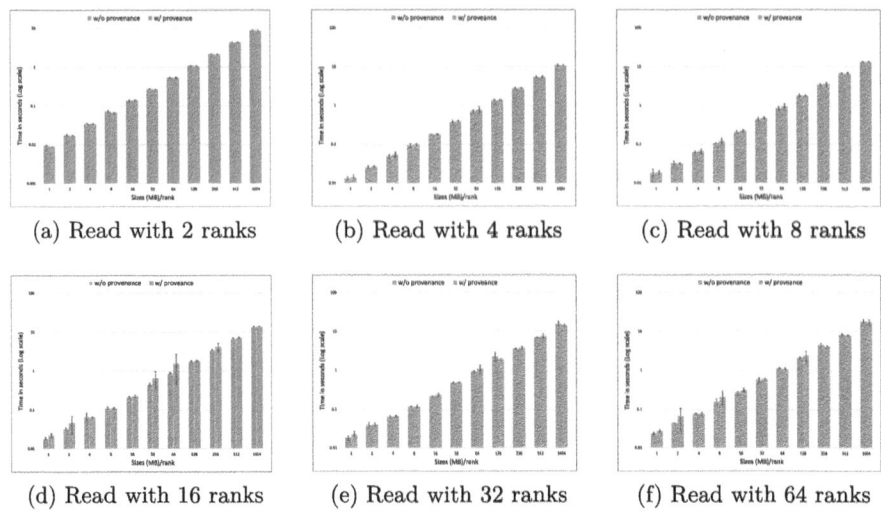

(a) Read with 2 ranks   (b) Read with 4 ranks   (c) Read with 8 ranks

(d) Read with 16 ranks   (e) Read with 32 ranks   (f) Read with 64 ranks

Fig. 6. Comparing read time on different data sizes with different numbers of ranks. "w/o provenance" means without vanilla read operations, and "w/ provenance" means using provenance data tracing in read operations.

and thus, the measured time for the two methods that use provenance I/O and vanilla I/O operations.

We summarize the time elapsed for I/O operations for different buffer sizes from 1 MB to 1 GB to 64 GB. For example, if we conduct the operation for 64 ranks and 1024 MB data, the file's total size will be 64 GB. For append operation, the size will be 128 GB for 64 ranks and 1024 MB.

We compare the results using read, write, and append data modes with different numbers of processes and different file sizes. Each process handles different data sizes ranging from 1 MB to 1GB, and the file size varies from 1 GB to 132 GB. We performed these operations using 1 to 64 ranks on the HPC system. The data from all processes are written to one HDF5 dataset and tested for read, write, and append operations. Figures 4, 5, 6 and 7 show the comparison between provenance (w/ provenance) and vanilla operations (w/o provenance) in write, read, and append operations, respectively. The comparison shows that I/O operation with provenance incurs low overhead.

5.2   Results

The experiment results are evaluated using the write, read, and append operations times (in milliseconds or seconds) with provenance collection and vanilla operations.

Figure 4 compares the results for all operations (write, read, and append) with a single rank from 1 MB to 1 GB data. In most cases, the provenance data showed negligible overhead (a few milliseconds) compared to vanilla operations.

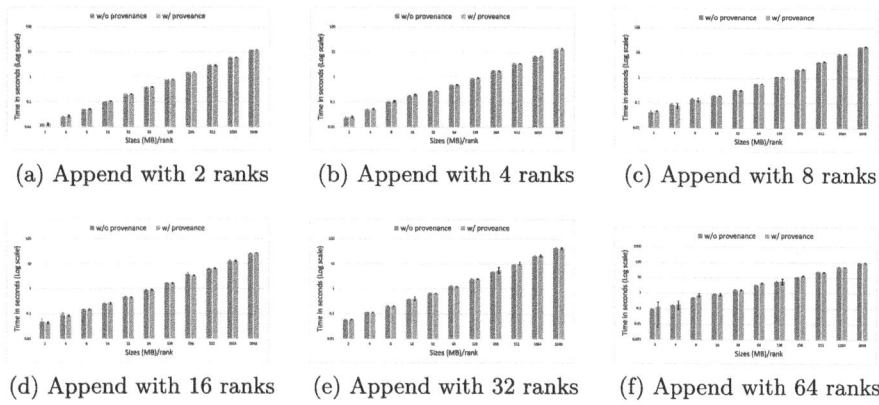

(a) Append with 2 ranks   (b) Append with 4 ranks   (c) Append with 8 ranks

(d) Append with 16 ranks   (e) Append with 32 ranks   (f) Append with 64 ranks

Fig. 7. Comparing append time on different data sizes with different numbers of ranks. "w/o provenance" means vanilla append operations, and "w/ provenance" means using provenance data tracing in append operations.

For read operations in 16 MB, provenance data shows 58 ms overhead, whereas for write operations in 256 MB, provenance data shows approximately 20 ms overhead. The append operation shows a maximum 19 ms delay with 1024 MB data size for provenance data tracing than vanilla append.

Figure 5 compares the results for all write operations with different sizes between 2 MB and 1024 MB data for each rank. For write operations, 4 ranks for 1024 MB, and 16 ranks for 512 MB data provenance data added 0.041 s and 0.35 s overhead, respectively. Similarly, in 32 ranks for 512 MB data, and 64 ranks for 1024 MB data, the provenance data added approximately 1.13 s and 1.32 s overhead, respectively. A maximum of 1.32 s is added for the write operation with provenance data.

The data read operations shown in Fig. 6, in most cases, the provenance added little (few milliseconds) overhead. With 16 ranks and 64 MB data, the read operation added approximately 0.67 s over the vanilla read operation. For 32 ranks with 512 MB data, 0.59 s are added over the vanilla read operation. In 16 ranks, 64 MB shows overhead for provenance data added 0.67 s, which is the maximum overhead.

Figure 7 shows the results for all append operations with different sizes between 2 MB and 2 GB data for each rank. The highest time for append operation is for 2 GB data in 64 ranks. Vanilla append operation takes around 99.7 s, whereas provenance data takes 98.2 s. Multiple append operations with 2 ranks and 4 ranks show little overhead, a maximum of 0.028 s, on the provenance data. However, for an append operation with 8 ranks and 16 ranks with data size 2048 MB, data provenance added 0.338 s and 0.693 s overhead. Similarly, in 64 ranks, for 256 MB data, a maximum of around 1.44 s overhead.

Our experiments show that blockchain-based provenance data collection does not add significant overhead compared to vanilla operations. A higher overhead of 1.44 s is observed when the appended size is 256 with 64 ranks. Blockchain-based provenance adds little overhead when there is a small amount of data (with 1 and 2 MPI ranks). In contrast, with data size 64 MB with the 16 MPI ranks, the provenance write operation added around 0.67 s. With data size 64 MB and 16 ranks, data provenance read operations added 0.67 s. Since data outcomes in read, write, and append operations are varied, the standard error of the samples is checked. From the figures, we can understand that the error bars overlap; this does not make us confident that the actual mean is different. In summary, our framework can provide provenance data in scientific research with minimal overhead for most of the common I/O patterns.

6   Conclusion

Our findings indicate that blockchain-enabled provenance with small write operations can add a small overhead of scientific data. We have developed a transparent strategy to trace the kernel level provenance in the HDF5 dataset. We show the significance of our solution by comparing the read, write, and append operations among the blockchain-enabled provenance with vanilla operations for different file sizes and different numbers of processes. Our results can provide provenance (within 1.44 s) overhead compared to vanilla operations.

Our future work includes evaluating blockchain-enabled provenance data for reproducibility in real scientific applications and extending it to other provenance-based I/O libraries. We will also explore ways to perform provenance-aware scientific research under different consistency models and optimize the algorithm to reduce overhead in the worst case.

Acknowledgment. This material is based upon work supported in part by the National Science Foundation under Grant Nos. EF-2150107 and 2005506. The University of Alabama and Comilla University, Bangladesh, partially supported this research. This work used Jetstream2 at Indiana University through allocation CIS230201 from the Advanced Cyberinfrastructure Coordination Ecosystem: Services & Support (ACCESS) program, which is supported by National Science Foundation grants #2138259, #2138286, #2138307, #2137603, and #2138296. Any opinions, findings, conclusions, or recommendations expressed in this material are those of the author(s) and do not necessarily reflect the views of the National Science Foundation.

References

1. Al-Mamun, A., Yan, F., Zhao, D.: Scichain: blockchain-enabled lightweight and efficient data provenance for reproducible scientific computing. In: 2021 IEEE 37th International Conference on Data Engineering (ICDE), pp. 1853–1858. IEEE (2021)
2. Androulaki, E., et al.: Hyperledger fabric: a distributed operating system for permissioned blockchains. In: Proceedings of the Thirteenth EuroSys Conference, pp. 1–15 (2018)

3. Boufford, N.: Computational experiment comprehension using provenance summarization. Ph.D. thesis, University of British Columbia (2024)
4. Cachin, C., et al.: Architecture of the hyperledger blockchain fabric. In: Workshop on Distributed Cryptocurrencies and Consensus Ledgers, Chicago, IL, pp. 1–4 (2016)
5. Carata, L., et al.: A primer on provenance: better understanding of data requires tracking its history and context. Queue **12**(3), 10–23 (2014)
6. Caviglione, L., Mazurczyk, W., Repetto, M., Schaffhauser, A., Zuppelli, M.: Kernel-level tracing for detecting stegomalware and covert channels in linux environments. Comput. Netw. **191**, 108010 (2021)
7. Cheah, Y.W., Canon, R., Plale, B., Ramakrishnan, L.: Milieu: lightweight and configurable big data provenance for science. In: 2013 IEEE International Congress on Big Data, pp. 46–53. IEEE (2013)
8. Dai, D., Chen, Y., Carns, P., Jenkins, J., Ross, R.: Lightweight provenance service for high-performance computing. In: 2017 26th International Conference on Parallel Architectures and Compilation Techniques (PACT), pp. 117–129. IEEE (2017)
9. Deelman, E., Berriman, B., Chervenak, A., Corcho, O., Groth, P., Moreau, L.: Metadata and provenance management. arXiv preprint arXiv:1005.2643 (2010)
10. Deelman, E., et al.: Managing large-scale workflow execution from resource provisioning to provenance tracking: the cybershake example. In: 2006 Second IEEE International Conference on e-Science and Grid Computing (e-Science 2006), pp. 14–14. IEEE (2006)
11. Halchenko, Y., et al.: Datalad: distributed system for joint management of code, data, and their relationship. J. Open Source Softw. **6**(63) (2021)
12. Liang, X., Shetty, S., Tosh, D., Kamhoua, C., Kwiat, K., Njilla, L.: Provchain: a blockchain-based data provenance architecture in cloud environment with enhanced privacy and availability. In: 2017 17th IEEE/ACM International Symposium on Cluster, Cloud and Grid Computing (CCGRID), pp. 468–477. IEEE (2017)
13. Mamun, A.A., Yan, F., Zhao, D.: Baash: lightweight, efficient, and reliable blockchain-as-a-service for HPC systems. In: Proceedings of the International Conference for High Performance Computing, Networking, Storage and Analysis, pp. 1–18 (2021)
14. McKiernan, E.C., et al.: How open science helps researchers succeed. elife **5**, e16800 (2016)
15. Murta, L., Braganholo, V., Chirigati, F., Koop, D., Freire, J.: noworkflow: capturing and analyzing provenance of scripts. In: Provenance and Annotation of Data and Processes: 5th International Provenance and Annotation Workshop, IPAW 2014, Cologne, Germany, 9–13 June 2014. Revised Selected Papers 5, pp. 71–83. Springer (2015)
16. Pan, B., Stakhanova, N., Ray, S.: Data provenance in security and privacy. ACM Comput. Surv. (2023)
17. Pasquier, T., et al.: If these data could talk. Sci. Data **4**(1), 1–5 (2017)
18. Ruan, P., Chen, G., Dinh, T.T.A., Lin, Q., Ooi, B.C., Zhang, M.: Fine-grained, secure and efficient data provenance on blockchain systems. Proc. VLDB Endow. **12**(9), 975–988 (2019)
19. Sivagnanam, S., Nandigam, V., Lin, K.: Introducing the open science chain: protecting integrity and provenance of research data. In: Practice and Experience in Advanced Research Computing 2019: Rise of the Machines (Learning). PEARC 2019. Association for Computing Machinery, New York (2019). https://doi.org/10.1145/3332186.3332203

20. Tang, H., Koziol, Q., Byna, S., Mainzer, J., Li, T.: Enabling transparent asynchronous I/O using background threads. In: 2019 IEEE/ACM Fourth International Parallel Data Systems Workshop (PDSW), pp. 11–19. IEEE (2019)
21. UNESCO: United nations educational,scientific and cultural organization (UNESCO) recommendation on open science (2021). https://www.unesco.org/en/open-science/about. Accessed 06 Dec 2023
22. Wilkinson, M.D., et al.: The fair guiding principles for scientific data management and stewardship. Sci. Data **3**(1), 1–9 (2016)
23. Zhao, D., Shou, C., Maliky, T., Raicu, I.: Distributed data provenance for large-scale data-intensive computing. In: 2013 IEEE International Conference on Cluster Computing (CLUSTER), pp. 1–8. IEEE (2013)
24. Zheng, Z., Xie, S., Dai, H.N., Chen, X., Wang, H.: Blockchain challenges and opportunities: a survey. Int. J. Web Grid Serv. **14**(4), 352–375 (2018)

Using Minicasts for Efficient Asynchronous Causal Unicast and Byzantine Tolerance

Laine Rumreich[(✉)] and Paolo A. G. Sivilotti

The Ohio State University, Columbus, OH 43210, USA
rumreich.1@osu.edu, paolo@cse.ohio-state.edu

Abstract. We present an implementation of asynchronous causally ordered unicast that requires linear space for message size, which is a significant improvement compared to the best existing algorithms which require quadratic space in the worst case. This algorithm is a modification of the Raynal-Shiper-Toueg algorithm and broadcasts a small control message, defined here as a *minicast*, to augment the unicast message to preserve causal ordering. The smaller message size is at the cost of additional traffic on the network. With the addition of cryptography in the form of digital signatures, this algorithm can be made tolerant to byzantine failures. For existing versions of causal unicast, byzantine tolerance has previously only been possible with the addition of bounded latency.

Keywords: reliable unicast · causal ordering · byzantine fault tolerance · asynchronous · minicast

1 Introduction

1.1 Motivation

The demand for data center capacity and distributed computing has increased dramatically in recent years, driven in part by the rise of AI and cloud computing. The development of robust distributed applications, however, is challenged by fundamental limitations such as the CAP Theorem, which proves that it is impossible to simultaneously achieve strong consistency, consistent availability, and partition tolerance [15]. While some systems choose to forgo strong consistency in favor of availability and partition tolerance, many modern services–such as distributed data stores, systems that require fair resource allocation, and interactive services–require stronger consistency guarantees. Stronger consistency is also desirable because it makes distributed systems easier to reason about and debug.

One approach to achieving stronger consistency guarantees is causal message ordering. With causal ordering, the order of message delivery respects causal

© The Author(s), under exclusive license to Springer Nature Switzerland AG 2025
H. R. Arabnia et al. (Eds.): CSCE 2024, CCIS 2256, pp. 65–81, 2025.
https://doi.org/10.1007/978-3-031-85638-9_5

dependencies between the sends. Prior work has demonstrated that causal ordering can be used to achieve database consistency and that consistent snapshots in which all messages are delivered in causal order can be obtained without any additional costs [2,7,28]. For distributed data stores, causal ordering enables automatic conflict resolution in the presence of concurrent writes [11]. For collaborative applications such as social networking, multiplayer online gaming, group editing of documents, event notification systems, and distributed virtual environments, causal ordering enables scaling to many users by minimizing conflicts and locks.

Causal ordering of broadcast messages is relatively easy to achieve compared to that of unicast messages. While message-size efficient (linear) algorithms exist for the former, the best-known algorithms for asynchronous causally ordered unicast are $O(n^2)$ in the worst case. Furthermore, byzantine-tolerant solutions exist for broadcast messages but have previously been impossible for asynchronous unicast messages. However, the combination of byzantine failures and fully asynchronous communication is a realistic system model and applicable to a variety of real-world scenarios. Therefore, efficiently supporting causal ordering of unicast messages in such a model is of considerable interest and practical applicability.

1.2   Contribution

This paper presents a novel algorithm for causal message ordering of unicast application messages. Our solution is a modification of the Raynal-Shiper-Toueg (RST) algorithm [26], whereby application messages are augmented with $O(1)$ broadcast control messages, defined here as *minicasts*. As with the RST algorithm, extra information is added to the unicast application messages related to message history in order to preserve causal ordering. The addition of minicasts allows for a reduction in the size of this history information sent with the application messages from $O(n^2)$ to $O(n)$, bringing the total volume of messages sent from $O(n^2)$ to $O(n+n)$, even in the worst case. Algorithms that are more recent than the RST algorithm, such as the KS algorithm [18], perform better in practice than RST but are also still $O(n^2)$ in the worst case. Recently, a $O(n)$ space algorithm for causally ordered unicast has been presented [23], but it uses locks and bounded latency to preserve message order. The message size complexity of this algorithm is similar to ours, but it is based on an underlying assumption of a synchronous system. The algorithm presented in this work not only requires only $O(n)$ space, but it does not rely on bounded latency.

The second contribution of this paper is a solution to the unicast causal ordering problem that is both asynchronous and byzantine tolerant. This solution is based on a slight modification of the Minicast Algorithm presented in the first part of the paper: a BCCH FIFO consistent broadcast [9] is used to send the minicast control messages. This additional layer of consistency, along with the addition of a message passing layer with cryptographic digital signatures, allows for asynchronous byzantine tolerance. Existing solutions for byzantine tolerant causally ordered unicast require bounded latency due to an impossibility result for byzantine tolerant causally ordered broadcast on asynchronous systems [22].

For example, a recent algorithm for byzantine tolerant unicast uses control messages together with bounded latency to achieve consistency [23]. The algorithm presented here allows for byzantine tolerance for causally ordered unicast without bounded latency. Circumventing the impossibility result for asynchronous systems is only possible with some strengthening of the model, such as the addition of secure cryptography as is done here.

2   Background

2.1   Causally Ordered Events

Causality between events is defined by the *happens before* [19] relation (denoted $\rightarrow$) on a set of events in a distributed computation. The happens-before relation is formally defined as the least strict partial order on events such that:

- For events a and b that occur on the same process, $a \rightarrow b$ if the occurrence of event a preceded the occurrence of event b.
- For events a and b corresponding to the send and delivery, respectively, of a single message, $a \rightarrow b$.

2.2   Causal Message Ordering: Safety and Liveness

Informally, the causal ordering of messages requires that the delivery of messages at any given process occurs in an order that is consistent with the causal ordering of their sends. That is, for any two messages sent to the same process, if one send happened before the other, that message must be delivered first.

More formally, causally ordered messages satisfy the following *strong safety* property:

Definition 2.1. *Strong Safety. Let i and j be two messages, and denote their corresponding sends (deliveries) as s_i and s_j (d_i and d_j). For messages i and j with the same destination, if $s_i \rightarrow s_j$, then $d_i \rightarrow d_j$.*

This safety property of causal ordering is a stronger requirement than FIFO channels. For example, consider the computation illustrated in Fig. 1. In this example, which respects FIFO delivery on each channel, the messages i and j have the same destination, s. Furthermore, the send of i (on process p) happens before the send of j (on process t), by virtue of the chain of messages highlighted in cyan. Causal ordering requires that i be delivered before j, but in this example, j is delivered first.

Since byzantine processes can lie about the order in which they receive messages, this strong safety property cannot be implemented in the presence of byzantine faults. Instead, a weaker property is used, in which the ordering on delivery is only guaranteed if a causal chain exists between corresponding sends which passes through only correct processes. This weaker version is defined as follows:

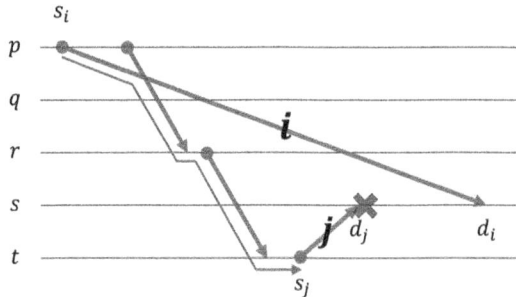

Fig. 1. An example of non-causally ordered messages i and j

Definition 2.2. *Weak Safety. Let i and j be two messages, and denote their corresponding sends (deliveries) as s_i and s_j (d_i and d_j). For messages i and j with the same destination, if $s_i \rightarrow s_j$ and there is a causal path from s_i to s_j passing through only correct processes, then $d_i \rightarrow d_j$.*

The liveness property of causal ordering is that messages eventually arrive at their destination. Notice that the message passing layer guarantees the liveness of the underlying channels. That is, all messages are eventually *received*. However, causal ordering typically involves buffering these messages and delaying their delivery in order to respect the ordering imposed by any happens-before relationships between sends. Thus, the liveness property for causal ordering requires that all messages are eventually *delivered*.

In the presence of byzantine faults, a weakening is again required: all messages between correct processes are eventually delivered.

2.3   Byzantine Tolerance

Asynchronous systems have no bounds on message delays or relative speeds of processes. Because of this, there is no way to distinguish between a "slow" message and a message that was not sent. For networks with the possibility of crash faults or byzantine nodes, faulty processes may deviate arbitrarily from the protocol, including by crashing at any point during execution, whereas correct processes behave exactly as specified by the algorithm. For networks with byzantine nodes, processes can fail to send messages when they should and can send spurious and contradictory messages [8].

To circumvent fundamental impossibility results, such as FLP [13], the computational model is often strengthened (or, equivalently, bounds are placed on the behavior of byzantine processes). For example, one might stipulate the existence of failure detectors [10], bounds on latency [12], or some cryptographically secure mechanism to guarantee identity [17]. Here, we assume that a byzantine process cannot impersonate another process or spawn new processes.

With such an assumption in place, many consensus problems become solvable even in the presence of byzantine faults. In particular, in this paper, we leverage the existence of a byzantine reliable broadcast primitive, such as the one in [8]. This broadcast primitive can be viewed as a message passing layer with the following properties:

Definition 2.3. *Byzantine Reliable Broadcast. A reliable broadcast protocol satisfies the following properties for all messages sent from any process p:*

1. *If p is correct, then all correct processes accept and agree on the value of the message*
2. *If p is faulty, either all correct processes accept and agree on the same value of the message or none of them accept the message*

3 Related Work

3.1 Causally Ordered Unicast and Byzantine Tolerance

The RST causal message ordering algorithm by Raynal, Schiper, and Toueg [26] was the first algorithm to solve the causal message ordering problem. It requires a space overhead of n^2 storage on each process, where n is the number of processes. In the RST algorithm, every process maintains a local $n \times n$ matrix, SENT. SENT[p, q] is the process's best knowledge of the number of messages sent by process p to process q. A process also maintains an array of the number of messages that have been delivered locally from every other process, DELIV. The algorithm also incurs a message size cost of $O(n^2)$ as each message is augmented with the local SENT matrix of the sender process. A process q that receives a message augmented with the matrix S delivers that message only if $\forall p : DELIV[p] \geq SENT[p, q]$. If a message cannot be delivered immediately, it is buffered until the condition above is met. When the message is delivered, the local SENT matrix is updated to be the element-wise maximum of SENT and the message's S matrix, for each element in SENT. In this way, information about messages that have been sent is propagated across the network.

Other variants [3,6,16,25,27] and improvements upon the RST algorithm [18] perform significantly better in practice, but still require $O(n^2)$ in the worst case. Additional algorithms for causal ordering of point-to-point messages in real-time applications have been proposed in [1,5] with similar message size complexity requirements. Another algorithm for causal ordering uses no control information at all and orders messages by flooding on an overlay topology [14].

One highly relevant variant of causally ordered unicast by Misra et al. is the Sender-Inhibition algorithm, which reduces the message size overhead to $O(n)$ by assuming a synchronous model [23]. The Sender-Inhibition algorithm uses one constant-size control message per application message. This algorithm also uses locks to prevent a process from having multiple outstanding sends, which reduces the concurrency of the protocol. A reliable and FIFO-ordered channel is used. *When* blocks are also used to execute blocks of code asynchronously with respect to each other in a fair manner and also allow for context switching between blocks. As this algorithm requires a synchronous underlying system, a bounded latency is assumed for messages.

Byzantine-tolerant causal ordering for unicasts is a topic of ongoing interest [20–22], but it has been shown that it is impossible to causally order messages under point-to-point communication in an asynchronous system with one or more Byzantine processes [22]. The addition of a requirement on the underlying network to have a known upper bound on the message latency can circumvent this impossibility result [22]. One example of a recent work that implements byzantine tolerant unicast on a synchronous system is the Channel Sync algorithm [23]. This algorithm uses timeouts and control messages after each send and after the delivery of each message. Application messages are delivered immediately after getting popped from the queue of messages, but control messages are only processed when it is safe to deliver the next message in the queue. All control messages have timers associated with them to time them out in case of Byzantine behavior of the sender or receiver.

The Channel Sync algorithm and other byzantine tolerant causal unicast algorithms use bounded latency to circumvent the known impossibility result. However, another option for circumventing this impossibility result is to use cryptography. A recent work by Misra et al. proved that it is possible to solve causal ordering of unicast messages in an asynchronous system with one or more Byzantine processes with the use of cryptography, as weak safety and liveness can be guaranteed [23]. The algorithm presented in this work uses this option for byzantine tolerance, unlike other algorithms that have been developed.

3.2   Causally Ordered Broadcast and Byzantine Tolerance

Bracha first developed a protocol for byzantine reliable broadcast [8]. In this protocol, three types of messages are used: *initial, echo,* and *ready.* An *initial* message means that p wishes to send a broadcast. An *echo* message means that its sender knows that p sent a message because it received either an *initial* message from p or enough *echo* or *ready* messages confirming it. A process sends a *ready* message only when it is ready to accept the message because it received enough *echo* or *ready* messages. Finally, when a process receives enough *ready* messages it accepts the message. All other correct processes are bound to accept the message at this point, regardless of whether they received an *initial* message from p.

A causally ordered version of this byzantine tolerant reliable broadcast was introduced by Auvolat et al. [4]. In this algorithm, an array of integers is used to track the number of messages that have been broadcast from every other process. That array is sent with each message to enforce causal ordering. Information about how many messages have been sent is transmitted directly to each process in this algorithm, rather than propagated. The algorithm presented in [24] implements crash fault-tolerant causal broadcast in asynchronous systems with a focus on reducing the control information required for each message.

4 Minicast Algorithm

4.1 System Model

A set of FIFO (logical) communication links is assumed where processes communicate by message passing. The communication links are assumed to be reliable, meaning messages cannot get lost or be duplicated and the identity of the sending processes is authenticated. The system is asynchronous, so there is no guarantee on how long messages may take to arrive. For this section, we assume the system is fault-free. In the next section, this assumption is weakened to permit byzantine failures.

4.2 Overview

The algorithm presented here describes a version of unicast that preserves causal ordering using a *minicast* message. A *minicast* is a small broadcast message and functions like a control message. Each unicast message is supplemented with this minicast message to share information with other processes directly. In this way, information about which messages have been sent is shared directly rather than propagated, and this algorithm can be viewed as a hybrid of unicast and broadcast.

To preserve causal ordering, processes track the number of minicast messages that have been received from every other process in a vector. This vector is also used to keep track of whether a received (i.e. buffered) message meets the delivery condition and thus can be delivered.

For notational convenience, we define a single-point exclusive ordering relation on vectors, $\leq_j$, below.

Definition 4.1. *Let v and u be vectors of equal length and let q be the index of an entry.*

$$\vec{v} \leq_j \vec{u} \text{ iff } \forall i \neq j,\ v_i \leq u_i.$$

4.3 Local Data Structures

- `deliveredMCs`: Vector of the number of minicasts delivered from every other process, used to establish causal ordering.
    - Initialized to 0 for all entries except p (the process's own entry), which is initialized to 1.
- `receivedUnicasts[i]`: Queue of unicast messages that have been received from process i but have not yet been ordered with minicasts from i.
    - Initialized as empty.
- `receivedMessages[i]`: Queue of messages (unicast and minicast) that have been received from process i but have not yet been delivered.
    - Initialized as empty.
    - Minicasts that correspond to a unicast are replaced in this queue by the unicast from `receivedUnicasts`.

4.4   Algorithm

Algorithm 1 Causally Ordered Unicast (Process p)

Initially
1: $deliveredMCs \leftarrow [0, 0, ..., 0]$
2: $deliveredMCs[p] \leftarrow 1$
3: $receivedUnicasts \leftarrow [\epsilon, \epsilon, ..., \epsilon]$
4: $receivedMessages \leftarrow [\epsilon, \epsilon, ..., \epsilon]$

Message Send
5: send message m to process $q \longrightarrow$
6:    **Send**($\langle m, deliveredMCs \rangle$) to q
7:    **Broadcast**($\langle q, deliveredMCs[p] \rangle$)
8:    $deliveredMCs[p] \mathrel{+}= 1$

Unicast Arrives
9: $\langle m, MCs \rangle$ arrives from process $q \longrightarrow$
10:    $receivedUnicasts[q].enqueue(\langle m, MCs \rangle)$

Minicast Arrives
11: $\langle r, msgNum \rangle$ arrives from process $q \longrightarrow$
12:    $receivedMessages[q].enqueue(\langle r, msgNum \rangle)$

Order Unicast in receivedMessages
13: $receivedMessages[q].front = \langle p, msgNum \rangle$
      $\wedge\ receivedUnicasts[q] \neq \epsilon \longrightarrow$
14:    $next \leftarrow receivedUnicasts[q].dequeue()$
15:    **if** $next.MCs[q] = msgNum$ **then**
16:       $receivedMessages[q].replaceFront(next)$
17:    **end if**

Unicast is Delivered
18: $receivedMessages[q].front = \langle m, MCs \rangle$
      $\wedge\ MCs \leq_q deliveredMCs \longrightarrow$
19:    $next \leftarrow receivedMessages[q].dequeue()$
20:    **Deliver**($next$)
21:    $deliveredMCs[q] \leftarrow next.MCs[q]$

Minicast is Delivered
22: $receivedMessages[q].front = \langle r, msgNum \rangle$
      $\wedge\ r \neq p \longrightarrow$
23:    $receivedMessages[q].dequeue()$
24:    $deliveredMCs[q] \leftarrow msgNum$

4.5   Description

The causally ordered unicast algorithm uses a series of guards to control operations. With the use of these guards, the algorithm switches between the blocks in a fair manner and only executes a block if the guard is true. The blocks are executed atomically.

Each channel is assumed to be FIFO, but unicast and minicast messages use different message passing layers. That is, the point-to-point channels used for unicasts are FIFO and the broadcast channels used for minicasts are also FIFO, but these two kinds of messages are not ordered with respect to each other. This separation has the advantage of making the algorithm (and its proof of correctness) more general. For example, it allows for network architectures that use different transmission media for these two kinds of communication. Most importantly, it means that the broadcast layer can be replaced by an independent broadcast protocol, such as byzantine tolerant broadcast as is done in the second part of the paper.

Unicast messages are augmented with a vector of how many minicasts have been (directly) received by other processes. Unicast messages are also supplemented with a broadcast message (i.e. a minicast) including the process of id of the destination and total message count.

Two queues are used to track when messages are received, one for unicasts (receivedUnicasts) and one for minicasts (receivedMessages). The queue of received unicasts is merged into the queue for minicasts based on the message number included with both minicast and unicast messages. This operation results in FIFO ordering between the two channels. Minicasts can safely be delivered if they are at the front of the queue as long as a unicast was not sent with it. Unicast messages can only be delivered when the delivery condition has been met. The delivery condition requires that the vector sent along with the message is smaller than the number of minicasts received directly from other processes at every value (except q, the sending process, which is always at least one more than the current value). This delivery condition ensures causal ordering of messages.

5   Proof of Causal Ordering

5.1   Safety

We show that the Minicast Algorithm in Sect. 4 satisfies strong safety as given in Definition 2.1. That is, we prove Theorem 5.5, which states that delivery events are causally ordered.

Lemma 5.1. *Consider any pair of processes p, q. For all messages (application and minicast) from q to p, the order of delivery events at p is the same as the order of send events at q.*

Proof. Given the FIFO channel for minicasts, the order of minicast receive events at p must be the same as the order of minicast send events at q. Additionally, the operations used to order unicast messages in the `receivedMessages`$[q]$ queue replace any minicast with its corresponding unicast from `receivedUnicasts` based on the message number, if one exists. Figure 2 illustrates how the `receivedUnicasts` and `receivedMessages` are combined to update `receivedMessages`$[q]$. A unicast message must be received if a minicast has been sent. This operation happens when a minicast with a destination of p is at the front of the queue, and the message cannot be delivered before this time. Since messages must be dequeued in order and are always delivered immediately after they are dequeued, the order of delivery events at p must be the same as the order of receive events at p and thus are the same as the send events at q. □

Definition 5.1. *For equal length vectors v_1 and v_2, $v_1 < v_2$ means that every element of v_1 is less than or equal to the corresponding element in v_2, and there exists at least one element of v_1 that is strictly less than the corresponding element in v_2.*

Lemma 5.2. *Let e_1 and e_2 be events (send or delivery). If $e_1 \rightarrow e_2$, then* `deliveredMCs`$(e_1) < $ `deliveredMCs`(e_2)

Proof. First, assume that e_1 and e_2 occur on the same process p. If e_1 is a delivery from process q, `p.deliveredMCs` is updated at the qth entry to be the new message number, which is guaranteed to be larger than the previous message number by Lemma 5.1. Since there is no way for `deliveredMCs` to decrease, `p.deliveredMCs`$(e_1) < $ `p.deliveredMCs`(e_2). If e_1

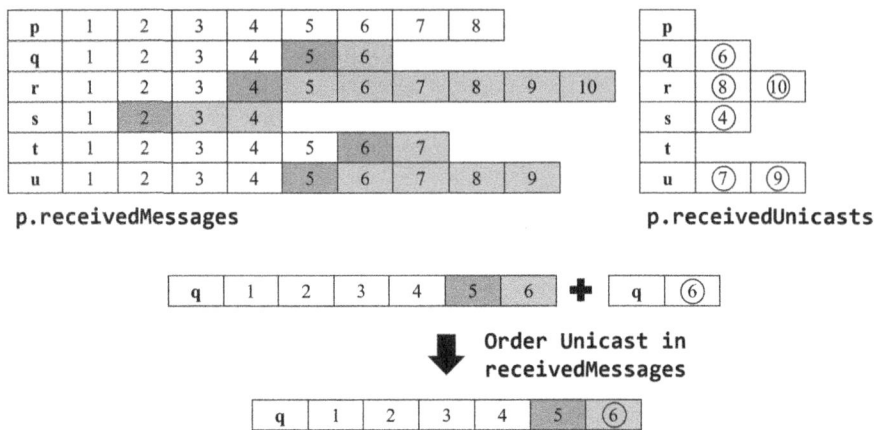

Fig. 2. The ordering of received unicast messages in the queue of `receivedMessages`

is a send, p.deliveredMCs is incremented at the pth entry. By the same argument, p.deliveredMCs(e_1) < p.deliveredMCs(e_2). Now in either case, p.deliveredMCs(e_1) < p.deliveredMCs(e_2).

Now assume events e_1 and e_2 happen on different processes and let e_1 be a send of message m at q and e_2 be the delivery of that message at process p. Because message m was sent from process $q(e_1)$, we know that m.MCs $=$ q.deliveredMCs(e_1). We also know that since m was delivered at $p(e_2)$, m.MCs $\leq_q$ p.deliveredMCs(e_2) based on the delivery condition. Additionally, p.deliveredMCs$[q](e_2)$ is immediately updated to be the message number, which is m.MCs$[q]$. Lastly, p.deliveredMCs$[p](e_2)$ must be larger than m.MCs$[p]$ because no message could have been sent out with the current value of p.deliveredMCs$[p]$. Hence, m.MCs < p.deliveredMCs(e_2) and q.deliveredMCs(e_1) < p.deliveredMCs(e_2).

Now for any e_1 and e_2 from any processes q and p, by definition, there must exist some chain of events that follow $\rightarrow$ between e_1 and e_2 such that they both occur on the same process or e_2 is the delivery of e_1. Therefore, for every two events e_1 and e_2 where $e_1 \rightarrow e_2$, q.deliveredMCs(e_1) < p.deliveredMCs(e_2). □

Lemma 5.3. *If $s_1 \rightarrow s_2$, then $s_1.MCs < s_2.MCs$*

Proof. Since any sends s_1 and s_2 are also events, from Lemma 5.2 we have: if $s_1 \rightarrow s_2$, then p.deliveredMCs(s_1) < q.deliveredMCs(s_2).

For brevity, we will refer to $m.MCs$ for message m sent by p at s_1 as $s_1.MCs$. Now, $s_1.MCs = p.deliveredMCs(s_1)$ based on the information supplied in the Send. Therefore, we have that $s_1 \rightarrow s_2$, then $s_1.MCs < s_2.MCs$.

Lemma 5.4. *For sends s_1 and s_2 with the same destination p, if $s_1.MCs < s_2.MCs$, then $d_1 \rightarrow d_2$.*

Proof. Let s_1 be sent from process q, and consider the qth component of s_1.MCs and s_2.MCs. Let s_2.MCs$[q]$ be x. Since s_2 has been delivered, p.deliveredMCs$[q]$ must have been updated to be equal to x.

Since s_1.MCs $< s_2$.MCs by construction, s_1.MCs$[q] \leq s_2$.MCs$[q]$. Now we have that s_1.MCs$[q] \leq x$, meaning it must be the xth message sent or some message sent before it. Now it must have been delivered by Lemma 5.1. $\square$

Theorem 5.5. *For sends s_1 and s_2 with the same destination, if $s_1 \to s_2$, then $d_1 \to d_2$. That is, delivery events are causally ordered.*

Proof. Lemmas 5.3 and 5.4.

5.2   Liveness

We prove that every message is eventually delivered. The proof is by contradiction. Assume there is some message that can never be delivered. The existence of such a message means there is some process p and some first, or globally minimal, message m (minicast or application) sent to p that can never be delivered. That is, m is such that all messages whose sends to p happened before the send of m are deliverable (otherwise m would not be globally minimal). We will show that message m can be delivered once it is received, hence the contradiction.

Case 1: m is a minicast

If m is a minicast (with no corresponding unicast) and there are no undelivered messages that happened before it, then it must be at the front of the receivedMessages$[q]$ queue if it has been received. The delivery condition for a minicast is that it is at the front of the queue, so it can be delivered.

Case 2: m is an application message For a process p, consider the most recently delivered message from each process. Figure 3 illustrates the receivedMessages queue and deliveredMCs for process p. The most recently delivered messages are shown in blue, which correspond to the values in deliveredMCs. Any message sent after the most recently delivered message from a process has not been delivered and is colored gray. All messages before it are white and have been delivered.

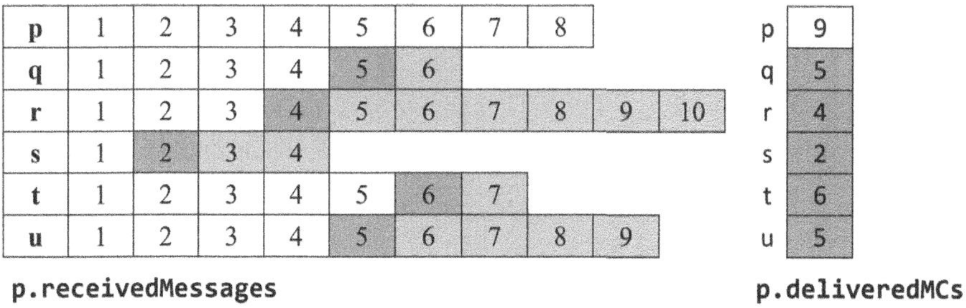

p	1	2	3	4	5	6	7	8		
q	1	2	3	4	5	6				
r	1	2	3	4	5	6	7	8	9	10
s	1	2	3	4						
t	1	2	3	4	5	6	7			
u	1	2	3	4	5	6	7	8	9	

p	9
q	5
r	4
s	2
t	6
u	5

`p.receivedMessages`   `p.deliveredMCs`

Fig. 3. Conceptual representation of the local data structures for process p

These most recent messages correspond to the value of deliveredMCs at each corresponding process. The messages immediately after the blue values are the first in the receivedMessages queue. These messages must eventually be application messages because minicasts are delivered when they are at the front of the queue.

These application messages could not have happened before m because otherwise they would have been delivered by construction. If one of these messages happened after m, then by Lemma 5.2 the value of deliveredMCs at that element would already be large enough for m.MC in that location. This only leaves messages that are concurrent with m.

Consider an arbitrary message from this group that is concurrent with m. The value of n.MC$[n]$ must be larger than the value of deliveredMCs$[n]$ by Lemma 5.1. Since m and n are concurrent, m.MC$[n] < n$.MC$[n]$. Now m.MC$[n] < n$.MC$[n]$ $<$ deliveredMCs$[n]$. Now m.MC$[n]$ must meet the delivery condition.

For each element in m.MC, this value must now be smaller than deliveredMCs and thus meet the delivery condition. Now it is clear that the guard for the delivery condition must become true eventually and is stable. Therefore, m must be delivered eventually. Since we have arbitrarily picked a minimal message, all minimal messages can be delivered. Every message will eventually become this minimal message by induction. Therefore, every message is eventually delivered.

6   Byzantine Tolerant Minicast Algorithm

6.1   System Model

As with the algorithm in Sect. 4, a set of FIFO (logical) communication links is assumed where processes communicate by message passing. Two separate channels are assumed per pair of processes, one for unicast messages and one for minicasts. The communication links are again assumed to be reliable, meaning messages cannot get lost or be duplicated and communication is authenticated. The system is asynchronous so there is no guarantee of how long messages may take to arrive. Since there may be byzantine nodes in this model, some processes may crash or behave arbitrarily. The number of byzantine nodes must be capped based on the BCCH algorithm [9] used for minicasts.

6.2   Overview

An additional assumption about the existence of a message passing layer that uses cryptography allows for byzantine tolerance in the previously presented Minicast Algorithm. The algorithm presented in this section uses the byzantine FIFO consistent broadcast channel (BCCH) [9] for the minicast so they are delivered in FIFO order and are tolerant to byzantine failures. The BCCH protocol satisfies the byzantine reliable broadcast properties of Definition 2.3 and furthermore ensures FIFO ordering by including a sequence number.

Only two sections of the Minicast Algorithm require modifications for byzantine tolerance. The rest are omitted.

6.3   Algorithm

Algorithm Byzantine Tolerant Causally Ordered Unicast (Process p)

Message Send

1: send message m to process q $\longrightarrow$
2:   $signature \leftarrow$ **Send_MPLayer**$(q, \langle m, deliveredMCs \rangle)$
3:   **BCCH_Broadcast**$(\langle q, signature, deliveredMCs[p] \rangle)$
4:   $deliveredMCs[p] \mathrel{+}= 1$

Minicast Arrives

5: $\langle r, signature, msgNum \rangle$ arrives from process q
   $\wedge$ **Verify**$(q, r, signature)$ $\longrightarrow$
6:   $receivedMessages[q].enqueue(\langle r, msgNum \rangle)$

6.4   Description

The byzantine tolerant version of this algorithm requires very few modifications. Most notably, minicast messages are sent using a byzantine tolerant FIFO channel for broadcast and are verified using a signature generated by a neutral message passing layer. This means that if a minicast is accepted, it was accepted by every process and a unicast message must have been sent. Any unicast messages that are sent without a corresponding minicast are discarded as part of the merging process of minicasts and unicasts. Minicast messages and unicast messages must be sent on separate channels due to the nature of byzantine tolerant broadcast. Not every process is required to receive the `initial` broadcast message from byzantine nodes, so FIFO ordering cannot be guaranteed for unicast messages sent on the same channel. As a result, an explicit merge of minicast and unicast messages is necessary.

7   Proof of Byzantine Tolerant Causal Ordering

7.1   Proof Of Causal Ordering

The proofs for both safety and liveness in Sect. 5 apply directly to the Byzantine Tolerant Unicast algorithm. Only weak safety can be shown for an algorithm with byzantine processes.

7.2   Proof Of Byzantine Tolerance

We define Byzantine Reliable Unicast (BRU) based on the validity and termination properties of Byzantine Tolerant Broadcast [4].

1. *BRU-Validity.* If a correct process BRU-delivers message m from p (possibly faulty), then p BRU-sent m
2. *BRU-Termination.* If a correct process BRU-sends message m to another correct process p, p BRU-delivers m

Proof. We will show that the algorithm meets the validity and termination criteria for byzantine tolerant unicast.

1. *BRU-Validity.* Given a correct process has BRU-delivered a message, because the delivery condition has been met, it has to have received both the unicast message m from p and a BCCH-broadcast (i.e. minicast) of the message from p.
2. *BRU-Termination.* If a correct process BRU-sends a unicast message and a minicast message to another correct process p, p will eventually have to receive this message based on the liveness and safety of BCCH-broadcast. If a minicast message is sent (and verified) with the application message destination as p, a unicast message must arrive eventually because of the Message Passing Layer. The unicast message will eventually be delivered based on the safety argument in the proof of causal ordering. If a unicast message is sent without a minicast, the sending process must be byzantine, and that message will eventually be ignored. Delivery of messages from other processes will not be delayed because no minicast was accepted.

8   Performance and Limitations

A major result of this work is a reduced overall complexity of causally ordered unicast in terms of total overhead summed over all messages. Previous solutions to the problem of causal ordering for asynchronous unicast messages required $O(n^2)$ of overhead space per message in the worst case. The algorithm presented here requires only $O(n)$ per unicast plus $O(log(n))$ per minicast, resulting in an overall complexity of $O(n + nlog(n))$ per application message. However, the encoding of process identifiers and message numbers sent with minicasts are not required for the Minicast algorithm if minicasts and unicasts occur on the same channel, so the overall complexity of the Minicast Algorithm can easily be reduced to $O(n)$ by sending minicasts of size $O(1)$. The complexity of the byzantine tolerant algorithm is $O(nlog(n))$.

A limitation of this algorithm is that the use of minicasts results in additional network traffic. Where traditional unicast requires only M messages sent, the algorithm presented here requires M unicast messages and M minicasts (each of which entails n messages).

The Minicast algorithm does not inhibit the degree of synchronization beyond what is necessary to enforce causal order because sends are never delayed. However, the overall latency of the algorithm is longer due to latency introduced by minicast control messages. The additional latency is only increased by these control messages. To show this, consider the proof of Liveness in Sect. 5. For the current minimal global message, the only messages preventing delivery are minicasts, which are delivered as soon as they are at the front of the queue. The Byzantine Tolerant Minicast algorithm has additional latency due to the underlying Bracha's BRB protocol [8] in the BCCH algorithm.

9   Conclusion

This paper demonstrates an improvement upon a previous implementation of asynchronous causal unicast from $O(n^2)$ in the worst case to $O(n)$. The addition of a minicast message, defined in this work as a small broadcast message, is used to preserve ordering and reduce message size. With this small broadcast message, the Minicast Algorithm is a blend between unicast and broadcast. The addition of the minicast results in a tradeoff of increased traffic on the network. A byzantine tolerant version of the Minicast Algorithm is also introduced. A message passing layer that uses cryptography is required, and allows the algorithm to circumvent the impossibility result for byzantine tolerant causally ordered unicast [23]. Byzantine tolerance in this algorithm is achieved using the BCCH [9] FIFO consistent broadcast channel for the minicast messages. The Byzantine Tolerant Minicast Algorithm is the first to achieve asynchronous byzantine tolerant causal unicast. The required message size is $O(nlogn)$ and there is added latency due to the BCCH protocol.

References

1. Adelstein, F., Singhal, M.: Real-time causal message ordering in multimedia systems. In: Proceedings of 15th International Conference on Distributed Computing Systems, pp. 36–43 (1995). https://doi.org/10.1109/ICDCS.1995.500000
2. Alagar, S., Venkatesan, S.: An optimal algorithm for distributed snapshots with causal message ordering. Inf. Process. Lett. **50**, 311–316 (1994). https://api.semanticscholar.org/CorpusID:12816143
3. Amir, Y., Dolev, D., Kramer, S., Malki, D.: Transis: a communication subsystem for high availability. In: [1992] Digest of Papers. FTCS-22: The Twenty-Second International Symposium on Fault-Tolerant Computing, pp. 76–84 (1992). https://doi.org/10.1109/FTCS.1992.243613
4. Auvolat, A., Frey, D., Raynal, M., Taïani, F.: Byzantine-tolerant causal broadcast. Theoret. Comput. Sci. **885**, 55–68 (2021). https://doi.org/10.1016/j.tcs.2021.06.021. https://www.sciencedirect.com/science/article/pii/S0304397521003662
5. Baldoni, R., Mostefaoui, A., Raynal, M.: Causal delivery of messages with real-time data in unreliable networks. Real-Time Syst. **10**(3), 245–262 (1996). https://doi.org/10.1007/BF00383387
6. Birman, K., Schiper, A., Stephenson, P.: Lightweight causal and atomic group multicast. ACM Trans. Comput. Syst. **9**(3), 272–314 (1991). https://doi.org/10.1145/128738.128742
7. Birman, K.P.: Building secure and reliable network applications. In: Masuda, T., Masunaga, Y., Tsukamoto, M. (eds.) Worldwide Computing and Its Applications, pp. 15–28. Springer, Heidelberg (1997)
8. Bracha, G.: Asynchronous byzantine agreement protocols. Inf. Comput. **75**(2), 130–143 (1987). https://doi.org/10.1016/0890-5401(87)90054-X. https://www.sciencedirect.com/science/article/pii/089054018790054X

9. Cachin, C., Guerraoui, R., Rodrigues, L.: Introduction to Reliable and Secure Distributed Programming, 2nd edn. Springer (2011)
10. Chandra, T.D., Toueg, S.: Unreliable failure detectors for reliable distributed systems. J. ACM **43**(2), 225–267 (1996). https://doi.org/10.1145/226643.226647
11. DeCandia, G., et al.: Dynamo: amazon's highly available key-value store. In: Proceedings of Twenty-First ACM SIGOPS Symposium on Operating Systems Principles, SOSP 2007, pp. 205–220. Association for Computing Machinery, New York (2007). https://doi.org/10.1145/1294261.1294281
12. Dwork, C., Lynch, N., Stockmeyer, L.: Consensus in the presence of partial synchrony. J. ACM **35**(2), 288–323 (1988). https://doi.org/10.1145/42282.42283
13. Fischer, M.J., Lynch, N.A., Paterson, M.S.: Impossibility of distributed consensus with one faulty process. J. ACM **32**(2), 374–382 (1985). https://doi.org/10.1145/3149.214121
14. Friedman, R., Manor, S.: Causal ordering in deterministic overlay networks. Israel Institute of Technology, Haifa, Israel (2004)
15. Gilbert, S., Lynch, N.: Brewer's conjecture and the feasibility of consistent, available, partition-tolerant web services. SIGACT News **33**(2), 51–59 (2002). https://doi.org/10.1145/564585.564601
16. Kaashoek, M., Tanenbaum, A.: Group communication in the amoeba distributed operating system. In: [1991] Proceedings. 11th International Conference on Distributed Computing Systems, pp. 222–230 (1991). https://doi.org/10.1109/ICDCS.1991.148669
17. Katz, J., Koo, C.Y.: On expected constant-round protocols for byzantine agreement. J. Comput. Syst. Sci. **75**(2), 91–112 (2009). https://doi.org/10.1016/j.jcss.2008.08.001
18. Kshemkalyani, A.D., Singhal, M.: Necessary and sufficient conditions on information for causal message ordering and their optimal implementation. Distrib. Comput. **11**, 91–111 (1998). https://api.semanticscholar.org/CorpusID:5724999
19. Lamport, L.: Time, clocks, and the ordering of events in a distributed system. Commun. ACM **21**(7), 558–565 (1978). https://doi.org/10.1145/359545.359563
20. Misra, A., Kshemkalyani, A.D.: Solvability of byzantine fault-tolerant causal ordering problems. In: Koulali, M.A., Mezini, M. (eds.) Networked Systems, pp. 87–103. Springer, Cham (2022)
21. Misra, A., Kshemkalyani, A.D.: Byzantine fault-tolerant causal ordering. In: Proceedings of the 24th International Conference on Distributed Computing and Networking, ICDCN 2023, pp. 100–109. Association for Computing Machinery, New York (2023). https://doi.org/10.1145/3571306.3571395
22. Misra, A., Kshemkalyani, A.D.: Causal ordering in the presence of byzantine processes. In: 2022 IEEE 28th International Conference on Parallel and Distributed Systems (ICPADS), pp. 130–138 (2023). https://doi.org/10.1109/ICPADS56603.2022.00025
23. Misra, A., Kshemkalyani, A.D.: Byzantine-tolerant causal ordering for unicasts, multicasts, and broadcasts. IEEE Trans. Parallel Distrib. Syst. **35**(5), 814–828 (2024). https://doi.org/10.1109/TPDS.2024.3368280
24. Mostéfaoui, A., Perrin, M., Raynal, M., Cao, J.: Crash-tolerant causal broadcast in o(n) messages. Inf. Process. Lett. **151**, 105837 (2019). https://doi.org/10.1016/j.ipl.2019.105837.   https://www.sciencedirect.com/science/article/pii/S0020019019301206
25. Prakash, R., Raynal, M., Singhal, M.: An adaptive causal ordering algorithm suited to mobile computing environments. J. Parallel Distrib. Comput. **41**(2), 190–204

(1997). https://doi.org/10.1006/jpdc.1996.1300. https://www.sciencedirect.com/science/article/pii/S0743731596913003

26. Raynal, M., Schiper, A., Toueg, S.: The causal ordering abstraction and a simple way to implement it. Inf. Process. Lett. **39**(6), 343–350 (1991). https://doi.org/10.1016/0020-0190(91)90008-6. https://www.sciencedirect.com/science/article/pii/0020019091900086

27. Schiper, A., Eggli, J., Sandoz, A.: A new algorithm to implement causal ordering. In: Bermond, J.C., Raynal, M. (eds.) Distributed Algorithms, pp. 219–232. Springer, Heidelberg (1989)

28. Schwarz, R., Mattern, F.: Detecting causal relationships in distributed computations: in search of the holy grail. Distrib. Comput. **7**, 149–174 (1994). https://api.semanticscholar.org/CorpusID:3065996

A Comparative Study of Two Matrix Multiplication Algorithms Under Current Hardware Architectures

Samuel Olatunde$^{(\boxtimes)}$ and Eduardo Colmenares

Department of Computer Science, McCoy College of Science, Mathematics and Engineering, Midwestern State University, Wichita Falls, TX 76308, USA
`psalmyz735@gmail.com`, `eduardo.colmenares@msutexas.edu`

Abstract. A widely used computationally intensive scientific kernel, the matrix multiplication algorithm is at the heart of many scientific routines. Resurging fields, such as artificial intelligence (AI), strongly benefit from fast and accurate processing of large matrices. Through the years, multiple efforts have been made to derive new algorithms capable of achieving better performance than the naive matrix multiplication approach $\Theta(n^3)$. One of those is Strassen's variant $\Theta(n^{2.81})$. This research compares the benefits and differences of using an optimal version of Strassen's algorithm versus the naive algorithm. The performance analysis makes use of the two most dominant high-performance computing (HPC) architectures available within the Lonestar6 cluster at Texas Advance Computing Center (TACC), the multi-core (CPU) and many-core (GPU) architectures.

Keywords: Matrix Multiplication · Strassen's · TACC · GPU · CUDA · C programming

1 Introduction

Matrix multiplication is at the core of many computational tasks within fields such as image processing, machine learning, artificial intelligence, data science, computer graphics, robotics, and physics. Due to its relevance in science, many scientists have made considerable efforts to study and create algorithms that perform better than the naive approach. One such algorithm is Strassen's algorithm.

Resurgent fields like artificial intelligence (AI), strongly rely on the fast and accurate multiplication of large matrices. Several of the current AI algorithms need to process massive amount of data not only once, but multiple times. In such contexts, any enhancements in performance without compromising accuracy are highly advantageous. One of the authors of this research has a strong interest in Mathematics and Computer Science, and the scenario described presents an ideal landscape for research and learning.

© The Author(s), under exclusive license to Springer Nature Switzerland AG 2025
H. R. Arabnia et al. (Eds.): CSCE 2024, CCIS 2256, pp. 82–96, 2025.
https://doi.org/10.1007/978-3-031-85638-9_6

This research seeks to achieve two major goals. Firstly, it aims to implement and compare the potential performance benefits of an optimal version of single-level Strassen's algorithm $\Theta(n^{2.81})$ against the traditional dot product matrix multiplication algorithm $\Theta(n^3)$. To facilitate a thorough comparison, performance analyses were conducted using cutting-edge computational resources, including the Lonestar6 facility at the Texas Advanced Computing Center (TACC). These analyses encompassed metrics from two prominent high-performance computing (HPC) architectures: multi-core (CPU) and many-core (GPU).

Secondly, the research examines how effectively the GPU, which has dominated the floating-point race since 2003 [8], accelerates each algorithm relative to the other. Does the GPU accelerate one more efficiently than the other? How does the speedup trend across different data sizes? All code implementations were carried out in C and CUDA-C for their respective architectures. The mathematical correctness of these methods was rigorously verified across a diverse range of problem sizes. Using execution time as the primary metric for performance evaluation, initial findings indicate that for small problem sizes, the naive approach exhibits superior performance compared to Strassen's approach. However, Strassen's algorithm surpasses the naive implementation as matrix sizes increase. A substantial performance boost is also observed when both algorithms are executed on the GPU.

2 Manual Analysis

The conventional matrix multiplication method, also known as the dot product approach, is widely known in the scientific community and well documented in multiple textbooks. For these reasons, if interested in this approach, the reader is referred to [11,12]. This section of the paper focuses on Strassen's algorithm. The divide-and-conquer approach serves as an alternative to the naive matrix multiplication algorithm. This method involves partitioning all matrices participating in the operation into equally sized block matrices, as outlined below:

$$A = \left[\begin{array}{c|c} a & b \\ \hline c & d \end{array}\right] \quad B = \left[\begin{array}{c|c} e & f \\ \hline g & h \end{array}\right]$$

Then we find the product by multiplying the corresponding rows by columns of the matrices:

$$C = A \cdot B = \left[\begin{array}{c|c} a & b \\ \hline c & d \end{array}\right] \cdot \left[\begin{array}{c|c} e & f \\ \hline g & h \end{array}\right] = \left[\begin{array}{c|c} ae + bg & af + bh \\ \hline ce + dg & cf + dh \end{array}\right]$$

If A and B are large enough, the divide-and-conquer approach can be applied recursively to the product of the sub-matrices. For simplicity and illustrative purposes, we assume that matrices A and B are 2×2. Note that in the computation described earlier, two multiplications and one addition are performed in each partition or quadrant of Matrix C, this results in a total of eight distinct multiplications and 4 distinct additions. Strassen's algorithm optimizes this by reducing the number of distinct multiplications to seven through the use of equivalent expressions for each partition:

$$
\begin{aligned}
ae + bg &= (a + d)(e + h) + d(g - e) \\
&\quad - (a + b)h + (b - d)(g + h) \\
af + bh &= a(f - h) + (a + b)h \\
ce + dg &= (c + d)e + d(g - e) \\
cf + dh &= a(f - h) + (a + d)(e + h) \\
&\quad - (c + d)e - (a - c)(e + f).
\end{aligned}
$$

The seven distinct products performed are:

$$
\begin{aligned}
p_1 &= (a + d)(e + h) \\
p_2 &= d(g - e) \\
p_3 &= (a + b)h \\
p_4 &= (b - d)(g + h) \\
p_5 &= a(f - h) \\
p_6 &= (c + d)e \\
p_7 &= (a - c)(e + f).
\end{aligned}
$$

We rewrite the partitions as sums/differences of these products below:

$$
\begin{aligned}
ae + bg &= p_1 + p_2 - p_3 + p_4 \\
af + bh &= p_5 + p_3 \\
ce + dg &= p_6 + p_2 \\
cf + dh &= p_5 + p_1 - p_6 - p_7.
\end{aligned}
$$

Therefore $C = A \cdot B =$

$$
\begin{aligned}
&\left[\begin{array}{c|c} ae + bg & af + bh \\ \hline ce + dg & cf + dh \end{array}\right] \\
&= \left[\begin{array}{c|c} p_1 + p_2 - p_3 + p_4 & p_5 + p_3 \\ p_6 + p_2 & p_5 + p_1 - p_6 - p_7 \end{array}\right]
\end{aligned}
$$

Although Strassen's algorithm reduces the number of distinct multiplications, it significantly increases the number of additions and subtractions. However, as the matrix size grows, the impact of these additional operations becomes negligible. This is because multiplication is computationally more expensive than addition. Consequently, the relative cost of the increased number of additions and subtractions diminishes when working with larger matrices.

The previous analysis was conducted for 2×2 matrices, but the same principle applies to larger matrices. They are partitioned into four equally sized blocks each, and the seven products are computed using these blocks during the divide phase. The products are then combined in the prescribed way to produce the resultant matrix during the conquer phase.

Strassen's algorithm ultimately resorts to the naive method. The point at which this transition takes place depends on the implementation. One possible choice is to recursively divide and conquer until the partition size is 2×2 and then perform the naive method, the alternative choice is to recursively divide and conquer to an earlier point (not a 2×2) and then apply the naive algorithm. Independent of the chosen Strassen's variant, each divide-and-conquer step is referred to as a level. Thus, a single-level Strassen's algorithm involves one divide-and-conquer step, two times is a double-level, and so forth. The term "multilevel Strassen's" is commonly used to describe performing multiple divide-and-conquer steps.

The focus of this paper is a single-level Strassen's algorithm. As mentioned in Sect. 8.3, future plans will include implementing and analyzing multilevel Strassen's algorithm.

3 Speedup

Speedup is a crucial performance evaluation metric in parallel computing, used to compare the performance improvement of a parallel approach with its serial counterpart [4].

According to [7], speedup is defined as the worst-case run time of the best sequential algorithm divided by the worst-case runtime of the parallel algorithm. Because the number of processes used by parallel systems can vary, references normally refer to the speedup achieved on a certain data size in terms of the number of processes/threads, S(p). It is given by

$$S(p) = \frac{t_{\text{serial}}}{t_{\text{parallel}}}, \tag{1}$$

where,

p: Number of threads
t_{serial}: Runtime of serial approach
t_{parallel}: Runtime of parallel approach using p threads.

4   Naive-Strassen Speedup Ratio

Inspired by speedup, a new metric was introduced to compare the two matrix multiplication approaches: the Naive-Strassen Speedup Ratio (NSSR). This metric evaluates how much faster Strassen's algorithm performs compared to the naive method for each data size, using the same number of threads. It is computed as follows:

$$NSSR(n) = \frac{t_{naive}}{t_{strassen}}, \tag{2}$$

where,

n : Order of matrices
t_{naive} : Runtime of naive method
t_{strassen} : Runtime of strassen's method.

5   Implementation

The code for this research is organized into four files: two for the serial and parallel implementations of the naive algorithm, and two for the serial and parallel implementations of Strassen's algorithm.

In all implementations, matrices were stored as dynamically allocated 2D arrays to accommodate large sizes and manage memory efficiently. This approach allows for flexible memory allocation at runtime, ensuring that memory is allocated only as needed.

To simulate floating-point operations while avoiding accuracy issues, we used single-precision data types and initialized test data with whole numbers. Further details are provided in the first paragraph of Sect. 6.2.

The serial code was written in C using traditional sequential programming techniques, while the parallel code was implemented in CUDA-C using methods learned from [1]. All parallel implementations utilize square, power-of-two, two-dimensional computational grids with two-dimensional blocks.

Additionally, load-balancing techniques were employed to ensure even data distribution among participant CUDA threads, and memory management techniques were used to prevent memory leaks.

5.1   Naive Algorithm

The implementation of the naive algorithm is straightforward in both its serial and parallel versions. In both cases, the matrices (arrays) are initialized, and the function "multMatrix(A, B, P)" is called to execute the respective version (serial or parallel) of the naive method.

In the serial implementation of multMatrix, three nested loops are utilized. The outer loops iterate over the rows and columns of matrix P, while the innermost loop performs the dot product operation for each element, resulting in the multiplication of corresponding elements from matrices A and B, and accumulation of the result in matrix P.

On the other hand, the parallel *multMatrix* function determines the number of threads needed in the x and y dimensions based on the block and grid sizes. It then uses nested loops to distribute the matrix multiplication task among these threads. Each thread computes its assigned part of the resulting matrix by iterating over rows and columns, performing the necessary multiplications and additions, and contributing to the final result in parallel.

5.2   Strassen's Algorithm

The implementation of Strassen's algorithm, on the other hand, is not as straight-forward as the naive method, as it involves multiple helper functions that are called repeatedly. The exact approach to achieving their tasks in serial and parallel implementations differs, but below are the helper functions used in our implementation of Strassen's algorithm:

- *matrixMultiplication*: Multiply two matrices using the naive method as described in [11,12] and return the result to the calling function.
- *getSlice*: Extract a sub-matrix (partition) from a larger matrix based on specified row and column offsets and return it. It is used to partition a larger square $(n \times n)$ matrix into four smaller, equally sized square matrices ($\frac{n}{2} \times \frac{n}{2}$) by allocating a new matrix and copying the relevant elements from the specified offsets. For example, given a 4×4 matrix

$$C = \begin{bmatrix} a & b & c & d \\ e & f & g & h \\ i & j & k & l \\ m & n & o & p \end{bmatrix},$$

calling the function with parameters C, 4 (the total number of columns or rows in C), 0 (the row offset), and 2 (the column offset) would extract the second quarter of C, denoted as C_2:

$$C_2 = \begin{bmatrix} c & d \\ g & h \end{bmatrix}.$$

- *addMatrices*: Add or subtract two matrices. The function takes in two input matrices and an integer that causes the function to add the matrices if its value is 1 and subtract the matrices if the value is 0. The resulting matrix is returned to the calling function.
- *combineMatrices*: Combine four sub-matrices into a larger matrix. For input, this function takes in four equally sized square matrices,

$$C_1 = \begin{bmatrix} a & b \\ e & f \end{bmatrix} \qquad C_2 = \begin{bmatrix} c & d \\ g & h \end{bmatrix}$$

$$C_3 = \begin{bmatrix} i & j \\ \hline m & n \end{bmatrix} \qquad C_4 = \begin{bmatrix} k & l \\ \hline o & p \end{bmatrix},$$

and combines them into one big output matrix

$$C = \begin{bmatrix} C_1 & C_2 \\ \hline C_3 & C_4 \end{bmatrix} = \begin{bmatrix} a & b & c & d \\ e & f & g & h \\ i & j & k & l \\ m & n & o & p \end{bmatrix}.$$

The final function in this implementation is called 'strassens.' This function uses the helper functions to achieve the process highlighted in Sect. 2.

5.3   Timing

To measure the execution time of both serial and parallel code, different techniques tailored to each scenario are utilized.

For the serial code, we utilize a macro leveraging the timeval struct specified in [10] to capture the EPOCH time in microseconds. Initially, the code records the current time before executing the matrix multiplication operation. Subsequently, after the completion of the multiplication, it captures the current time once again. By subtracting the time before and after the multiplication, the code effectively estimates the execution time of the matrix multiplication operation.

On the other hand, for the parallel code, we harness the CUDA runtime API outlined in [3] to precisely time the execution. This process involves the utilization of CUDA events to mark the start and end of the computation accurately. Initially, two CUDA events, named start and stop, are created to denote the beginning and end of the computation, respectively. The time is recorded just before invoking the matrix multiplication computation on the GPU. Upon the completion of the computation, the current time is recorded again. Synchronization ensures that all GPU tasks are finalized before calculating the elapsed time between the start and stop events. Finally, the elapsed time in milliseconds is obtained, and multiplied by 1000 to obtain the duration in microseconds.

6   Methodology

6.1   Testing Environment (Cluster)

All but two of the tests were conducted on the Lonestar6 cluster at the Texas Advanced Computing Center (TACC). The reason for this will be discussed later in this section.

The following specifications are taken from [5]. Lonestar6 boasts a powerful compute infrastructure with 560 compute nodes, each offering 5 TFlops of peak performance. Each node is equipped with two AMD EPYC 7763 64-core processors ("Milan"), providing a total of 128 cores per node across two sockets. The processors operate at a base clock rate of 2.45 GHz, which can boost up to 3.5 GHz for enhanced performance. Additionally, each node is outfitted with 256 GB of DDR4 memory, ensuring ample capacity for demanding computational tasks. The cache hierarchy includes a 32KB L1 data cache per core, 512KB L2 cache per core, and 32 MB L3 cache per core complex, with a total of 256 MB L3 cache per node [5].

The GPU nodes on Lonestar6 are particularly noteworthy, featuring 84 A100 GPU nodes and 4 H100 nodes. Each A100 GPU node hosts three NVIDIA A100 PCIE GPUs with 40 GB HBM2 memory each, while each H100 GPU node supports two NVIDIA H100 PCIE GPUs with 80 GB HBM2e memory per GPU. These GPUs offer impressive peak performance capabilities, with the A100 GPUs delivering 9.7 TFlops in double precision and 312 TFlops in FP16 precision using Tensor Cores, and the H100 GPUs boasting a peak performance of 26 TFlops in double precision and 1513 TFlops in FP16 precision using Tensor Cores [6].

6.2   Methods

The goal of this research was to evaluate performance rather than numerical stability. We initialized test matrices with the whole number 4.0f, as whole numbers can be precisely represented in the floating-point format. The tests were divided into two major phases: validation and scale-up.

In the validation phase, we took the following steps to ensure mathematical correctness: 1. Ran all versions (serial and parallel) of both algorithms (naive and Strassen's) with matrices of order 4 and recorded the output. 2. Computed the product of the same matrices by hand. 3. Compared the answers from step 2 with the outputs from step 1. If the answers matched, we proceeded to the scale-up phase; if not, we made necessary adjustments to the code until the answers were correct.

In the scale-up phase, we ran and timed all versions of both algorithms with square matrices of orders 512, 2048, 8192, and 32768. These tests were further divided into serial and parallel. For the serial tests, we executed the code for both algorithms with each data size.

The tests were submitted as jobs to the 'normal' queue on Lonestar6 to run on one of the CPU nodes with a maximum job duration of 48 h. However, the serial versions of both the naive and Strassen's algorithms required more time to process matrices of order 32768. Consequently, we had to transfer these specific computations to a local computer. As a result, two of our tests were not conducted on the cluster, exceeding its computational constraints, which led to an anomaly in our results.

All parallel tests were successfully executed on the "gpu-a100" queue of Lonestar6. Each problem size was analyzed using multiple square computational grid sizes, starting with a 32×32 grid and increasing by a factor of 4 in each dimension until the grid size matched the problem size. At this point, each thread was assigned to a single data element of the output matrix, and we did not increase the number of threads further to avoid performance degradation from idle threads.

To provide additional validation, we summed the product matrix after each run of both algorithms and compared the sums for matching data sizes to ensure their equality. This approach was feasible because numerical stability was assured through careful initialization.

For all data sizes and thread sizes, we recorded the runtimes in a spreadsheet and analyzed the performance.

6.3   Test Environment (Local Computer)

The local computer is equipped with a 64-bit Ubuntu 16.04 LTS operating system, running on an IntelXeon® Xeon® CPU E5-1607V4. This processor, belonging to the Intel® Xeon® Processor E5 v4 Family, boasts a 14 nm lithography and is specifically tailored for server applications. Featuring 4 cores and 4 threads, it operates at a base frequency of 3.10 GHz and incorporates a 10 MB cache. Sporting a Thermal Design Power (TDP) of 140 W, it was initially released in Q2'16, although it has since been discontinued. It supports a maximum memory size of 1.5 TB and is compatible with DDR4 memory types, including 1600, 1866, and 2133. With 4 memory channels and a peak memory bandwidth of 68 GB/s, it facilitates Error-Correcting Code (ECC) memory and boasts 46-bit Physical Address Extensions. Employing FCLGA2011 sockets, it is tailored for single-socket (1S) configurations and offers a maximum of 40 PCI Express lanes. Additionally, it incorporates Intel® Transactional Synchronization Extensions, supports a 64-bit instruction set, and extends its capabilities with Intel® AVX2 instruction set extensions. Furthermore, it includes an array of advanced technologies such as Intel® AES New Instructions, Secure Key, Intel® OS Guard, and Execute Disable Bit, bolstering its security and reliability features [9].

7   Results and Discussion

Table 1 and Table 2 present the serial and parallel execution times for both matrix multiplication approaches, naive and Strassen. For both tables the results are in seconds.

The second column of Table 2 shows the square size of the CUDA computational grid, e.g., 512 means that the computational grid is constituted by a 512×512 two dimensional logical distribution of the CUDA threads, this means a total of 262144 threads for this case.

A CUDA computational grid is composed of threads that are organized into blocks. Each block can contain a maximum of 1024 threads. It's important to note that the maximum number of threads per block does not correspond to the dimensions of the grid. Instead, the grid dimensions are determined by the total number of threads distributed across blocks, taking into account the organization along the logical x-axis and y-axis.

Table 1. Serial Runtimes in Seconds

Square Matrices Dimensions	Naive	Strassen
512	0.506	0.482
2048	36.601	34.610
8192	6149.945	3351.459
32768	528946.638	727212.050

Table 2. Parallel Runtimes in Seconds

Square Matrices Dimensions	Square GPU Grid Dimensions	Naive	Strassen
512	32	0.315	0.184
	128	0.029	0.025
	512	0.008	0.017
2048	32	17.707	5.807
	128	1.104	0.531
	512	0.368	0.178
	2048	0.332	0.173
8192	32	1135.050	359.166
	128	73.373	23.311
	512	17.215	4.974
	2048	14.472	3.962
	8192	14.859	3.953
32768	32	76259.287	22971.441
	128	4792.818	1436.204
	512	1994.226	285.446
	2048	1026.350	275.510
	8192	979.290	219.480
	32768	995.637	222.450

Figures 1, 2 and 3 are generated from the acquired data, which is shown in Table 1 and 2.

For the analysis, square matrices of orders 512, 2048, 8192, and 32768 were considered. The matrices were categorized into four different groups: small (512), medium (2048, 8192), and large (32768). These problem sizes and their corresponding categories represent the x-axis of Figs. 1, 2 and 3.

The top-right section of Figs. 1, 2 and 3 shows a legend with values of 1, 32, 128, 512, 2048, 8192, and 32768. These numbers make reference to the dimensions of the square CUDA computational grid used to process a given problem size, e.g., 128 in the legend indicates that the CUDA computational grid in charge of processing a given problem size will use a logical square layout of 128×128 threads, this means a total of 16384 participant CUDA threads.

7.1   Speedup

Figure 1 shows the speedup achieved by employing the naive algorithm across various data sizes and computational grid configurations. Remember, speedup compares CPU to GPU performance. As illustrated in Fig. 1, for smaller data sizes (512 and 2048), the speedup increases as the thread count (size of the computational grid) increases, reaching a maximum of 62.5 (indicating that the GPU performed the algorithm 62.5 times faster than the CPU) for 512 and 110.3 for 2048. This demonstrates a directly proportional relationship between the number of threads and the speedup achieved for these smaller data sizes.

For larger data sizes (8192 and 32768), the speedup significantly increases with thread size, achieving a maximum of 424.9 for 8192 and 540.1 for 32768. However, there is a noticeable reduction in speedup on the last (rightmost) bar for these data sizes. At this point, the thread count equals the large data size, which likely causes congestion in the GPU, thereby negatively impacting performance.

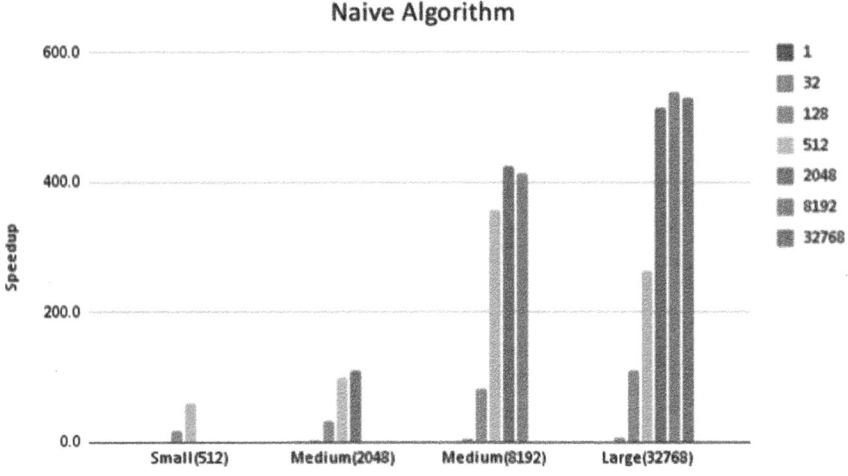

Fig. 1. Speedup of Naive Algorithm

Figure 2 illustrates the remarkable speedup achieved through the implementation of Strassen's algorithm across various data sizes and computational grid configurations. A trend similar to that of the naive algorithm's speedup is observed. As the thread count increases, the speedup rises for smaller matrices and continues to do so for larger matrices until the thread count matches the data size. A significantly higher speedup was observed across all data sizes starting from 2048, with the most notable performance at 32768, achieving a speedup of 3313.3 using a 8192 order computational grid. This indicates that the GPU significantly accelerates Strassen's algorithm relative to the naive algorithm-a surprising result given the additional operations (copy, add, multiply, slice, combine) involved in the implementation of Strassen's method.

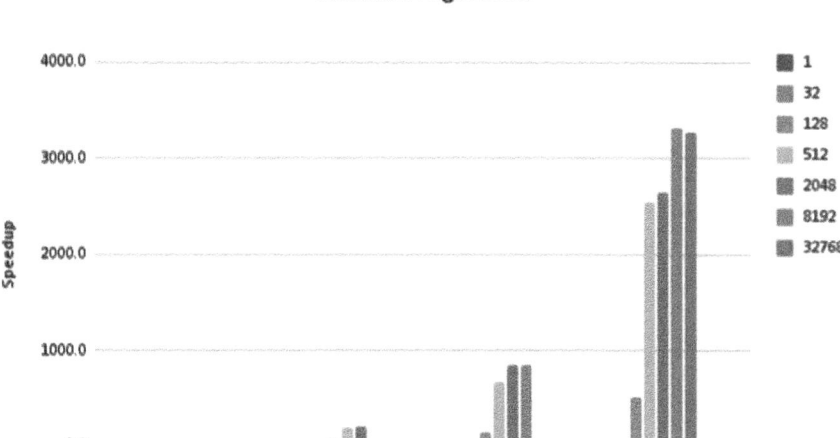

Fig. 2. Speedup of Strassen's Algorithm

7.2   Naive-Strassen Speedup Ratio ($NSSR$)

The Naive-Strassen Speedup Ratio (NSSR) depicted in Fig. 3 provides a direct comparison of the performance between Strassen's algorithm and the naive approach across various data sizes and thread counts. In the serial execution (single thread), there is a noticeable performance increase up to matrices of order 8192, followed by a decline at order 32768. This reduction in performance is likely due to the change in computing machines, necessitated by the computational constraints of Lonestar6, as discussed in Sect. 6.2.

For the parallel analysis of smaller data sizes (512 and 2048), Strassen's algorithm initially outperforms the naive method when using a computational grid of order 32, but its performance steadily decreases as the grid size increases. Conversely, for the larger data sizes, there is a generally steady increase in NSSR as the thread size increases. An interesting observation in data sizes 2048 and 32768 is the presence of standout high bars, indicating a potentially optimal configuration. Further investigation revealed that at these points, the difference between the data size and the computational grid size is a factor of 64 in both dimensions, suggesting an optimal grid configuration for Strassen's algorithm to outperform the naive method. Additional tests with other data sizes were conducted to verify this observation, but no consistent trend was found across the other data sizes.

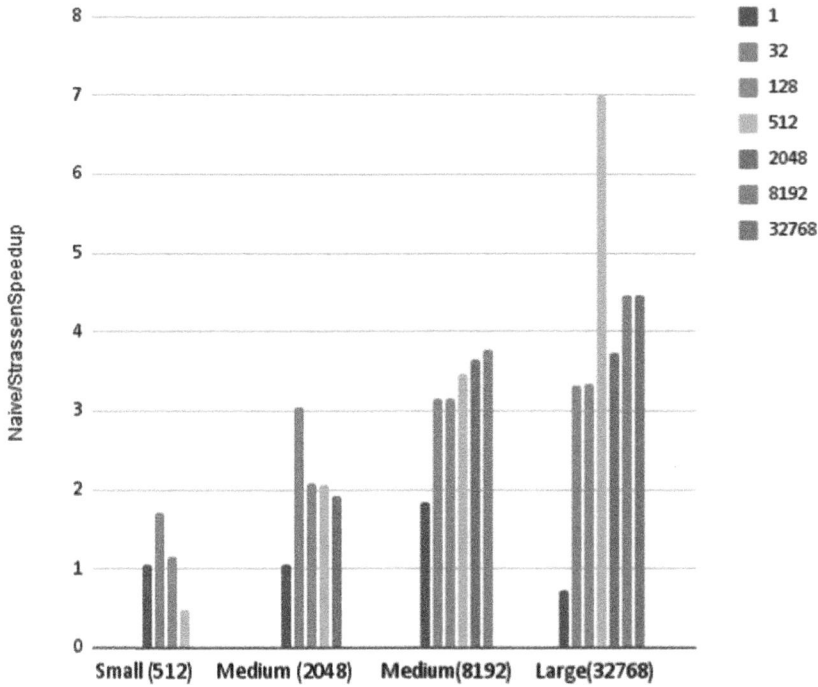

Fig. 3. Naive-Strassen Speedup Ratio ($NSSR$)

8 Conclusions

8.1 Algorithmic Insights

The Naive-Strassen Speedup Ratio (NSSR) offers a clear comparison between Strassen's algorithm and the naive approach across various data and thread sizes. Strassen's algorithm, despite an initial performance dip, consistently outperforms the naive method, particularly with larger data sizes. For instance, Strassen's method multiplies matrices of order 32,768 approximately 6.99 times faster than the naive method. This underscores the potential benefits of adopting Strassen's method more widely. However, Strassen's method involves trade-offs that may impact its practicality. For instance, it is less suitable in systems with limited memory or for matrix multiplication by hand.

8.2 Architectural

Both Strassen's algorithm and the naive approach achieve significant speedups across various data sizes, with the GPU accelerating Strassen's algorithm more effectively than the naive method. The maximum speedup of 540.1 for the naive method and 3313.3 for Strassen's method highlights the value of parallelizing algorithms, particularly matrix multiplication. This underscores the importance of leveraging GPU resources to optimize performance in algorithmic implementations like neural networks, where improving small but computationally intensive operations, such as matrix multiplication, guarantees substantial reductions in processing time.

Additionally, our analysis reveals a sublinear speedup for both algorithms, where performance initially increases sharply but levels off as the thread count matches the data size. This suggests bottlenecks not only within the parallelization strategy but also in the hardware. These results call for a closer examination of the underlying factors from an algorithmic standpoint and provide valuable insights for future optimizations and enhancements, some of which are outlined in the next subsection.

8.3   Future Work

In extending this project, the primary focus will be on evaluating the performance and possibly identifying the optimal implementation of the Multi-level Strassen's Algorithm. The aim is to determine whether a universal approach exists for the number of recursive steps or if this varies with data size. Additionally, the project will seek to optimize space complexity and investigate numerical stability. As mentioned in Sect. 5, multiple kernels are launched multiple times, resulting in significant overhead from kernel launches. This overhead becomes more pronounced with an increasing number of recursive steps. Techniques such as kernel fusion will be explored to mitigate this overhead.

References

1. Kirk, D.B., Hwu, W.W.: Programming Massively Parallel Processors: A Hands-on Approach, 4th edn. Morgan Kaufmann (2020)
2. Inside Code: Strassen algorithm for matrix multiplication (divide and conquer). YouTube. https://www.youtube.com/watch?v=OSelhO6Qnlc. Accessed 12 Apr 2024
3. CUDA Toolkit Documentation: CUDA Runtime API. NVIDIA. https://docs.nvidia.com/cuda/cuda-runtime-api/index.html. Accessed 12 Apr 2024
4. Pacheco, P.: An Introduction to Parallel Programming, 2nd edn. Morgan Kaufmann (2011)
5. TACC User Portal: Lonestar6 User Guide - System Architecture. https://docs.tacc.utexas.edu/hpc/lonestar6/#system-compute. Accessed 12 Apr 2024
6. TACC User Portal: Lonestar6 User Guide - GPU Accelerators. https://docs.tacc.utexas.edu/hpc/lonestar6/#system-gpu. Accessed 12 Apr 2024
7. Akl, S., Bruda, S.: Parallel Real-Time Optimization: Beyond Speedup. Technical report No. 99-421 (1999)
8. Oxford Numerics (2024). https://www.oxfordnumerics.co.uk/images/ON/gpgpu-floating-point-operations-per-second.png. Accessed 16 Apr 2024

9. Intel: Intel® Xeon® Processor E5-1607 v4 (10M Cache, 3.10 GHz) - Product Specifications. https://www.intel.com/content/www/us/en/products/sku/93101/intel-xeon-processor-e51607-v4-10m-cache-3-10-ghz/specifications.html. Accessed 16 Apr 2024

10. Gupta, S.: Struct timeval in C. http://www.ccplusplus.com/2011/09/struct-timeval-in-c.html. Accessed 16 Apr 2024

11. Anderson, J.: Applied Linear Algebra Lesson 11A: Matrix-matrix Multiplication (2023). https://static1.squarespace.com/static/53bc694ee4b00ad4e0bd6d55/t/625d78d0495a0a2b81f76721/1650292944748/Anderson_Applied_Linear_Algebra_Lesson_11A_Matrix_matrix_Multiplication_draft_v20220329.pdf. Accessed 14 June 2024

12. Pierce, R.: How to Multiply Matrices. Mathsisfun.com (2017). https://www.mathsisfun.com/algebra/matrix-multiplying.html. Accessed 14 June 2024

Is Manual Code Optimization Still Required to Mitigate GPU Thread Divergence? Applying a Flattening Technique to Observe Performance

Lucas Vespa[(✉)]

University of Illinois, Springfield, USA
lvesp2@uis.edu

Abstract. We examine the impact of manual elimination of thread divergence in GPU code through removal of all branches using a flattening technique. The goal is to investigate the necessity of manual mitigation of thread divergence on GPU, compared with automated, modern compiler optimization and architectural improvements. We apply our previously presented flattening technique called Algorithm Flattening (AF), which eliminates all branches, producing divergence-free code with increased ILP at the expense of minor to moderate increased instruction overhead. We observe the effect of said optimization on kernel performance across historical architectures and compilers, up to recent offerings. We theorize that modern GPU improvements will eventually eliminate the need for programmer intervention of thread divergence coding issues for GPU, although further study is necessary.

Keywords: Thread Divergence · General Purpose GPU · High Performance Computing · Algorithm Flattening · Branch Elimination

1 Introduction

GPU performance suffers in the presence of thread divergence due to branches. Optimizations need to be applied to GPU code in order to mitigate said divergence and improve performance. But how much of this optimization needs to be applied manually by the programmer. GPUs have come a long way in recent years in terms of hardware and compiler design. Given that GPU design still contains some variation of SIMD constraints, it would follow that hardware and compiler optimization for mitigating thread divergence due to branches would be a priority for those working with the design and workflow optimization of GPUs.

In this work, we intend to do a preliminary study of how far GPUs have come in terms of hardware and compiler optimizations to mitigate the effect that branched code has on thread divergence, without special coding techniques or optimizations that the programmer must implement. Branch Divergence can

© The Author(s), under exclusive license to Springer Nature Switzerland AG 2025
H. R. Arabnia et al. (Eds.): CSCE 2024, CCIS 2256, pp. 97–108, 2025.
https://doi.org/10.1007/978-3-031-85638-9_7

severely degrade GPGPU performance [1]. Although many methods have been proposed to mitigate this problem, highly divergent branch-based code still limits how much these methods can help. Our first task in this work is to demonstrate how to modify divergent source code in order to create divergent free code.

Historically, branches cause performance issues in many systems, which is why a great deal of work has been done to try and mitigate their effects. Unlike CPU multiprocessors, GPUs are massively parallel with thousands of processing elements. This huge number of processors still has to fit on chip, which is why comprises must be made in the independence of individual processors on a GPU. Some processors share instructions, and with divergence in instruction paths, some processors in a group of instruction tied processors will be idle at times.

We previously presented an extreme de-optimization for CPU [2] which completely eliminates branches, and historically resulted in a significant optimization for general purpose GPU applications, especially applications which had previously not been suitable for GPU implementation due to thread divergence. Our optimization removes all branches from code blocks and replaces each block with a reduced equation. The equation evaluates all branches simultaneously using arithmetic operations. We call our method Algorithm Flattening (AF). Use of AF eliminates thread divergence.

Our second task in this work is to compare performance of un-optimized CUDA code on NVIDIA GPUs, with that of CUDA code with all branches eliminated. Our intention is to see if modern hardware and compiler techniques have overtaken such manual optimization, and if performance issues with thread divergence do to branched code are mostly handled by such integrated optimization.

The remainder of this work is organized as follows. Section 2 presents background information on GPU architecture and considerations, and related work in the area of branch elimination. This section details some work in thread divergence which has been potentially been considered during GPU development and optimization. Our algorithm for branch elimination is detailed in Sect. 3. Much of this description comes from our previous paper [2]. Results are presented in Sect. 4 and the paper is concluded in Sect. 5.

2   Discussion of Thread Divergence Issues and Optimization

Modern GPUs are essentially massively parallel multiprocessors. Although these multiprocessors are becoming less and less limited in the way they can process data, they still tend to use some variant of an SIMD arrangement [3,4]. The limitations of these arrangements have been mitigated in many ways in recent years. However, there is typically still some sort of constraints on the way groups of processors can access instructions, such that not all processors can execute different instructions. This is simply a necessity of packing so many processors on chip. This works well with many applications, especially when there is little divergence. It follows that if processors share instructions in some way, but can access different data, then branches will affect performance of these processors, as some processors may not be able to execute code on their given data, based on the flow of instructions according to decisions made by certain branched code.

The following is a study of techniques which can reduce the impact of branches. Some of these techniques are more general and suitable for any platform, while others are specifically designed for SIMD. The reason for this study is two-fold. First, we wish to present some background on branches and how they affect code execution on various platforms. Second, we want to show the myriad of work which, much of which has been integrated into GPU design and work-flow. In other words, GPU hardware and compilers have been changed to include many of these optimizations at various levels.

Hijma et al. [5] present an excellent summary of branch optimization techniques on GPU, which includes our previously presented method called Algorithm Flattening. Since this method completely eliminates thread divergence on GPU, we plan to use this method to compare performance against raw GPU code. Hijma et al. present a section on branching issues, and much of this presentation has been considered by the GPU industry at this point.

Some techniques involve analyzing [1,6] and merging conditions [7–9], reordering conditions [10], replicating code or code addition [11], factoring code [12], distributing branch code [13–15], hardware based predicated execution [16,17], and warp scheduling [18,19].

Anido et al. [20] reduce the number of branches executed using Guarded Instructions and Pseudo Branches, which selectively execute instructions based on register values. Pseudo Branch instructions require an additional tag that allows control to be skipped to a destination point, so the SIMD device must have the appropriate hardware. Carrillo et al. [13] describe two optimizations for general purpose GPU using code splitting. Loop Splitting takes a loop and breaks it into two or more smaller loops. Branch Splitting involves breaking segments of a branch off into separate kernels. The purpose of splitting code is to reduce the hardware load. For data-dependent loops, Sarkar and Mitra [15] split code by discovering if a significant pattern exists in the control flow over a period of iterations. Branch behavior determines where code is split and how many kernels result. Han and Abdelrahman [12] present an optimization method known as Iteration Delaying. Similar to Guarded Instructions and Branch Splitting, segments of branches are gated. Unlike the other methods, Iteration Delaying delays segments from executing, so that similar segments are executed together.

Code Replication, an optimization technique described by Mueller and Whalley [11], simplifies control flow by replicating segments of code. Han and Abdelrahman [12] also present an optimization method known as Branch Distribution in which common code between branches is replicated outside of the branches. In Branch Distribution and Code Replication, new code is added which creates an optimization for SIMD but a de-optimization for CPU. However, these methods simply reduce the time penalty due to thread divergence, but do not actually eliminate branches.

Chakroun et al. [21] reduce thread divergence in a branch and bound algorithm accelerated on a GPU. As part of their method, they remove several single level if-else statements through a method equivalent to α (Eq. (1)) for case $n = 0$ only.

Other methods of SIMD optimization such as hardware Predicated Execution [16] can be used to reduce the number of branch operations executed in a program, but require run time intervention. Reissmann et al. [17] implement a predicated branch restructuring algorithm for unstructured code. Yu et al. [19] redesigns PDOM stack hardware and implements a multi-level scheduling protocol to run more warps at once and re-converge threads earlier. Rogers et al. [18] offer a hardware solution that profiles memory accesses and dynamically reschedules warps to reduce the frequency of re-referencing data. Rogers et al. [18] note that their method is not intended to solve divergence but is a viable option in the ongoing effort to optimize GPU code.

Fung et al. [14] attempt to improve the efficiency of how branches are executed by regrouping threads. Liang et al. [22] demonstrate that performance gains from thread regrouping is more accurately measured with thread modeling and basic block vector metrics. This in-depth analysis of thread-level control flow divergence can guide optimization strategies. In support of general purpose GPU optimization techniques, Yu et al. [23] compare threads by calculating the degree of similarity in their execution paths and represent these values on a grayscale. Yu et al. [23] visualize this evaluation as a graphed matrix where thread divergence is easily identified from the variability in tones.

Lin et al. [24] assess divergence at run time and implement a thread-data remapping algorithm to reduce global memory accesses. Thread-data remapping avoids source code optimization and does not eliminate branches. For specific programs where random selection determines control flow, like the Fractal Flames algorithm, Schied et al. [25] propose randomizing the data instead to achieve intra-warp synchronicity, thus eliminating branches. Huang and Yang [26] redesign parallel loops so that idle threads can execute ensuing iterations tasked to non-idle threads.

Branch fusion [1] optimizes code by "weaving" together divergent branches with similarities. Multiple branches can also be merged together through Conditional Merging [7–9], reducing the total number of paths. This technique trades precision for performance and is recommended for error-tolerant applications [9]. Reordering of branches may also result in increased performance in the average case [10]. Branch reordering is a general optimization suitable for CPU or GPU implementation.

Grigorian and Reinman [27] offer a neural network solution that automatically identifies divergent kernels, trains Artificial Neural Networks, and approximates target kernels with branch-less code. Although branches are eliminated, this method can be intensive and produce only approximate results, so it is not suitable for compiler implementation.

We have previously proposed a method of optimization call Algorithm Flattening, which completely eliminates divergent code [2], and therefore all overhead associated with handling branches and divergent threads. The goal from here on out in this paper is to implement this optimization, which completely eliminates thread divergence, and compare performance against compiler only optimized code o various architectures. This will give us insight into the extent to which modern GPU architectures and compilers are capable of addressing thread divergence without developer interference.

3   Manual Intervention for Complete Thread Divergence Elimination

By using a method called Algorithm Flattening (AF), we are able to replace branch statements with equivalent mathematical expressions that GPUs can process more efficiently. As a preview of how AF works, observe Eq. 2, which is the flattened version of the code at the beginning of Sect. 3.4.

3.1   Applying Preliminary AF to Simple Branches

The basic idea behind Algorithm Flattening is to represent an entire branch with a mathematical expression, beginning with a simple non-optimized flattening process. A basic flattened equation results from the summation of the product of each assignment and its corresponding evaluated expression. The result is that one expression can be executed that represents the whole branch. For example, the following if statement:

$$if(e) \ \{x = p; \}$$

can be represented by the expression:

$$x = (e)p + (!e)x$$

where e represents the expression being evaluated, p is the assignment value if e is true, and x is the assignment value when e is false. When the expression is evaluated two outputs are possible; x = p or x is unchanged (x = x).

if e is true,

$$x = (1)p + (0)x \longrightarrow x = p$$

and if e is false,

$$x = (0)p + (1)x \longrightarrow x = x$$

More complex branches such as if-else, nested if-else statements and chains, switches, etc., can also be generalized. This if-else:

$$if(e) \ \{x = p; \} \ else \ \{x = q; \}$$

becomes:

$$x = (e)p + (!e)q$$

The flattening of a nested if-else statement into a mathematical expression requires substitution. For example, the nested if-else condition described below:

```
if(e1) {
    if(e2) {x = p;} else {x = q;}
} else {
    x = r;
}
```

can be flattened by first splitting the code into two distinct parts. The first part is the inner or nested if-else condition. Once we convert the entire nested part of the code, we can treat it as an outcome for the parent conditional. Then flattening the remaining parent conditional is the same process as before, with the added step of substituting in the nested conditional as one of the parent conditional's specific outcomes. This can of course be automated recursively. The AF result is as follows:

$$x = e1((e2)p + (!e2)q) + (!e1)r$$

3.2 Generalized Preliminary AF for All Branches (A Starting Point)

$$\alpha = \sum_{i=0}^{n} x_i \cdot y_i = (x_0 \cdot y_0 + x_1 \cdot y_1 + ...x_n \cdot y_n)$$

$$\beta = \prod_{i=0}^{n} x_i \cdot y_i = (x_0 \cdot y_0 \cdot x_1 \cdot y_1 \cdot ...x_n \cdot y_n) \tag{1}$$

$$where \ y_i = \alpha \ \vee \ \beta \ \vee \ assigned\_value$$

Equation 1 shows the non-optimized and unreduced, generalized format for performing AF on any code block. The finalized AF equation is either a sum or product with other sums and products embedded. A pseudo-algebraic reduction, as well as other optimizations make AF much more efficient as shown shortly.

3.3 Optimized and Reduced AF

The most common instruction in an AF reduced equation is multiply-add. AF also reduces instructions because of the multiply-add operation within GPUs which allows multiple parts of the expression to be evaluated in one cycle. Also, flattened expressions can reduce instructions by omitting redundant variable assignments, namely assignment to zero. Algebraic reduction is another method to further reduce an AF expression. Other possibilities for reduction exist in many cases. For example, it is known that:

$$(e)a + (!e)b = e(a - b) + b$$

Which is often reduced further if constants, multiples or other factors reduce algebraically. Also, branch reordering can be used to reduce AF equations. This is in contrast to standard forms of branch reordering which concentrate on reducing the average path through branched code. This intuitive kind of optimization makes no difference for the performance of an AF equation. Reordering to reduce AF involves choosing an order which allows an AF equation to fully reduce. Branch reordering, which in an if-else statement actually involves inverting the conditional expression, can be represented as follows:

$$e(a - b) + b = !e(b - a) + a$$

It should be noted that reordering and inversion can often be achieved algebraically without knowing the above reordering equality by recognizing any variation of the following equivalence:

$$-e + 1 \equiv !e$$

This is demonstrated in the first form of reduction in Sect. 3.4.

3.4   Further Complexities

The following is a more complex conditional code block derived from [28]:

```
if(n == 0) {x = a; }
else if(n == 1) {x = a + 1; }
else if(n == 2) {
      if(m == 1) {x = b; }
      else {x = b + 1; }
}
else {x = 0; }
```

The first step of conversion is to identify the nested conditionals as follows:

$$if(m == 1) \{x = b; \} \ else \ \{x = b + 1; \}$$

Initial flattening uses Eq. 1:

$$x = (m == 1) \cdot b + (m \neq 1) \cdot (b + 1)$$

Which is reduced as follows using $[e(a\text{-}b)+b]$:
$$x = (m == 1) \cdot (b - (b + 1)) + b + 1 \equiv$$

$$x = (m == 1) \cdot (-1) + b + 1 \equiv$$
$$x = [-(m == 1) + 1] + b \equiv \qquad Note: \text{-}e + 1 \equiv !e$$
$$x = [!(m == 1)] + b \equiv$$
$$x = (m \neq 1) + b$$

This is simplified quicker with branch reordering using $[!e(b\text{-}a)+a]$ rather than $[e(a\text{-}b)+b]$:
$$x = (m \neq 1) \cdot (b + 1 - b) + b \equiv$$

$$x = (m \neq 1) \cdot (1) + b \equiv$$
$$x = (m \neq 1) + b$$

After nested control flow is flattened, parent conditionals are flattened while substituting the converted nested conditional for the parent conditional's outcome. This leads to the basic AF equation: $x = (n == 0) \cdot a + (n == 1) \cdot (a + 1) + (n == 2) \cdot ((m \neq 1) + b)$

Which is simplified to Eq. 2.

$$x = !(n >> 1) \cdot (n + a) + (n == 2) \cdot ((m \neq 1) + b) \tag{2}$$

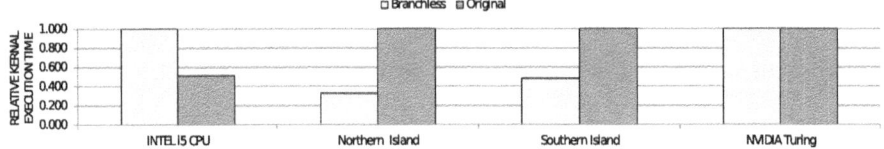

Fig. 1. Relative execution time for experiment code. Branched version is compared to the flattened, branch-less version on four different processors. The processors and compiler scenarios are described in Sect. 4.

4   Results

The following four scenarios are used to test the effect of programmatic elimination of branches on thread divergence and performance of modern GPU architectures and compilers. The test code for all scenarios is the branched code outlined in Sect. 3.4 and the flattened code shown in Eq. 2. We use this code because we have legacy results for this on older GPU/compiler combinations. It would be difficult to set up these experiments again due to the difficulty of installing the proper support systems. It is also a good example of an efficient complete flattening of branches that does not introduce too much additional instruction overhead.

Figure 1 shows the relative performance for each scenario. Each uses a specific processor and set of compile tools as detailed below. In each scenario, the branched code and flattened, branch-less code are both executed on the processor. Relative performance of the kernel is used so that each scenario shows a percentage improvement for simplicity, and so that scenarios can be easily compared to each other. In this work we will simply observe kernel execution time. In future work, we will thoroughly examine compiler and architectural issues affecting performance.

4.1 Core I5 Architecture CPU Scenario

This scenario utilizes an Intel I5 CPU and code written in C. This scenario is designed to clarify that complete elimination of all branches through a flattening algorithm such as ours is a de-optimization for CPU. Through branch removal and code flattening, ILP is increased and branches are eliminated. However, the trade-off is typically that the overall instruction count increases from the average case. If these instructions are executed linearly, then overall execution time will increase.

According to Fig. 1, the overall execution time for the test code running on CPU is doubled when branches are removed with the flattening method. This is in line with the instruction count vs. ILP trade-off aforementioned. The increased instruction count has a limited effect on GPU compared to CPU, as the increased ILP and branch removal have a greater effect on performance.

4.2 Northern Island Architecture GPU Scenario

This scenario utilizes an AMD GPU. This is a slightly older GPU running on the Northern Island architecture from AMD. The code for this is written in OpenCL.

According to Fig. 1, the overall execution time of the flattened, branch-less code is approximately 33% of the un-optimized code. The Northern Island architecture, along with the older OpenCL compiler used for this scenario are not implementing any similar optimization at the compiler or hardware level.

The Northern Island Architecture uses one set of sixteen, four-way or five way VLIW arranged processing elements. The VLIW processors of the Northern Island architecture benefit more from the instruction level parallelism (ILP) introduced by the Algorithm Flattening optimization.

4.3 Southern Island Architecture GPU Scenario

This scenario utilizes an AMD GPU. This is a GPU running on the Southern Island architecture from AMD. This is a newer architecture than the previous scenario. The code for this is written in OpenCL.

According to Fig. 1, the overall execution time of the flattened, branch-less code is approximately 50% of the un-optimized code. The Southern Island architecture, along with the OpenCL compiler used for this scenario, clearly benefit from manual removal of branches.

Even without the VLIW layout of the vector processors in this architecture, we still see an improvement in the performance using the manually optimized code, which eliminates thread divergence pre-compile. Although admittedly, this architecture cannot take advantage as much of the increased ILP. This is because The Southern Island Architecture uses four sets of sixteen SIMD arranged processing elements per multiprocessor, whereas the Northern Island Architecture uses one set of sixteen, four-way or five way VLIW arranged processing elements.

4.4   Turing Architecture GPU Scenario

This scenario utilizes an NVIDIA GPU using the Turing architecture. The code is written using CUDA C.

According to Fig. 1, the overall execution time of the flattened, branch-less code is nearly identical to the original branched code. An initial look at this result seems to indicate that the newer architecture, coupled with the more advanced compiler version makes manual mitigation of thread divergence less necessary.

There could be various reasons that we do not see a performance improvement from manually eliminating branches, and therefore eliminating thread divergence before code compilation. This could be a smarter compiler, or it could be due to the optimizations put in place in the hardware, as NVIDIA has been addressing thread divergence in their architectures for years.

This more or less answers our question as to whether or not manual removal of branches is always a performance boost for GPUs. We have identified a scenario where it does not improve performance. But there are many questions that remain about this happens that we hope to answer in our future work.

5   Conclusion

In this preliminary study, we have applied our flattening technique to GPU code to address thread divergence through program pre-processing. We have observed that modern GPU improvements have changed the impact of such manual intervention on GPU performance.

Clearly, modern built-in optimizations are helpful for mitigating thread divergence due to branches. The last results scenario using the Turing architecture demonstrates this. In our future work, we will investigate the compiled code and determine which factors of modern optimization are contributing to this improvement.

References

1. Coutinho, B., Sampaio, D., Pereira, F., Meira, W.: Divergence analysis and optimizations. In: 2011 International Conference on Parallel Architectures and Compilation Techniques (PACT), pp. 320–329 (2011)
2. Vespa, L., Bauman, A., Wells, J.: Algorithm flattening: complete branch elimination for GPU requires a paradigm shift from CPU thinking. In: 2015 IEEE High Performance Extreme Computing Conference (HPEC), pp. 1–6 (2015)
3. Flynn, M.: Some computer organizations and their effectiveness. IEEE Trans. Comput. C-21(9), 948–960 (1972)
4. Zhang, W., Bao, T., Zang, B., Zhu, C.: Data pipeline optimization for shared memory multiple-simd architecture. In: Proceedings of the 19th International Conference on Languages and Compilers for Parallel Computing, pp. 49–63 (2007)
5. Hijma, P., Heldens, S., Sclocco, A., van Werkhoven, B., Bal, H.E.: Optimization techniques for GPU programming. ACM Comput. Surv. 55(11) (2023)

6. Bodík, R., Gupta, R., Soffa, M.L.: Interprocedural conditional branch elimination. In: Proceedings of the ACM SIGPLAN 1997 Conference on Programming Language Design and Implementation, pp. 146–158 (1997)

7. Kreahling, W., Whalley, D., Bailey, M., Yuan, X., Uh, G.-R., van Engelen, R.: Branch elimination via multi-variable condition merging. In: Kosch, H., Böszörményi, L., Hellwagner, H. (eds.) Euro-Par 2003. LNCS, vol. 2790, pp. 261–270. Springer, Heidelberg (2003). https://doi.org/10.1007/978-3-540-45209-6_40

8. Kreahling, W.C., Whalley, D., Bailey, M.W., Yuan, X., Uh, G.-R., van Engelen, R.: Branch elimination by condition merging. Softw. Pract. Exp. **35**(1), 51–74 (2005)

9. Sartori, J., Kumar, R.: Branch and data herding: reducing control and memory divergence for error-tolerant GPU applications. IEEE Trans. Multimedia **15**(2), 279–290 (2013)

10. Yang, M., Uh, G.-R., Whalley, D.B.: Improving performance by branch reordering. In: Proceedings of the ACM SIGPLAN 1998 Conference on Programming Language Design and Implementation, pp. 130–141 (1998)

11. Mueller, F., Whalley, D.B.: Avoiding conditional branches by code replication. In: Proceedings of the ACM SIGPLAN 1995 Conference on Programming Language Design and Implementation, pp. 56–66 (1995)

12. Han, T.D., Abdelrahman, T.S.: Reducing branch divergence in GPU programs. In: Proceedings of the Fourth Workshop on General Purpose Processing on Graphics Processing Units, pp. 3:1–3:8 (2011)

13. Carrillo, S., Siegel, J., Li, X.: A control-structure splitting optimization for GPGPU. In: Proceedings of the 6th ACM Conference on Computing Frontiers, pp. 147–150 (2009)

14. Fung, W., Sham, I., Yuan, G., Aamodt, T.: Dynamic warp formation and scheduling for efficient GPU control flow. In: 40th Annual IEEE/ACM International Symposium on Microarchitecture, MICRO 2007, pp. 407–420 (2007)

15. Sarkar, S., Mitra, S.: A profile guided approach to optimize branch divergence while transforming applications for GPUs, pp. 176–185 (2015)

16. Park, J.C.H., Schlansker, M.: On predicated execution (1991)

17. Reissmann, N., Falch, T.L., Bjrnseth, B.A., Bahmann, H., Christian Meyer, J., Jahre, M.: Efficient control flow restructuring for GPUs. In: 2016 International Conference on High Performance Computing Simulation (HPCS), pp. 48–57 (2016)

18. Rogers, T.G., O'Connor, M., Aamodt, T.M.: Divergence-aware warp scheduling. In: 2013 46th Annual IEEE/ACM International Symposium on Microarchitecture (MICRO), pp. 99–110 (2013)

19. Yu, L., Tang, X., Wu, M., Chen, T.: Improving branch divergence performance on GPGPU with a new PDOM stack and multi-level warp scheduling. J. Syst. Architect. **60**, 01 (2013)

20. Anido, M.L., Paar, A., Bagherzadeh, N.: Improving the operation autonomy of SIMD processing elements by using guarded instructions and pseudo branches. In: DSD 2002: Proceedings of the Euromicro Symposium on Digital Systems Design, pp. 148–155. IEEE Computer Society (2002)

21. Chakroun, I., Mezmaz, M., Melab, N., Bendjoudi, A.: Reducing thread divergence in a GPU-accelerated branch-and-bound algorithm. Concurr. Comput. Pract. Exp. **25**(8), 1121–1136 (2013)

22. Liang, Y., Satria, M.T., Rupnow, K., Chen, D.: An accurate GPU performance model for effective control flow divergence optimization. IEEE Trans. Comput.-Aided Des. Integr. Circuits Syst. **35**, 1165–1178 (2016)

23. Yu, Z., Eeckhout, L., Xu, C.: Thread similarity matrix: Visualizing branch divergence in GPGPU programs. In: 2016 45th International Conference on Parallel Processing (ICPP), pp. 179–184 (2016)
24. Lin, H., Wang, C.-L., Liu, H.: On-GPU thread-data remapping for branch divergence reduction. ACM Trans. Archit. Code Optim. **15**(3) (2018). https://doi.org/10.1145/3242089
25. Schied, C., Hanika, J., Dammertz, H., Lensch, H.: Chapter 18 - high-performance iterated function systems. In: Mei, W., Hwu, W. (eds.) GPU Computing Gems Emerald Edition, pp. 263 – 273. Morgan Kaufmann, Boston (2011)
26. Huang, M., Yang, W.: Partial flattening: a compilation technique for irregular nested parallelism on GPGPUS. In: 2016 45th International Conference on Parallel Processing (ICPP), pp. 552–561 (2016)
27. Grigorian, B., Reinman, G.: Accelerating divergent applications on SIMD architectures using neural networks. ACM Trans. Architect. Code Optim. **12**(1) (2015)
28. Vespa, L., Mathew, M., Weng, N.: P3FSM: portable predictive pattern matching finite state machine. In: 20th IEEE International Conference on Application-specific Systems, Architectures and Processors, Boston, MA, USA, pp. 219–222 (2009)

Towards Automatic, Predictable and High-Performance Parallel Code Generation

Lenore Mullin[1] and Gaétan Hains[2]([✉])

[1] University at Albany (SUNY), 1400 Washington Ave, Albany, NY 12222, USA
`lmullin@albany.edu`
[2] LACL, Université Paris-Est, 94000 Créteil, France
`gaetan.hains@u-pec.fr`

Abstract. High-performance architectures have complex features so that reliable production of parallel software is beyond the reach of many Computer Science graduates. Compilers alone cannot guarantee the highest performance and multiple APIs with complex performance features are difficult to master. As a first step towards more comprehensive solutions we are building key elements of a pre-compiler system that will automatically produce predictable, scalable and high-performance code from declarative tensor expressions. In this paper we summarize and analyze a large set of timing experiments of matrix multiplication variants that are mapped to vectorized and multithread code. The analysis covers two high-end target architectures and exhaust a whole space of code, compiler, pragma and parallelism parameters. Our analysis shows how the best choice of parameters is produced from a small set of tests that can converge in a matter of seconds and then predict performance of larger instances to within 25% or much less. Inefficient choices of parameters is also shown to be reliably predicted from small tests, so that our design for a precompiler is guaranteed to be a realistic and portable tool. The generality of our Mathematics of Arrays tensor algebra, and very broad applicability of tensor operations (signal processing, scientific computing, AI, etc.) supports our claim that these experiments and design can be generalized to a general purpose parallel programming tool.

Keywords: Software Tools · Environments · Parallel · Distributed Platforms · Performance Analysis · Evaluation · Prediction

1 Introduction

The MoA (Mathematics of Arrays) algebra [3,4,6,7] is a unifying formalism for expressing arrays/tensors of any dimension and field operations on them. It replaces the figures and pointwise expressions of linear algebra textbooks with combinators. Its transformations allow the formal and correct exploration of all symetries of a given field operation on arrays, thus defining all potential transformations and compilations of linear-algebra algorithms. Our key motivation is

© The Author(s), under exclusive license to Springer Nature Switzerland AG 2025
H. R. Arabnia et al. (Eds.): CSCE 2024, CCIS 2256, pp. 109–119, 2025.
https://doi.org/10.1007/978-3-031-85638-9_8

to allow future users to concentrate on a single declarative formalism and use automatic or semi-automatic tools to leverage *without special training and waste of time* the complex combinations of algorithm variant, compiler flags, directives, pragmas and other features of HPC practice.

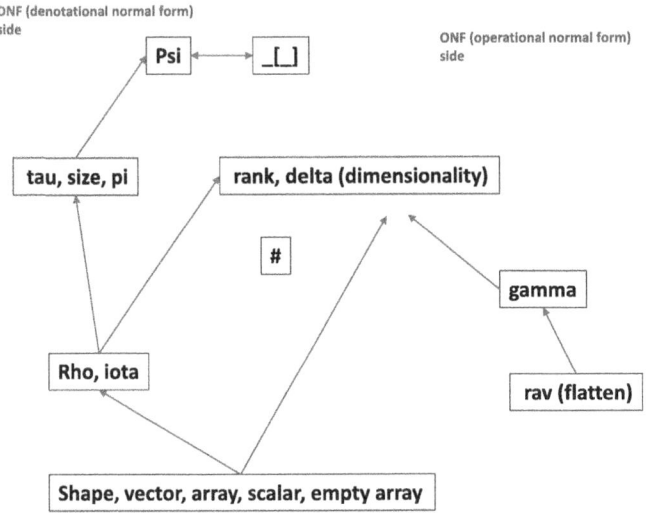

Fig. 1. MoA operators

The core hypothesis is that (a) exploring this space need only be based on MoA operators (Fig. 1), array shapes and a subset of compilation + architecture features and (b) parallel architectures are themselves arrays of vector-, memory- and computational units so that the best possible performance can be found by reshaping the dataflow dag with (some of) those dimensions.

In the work presented here we have chosen to concentrate on algorithmic- and architectural foundations: dense matrix multiplication, vectorization and (single-node) SMP multi-threaded parallelism. We hope to convince the reader of the interest of such a balanced approach that is a form of "portable and scalable parallel no-coding" yet can use a very general source language and can predictably yield relatively high performance.

2   From Arrays/tensors to C Code

The restriction to matrix multiplication (MM) is acceptable because the operation can be generalized to include the Kronecker Product (KP), Hadamard Product (HP), and scalar operations [2] all core for many important algorithms.

For our given initial "algorithm" (array expression) we produce algorithm "variants" by algebraic transforms in MoA and each of them corresponds to a set of C for-loops. The variants are produced from the naive algorithm by so-called *dimension lifting* which is a generalized form of row- and column-blocking for matrix algorithms as used for example in the Bisseling-McColl BSP algorithms [1]. Our transformation is currently not mechanized but will be in the future.

Define $\mathbf{A}$ as an $m \times n$ matrix, $\mathbf{B}$ as $n \times p$, and $\mathbf{C}$ as $m \times p$. Let the following notation denote the 2-d Matrix Multiplication. $\mathbf{C} = \mathbf{A} \bullet \mathbf{B}$. In MoA notation, the shapes are:

$$\rho \mathbf{A} = \langle m, n \rangle \quad \rho \mathbf{B} = \langle n, p \rangle \quad \rho \mathbf{C} = \langle m, p \rangle \tag{1}$$

Next, define the valid indices of the matrices:

$$\forall\, i, j, k \ni \left\{ 0 \leq i < m \quad 0 \leq j < p \quad 0 \leq k < n \right. \tag{2}$$

$\mathbf{C} = \mathbf{A} \bullet \mathbf{B}$ is defined by the MoA psi expression, given the shapes above.

$$< i > \psi \mathbf{C} \equiv +_{red}(< i, \ k > \psi \ \mathbf{A} \times (< k > \psi B)) \tag{3}$$

When reduced to its so-called denotational normal form (DNF), γ_{row} is applied thus producing the MoA Operational Normal Form (ONF) yielding the following generic "program" where arrays are mapped to 1D row-major order:

$$\mathbf{C}[(i \times p) + j] := \sum_{k=0}^{n-1} \mathbf{A}[(i \times n) + k] \times \mathbf{B}[(k \times p) + j] \tag{4}$$

The concept of **dimension-lifting** is defined by partitioning one or more dimensions into two levels. That is, given any shape s, s.t. $\tau s = \delta \xi$. The number of components in dimension i, i.e. s_i is partitioned into np parts, thus defining new shapes $s_i \rightarrow < np, \ s_i/np >$ or $< s_i/np, \ np >$. This means that every loop in the ONF can be partitioned into one or more loops to match components of the architecture chosen. Begin by partitioning the rows loop of $\mathbf{A}$ into a two parts: one loop that indexes the processors and the other loop defines how many rows are done sequentially within that processor. The next step is to map these loops to OpenMP menmonics that support the theoretical partitioning in a general way. Also it is essential that the mnemonics chosen provide performance scalability across architectures. Once that is done, the columns loop of $\mathbf{B}$ and $\mathbf{C}$ are partitioned into two loops, one that defines the vector register length, and the other, how many components of the columns must be loaded into the vector register. Figure 2 shows the sequential program and Fig. 3 the same dimension-lifted over rows.

Exploring a whole set of dimension-lifted forms, so-called binary transposes and loop interchanges, we have used OpenMP directives and SSE instructions to turn them into different parallel algorithm variants. The rest of the paper summarizes how we systematically explored the performance of all variants and their implementations, then how this can lead to a tractable static search problem.

Identifying pragmas and C flags that consistently worked across compilers and machines was a challenge. Although there were numerous flags, and OpenMP directives, most turned out to be merely "suggestions", hence mostly useless.

```
#include <stdio.h>
#include <sys/time.h>
void mm(double *C, double *A, double *B,
    int m, int p, int n)
{
  int i,j,sigma;
    for (i=0;i<m;i++)
      {for (sigma=0; sigma<n; sigma++)
        {for (j=0;j<p;j++)
          {
            C[j+i*p]=C[j+i*p]
            +A[(i*n)+sigma]*B[(sigma * p)+j];
          }
        }
      }
}
```

Fig. 2. mm.c

3 Timing Experiments

Experiments were run using a single node of two machines provided by Stony Brook University's Ookami computer center: Fujitsu's A64FX (in short "Fujitsu") and Intel's Skylake (in short "Intel"). The A64FX was developed by Riken and Fujitsu for the Japanese path to exascale computing. Skylake, is Intel's codename for its 6th generation Core microprocessors. Skylake is a microarchitecture redesign of 14 nm manufacturing technology. More details:

Characteristics	Fujitsu A64FX	Intel Skylake
Architecture	Arm.2−A+SVE	x86_64
CPUs (cores)	48	36
Threads/CPU	1	1
CPU MHz	2000MHz	1764.320MHz
L1 cache	64KB	32KB

We used three compilers: gcc on both machines, and fcc (Fujitsu C compiler) and icc (Intel C compiler) on the A64FX and Skylake respectively. It is beyond the scope of this paper to discuss all compilation-execution choices we made. We rather show how automated optimization can make such issues invisible to the impatient or untrained programmer.

Our timing experiments measured combinations of multi-threaded execution and vectorization. One aspect of experiments was to use flags that were basically

```
#include <stdio.h>
#include <sys/time.h>

  void ip_rows(double *C, double *A, double *B,
      int sizel, int sizer, int sizeres, int np, int shr0)
  {
    int i,j,k,ip,sigma;
    //  for (i=0;i<sizel;i++)
    for (k=0;k<np;k++)
      {for (ip=0;ip<(sizel/np);ip++)
      {for (sigma=0; sigma<shr0; sigma++)
        {for (j=0;j<sizer;j++)
          {
            //C[j+i*sizer]=C[j+i*sizer]+A[(i*shr0)+sigma]*B[(sigma * sizer)+j];
            C[j+(ip+(sizel/np)*k)*sizer]=C[j+(ip+(sizel/np)*k)*sizer]
            +A[((ip+((sizel/np)*k))*shr0)+sigma]*B[(sigma * sizer)+j];
          }
        }
      }
        }}
```

Fig. 3. ip_rows.c

the same across platforms. Another set of experiments could identify what flags to extend given the plethora of flags available on each compiler. We use, typically, fast or O3 to vectorize, a flag to identify which architecture, a flag to identify OpenMP. The only ones we used were prefetch and unroll. There would be a set of experiments to identify what the best prefetch size should be and the amount of loops to unroll, obviously related to the data and instruction cache sizes.

Building upon ideas of shapes and optimizing memory processor layouts [5], blocks in Fujitsu experiments fit the L1 Cache (64KiB/core), or 48 by 48 doubles. With two levels of memory we were able to predict speedups using vector registers and multiple processors.

Matrices of sizes up to 5000×5000 were used and nearly all combinations of pragmas, threads-cores and algorithm variants were tried. A typical timing plot is Fig. 4 that maps OpenMP acceleration vs number of cores. Some spikes were observed but most curves were smooth as confirmed by the data analysis below.

4   Performance Tuning, Analysis

Despite some unexpected effects (such as gcc being systematically faster than fcc on its own Fujitsu architecture), all static program and compilation parameters had a monotonic effect on speed. If a discrete variable like the choice of algorithm variant, then one of them systematically outperformed the others, and if a numerical variable like the number of threads, then behaviour was almost completely monotonic. Observe however that the largest 5000×5000 matrix sizes is an observed limit on our hardware nodes for scalability.

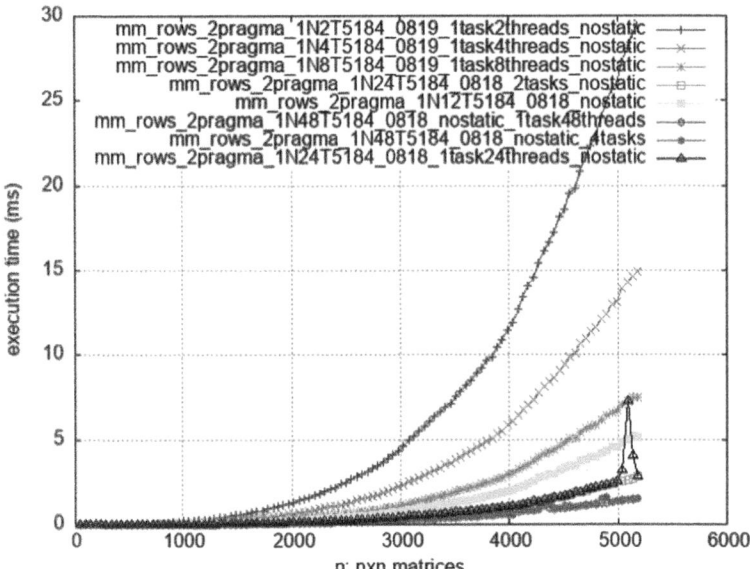

Fig. 4. Scalable OpenMP for 2–48 cores

One global result is that gcc, surprisingly outperformed fcc on Fujitsu but icc, as expected outperformed gcc on Intel (Fig. 5). Our Fujitsu experiments were often slower, which indicates that our C-code approach may not be sufficient to leverage the A64FX's peak rate. But this does not affect our conclusion: the choice of compiler can be made from a small set of runs.

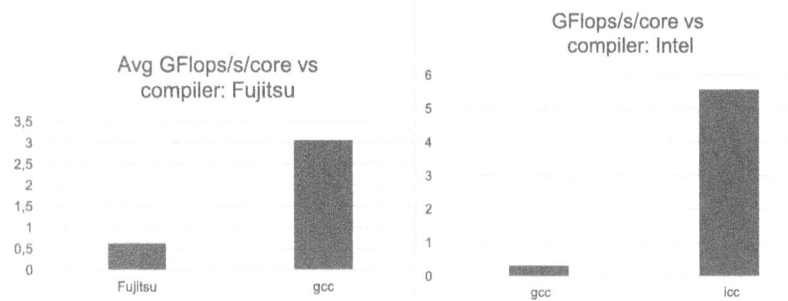

Fig. 5. Average speed vs compiler, Fujitsu/Intel

Then came the choice of fastest algorithm variant, which depends on the architecture as seen in Fig. 6. A row-wise approach performed systematically better on Fujitsu, whereas for Intel the choice was more difficult, favoring a large 48 × 48 square blocks dimension-lifting. In any case, choosing the algorithm

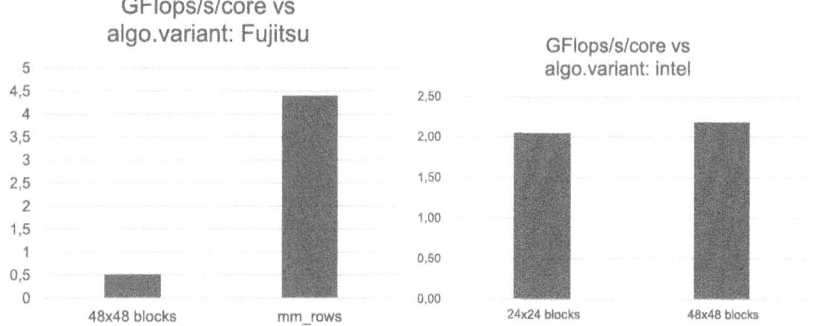

Fig. 6. Speed of algorithm variants, Fujitsu/Intel

variant with best overall performance never led to a slower run, only possibly no better than another algorithm variant.

We also analysed the "local" (per core) speed's evolution with the growing number of threads in a multicore execution. For each architecture that leads to two curves or sets of points, "slow" ones from the slower algorithm variants and "fast" ones from the other. If we concentrate on the fast (upper) curve, we observe as always an overhead for increased parallelism (synchro-communication). For the Fujitsu runs the decrease in efficiency is lesser, about 25% at 48 cores while the faster Intel runs have larger *relative* overhead of about 47% at only 24 cores (Fig. 7).

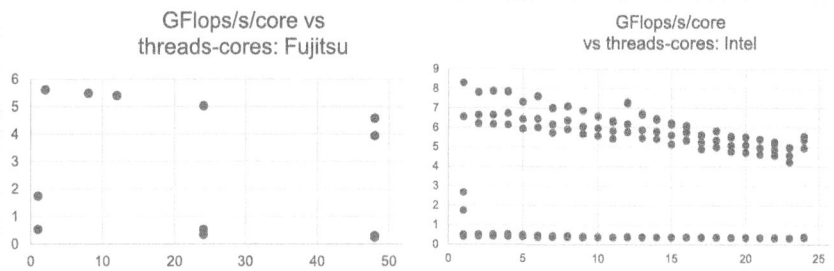

Fig. 7. Parallel efficiency, Fujitsu/Intel.

That fits traditional quantitative understanding of parallel execution: faster processor speeds make the cost of synchro-communication relatively higher. Most important: it is relatively smooth and predictable.

5   Design for a Static Codegen Tool

Having tested all combinations of program and compilation parameters, and observed that they all had a (almost always) monotonic effect on performance, it was possible to apply a naive steepest descent approach to select the best parameter values. That is illustrated in Fig. 8 for the Intel architecture, but worked equally well for Fujitsu. Our final goal is the design of a code generation tool that would quickly and reliably select those parameters from a set of (MoA-generated) algorithm variants, and expert-selected sets of compilation directives, pragmas and the like. It is surely not realistic to expect the user of such a tool to wait for hundreds of test runs to complete, even if their analysis is straightforward. So it is necessary to drastically cut down on the search space for that optimization.

Choosing static parameters (Intel) : [compiler ; common subexpression elim./not ; algorithm variant, ; prefetching/not]

Comparison	vectorized	Source code	Compiler	com-subex remv by hand	Prefetching	Threads	Avg Gflops/s	Avg GFlops/s/core	statistics
Compiler?	Y	24B/48B/rows	icc	Y/N	Y/N	2-24	61,10 +/- 33,01	5,21 +/- 1,44	Avg +/- sdev
			gcc				4,69 +/- 2,23	0,43 +/- 0,27	

Comparison	vectorized	Source code	Compiler	com-subex remv by hand	Prefetching	Threads	Avg Gflops/s	Avg GFlops/s/core	statistics
com-subex rem ?	Y	24B/48B/rows	icc	Y	Y/N	2-24	62,27 +/- 32,35	5,21 +/- 1,44	Avg +/- sdev
				N			5,92 +/- 1,23	5,92 +/- 1,23	

Comparison	vectorized	Source code	Compiler	com-subex remv by hand	Prefetching	Threads	Avg Gflops/s	Avg GFlops/s/core	statistics
Source code ?	Y	24x24 blocks	icc	Y	Y/N	2-24	67,50 +/- 31,08	5,61 +/- 0,64	Avg +/- sdev
		48x48 blocks					76,93 +/- 33,69	6,51 +/- 0,92	
		mm_rows					42,39 +/- 20,05	3,48 +/- 0,32	

Comparison	vectorized	Source code	Compiler	com-subex remv by hand	Prefetching	Threads	Avg Gflops/s	Avg GFlops/s/core	statistics
Prefetching?	Y	48x48 blocks	icc	Y	Y	2-24	78,55 +/- 32,50	6,48 +/- 0,89	Avg +/- sdev
					N		75,38 +/- 34,69	6,54 +/- 0,95	

Best static parameters : Intel

Acceleration	vectorized	Source code	Compiler	com-subex remv by hand	Prefetching
Best configuration	Y	48x48 blocks	icc	Y	Y

Fig. 8. Selection of best static parameters

This can be done as follows: 1. assume that compiler flags, pragmas come in a small number and have few if not only two possible values 2. assume 2^k such parameter values exist, 3. observe that algorithm variants are also in small numbers because the size of blocks and number of dimensions in the algorithm are small, generating another small-dimensional space of combinations, assume there are k' algorithm variants, 4. reduce the search space for the optimal number of threads and scalability with data size, by observing that (until a hardware-dependent limit like our 5000×5000 matrices) timing curves are not only smooth but very predictable. As a result only a few test runs are necessary to extrapolate along the dimension of threads-core and data size. If the above observations 1–4 are confirmed, then only about $k' * 2^k$ test runs on *small* matrices can predict

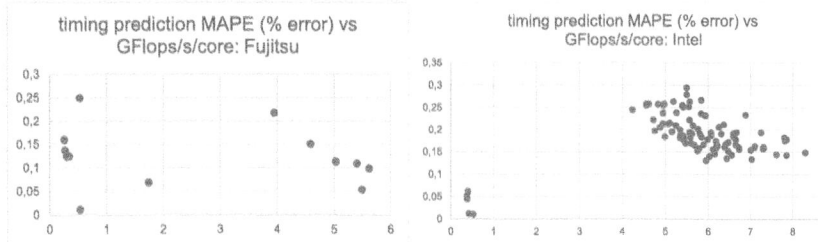

Fig. 9. Speed prediction error vs net Flop rate, Fujitsu/Intel.

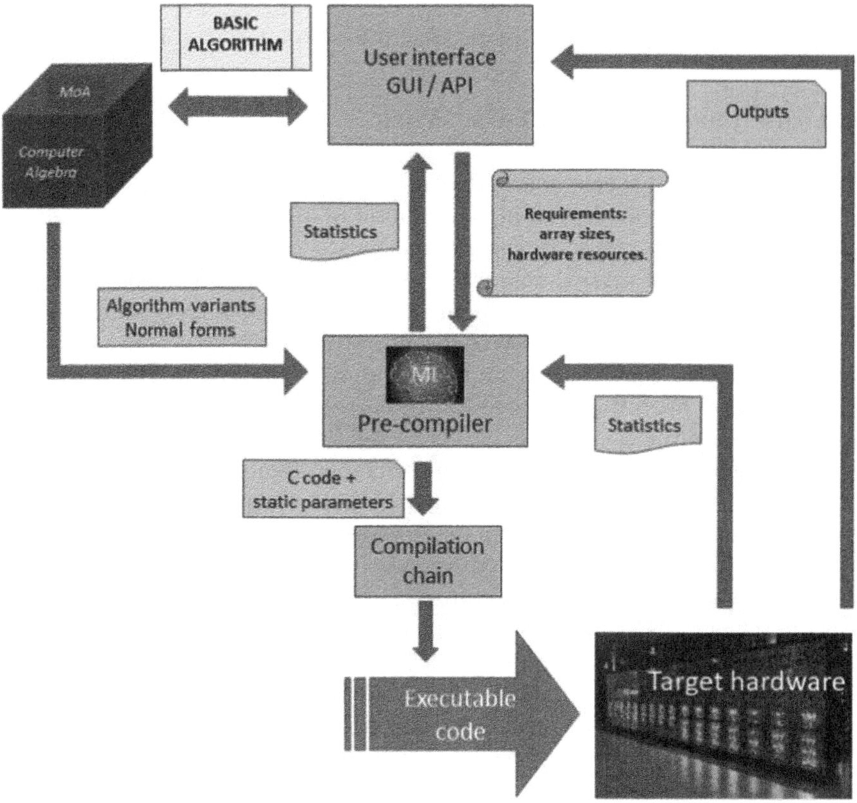

Fig. 10. Proposed system architecture

performance on all possible tests and thus allow the choice of optimal parameters with that many speed tests. Given that our runs take in the order of dozens of ms, that would mean no more than $k' * 2^k * 100$ ms (possibly much less than an hour) plus some extremely fast sequential data analysis to produce the static choice of optimal parameters *and* predict their effect on speed for larger runs.

Since the proposed system will not systematically test all combinations of algorithm variants and statics parameters, it will do so on a limited set of tests and depend on their extrapolated performance prediction. To gain confidence in the quality of this prediction, we tried curve fitting on all speed tests: for $n \times n$ matrices and 3 (sometimes only 2 or 1) points we have extrapolated to a whole set of 9–100 points on their runtime vs problem size curve. The quality of prediction is then rather good with mean average percent errors less than 30% and often less than 15% (Fig. 9). This means that even the fastest runtime measurements can be approximated to within less than 1/3, giving the user and static analysis tool a very good estimate on which to base their choices of algorithm variant, architecture and compilation parameters.

A preliminary design for our code generation tool is shown in Fig. 10.

6   Conclusions and Future Work

The vision behind this research is that of a system with which the application scientist or engineer can use a functional subset of his/her favorite language and, in so doing, have the ability to generate optimized code with very high productivity. The shapes of arrays, and sub-arrays (blocks) are assumed sufficient to define the parallel operations, communications *and their mapping* to the parallel architecture because, despite heterogeneous hardware, its structures are mostly made of arrays of computation units. A summary of this approach could be "mapping array operation parts to hardware array parts automatically, based on size-shape information."

We explore the central notion of predictable high performance for MoA-generated code by an exploration of matrix-multiplication variants producing vectorized and multi-threaded from "stereotyped" C code that is equivalent to MoA declarative expressions: nested for-loops whose bounds are defined by the arrays/blocks shapes and MoA operators.

Some dimensions of the problem are mostly predictable and easily extrapolated: scalability and amount of parallelism. Others appear unpredictable but their small exploration space makes them tractable: choice of algorithm variant, compiler flags, OpenMP pragmas etc. One key decision that we make in this respect is *not* to treat the program as an enumerated dataflow dag. If that were the case, our search problem would become intractable. Instead we observe that parallel array programs are highly symmetric, and only explore their shape- and dimension-induced variations.

The next steps in this research should determine whether our designs scale to multiple nodes using MPI, to explore their behaviour on very large multicore nodes (such as the 8 CPU Intel Cooper lake, 224 cores, 6To RAM SMP node available at CRIANN, Normandy) and design an MPI, GPU adaptation of our approach which is currently restricted to vectorization + multicore parallelization. Then we will explore more matrix algorithm variants via Strassen schemes, generalize to all MoA-expressible expressions and automate the process.

Acknowledgments. This work is supported by Stony Brook University's Ookami Supercomputing Center. The Ookami computing center is supported by the US NSF grant #1927880. The authors gratefully acknowledge the generous support of the Ookami community. In particular, we thank Eva Siegemann, Tony Curtis, Ben Michalowicz, David Carlson for their many programming suggestions on Ookami's Slack Channel, and others who spent their time talking to us during office hours.

Disclosure of Interests. The authors have no competing interests to declare that are relevant to the content of this article.

References

1. Bisseling, R.H.: Parallel scientific computation: a structured approach using BSP and MPI. Oxford University Press, Oxford (2004)
2. Grout, I., Mullin, L.: Realization of the kronecker product in VHDL using multi-dimensional arrays. In: 2019 7th International Electrical Engineering Congress (iEECON), pp. 1–4 (2019)
3. Hains, G., Mullin, L.M.R.: Parallel functional programming with arrays. Comput. J. **36**(3), 238–245 (1993)
4. Mullin, L.M.: A Mathematics of arrays. Ph.D. thesis, Syracuse University, Syracuse, NY (1988)
5. Mullin, L.M.R.: From array algebra to energy efficiency on GPUs. Technical report, HLPP2023: Cluj-Napoca (RO) (2023). https://doi.org/10.48550/arXiv.2306.11148. Accessed 23 Aug 2024
6. Thomas, S., Mullin, L., Swirydowicz, K., Khan, R.: Threaded multi-core GEMM with moa and cache-blocking: Preprint (2022). https://www.osti.gov/biblio/1848079. Accessed 23 Aug 2024
7. Thomas, S., Mullin, L., Swirydowicz, K.: Improving the performance of DGEMM with MoA and cache-blocking. Technical report, National Renewable Energy Laboratory (NREL), Golden CO (USA) (2022)

Attack Graph Generation on HPC Clusters

Ming Li$^{(\boxtimes)}$ (ID) and John Hale (ID)

The University of Tulsa, Tulsa, OK 74104, USA
{ming-li,john-hale}utulsa.edu

Abstract. Attack graphs (AGs) are graphical tools to analyze the security of computer networks. By connecting the exploitation of individual vulnerabilities, AGs expose possible multi-step attacks against target networks, allowing system administrators to take preventive measures to enhance their network's security. As powerful analytical tools, however, AGs are both time- and memory-consuming to be generated. As the numbers of network assets, interconnections between devices, as well as vulnerabilities increase, the size and volume of the resulting AGs grow at a much higher rate, leading to the well-known state-space explosion. In this paper, we propose the use of high performance computing (HPC) clusters to implement AG generators. We evaluate the performance through experiments and provide insights into how cluster environments can help resolve the issues of slow speed and high memory demands in AG generation in a balanced way.

Keywords: Attack Graph · High Performance Computing · Cybersecurity

1 Introduction

Attack graphs (AGs) visualize possible paths attackers can take to compromise computer networks [1], cyber-physical systems (CPSs) [2], IoT [3], and even networks of Docker containers [4]. AGs allow users to logically connect individual vulnerabilities to reveal multi-step attacks, which might be unseen if each vulnerability is handled separately. AGs are generated with input information modeling network assets, their interconnections and vulnerabilities. AG generators typically output node and edge sets, and other relevant information. AG structure can be analyzed, which identifies nodes, edges and vulnerabilities that are pivotal to achieve attackers' goals. By applying probability based approaches [5], the likelihood of different attack paths can be compared. Accordingly, system administrators are informed of more valuable intelligence of the weakness in their system. They can concentrate the limited time, money and man-power on addressing the most pressing security needs.

The generation of AGs is the most challenging aspect in their application. Starting from some initial states, the input set of vulnerabilities are repeatedly applied to derive new states. Most AGs have a tree-like structure. The

© The Author(s), under exclusive license to Springer Nature Switzerland AG 2025
H. R. Arabnia et al. (Eds.): CSCE 2024, CCIS 2256, pp. 120–129, 2025.
https://doi.org/10.1007/978-3-031-85638-9_9

farther away from the tree root, the more nodes are branched out. The earliest AG models, such as [6] and [7], permute all the vulnerabilities to enumerate every possible attack path. Each AG node in these models represents a network state, describing the security status of all the network entities. Each edge is the exploitation of one or more vulnerabilities, and causes a transition between two states. While these models provide the most detailed security evaluation, they suffer from the exponential growth of the state space as the input size increases [7]. To address the issue of state-space explosion, later research proposed more scalable AG models, such as logical AGs [1,8]. In these models, each AG node just represents a specific pre- or post-condition, a vulnerability, or a privilege of an attacker on a certain host. The edges are causal connections between nodes and are not associated with any exploitation operations. Logical AGs and their variations [9,10] often assume that attackers will never relinquish a privilege already acquired from previous attack steps, therefore, further reduce the state space to be explored in the generation process. The generators for logical AGs and its variations are demonstrated to be polynomial over their input size, which are more efficient than those for state-enumeration AGs. While the generation complexity of novel AG models are reduced because of simplified model definition and the monotonicity assumptions, they are not completely free of the scalability issue. When such models are applied to analyze the security posture of large-scale networks, the total computation task and the required memory capacity still easily overwhelm single PCs and small-scale servers. [11–13] introduced parallelism into the AG generation process, however, their efforts are limited in the environment of single computers. Although distributed AG generation is not a novel idea, to the best of our knowledge, there is no AG generator aiming to run on high performance computing (HPC) clusters, let alone acquiring any useful performance data. We observe that AG generation should be treated as other computation intensive tasks and seek the help of HPC.

In this research, we design a parallel algorithm for AG generation that utilizes OpenMPI processes and OpenMP threads to break down the generation task and explore partial state space in parallel. We conduct the performance evaluation on OSCER, an HPC cluster from University of Oklahoma [14]. Our research fills the aforementioned gap and provides design and engineering knowledge to industry and academia that need effective solutions to AG generation.

2   Related Research

Research efforts to address the scalability issue of AG models can be partitioned into two tracks. One track simplifies AG definition to reduce the complexity of the generation process, which is represented logical AGs. The other track applies multi-threaded programming to accelerate the exploration of AG state space. Typical platforms are either single PCs or small servers.

2.1   Logical AGs

Two consecutive papers [1] and [8] established the foundation of logical AG models. The nodes in these AGs are categorized as SINK, AND and OR nodes, representing input facts, vulnerability exploitations and derived facts. As exploitations are defined as a special type of nodes, edges in logical AGs only represent dependence between nodes. Backtracking is one of the culprits that cause state-space explosion in state-enumeration AG models. To address this, logical AGs assume that attackers will never relinquish any privileges they have already acquired. This monotonicity assumption helps eliminate unnecessary permutations of exploitations during state-space exploration, giving logical AGs and its variations [9,10] an advantageous polynomial time complexity for generation.

2.2   Multi-threaded AG Generation

Multi-threaded programs are implemented in [13,15,16] to accelerate AG generation. The data structure to store the resulting AG is shared among the participating threads, which are either OpenMP threads [13] or CUDA warps [16]. Each thread starts with a few nodes fetched from the initial frontier prepared by a master thread and explores its partial state space. In [16], to take advantage of GPU's computational power, the SIMD threads in each warp further accelerates loops inner to the outer-loop that expand AG nodes. In [15], work-stealing is proposed to balance the workload among the threads, which further reduces the execution time. While these designs are able to accelerate AG generation, they are implemented on either a single PC or a small server, and the performance worsens sharply as the memory demands exceed the available capacity.

Our research extends the multi-threaded scheme by proposing an AG generation algorithm targeting HPC clusters. Modern HPC clusters have ample memory on each node, satisfying the needs of many memory-intensive programs. To the best of our knowledge, however, no existing research ever deployed AG generators on HPC clusters.

In [11], a distributed AG generator is proposed. The authors apply reachability hyper-graph partitioning to divide the target network into groups of networked software applications. Each group is assigned as a task to a search agent to derive a part of the AG. The multiple agents communicate with one another through TCP sockets and access a virtually shared memory to avoid redundant expansion of nodes that are already processed. While this AG generator is designed to execute with distributed computing agents, the experiments yielding a speedup of X2.65 were actually conducted on a single computer with a quad-core Intel processor. More experiments are needed to evaluate if this distributed AG generator can perform equally well on a real distributed platform, especially after adding the overhead from TCP/IP communication between search agents and from accessing the virtually shared memory.

In [12], the authors proposes parallel AG generation in Spark. Utilizing multiple Spark executors enables each to generate a distinct sub-AG. Following parallel execution, these subgraphs are merged into a comprehensive resulting AG.

To optimize the parallelization efficiency, a multilevel k-way partition algorithm divides the input network into smaller segments according to topology, which significantly reduces the workload added to each executor. While the experiments in [12] on a single computer indicate that the Spark-based scheme outperforms a distributed AG generation algorithm, crucial experiment details, such as the implementation specifics of the baseline AG generator being compared, and the dimensions of each target AG, are omitted.

Different from these existing efforts to parallelize AG generation, we not only deploy our parallel AG generator crossing multiple nodes on an HPC cluster, but also tune the platform parameters to examine the impacts of the hardware configuration on the performance and cost. Furthermore, we profile the execution times of different components in our AG generator to identify the most critical one and propose further optimizations to speed it up.

3   AG Model and Parallel Generation

This section introduces the AG model used by this paper and applies it to an example network. It then presents a parallel algorithm for the model's AG generator to be deployed on HPC clusters.

3.1   AG Model

Our AG model follows the design in [15]. The model defines an AG as a tuple:

$$AG = \{V, E\}, \tag{1}$$

where V is the set of nodes and E is the set of directed edges. Each node represents the set of properties of network assets relevant to attacks. Each edge represents the exploitation of one or more vulnerabilities, causing a state transition from one node to the other. To build an AG for a target network, the input must include:

– A list of assets, which encompasses network devices and software entities.
– A list of vulnerabilities. Each vulnerability is formatted as a set of pre-conditions and a set of post-conditions.
– A set of initial properties of network assets, which essentially defines the root node of the AG. According to [15], the AG tree structure originates from the root node, and all derived nodes are either intermediate states or target states after attacks are carried out successfully.

As an example, Fig. 1(A) shows a small network with three servers. The security policy regulates that any user from the Internet can only use the web or file service. The database server only provides backend service to the other two servers. The web server and the file server both have vulnerable services that might be used by an attacker to gain root privileges. In addition, the database server has a bug in its OS, which might be exploited by an attacker that has a

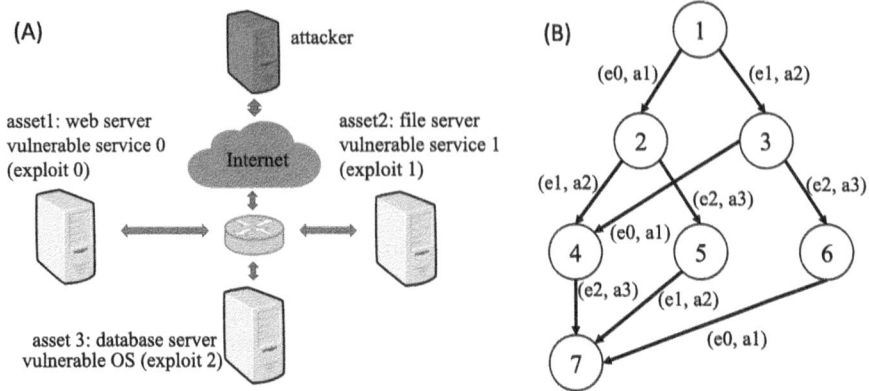

Fig. 1. A target network (A) and its AG (B)

foothold on either the web server or the file server. With the given input information, the AG is generated as in Fig. 1(B). Considering that the attacker may
choose the database server as the final goal, the AG shows that the exploitation
2 on the database server always conditions on either exploitation 0 on the web
server or exploitation 1 on the file server. Thus, this AG helps security administrator to identify all the possible multi-step attacks that can compromise the
database server.

3.2 Parallel AG Generator on HPC Clusters

To generate AGs on HPC clusters, we design a parallel algorithm in Fig. 2, which
comprises three distinct phases.

In phase 1 (lines 1–9), the initial AG state (Note: AG state is used hereafter
instead of AG node to avoid confusing with cluster node) and its derived states
are expanded by each cluster node locally to fill a per-node queue (Q) with
more unexpanded states. The queue is identical on each cluster node as they
take identical input. When the size of the per-node queue grows greater than a
threshold T, the multi-threaded phase 2 (lines 10–12) begins. Suppose comm_sz
is the number of cluster nodes and n_threads is the number of threads from
each node, then the total number of threads in the multi-threaded phase is
comm_sz*n_threads. Each thread maintains its own queue (threadQ), with an
initial size equal to the per-node queue size (Q.size()) divided by the total number
of threads. The partition of the unexpanded states in the per-node queue is cyclic,
aiming to divide the AG state space evenly among all the threads.

As inter-node communication is more expensive than local computations, in
phase 1 and 2, each cluster node explores its partial state space independently. In
phase 3 (lines 13–16), a master node merges all the partial graphs into a complete
AG. The merging needs to remove duplicate nodes and edges through hashing
methods. With comm_sz nodes, the merging requires a total of comm_sz-1 inter-
node communications, which might add a long latency to the total execution

```
Input:
    root: initial state of the target network
    exploits: set of vulnerabilities
    comm_sz: number of compute nodes from the cluster
    n_threads: number of threads from each compute node
Output:
    V: the set of AG states
    E: the set of AG edges
```

01 unexpanded state set $Q \leftarrow \{root\}, V \leftarrow \{root\}, E \leftarrow \emptyset$
02 while $Q.size() < T$:
03   state $q \leftarrow Q.pop()$
04   for-each e in exploits:
05   if e not applicable to q: continue
06          $q_{derived} \leftarrow apply\ postcondition\ of\ e\ on\ q$
07   if $q_{derived}$ is never discovered:
08            $Q \leftarrow Q \cup \{q_{derived}\}, V \leftarrow V \cup \{q_{derived}\}$
09          $E \leftarrow E \cup \{q\ to\ q_{derived}\}$
10 **multi-threaded**: $threadQ \leftarrow fetch\ Q.size()/(comm\_sz * n\_threads)$ states from Q
11 **multi-threaded:** while $threadQ.size() > 0$:
12 **multi-threaded:**   pop and expand a state, then update V and E in critical sections
13 if this node is master node:
14   for-each coworker node i:
15        $V \leftarrow V \cup V_{node\,i}$ with duplicate states removed
16        $E \leftarrow E \cup E_{node\,i}$ with duplicate edges removed

Fig. 2. Parallel algorithm to generate AG on HPC clusters

time. If no merging is required, however, each node can keep its partial AG in the local memory or store it into an AG database.

4 Performance Evaluation

The parallel AG generation on HPC clusters is implemented with a hybrid of Message Passing Interface (MPI) and Open Multi-Processing (OpenMP), both of which are available in most HPC environments. Specifically, each cluster node in the algorithm is embodied by an OpenMPI process. Each OpenMPI process forks multiple OpenMP threads for the multi-threaded phase in the algorithm.

4.1 Performance Evaluation

The AG to be generated targets a network with a tree structure in Fig. 3. The attacker from the Internet has the option to compromise any of the servers. With a compromised server as a foothold, the attacker can attack any of the workstations connected to the server via a LAN. The target network has 150 computers, 20% of which have a vulnerability to be exploited. The generated AG has 5,859,375 states and 56,640,625 edges. The storage cost is 13.5 GB, which is not small compared with the limited memory capacity of single computers.

As the baseline configuration, two compute nodes are employed to test, each with the number of threads tuned from 2 to 40, which matches the maximum

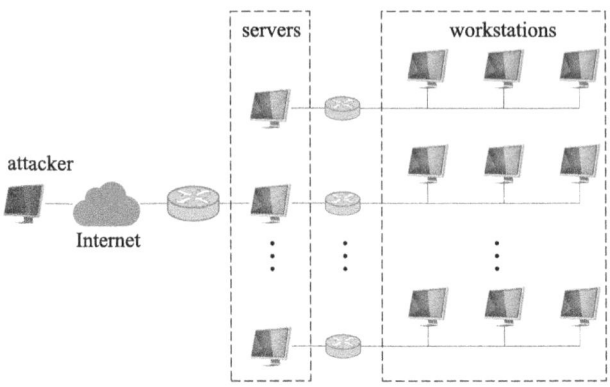

Fig. 3. Target network for AG generation in performance evaluation

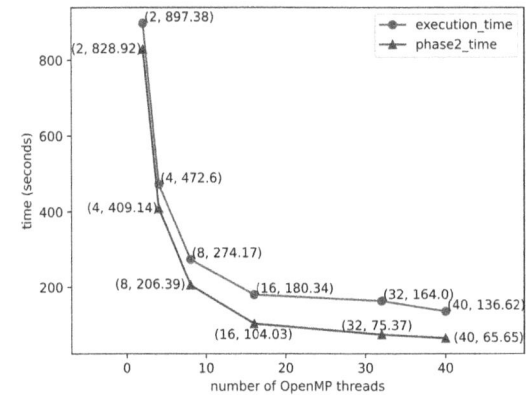

Fig. 4. Baseline performance with two compute nodes. Each node has 40 CPUs (Intel Xeon E5-2650 @2.3Ghz) and one 32 GB memory.

number of CPUs per-node. Figure 4 shows that as the number of threads in the multi-threaded phase increases, the total execution time decreases. Considering only phase 2, its execution time reduces about 50% each time the number of threads doubles, demonstrating the effectiveness of intra-node parallelism in accelerating the AG generation process. Based on the algorithm in Fig. 2, there is only one MPI send/recv communication between node 0 (master) and node 1 during phase 3 to merge partial AGs. For the case of 40 OpenMP threads per-node, phase 1 takes 0.48 s, phase 2 takes 65.65 s, phase 3 takes 69.47 s and the total is 136.62 s. Phase 1 takes a very short duration to prepare the workload for the multi-threaded phase 2. Phase 3 contributes the largest amount to the total execution time. Further profiling the sub-steps in phase 3 shows that MPI communication preparation takes 0.48 s, MPI send/recv takes 23.95 s, AG state merging takes 2.58 s and AG edge merging takes 42.29 s. While the time for MPI send/recv is a necessary cost due to communication, AG edge merging occurs only on the master node but adds the largest overhead, implying that further optimization is required.

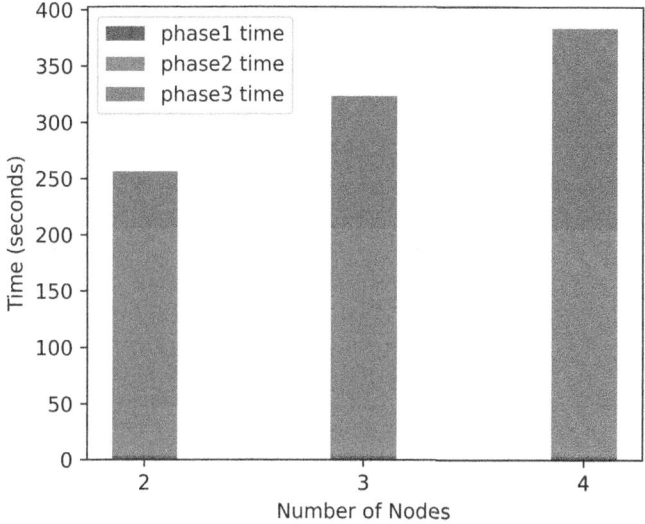

Fig. 5. Tune the number of compute nodes. Node configuration: 8 OpenMP threads; 32 GB memory per-node; CPU-Intel Xeon E5-2650 @2.3Ghz.

The next experiment tunes the number of invoked compute nodes. Specially, the execution times of the three phases are compared under 2-node, 3-node and 4-node settings. As Fig. 5 suggests, invoking more compute nodes increases the overall execution time. From 2 nodes to 4 nodes, the three settings spend approximately equal time on phase 1 and 2. However, phase 3 becomes more expensive. This trend is attributed to a larger overhead on MPI send/recv communication between compute nodes. For example, under 4-node settings, node 1, 2 and 3 must send their AG states and edges (essentially the partial AG itself) to node 0 for merging. In an application setting where merging partial AGs is not required, the time of phase 3 will not be a factor. As a result, the total execution time is expected to be non-increasing even if more compute nodes are enlisted.

On the other hand, although the total running time is unsatisfactory due to the implementation of phase 3, the benefits of running with multiple HPC nodes to mitigate the pressure of memory usage should not be overlooked. Our experimental AG needs 13.5 GB of storage. A typical OSCER compute node provides about 30 GB memory, which can be shared by at most 2 of our MPI processes. Mapping more processes to each node results in unsuccessful launching of the MPI program. With these processes more sparsely distributed, such as one process per-node in the conducted experiments, a master node has enough space for the storage of two partial AGs: one for itself and the other for buffering the AG received from other nodes. Execution time is not the only goal of an efficient solution to AG generation. Designing an AG generator to run on HPC clusters will need to strike a balance between minimizing execution time and distributing storage cost on participating nodes.

4.2   Optimization

To reduce the overhead of merging AGs, we propose the following options to accelerate phase 3 of our AG generator.

- Option 1: create multiple threads on the master node, and let each thread receive and merge one partial AG. This option means each thread on the master node must have its own buffer to store a partial AG, which results in a higher memory demand on the master node.
- Option 2: create a multi-threaded software pipeline on the master node. Some master threads serve as producers only receiving new partial AGs, while others as consumers simultaneously merge received ones into the complete AG.
- Option 3: create a hierarchical merging process, which aims to accelerate when more than four nodes are invoked. For instance, the even ID-ed processes merge into the adjacent odd ID-ed first, then the odd ID-ed ones merge together to build the complete AG.

As of the writing of this paper, experiments are underway to evaluate these optimization options. Option 3 is tested with the same cluster setting as the experiments already conducted. Both option 1 and 2 require more memory than the current implementation, and they are being tested on OSCER's large memory queues.

5   Conclusions and Future Work

To address the scalability issue of AG generation, this paper presents a parallel algorithm and its implementation on HPC clusters. The proposed algorithm partitions the generation process into three phases. Phase 1 runs a single thread per-node to prepare enough workload for multiple threads. Phase 2 runs a hybrid of MPI processes and OpenMP threads to accelerate the exploration of partial AGs. Phase 3 merges partial AGs into a complete one through MPI communications. The experimental results reveal that AG generation on HPC clusters can achieve an equilibrium between accelerating the generation process and reducing the memory demands on the computing device. For subsequent research, we will complete the design and experiments that optimize the merging of partial AGs. In addition, we will explore possible solutions to eliminate the need to merge partial AGs on a master node, for instance, via building a distributed database to store AG nodes and edges.

Acknowledgments. The computing of this project was performed at the OU Super-computing Center for Education & Research (OSCER) at the University of Oklahoma (OU). OSCER Research Computing Facilitator Thang Ha provided valuable technical expertise.

References

1. Ou, X., Govindavajhala, S., Appel, A.W., et al.: MulVAL: a logic-based network security analyzer. In: USENIX Security Symposium, Baltimore, MD, vol. 8, pp. 113–128 (2005)
2. Ibrahim, M., Al-Hindawi, Q., Elhafiz, R., Alsheikh, A., Alquq, O.: Attack graph implementation and visualization for cyber physical systems. Processes **8**(1), 12 (2019)
3. Yiğit, B., Gür, G., Alagöz, F., Tellenbach, B.: Cost-aware securing of IoT systems using attack graphs. Ad Hoc Netw. **86**, 23–35 (2019)
4. Ibrahim, A., Bozhinoski, S., Pretschner, A.: Attack graph generation for microservice architecture. In: Proceedings of the 34th ACM/SIGAPP Symposium on Applied Computing, pp. 1235–1242 (2019)
5. Poolsappasit, N., Dewri, R., Ray, I.: Dynamic security risk management using bayesian attack graphs. IEEE Trans. Dependable Secure Comput. **9**(1), 61–74 (2011)
6. Phillips, C., Swiler, L.P.: A graph-based system for network-vulnerability analysis. In: Proceedings of the 1998 Workshop on New Security Paradigms, pp. 71–79 (1998)
7. Sheyner, O., Haines, J., Jha, S., Lippmann, R., Wing, J.M.: Automated generation and analysis of attack graphs. In: Proceedings 2002 IEEE Symposium on Security and Privacy, pp. 273–284. IEEE (2002)
8. Ou, X., Boyer, W.F., McQueen, M.A.: A scalable approach to attack graph generation. In: Proceedings of the 13th ACM Conference on Computer and Communications Security, pp. 336–345 (2006)
9. Ingols, K., Lippmann, R., Piwowarski, K.: Practical attack graph generation for network defense. In: 2006 22nd Annual Computer Security Applications Conference (ACSAC 2006), pp. 121–130. IEEE (2006)
10. Jajodia, S., Noel, S., O'berry, B.: Topological analysis of network attack vulnerability. Managing Cyber Threats: Issues, Approaches, and Challenges, pp. 247–266 (2005)
11. Kaynar, K., Sivrikaya, F.: Distributed attack graph generation. IEEE Trans. Dependable Secure Comput. **13**(5), 519–532 (2015)
12. Cao, N., Lv, K., Hu, C.: An attack graph generation method based on parallel computing. In: International Conference on Science of Cyber Security, pp. 34–48. Springer (2018)
13. Li, M., Hawrylak, P., Hale, J.: Concurrency strategies for attack graph generation. In: 2019 2nd International Conference on Data Intelligence and Security (ICDIS), pp. 174–179. IEEE (2019)
14. OSCER Homepage. https://ou.edu/oscer. Accessed 01 May 2024
15. Li, M., Hawrylak, P., Hale, J.: Strategies for practical hybrid attack graph generation and analysis. Digit. Threats Res. Pract. **3**(4), 1–24 (2022)
16. Li, M., Hawrylak, P.J., Hale, J.: Implementing an attack graph generator in CUDA. In: 2020 IEEE International Parallel and Distributed Processing Symposium Workshops (IPDPSW), pp. 730–738. IEEE (2020)

Analyzing the Influence of File Formats on I/O Patterns in Deep Learning

Betzabeth Leon[1]([✉])(ID), Edixon Parraga[1](ID), Sandra Mendez[2](ID),
Dolores Rexachs[1](ID), Remo Suppi[1](ID), and Emilio Luque[1](ID)

[1] Computer Architecture and Operating Systems Department, Universitat
Autònoma de Barcelona (UAB), Bellaterra, Barcelona, Spain
{betzabeth.leon,edixon.parraga,dolores.rexachs,remo.suppi,
emilio.luque}@uab.es
[2] Computer Sciences Department, Barcelona Supercomputing Center (BSC),
Barcelona, Spain
sandra.mendez@bsc.es

Abstract. Deep Learning applications have become an important solution for analyzing and making predictions with massive amounts of data in recent years. However, this type of application introduces significant input/output (I/O) loads on computer systems. Moreover, when executed on distributed systems or parallel distributed memory systems, they handle much information that must be read during training. This persistent and continuous access to files can overwhelm file systems and negatively impact application performance. A file format defines how information is stored, and the choice of a format depends on the use case. Therefore, it is important to analyze how the file format influences the training stage when loading and reading the dataset, as opening and reading many small files could affect application performance. Thus, this paper will analyze the I/O pattern of different file formats used in deep learning applications to characterize their behavior.

Keywords: Parallel I/O · I/O Analysis · Distributed Deep Learning

1 Introduction

The large volumes of data required for training models in deep learning (DL) applications running in High-Performance Computing (HPC) systems generate significant I/O loads. This can impact the I/O system's performance, especially during training with intensive, simultaneous, and persistent file access. Efficient I/O utilization becomes challenging, potentially causing high training latency and overhead, particularly when datasets exceed main memory capacity.

This research has been supported by the Agencia Estatal de Investigación (AEI), Spain and the Fondo Europeo de Desarrollo Regional (FEDER) UE, under contract PID2020-112496GB-I00.
The authors thankfully acknowledge RES resources provided by CESGA in FinisTerrae III to RES-DATA-2022-1-0014.

© The Author(s), under exclusive license to Springer Nature Switzerland AG 2025
H. R. Arabnia et al. (Eds.): CSCE 2024, CCIS 2256, pp. 130–136, 2025.
https://doi.org/10.1007/978-3-031-85638-9_10

Understanding DL I/O patterns is important for evaluating and improving I/O performance in HPC systems. To manage I/O operations, a multi-layered software stack is configured, incorporating components such as I/O libraries, middleware, and file systems, which work together along the I/O path from compute nodes to storage devices. The efficiency of I/O patterns depends on how these layers are configured, as they can significantly influence the system's ability to utilize its performance capacity fully. The complexity of achieving optimal I/O performance is further compounded by the numerous tunable parameters within parallel I/O stacks, which can vary significantly across different systems and application use cases, as noted by the authors of [1]. With emerging workloads like artificial intelligence and big data analytics introducing more diverse and unpredictable I/O behaviors, understanding and modeling extreme-scale I/O performance becomes indispensable, as the authors of [4] emphasize.

One concept related to I/O libraries that can determine how a file is accessed and, therefore, impacts the I/O pattern is the file format, which usually depends on the application context. File formats like HDF5 are common in HPC and DL; this format also has the advantage of having a library that provides optimization techniques that can be applied depending on the I/O pattern. However, there are file formats specific to DL, such as TFRecord, NPZ, and CSV, among others, that are not designed to run on HPC parallel file systems.

Therefore, their optimization relies on how the HPC users or administrators configure the I/O software stack. Consequently, based on the above, this work will characterize specific file formats and their impact on the I/O patterns of DL applications. The file formats selected are NPZ, TFRecord, and HDF5. This study aims to characterize these formats and monitor their behavior according to the format type, describing the file access patterns to analyze their impact. This information can help decide which format to use and whether any preprocessing is necessary.

2   Motivation

I/O operations are a known performance bottleneck of HPC applications, as described by the authors of [5], who highlight the complexity and time-consuming nature of tuning the I/O stack for optimal performance. Figure 1 illustrates a software stack for DL applications composed of several software layers needed to manipulate I/O operations. The file format is an important element, often managed by I/O libraries. In DL applications, I/O operations such as data loading and reading are typically performed at the framework level, utilizing file formats like HDF5, TFRecord, and NPZ. These formats are then processed at lower levels of the software stack, where the impact of the file format becomes more apparent.

To compare this impact, we will use the DLIO benchmark, which emulates the loading and reading of data in different file formats. We will focus on three popular formats in DL applications: NPZ, TFRecord, and HDF5. Despite having similar configurations and workloads, these formats may exhibit different behaviors in their access patterns. These differences can significantly affect performance and resource usage.

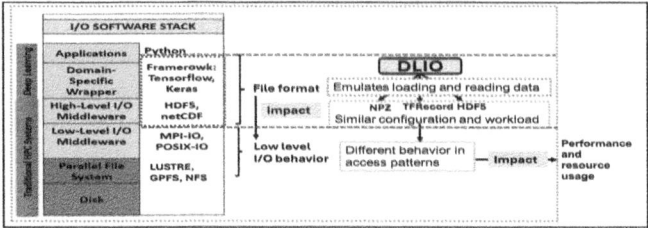

Fig. 1. Influence of File Formats on I/O Performance and Access Patterns

In the present study, we consider that even if we have files in these three formats with similar workloads, their access patterns will differ due to their intrinsic nature. These differences will significantly affect I/O performance and system resource utilization. By analyzing these effects, we can identify the advantages and disadvantages of each format concerning I/O efficiency and resource usage, guiding the selection of the most appropriate file format based on the specific context of the DL application.

3   I/O Pattern Analysis

Understanding the file access pattern can help make predictions to optimize the application's I/O or implement strategies to minimize the I/O impact on the application performance. In this work, to understand the I/O patterns' behavior, we represent them from two points of view: spatial and temporal:

- Spatial Pattern: This represents the logical view of how the file is accessed by processes at each position (file offset).
- Temporal Pattern: Shows the order in which processes access the file during the execution of the application.

3.1   File Formats

The HDF5, NPZ, and TFRecord file formats were selected for this work because they are commonly used in deep learning.

- NPZ is a Numpy file format that provides matrix data storage using gzip compression.
- TFRecord is a simple format for storing a sequence of binary records native to TensorFlow. It facilitates the combination of multiple datasets.

- HDF5 is a file format for storing scientific data. It allows data to be stored in a file and organized in a structured manner. It supports the insertion of metadata for self-description, which means that each file and dataset can have associated metadata that describes the data.

To mimic specific DL I/O patterns, we utilized DLIO, a Data-Centric Benchmark for scientific DL applications [3]. DLIO is a representative benchmark constructed based on the I/O profiling of selected workloads, accurately emulating the I/O behavior typical in modern scientific deep learning applications. We have designed experiments using a specific workload and a determined degree of parallelism. The data is stored in three formats: HDF5, NPZ, and TFRecord. This will allow us to analyze how each of these formats affects the I/O patterns and assess their impact on the performance of input/output operations.

3.2 Access Mode

Regarding the access mode, the multi and shared types were chosen in this work. Figure 2(a) shows the multi-access type corresponding to the I/O strategy of one file per process, where each process accesses a file independently, requiring no synchronization between I/O operations. Figure 2(b) shows the shared access type, where all processes access a single shared file.

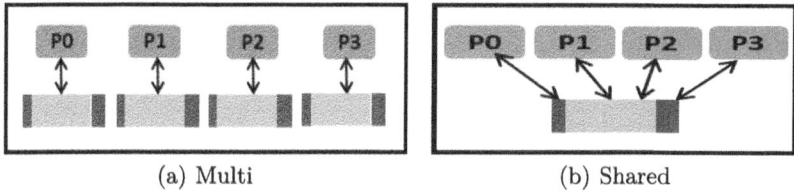

(a) Multi   (b) Shared

Fig. 2. File Access Mode

4   Experimental Results

The following section presents the experimental results. This experimentation aims to identify and compare the I/O pattern behavior of dataset reading using the NPZ, TFRecord, and HDF5 file formats. The access mode for NPZ and TFRecord was multi, where each process independently accesses its file. For HDF5, the access mode was shared, where all processes access different segments within the same file. The file system used was LUSTRE with a single data server, and the experiment configuration is shown in Table 1. We use Darshan 3.4.3, a scalable HPC I/O characterization tool, as a monitoring tool [2].

Figure 3 shows the spatial and temporal pattern for the three file formats, where the x-axis represents the number of I/O processes, the y-axis represents the

Table 1. Configuration Experimentation

File Format	Nodes	Processes IO	IO Total (GiB)	GiB per proc	No. of Files
NPZ	1	4	8.75	2.18	4
TFRecord	1	4	8.74	2.18	4
HDF5	1	4	8.73	2.18	1

temporal order, the z-axis represents the file offset, and the color-bar represents the request size of the read operations.

Regarding the results, the spatial and temporal data read pattern of the NPZ file with the multi-access mode is shown in Fig. 3(a). A total of 565 operations per process were performed, of which 561 had a size of 4 MiB, and the rest were very small metadata-related operations. In the case of the reads from the TFRecord file with multi-access mode, shown in Fig. 3(b), each process performed a total of 8947 reads of size 256 KiB, with no metadata reads observed. In both NPZ and TFRecord cases, it was observed that the read sizes were regular, and the Offset increased from the beginning to the end of the file, except for the metadata reads in NPZ.

In the case of reads from the HDF5 file, each process performed a total of 4489 reads, of which 16 operations were small metadata reads. The rest of the reads were 512 KiB in size. Figure 3(c) shows shared access to the same file, with each process accessing a different file offset to perform the read operations.

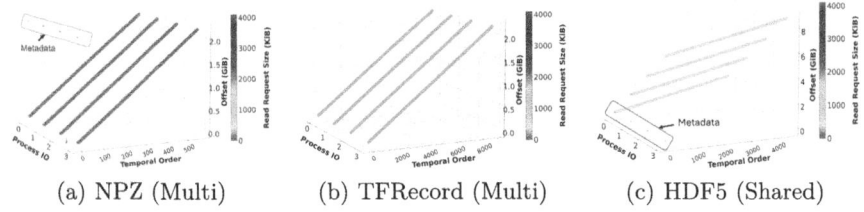

(a) NPZ (Multi)   (b) TFRecord (Multi)   (c) HDF5 (Shared)

Fig. 3. Spatial and Temporal Pattern of I/O Operations DLIO app. File System: LUS-TRE

It was observed that NPZ and HDF5 include a set of small operations generally used as metadata, which is then used in the reading stage to obtain information about the file's data layout. Formats like HDF5 include a larger number of operations related to metadata. Additionally, the file size and the operation size at the POSIX-IO level depend on the parameters set for the HDF5 library. The NPZ format has a very low number of metadata operations; it takes information from the file system, where the data will be written to perform operations the same size as the file system's block size. In the case of TFRecord, this format does not perform metadata-related operations (at least not explicitly), and the operation size corresponds to the transfer size of TensorFlow's buffer.

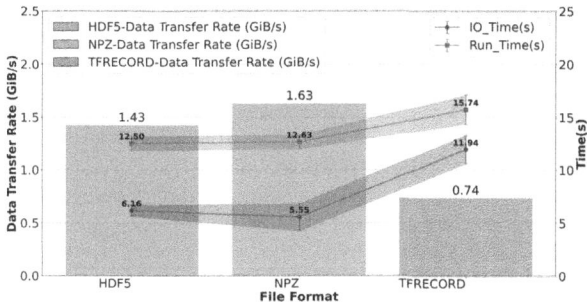

Fig. 4. Comparative Performance Analysis: I/O Time, Runtime, and Data Transfer Rate Across Different File Formats

4.1   Impact of File Format on Loading and Reading the Dataset: Bandwidth and Time

Figure 4 compares the file formats for bandwidth, I/O time, and execution time. HDF5 and NPZ exhibit similar performance regarding I/O time, execution time, and bandwidth. TFRecord, on the other hand, have significantly higher I/O and execution times, suggesting that this format might not be the most efficient for applications that require fast read/write and execution speeds. This evaluation can help select the most suitable file format according to specific performance and efficiency requirements in data handling.

5   Conclusions

This study analyzed the I/O patterns of HDF5, NPZ, and TFRecord formats in deep learning applications. The results show that, although file sizes may be similar, the I/O patterns at the POSIX-IO level differ, impacting performance due to variations in operations and metadata of each format. Despite having comparable file sizes, HDF5, NPZ, and TFRecord's internal structure and access methods lead to distinct I/O behaviors. These differences manifest in how each format handles read and write operations and in the overhead introduced by metadata management. The study underscores the importance of selecting the appropriate file format to optimize dataset loading and reading in deep learning (DL) applications. Different formats can lead to substantial differences in I/O efficiency, directly affecting the overall times. Addressing these bottlenecks can improve the configuration of the I/O system, such as optimizing buffer sizes, adjusting prefetching strategies, and fine-tuning the underlying file system parameters. Future research will analyze the impact of file formats' temporal and spatial patterns on IOPS and bandwidth metrics to design I/O optimization techniques.

References

1. Bababa, A., Wang, X., Niethammer, C., Gracia, J.: Improving the I/O performance of applications with predictive modeling based auto-tuning. In: 2021 International Conference on Engineering and Emerging Technologies (ICEET), pp. 1–6 (2021). https://doi.org/10.1109/ICEET53442.2021.9659711
2. Carns, P., et al.: Understanding and improving computational science storage access through continuous characterization. ACM Trans. Storage **7**(3) (2011). https://doi.org/10.1145/2027066.2027068
3. Devarajan, H., Zheng, H., Kougkas, A., Sun, X.H., Vishwanath, V.: DLIO: a data-centric benchmark for scientific deep learning applications. In: 2021 IEEE/ACM 21st International Symposium on Cluster, Cloud and Internet Computing (CCGrid), pp. 81–91 (2021). https://doi.org/10.1109/CCGrid51090.2021.00018
4. Neuwirth, S., Paul, A.K.: Parallel I/O evaluation techniques and emerging HPC workloads: a perspective. In: 2021 IEEE International Conference on Cluster Computing (CLUSTER), pp. 671–679 (2021). https://doi.org/10.1109/Cluster48925.2021.00100
5. Rajesh, N., Bateman, K., Bez, J.L., Byna, S., Kougkas, A., Sun, X.H.: TunIO: an AI-powered framework for optimizing HPC I/O. In: 2024 IEEE International Parallel and Distributed Processing Symposium (IPDPS), pp. 494–505. IEEE (2024)

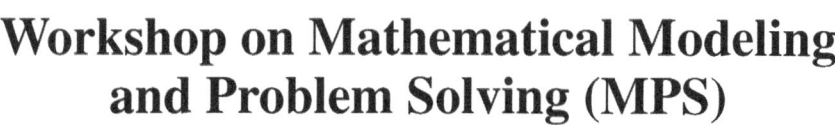

Workshop on Mathematical Modeling and Problem Solving (MPS)

Inference of Cell–Cell Interactions Through Spatial Transcriptomics Data Using Graph Convolutional Neural Networks

Takahiro Hiura[1,2P], Shigeto Seno[3(✉)] [iD], and Hideo Matsuda[3] [iD]

[1] School of Engineering Science, Osaka University, Osaka, Japan
[2] Nara Institute of Science and Technology, Nara, Japan
[3] Graduate School of Information Science and Technology, Osaka University, Osaka, Japan
{senoo,matsuda}@ist.osaka-u.ac.jp

Abstract. Understanding cell–cell interactions is crucial for unraveling the complexities of multicellular organisms and holds promising implications for advancements in medical science. These interactions, mediated through specific ligand-receptor pairs, remain partially identified. The rapid evolution of gene expression analysis technologies, especially spatial transcriptomics, now allows for the precise capture of gene expression while maintaining cellular localization. While studies using spatial transcriptomics data to visualize known cell–cell interactions are achieving great success, their application to infer unknown cell–cell interaction pairs has not yet been fully investigated.

In this study, we introduce a novel approach utilizing Graph Convolutional Neural Networks (GCNN) to infer cell–cell interactions from spatial transcriptomics data. Previous efforts have demonstrated the utility of GCNNs for data obtained through the continuous FISH (fluorescence *in situ* hybridization) method. We propose an alternative strategy to adapt GCNN-based cell–cell interaction prediction methods to data acquired by *in situ* capture methods. Additionally, we address the challenge of properly generating training data for the model, implementing a solution that significantly enhances the estimation process. Our findings reveal that the method used to transform Spatial Transcriptomics data into a graph significantly impacts the accuracy of interaction predictions, with prediction accuracies ranging from 80% to 90% under certain conditions.

Keywords: GCNN (Graph Convolutional Neural Network) · cell–cell interaction · Spatial Transcriptomics analysis

1 Introduction

Cell–cell interactions play an essential role in cell differentiation, immune disorders, and homeostasis, and their abnormalities are known to be involved in

© The Author(s), under exclusive license to Springer Nature Switzerland AG 2025
H. R. Arabnia et al. (Eds.): CSCE 2024, CCIS 2256, pp. 139–152, 2025.
https://doi.org/10.1007/978-3-031-85638-9_11

cancer and autoimmune diseases. Understanding the complex network of cell–cell interactions is a matter of fundamental biological interest and profound clinical relevance. cell–cell interactions are usually mediated by specific pairings between ligands (signal molecules secreted by a kind of cell) and receptors (molecules on the surface of the other cell that specifically recognize and bind the ligand). Historically, cell–cell interaction studies have been dominated by biological experiments and protein conformational approaches. These methods still provide valuable insights into cell–cell interactions but have yet to be limited by throughput and resolution. The advent of gene expression profiling technologies, such as microarray and RNA-seq technologies, has made it possible to analyze the expression of thousands of genes simultaneously, a first step toward high-throughput analysis. The principle of estimating cell–cell interactions from gene expression profiles is based on analyzing the expression patterns of the molecular messages (ligands and receptors) that cells use to communicate with each other. Estimating interactions from gene expression is an indirect approach and has been used by Kirouac et al. [11], Rieckmann et al. [13], and Joost et al. [9].

Recently, single-cell RNA sequencing (scRNA-seq) and Spatial Transcriptomics technologies have demonstrated synergy with cell–cell interaction analysis. Gene expression profiling at the level of individual cells has made it possible to visualize the possibility that ligand-receptor pairs are actually used for cell-to-cell communication in specific cell-type pairs. Various methods such as CellChat [7], CellPhoneDB [5], and NicheNet [3] have been proposed as tools for extracting and visualizing cell–cell interactions and are beginning to become standard analysis methods in papers dealing with single cells. These methods essentially use information on ligand-receptor pairs that are known to interact (information on known ligand-receptor pairs is stored in various databases). The gene expression profiles at the individual cell level provide a detailed snapshot of which genes are "on" or "off" in each cell and search for ligand-receptor pairs that are commonly "on" among a given cell population. This principle is equally applicable to Spatial Transcriptomics data. Spatial Transcriptomics data can provide spatial information on gene expression (such as whether cells are in physical proximity) and thus also provide insight into the mode of cell–cell interaction (CellChat v2 [8], Giotto [4], stLearn [12]).

Thus, analyses using known cell–cell interaction information are much used in single-cell gene expression data and Spatial Transcriptomics, whereas studies attempting to determine unknown cell–cell interactions are still in their infancy. There are many types of receptors and ligands, and only specific pairs can signal, but only a few are known to signal. There are still many unknown LR-pairs, so developing methods to estimate unknown cell–cell interactions is also an important issue. In particular, if cell–cell interactions can be estimated from Spatial Transcriptomics data, a new technique that can even provide information on cell location, different types of interactions can likely be identified. There are few such efforts yet, but one is GCNG (Graph Convolutional Neural networks for Genes) [16]. This is a supervised learning method that takes into account the spatial information of the cell and analyses it using GCN (Graph Convolutional Network) [10,14]. The main advantage of GCN is that even when spatial relationships are not perfect, the convolution capabilities of neural networks and GCNG actually improve the accuracy over unsupervised methods.

In this study, we attempted to extend the GCNN-based supervised learning method for estimating cell–cell interactions to a broader range of Spatial Transcriptomics data; the GCNG method has been validated on Spatial Transcriptomics data using the continuous FISH method in that paper. Continuous FISH has the advantage of high spatial resolution and the ability to measure sub-cellular levels, but the number of genes that can be observed is generally smaller. In contrast, the *in situ* capture method has low spatial resolution and measures expression profiles at each 'spot' at the oligo-cellular levels but has the advantage of being able to measure a wide variety of genes. This is a widely used technique, as exemplified by Visium. The proposed method uses the GCNG method as a reference and devises a method for creating a graph structure that enables supervised learning of cell–cell interactions even with Spatial Transcriptomics data from the *in situ* capture method. The large number of genes that can be observed means that there is a high possibility of picking up unknown LR-pairs.

Another issue in this study is how the training data are given to train the model. The following information is given for training in the supervised learning of cell–cell interactions from Spatial Transcriptomics.

(1) Expression profiles of gene A and gene B in each spot
(2) Location of the spots
(3) Label for whether there is a known interaction between genes A and B (positive or negative example).

The GCNG method uniformly treats all known LR-pairs as positive examples. However, depending on the specific conditions and organizational context in which data are collected, some LR-pairs generally recognized as interactive may not actually engage in interactions. Including these as positive examples could compromise the quality of the training data and diminish model accuracy. To address this issue, our approach leverages the method for extracting and visualizing known cell–cell interactions. This enables the pre-identification of LR-pairs specific to our dataset. Consequently, we classify only those pairs that demonstrate interaction with a high degree of confidence as positive examples.

We velified our approach using Visium data measuring brain and kidney tissue. The results showed that LR-pairs could be identified accurately even in Spatial Transcriptomics data obtained by *in situ* capture methods such as Visium. GCN showed better generalization performance than general supervised learning, which does not consider spatial information. It was also found that how spatial information is represented in the graph structure is an important issue affecting the type of LR-pairs detected. These involve signaling between more distant locations by secretion, such as autocrine and paracrine.

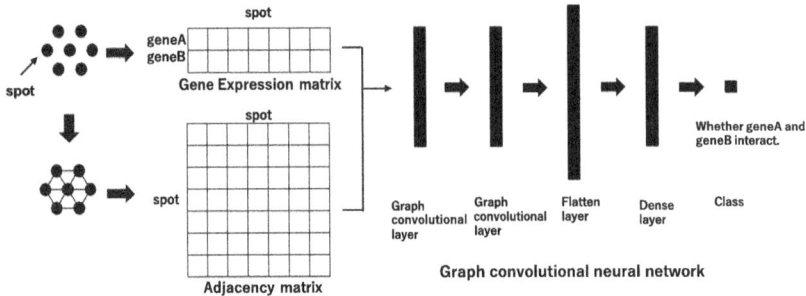

Fig. 1. Overview of the proposed method

2   Methods

2.1   Overview of Proposed Method

We propose a method to predict unknown ligand-receptor interaction pairs (LR-pairs) using Spatial Transcriptomics data of *in situ* capture methods, specifically Visium [15] data. Visium data are measured as expression data per spot containing multiple cells rather than expression data per cell. To solve the problem of Visium data not providing gene expression data for each cell, we propose a method to convert Visium data into a graph by treating each spot as a node and connecting adjacent spots with edges. Since there are several possible ways of connecting the edges, we will examine the effect of the edge connection policy on the results (details will be described later). The model of the proposed method is illustrated in Fig. 1. This structure of the model was created concerning GCNG [16]. In the same way, our model consists of two graph convolutional layers, one flatten layer, one dense layer, and one sigmoid function output layer for classification. Our model takes the adjacency matrix of spots and the expression information of gene pairs as input and learns and infers whether there is an interaction between these pairs.

The graph convolution layer is defined by the following equation.

$$Z = \mathbf{D}^{-\frac{1}{2}}(\mathbf{A} + I)\mathbf{D}^{-\frac{1}{2}}XW + \mathbf{b} \tag{1}$$

$\mathbf{A}$ is an adjacency matrix calculated from coordinates from spots, and $\mathbf{D}$ is degree matrix. The adjacency matrix represents the connectivity of spots for the graph convolution. When an edge exists between node i and j, $A_{i,j} = A_{j,i} = 1$, and 0 if no edge exists. X is the expression matrix of dimension "number of spots × 2" and W is the weights of the convolution kernel of dimension "2 × 32". $\mathbf{b}$ is a bias vector term of dimension "1 × 32". The output Z of the convolution layer consists of the dimension "number of spots × 32" and represents the embedding vector of all spots. The flatten layer receives the output of the graph convolution layer and transforms the matrix into a vector form.

The next layer is the dense layer, whose activation function uses the ReLU function. And the final layer is also a dense layer, but the number of units in the output is one, and its output is put into a sigmoid function, the activation function, which can predict the label of the input graph. The sigmoid function is defined as follows.

$$\text{Sigmoid}(x) = \frac{1}{1 + e^{\beta x}} \qquad (2)$$

β represents a parameter.

The objective function of the whole model is as follows. We consider binary cross-entropy as a loss function.

$$F = -\sum_{k=1}^{N} y_k \log(G_\Theta(x)) + (1 - y_k)\log(1 - G_\Theta(x)) \qquad (3)$$

The training labels used for learning are represented by the vector $\mathbf{y}$ of length N, where N indicates the total number of candidate LR-pairs. y_k is the k-th element of $\mathbf{y}$ and the label for the k-th gene pair, where it is 1 if the interaction is known, and 0 otherwise. Θ denotes all parameters that need to be optimized.

2.2 Workflow of the Proposed Method

Here, we describe the procedure for preparing training labels, transforming Visium spatial information into a graph (adjacency matrix), and the steps for training a graph convolutional network. The input data from Visium consists of expression information $\mathbf{X}$ for each spot (Matrix of size "number of gene types × number of spots"), and spatial information $\mathbf{C}$ (Matrix of size "number of spots × 2 (x,y coordinates in the 2D image)").

Preparing Training Labels of Interaction. If an interaction is known for a gene pair, it is listed in the database. If not listed in the database, the interaction is absent or unknown. This problem is called positive-unlabeled learning in the field of supervised learning [6]. In this study, however, we simply assume a positive example when the gene pair is listed in the database and a negative example when it is not. On the other hand, the focus of this study is on the treatment of positive examples. Gene interactions do not always observed, but depend on data such as organisation and conditions. If both of gene pair with known interactions are treated as positive examples, patterns in which almost none of the genes are expressed will also be learnt as positive examples. Therefore, in this study, only pairs for which interactions can be observed in the data used for learning are treated as positive examples in the data.

CellPhoneDB [5] has a statistical framework to predict cell–cell interactions between cell types from gene expression profiles of single cell. Although Visium data provide not cell-by-cell expression data but only spot-by-spot expression levels, CellPhoneDB is capable of estimating interactions between cells, as well as interactions between spots, similar to its functionality for cell–cell interaction prediction. In this way, we applied CellPhoneDB to Spatial Transcriptomics data $\mathbf{X}$, and the matrix $\mathbf{S}$ is obtained. This matrix $\mathbf{S}$ is a matrix with dimensions "number of known gene pairs" by "number of combinations of spot types," where each element represents the likelihood of interaction between that gene pair. Here, by introducing a significance level α, we decide to treat as positive examples those pairs that meet the criteria, i.e., pairs that are judged to be interacting with high confidence in this data. In this way, the vector of training labels $\mathbf{y}$ is prepared.

Transforming Spatial Information of Visium Spots to Graphs. For the purpose of graph convolutional neural networks, the spatial information of Visium spots is represented in a graph, connecting spots that are related (close in distance or similar in properties). The adjacency matrix $\mathbf{A}$ is a matrix "number of spots $\times$ number of spots", constructed from $\mathbf{C}$ representing the position data of each spot in Visium. The spatial distance between spots is calculated using the simple Euclidean distance. The following four types of adjacency matrices are considered.

1. A case in which each spot is considered as adjacent only to itself (**Pattern 1**).
2. A case in which two adjacent spots are considered adjacent to each other (**Pattern 2**).
3. A case in which a spot is considered adjacent up to two adjacent spots ahead (**Pattern 3**).
4. A case of connecting adjacent spots in each cluster (**Pattern 4**).

In Pattern 1, the adjacency matrix is a unit matrix. This would increase the likelihood that the model can detect interactions within the microenvironment of the spot and Autocrine-type interactions. Pattern 2 is the simplest connection, and other patterns are evaluated on this basis. Pattern 3 would lead to a model that is more likely to detect LR-pairs interacting at greater distances, since each spot is connected to a more distant spot. Pattern 4 is the case where adjacency is considered for each cluster. This approach is somewhat unique, involving the preliminary classification of spots with similar expression profiles in $\mathbf{X}$ through clustering. An adjacency matrix is created by connecting only adjacent spots in the same cluster. We consider that models using this adjacency matrix are well suited to detect interactions that occur within the same cell. One advantage of our proposed method is that, by creating various adjacency graphs and training model in this way, it is possible to consider which LR-pairs are easy to detect for each model.

Model Learning and Inference. From a given set of Visium data (gene expression profiles of spots $\mathbf{X}$ and spatial coordinates $\mathbf{C}$), we construct the adjacency matrix $\mathbf{A}$ and teacher labels $\mathbf{y}$) using the methods described above. During training and testing, we perform cross-validation. That is, the split data $\mathbf{X}_{\text{train}}$ and $\mathbf{A}$ are used as inputs to train the GCNN to learn $\mathbf{y}_{\text{train}}$. Once the model training is complete, inputting the expression profiles of any gene pair from the reserved test set $\mathbf{X}_{\text{test}}$ allows the model to output a value between 1 to 0, indicating whether an interaction exists between those pairs or not.

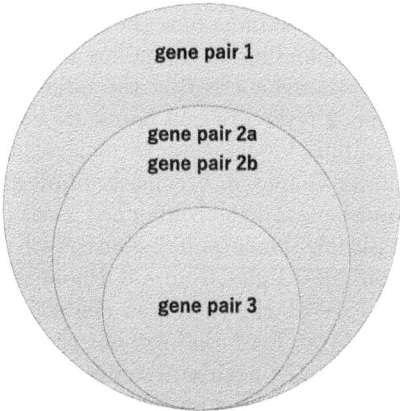

Fig. 2. Inclusion relationship of positive examples in gene pair 1, 2a, 2b, and 3. Gene pair 1 includes all known LR-pairs and gene pair 3 includes only interaction with high confidence at the data.

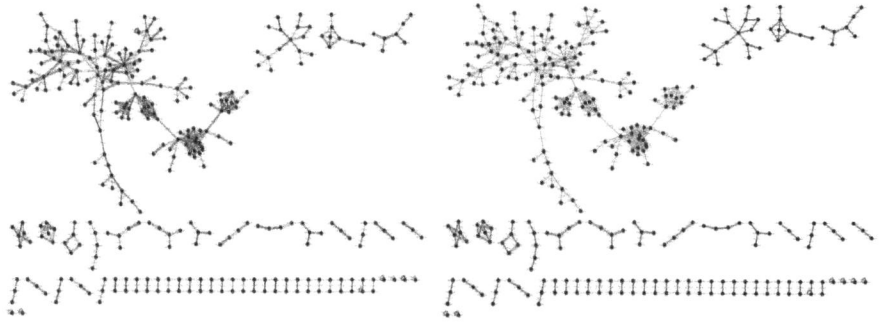

Fig. 3. Data splitting for training and testing. Random split for 3-fold cross validation (left, gene pair 2a). All ligand and receptors are separated exclusively as training and test gene sets for 2-fold cross validation (right, gene pair 2b)

3 Experiments

3.1 Overview

Since there are currently few methods for estimating unknown LR-pairs that interact using *in situ* capture data, we treat SVM (Support Vector Machine) and Random Forest as conventional methods. Although these methods are used in a situation where spot adjacencies cannot be taken into account, we considered that they could serve as a benchmark for measuring the benefits of using GCNNs. Because SVM and RandomForest require a one-dimensional vector as input, the expression matrix is transformed into a one-dimensional vector as input. Performance of these models is evaluated using Accuracy, Specificity, and Sensitivity.

In Experiment 1 and 2, we examine how the results of the conventional and proposed methods change depending on the policy to create the training labels. In this experiment, the method for creating the adjacency matrix used in the GCNN is fixed to **Pattern 2** (two adjacent spots are connected to each other). Here, we prepared the training labels using three levels of confidence as shown in Fig. 2 (Gene pair 1, 2, 3). Gene pair 1 consists of all known interacting pairs treated as positive examples even if the confidence levels of interaction obtained from CellPhoneDB are all low. Gene pair 2 consists of positive examples at a moderate level. Based on the results from CellPhoneDB, pairs for which the confidence of interaction exceeds the threshold (judged to be significant at the significance level $\alpha = 0.05$) at least one set of spots are treated as positive examples. Gene pair 3 consists of positive examples at a high level. According to the results from CellPhoneDB, pairs for which the significant interactions are observed in the majority of spots are treated as positive examples.

Furthermore, to more thoroughly evaluate the generalization capability of the GCN considering spatial information, we considered two methods for splitting the data into training and testing sets. Figure 3 illustrates the split of gene pairs into training and test data. Splitting is done for positive examples, and a negative example is added to each after splitting. Each node represents ligands, receptors and positive LR-pairs are connected by edges. In other words, each edge represents an interaction relationship and this edge is divided into two parts, one for training and the other for testing. As the model is trained by cross-validation, we split the data as many times as the number of splits and specify the training data and the test data from them. The split of the data in "gene pair 2a" is shown in the left panel of Fig. 3. It is a 3-fold cross-validation. As indicated by the three colors, the gene pairs are divided into three datasets, each dataset containing the same number of nodes. The split of the data in "gene pair 2b" is shown in the right panel of Fig. 3. It can be seen that each dataset split for cross-validation consists of different nodes. This is achieved by assigning each connected graph to each dataset in the order of the number of nodes contained. In this study, we decided to perform a 2-fold cross-validation in order to balance the number of nodes.

In experiment 3, we compared the results of the proposed method with the use of four patterns of the adjacency matrix and discussed the LR-pairs that resulted in different predictions. "Gene pair 2b" is used for the training and test data. This experiment allows to examine the effect of the policy to create the adjacency matrix on the results. We also paid attention to how the gene pairs that can be correctly predicted using each adjacency matrix are expressed.

To implement GCNN, we use python and "spektral" package. SVM and Random forests are used implemented in Sckit-learn library.

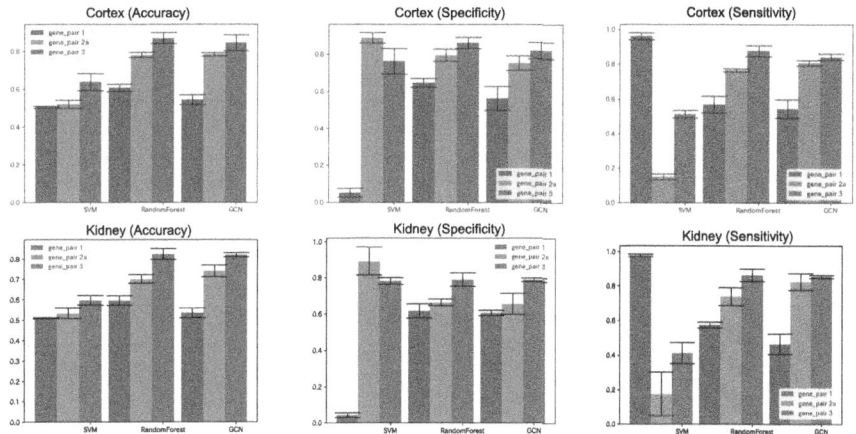

Fig. 4. Results of experiment 1 (adult mouse cortex and kidney). Comparison of accuracy between models and methods selecting positive examples using the confidence of interaction.

3.2   Dataset Used

In this study, we utilize the Visum dataset obtained from adult mouse cortex published by 10x Genomics [2]. This Visum dataset contains expression data for 17,145 genes in 2,264 spots. The number of positive examples extracted from this dataset vir CellPhoneDB have 845 (gene pair 1), 362 (gene pair 2), and 203 (gene pair 3), respectively. The same number of negative examples, split in the ratio 2:1 between training and test data. Gene pair 2b is a dataset for 2-fold cross-validation consisting of two datasets, with the total number of positive and negative samples being 256 and 468, respectively.

As a reference, we also show the results of an experiment using Visium data obtained from mouse kidneys [1].

4   Results and Discussion

4.1   Experiment 1

The results of experiments 1 are shown in Fig. 4. The top three columns show the results of Cortex data, and the bottom three columns show the results of Kidney data. From left to right, Accuracy, Specificity, and Sensitivity are shown, respectively.

Blue represents the results when gene pair 1 was used for positive examples, orange represents for gene pair 2a, and green represents when gene pair 3 are input to the model. The graphs indicate that the accuracy increases in order of gene pair 1, 2a, and 3 for all methods. It can also be seen that Specificity and Sensitivity increased for RandomForest and GCN. Comparing the proposed method (GCN) with the conventional method, the results for Accuracy are better than those of SVM and about the same as those of Random Forest.

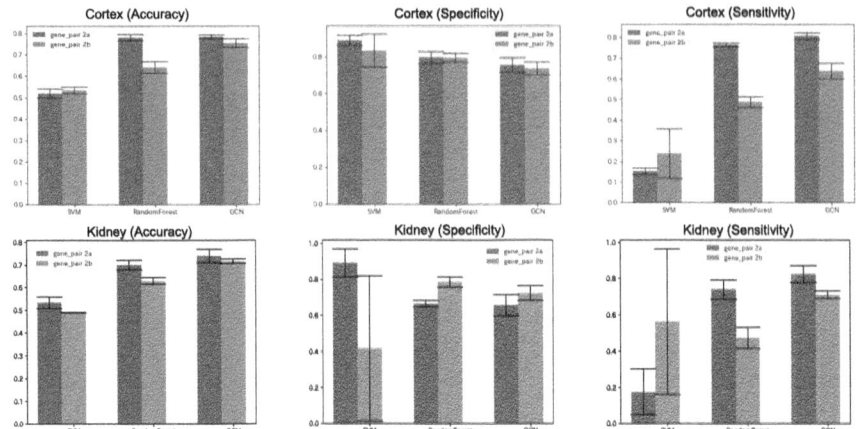

Fig. 5. Results of experiment 2 (adult mouse cortex and kidney). Comparison of accuracy between training and test data separation strategy.

It was confirmed that the selection of only LR-pairs that are actually expressed in the data as positive examples is an important one that affects the accuracy of the model, and that LR-pairs that are expressed over a wide range provide better quality training data.

4.2   Experiment 2

The results of experiments 2 are shown in Fig. 5. The top three columns show the results of Cortex data, and the bottom three columns show the results of Kidney data. From left to right, Accuracy, Specificity, and Sensitivity are shown, respectively. This experiment assesses the impact of the method of splitting the training and test data on estimation accuracy.

Overall, the results tend to be worse when gene pair 2b is used than when gene pair 2a is used. Looking at the Accuracy, we see that when gene pair 2a is used, the results of RandomForest and GCN are about the same. In contrast, when gene pair 2b is used, Random Forest's accuracy drops by 1.5–2.0, while GCN maintains a similar accuracy.

It is thought that when ligand or receptor A is included in the training data, RandomForest learns by capturing the tendency of receptor or ligand that interact with A in the training data, so it may be strong for a dataset such as gene pair 2a, but weak for a dataset such as gene pair 2b. This could also be considered a sort of information leakage in supervised learning, as warned in the GCNG article. In contrast, GCN learns to understand the relationship between interacting LR-pair, so it should be able to make predictions with similar accuracy on a data set such as gene pair 2b. Thus, the GCN-based model can make predictions with the same level of accuracy even for data containing ligand and receptor that are not in the training set, indicating that our method has high generalization performance.

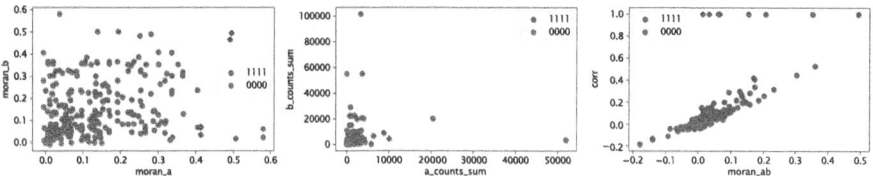

Fig. 6. Characteristics of LR-pairs in predicted patterns 0000 and 1111 (adult mouse cortex)

4.3   Experiment 3

When the adjacency matrices created by Pattern 1, 2, 3, and 4 were used to calculate Accuracy, Specificity, and Sensitivity, the results were similar for each adjacency matrix (data not shown). However, in each adjacency matrix, the LR-pairs that could be correctly predicted as positive examples were different, and this was thought to be influenced by how the genes were expressed.

Therefore, we investigate the characteristics of the LR-pairs obtained with the adjacency matrix of each pattern. Encode and demonstrate which patterns of LR-pairs were successfully predicted and which pairs could not be predicted using a binary sequence. The labels 0000 and 1000 are 4-bit numbers that represent the adjacency matrices (Pattern 1, 2, 3, and 4) starting from the top digit, and are 1 if they can be predicted for each adjacency matrix and 0 if not. That is, the label 0000 represents LR-pairs that could not be predicted correctly in all adjacency matrices, and the label 1000 represents LR-pairs that could be predicted correctly only in the adjacency matrix of Pattern 1.

To analyze characteristics from the expression of gene pairs, we compute the correlation coefficient, Moran I, and the sum of the expression levels for the LR-pairs that are correctly predicted as positive examples for each prediction pattern. Moran I is a spatial autocorrelation measure characterized by the correlation of signals between neighboring locations in space. A value of Moran I close to 0 indicates that the expressed spots are distributed, and a value close to 1 indicates that the expressed spots are densely packed.

Figure 6 shows the results of these plots. When considering the interaction between "gene a" and "gene b", "moran a" and "moran b" are the Moran I of "gene a" and "gene b" for all spots, and a value close to 0 indicates that the expressed spots are distributed, and a value close to 1 indicates that the expressed spots are clustered. "count sum a" and "count sum b" are the sum of the expression levels of "gene a and b" at each spot. "moran ab" is the moran I between the expression of the two genes, and corr is the correlation coefficient of the expression vectors of the two genes.

The label 0000 is a LR-pair that cannot be correctly predicted as a positive example in all adjacency matrices and experimental results suggest that the following two features may be responsible for the difficulty in prediction.

–   Low expression of at least one of the genes

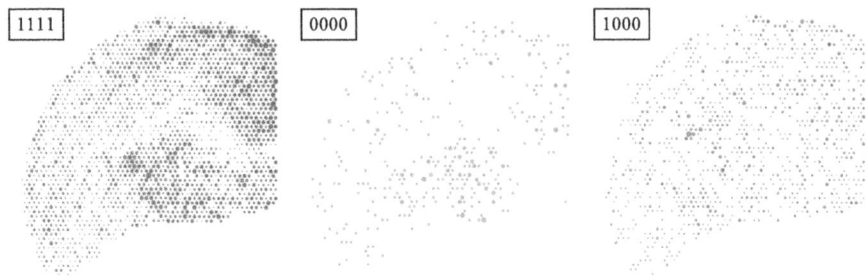

Fig. 7. The actual spatial expression pattern of the LR-pair in the mouse cortex data. Red circle indicates the expression level of gene A, while blue represents the expression level of gene B. (Color figure online)

– No correlation between the two genes

Figure 7 shows the spatial expression patterns of the specifically identified LR-pairs. The expression levels of 1111 shows strong expression of both genes overall, whereas in the case of 0000, only one of the genes is expressed. From label 1000, it seems that the model using the adjacency matrix Pattern 1 may be better at predicting LR-pairs that have the characteristics described above that make prediction difficult. The adjacency matrix of Pattern 1 is a unit matrix in which each node is connected to only itself by an edge. The two characteristics described above indicate a graph in which each node has few features and the relationship between nodes is thin, and it is thought that convolution of such a graph will reduce the feature values of each node, making prediction difficult. On the other hand, since the adjacency matrix of Pattern 1 is a unit matrix, the feature size after convolution is not so small, and it is thought that it tends to predict better than others for graphs with the above features. Conversely, models using the adjacency matrix of Pattern 1 tend to have difficulty predicting LR-pairs for other expression patterns because they cannot account for adjacencies. One advantage of the proposed method is that it can take into account LR-pair features that are easily predicted by the adjacency matrix creation policy.

5   Conclusion

In this study, we proposed a method for estimating cell–cell interactions using GCN, tailored to Visium data. This approach leverages more cost-effective spatial transcriptomics data to predict interactions. We assessed the impact of different configurations of the input adjacency and expression matrices on the model's predictions by experimenting with various patterns. Experiment 1 highlighted that the strategy for constructing the training labels significantly influences model accuracy. In Experiment 2, we demonstrated that our method considering spatial information effectively handles unknown ligands or receptors and exhibits strong generalization capabilities. In Experiment 3, while changes in the adjacency matrix did not affect the overall accuracy, variations in the types of detected LR pairs did arise due to different interaction styles. This suggests that interactions occurring within the same cell or between adjacent cells, such as autocrine or juxtacrine interactions, are better predicted using a compact adjacency matrix. Conversely, interactions between distant cells, such as paracrine or endocrine interactions, tend to be more accurately estimated with graphs that connect a broader range of areas.

Although some parameters, like the number of graph convolutions, were consistent with those used in GCNG, their optimality for Visium data remains uncertain; thus, re-evaluating these settings could enhance accuracy. Furthermore, some LR-pairs consistently predicted as negative across all adjacency matrix configurations might actually represent undiscovered interactions, investigating which poses an important avenue for future research.

Acknowledgments. This work was partially supported by JSPS KAKENHI Grant Numbers JP22H05085, JP22K12246 and JP23K21389.

Disclosure of Interests. The authors have no competing interests to declare that are relevant to the content of this article.

References

1. 10x genomics, mouse kidney section (coronal), spatial gene expression dataset by space ranger 1.1.0 (2020)
2. 10x genomics, adult mouse brain (ffpe), spatial gene expression dataset by space ranger 1.3.0 (2021)
3. Browaeys, R., Saelens, W., Saeys, Y.: Nichenet: modeling intercellular communication by linking ligands to target genes. Nat. Methods **17**(2), 159–162 (2020). https://doi.org/10.1038/s41592-019-0667-5
4. Dries, R., Zhu, Q., Dong, R., Eng, C.H.L., Li, H., et al.: Giotto: a toolbox for integrative analysis and visualization of spatial expression data. Genome Biol. **22**, 1–31 (2021). https://doi.org/10.1186/s13059-021-02286-2
5. Efremova, M., Vento-Tormo, M., Teichmann, S.A., Vento-Tormo, R.: Cell PhoneDB: inferring cell-cell communication from combined expression of multi-subunit ligand-receptor complexes. Nat. Protoc. **15**(4), 1484–1506 (2020). https://doi.org/10.1038/s41596-020-0292-x
6. Elkan, C., Noto, K.: Learning classifiers from only positive and unlabeled data. In: Proceedings of the 14th ACM SIGKDD International Conference on Knowledge Discovery and Data Mining, pp. 213–220 (2008)
7. Jin, S., Guerrero-Juarez, C.F., Zhang, L., Chang, I., Ramos, R., et al.: Inference and analysis of cell-cell communication using cell chat. Nat. Commun. **12**(1), 1088 (2021). https://doi.org/10.1038/s41467-021-21246-9
8. Jin, S., Plikus, M.V., Nie, Q.: Cellchat for systematic analysis of cell-cell communication from single-cell and spatially resolved transcriptomics. BioRxiv, pp. 2023–11 (2023). https://doi.org/10.1101/2023.11.05.565674
9. Joost, S., Jacob, T., Sun, X., Annusver, K., La Manno, G., et al.: Single-cell transcriptomics of traced epidermal and hair follicle stem cells reveals rapid adaptations during wound healing. Cell Rep. **25**(3), 585–597 (2018). https://doi.org/10.1016/j.celrep.2018.09.059

10. Kipf, T.N., Welling, M.: Semi-supervised classification with graph convolutional networks. ArXiv Preprint ArXiv:1609.02907 (2016). https://doi.org/10.48550/arXiv.1609.02907
11. Kirouac, D.C., Ito, C., Csaszar, E., Roch, A., Yu, M., et al.: Dynamic interaction networks in a hierarchically organized tissue. Mol. Syst. Biol. **6**(1), 417 (2010). https://doi.org/10.1038/msb.2010.71
12. Pham, D., Tan, X., Xu, J., Grice, L.F., Lam, P.Y., et al.: stlearn: integrating spatial location, tissue morphology and gene expression to find cell types, cell-cell interactions and spatial trajectories within undissociated tissues. Nat. Commun. **14**(1), 7739 (2023). https://doi.org/10.1038/s41467-023-43120-6
13. Rieckmann, J.C., Geiger, R., Hornburg, D., Wolf, T., Kveler, K., et al.: Social network architecture of human immune cells unveiled by quantitative proteomics. Nat. Immunol. **18**(5), 583–593 (2017). https://doi.org/10.1038/ni.3693
14. Seo, Y., Defferrard, M., Vandergheynst, P., Bresson, X.: Structured sequence modeling with graph convolutional recurrent networks. In: Neural Information Processing: 25th International Conference, ICONIP 2018, Siem Reap, Cambodia, December 13-16, 2018, Proceedings, Part I, vol. 25, pp. 362–373. Springer (2018)
15. Ståhl, P.L., Salmén, F., Vickovic, S., Lundmark, A., Navarro, J.F., et al.: Visualization and analysis of gene expression in tissue sections by spatial transcriptomics. Science **353**(6294), 78–82 (2016). https://doi.org/10.1126/science.aaf2403
16. Yuan, Y., Bar-Joseph, Z.: GCNG: graph convolutional networks for inferring gene interaction from spatial transcriptomics data. Genome Biol. **21**(1), 1–16 (2020). https://doi.org/10.1186/s13059-020-02214-w

Natural Product-Like Compound Generation with Chemical Language Models

Koh Sakano, Kairi Furui[ID], and Masahito Ohue[✉][ID]

School of Computing, Institute of Science Tokyo, Yokohama, Kanagawa, Japan
{sakano,furui}@li.comp.isct.ac.jp, ohue@comp.isct.ac.jp

Abstract. Natural products are substances produced by organisms in nature and often possess biological activity and structural diversity. Drug development based on natural products has been common for many years. However, the intricate structures of these compounds present challenges in terms of structure determination and synthesis, particularly compared to the efficiency of high-throughput screening of synthetic compounds. In recent years, deep learning-based methods have been applied to the generation of molecules. In this study, we trained chemical language models on a natural product dataset and generated natural product-like compounds. The results showed that the distribution of the compounds generated was similar to that of natural products. We also evaluated the effectiveness of the generated compounds as drug candidates. Our method can be used to explore the vast chemical space and reduce the time and cost of drug discovery of natural products.

Keywords: Natural product · Chemical language model · Deep learning · Drug discovery

1 Introduction

Natural products derived from plants and microorganisms have garnered significant attention for their beneficial properties and diverse biological activities [6,8]. These compounds are known for their complex structures and large molecular weights. Because they are biosynthesized within living organisms, many of them display potent biological activities and are often used as lead compounds in drug development. Between 1981 and 2002, natural products accounted for over 60% and 75% of the new chemical entities (NCEs) developed for cancer and infectious diseases, respectively [22]. Moreover, approximately half of the drugs currently available on the market are derived from natural products [7], underscoring their vital role in drug discovery and development.

The unique molecular structures of natural products, which are rarely found in synthetic compounds, contribute to their biological activity [8]. The golden age of natural products drug discovery began in the 1940s with the discovery of penicillin. Many drugs were discovered from microbes, especially actinomycetes

© The Author(s), under exclusive license to Springer Nature Switzerland AG 2025
H. R. Arabnia et al. (Eds.): CSCE 2024, CCIS 2256, pp. 153–166, 2025.
https://doi.org/10.1007/978-3-031-85638-9_12

and fungi, until the early 1970s. However, from the late 1980s to early 1990s, new drug discoveries from natural products declined [25]. Pharmaceutical companies began to withdraw from natural product research due to the emergence of combinatorial chemistry and high-throughput screening (HTS), which allowed for artificial creation of chemical diversity. Additionally, the complexity of natural product structures made synthesis and derivatization difficult, complicating lead compound optimization [20,31]. Despite these challenges, natural products have recently been reassessed and are once again gaining attention as valuable resources in drug discovery due to their diverse structures and biological activities [25].

In recent years, advances in deep learning-based molecular generation have been used for the discovery of novel pharmaceuticals [2]. This approach involves the virtual generation of compounds on computers, with the aim of identifying useful candidate molecules. However, because the training process typically utilizes general chemical databases comprising relatively small molecules such as PubChem [17], there are challenges to generate large and complex compounds similar to natural products. Consequently, this limitation narrows the chemical space that can be explored [15].

In this study, we propose a molecular generation model capable of producing natural product-like compounds. By generating a group of molecules using a model that has learned the distribution of natural products, we aim to facilitate the search for lead molecules in drug discovery and reduce the costs of natural product-based drug development.

A closely related previous study to this research is the work of Tay *et al.*, who used a recurrent neural network (RNN) to generate natural products [33]. They trained an RNN equipped with LSTM units on natural products from the COCONUT database [32] and developed a model capable of generating compounds similar to natural products. They showed that the distribution of the NP Score of the compounds generated was similar to that of the natural products in COCONUT. This study aims to create a more high-performance model using Transformers compared to the approach of Tay *et al.*, and further evaluates whether the generated library is useful as a candidate for pharmaceuticals.

2   Methods

2.1   Fine-Tuning and Chemical Language Models

Fine-tuning language models is a technique that refines models, initially trained on extensive datasets, to excel in particular tasks, tailoring them to specialized requirements. In this study, we fine-tuned chemical language models using a natural product dataset. A chemical language model refers to a model that processes string representations of molecules, e.g., simplified molecular-input line-entry system (SMILES) [34] and self-referencing embedded strings (SELFIES) [18]. Examples of these string representations are shown in Fig. 1. We hypothesized that since pre-trained models have already learned chemical structures, we can efficiently construct a model capable of generating natural product-like compounds.

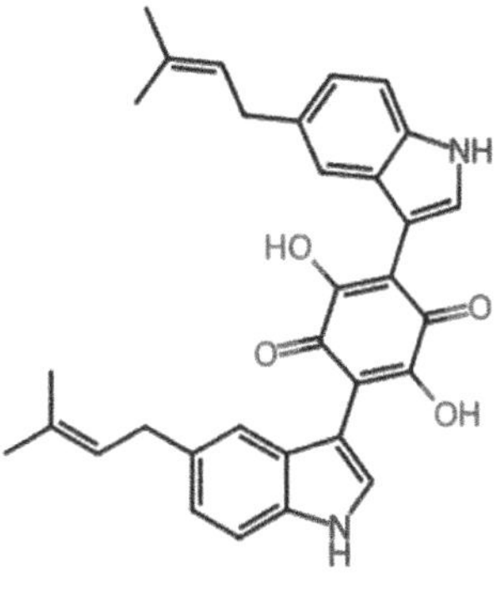

SMILES

O=C1C(O)=C(C(=O)C(O)=C1C2=CNC=3C=CC(=CC32)CC=C(C)C
)C4=CNC=5C=CC(=CC54)CC=C(C)C

SELFIES

[C][C][Branch1][C][C][=C][C][C][=C][C][=C][NH1][C]
[=C][Branch2][Ring2][=N][C][=C][Branch1][C][O][C][
=Branch1][C][=O][C][Branch2][Ring1][#Branch1][C][=
C][NH1][C][=C][C][=C][Branch1][Branch2][C][C][=C][
Branch1][C][C][C][C][=C][Ring1][=C][Ring1][O][=C][
Branch1][C][O][C][Ring2][Ring1][#Branch1][=O][C][R
ing2][Ring1][=N][=C][Ring2][Ring1][P]

Cochliodinol

Fig. 1. Examples of SMILES and SELFIES encoding (cochliodinol, a natural product compound)

2.2 Dataset

We used the COCONUT database, which encompasses approximately 400,000 natural products [32]. As a preprocessing step, we standardized the SMILES strings and removed large compounds (with an atom count greater than 150 or more than 10 rings). Subsequently, we employed a technique that enumerates SMILES by randomizing the traversal order of the molecular graph [3], augmenting the data by approximately nine times. The final dataset included approximately 3.6 million entries and was used for the fine-tuning process.

2.3 Models

We selected pretrained models that satisfy the following criteria:

- It has been trained on a dataset of significant size.
- It is a decoder-only model that utilizes only the decoder of a transformer architecture.

We selected two models, smiles-gpt [1] and ChemGPT [11]. The details of the models are shown in Table 1. Both models used the PubChem-10M dataset [5] for pretraining (smiles-gpt used the first 5 million molecules of PubChem-10M), and their architecture is based on GPT. They differ in the molecular string representation used: smiles-gpt employs SMILES, whereas ChemGPT uses SELFIES.

2.4 Training

We fine-tuned the models on the natural product dataset using the AdamW optimizer [21]. The learning rate was set from 5.0×10^{-4} to 5.0×10^{-8} (using a cosine annealing schedule) for smiles-gpt and 5.0×10^{-5} for ChemGPT. The

Table 1. Pretrained models used in this study.

Model	Molecular representation	Pretraining dataset	Architecture	Number of parameters
smiles-gpt	SMILES	PubChem-10M (first half)	GPT-2 [28]	24.8M
ChemGPT	SELFIES	PubChem-10M	GPT-Neo [4]	19M

batch size was set to 256 and 32 for smiles-gpt and ChemGPT, respectively. Due to the lengthy nature of SELFIES and their substantial byte size, the use of SELFIES in ChemGPT necessitated a reduction in batch size due to the constraints imposed by GPU memory capacity. This training was conducted on four GeForce RTX 3090 GPUs.

3   Results and Discussion

3.1   Evaluation of Generated Molecules

We calculated validity, uniqueness, novelty, internal diversity [26], and Fréchet ChemNet Distance (FCD) [27] for the 100 million molecules generated and made public in a previous study [33], as well as for the 100 million molecules generated by fine-tuned ChemGPT and smiles-gpt.

- Validity: The ratio of valid molecules to the total number of generated molecules. A valid molecule is one that can be parsed by RDKit [19].
- Uniqueness: The ratio of unique molecules to the total number of generated molecules.
- Novelty: The ratio of molecules that do not exist in the COCONUT database.
- Internal diversity: The average pairwise Tanimoto similarity between the generated molecules, calculated using Morgan fingerprints with a radius of 2 and 1024 bits. This metric was calculated using MOSES [26].
- FCD: A metric of the distance between the distribution of generated molecules and that of training dataset. A smaller FCD indicates that the set of generated molecules are closer to the training data distribution.

The results are shown in Table 2. smiles-gpt achieved results close to those of a previous study [33]. Compared to Tay *et al.*, the smaller FCD suggests that more compounds similar to natural products were generated, indicating sampling from a smaller chemical space that is better adapted to the space of natural products. In this respect, it has managed to generate compounds more closely resembling natural products than the previous study.

ChemGPT exhibited high validity, which is believed to be due to the use of SELFIES. However, the significantly large FCD indicates that the distribution of natural products was not captured accurately. Although high uniqueness and novelty are numerically positive outcomes, the magnitude of FCD suggests sampling from a broader chemical space, resulting in the generation of compounds that appear to be nearly random.

Table 2. Values of metrics for the generated set of 100 million molecules.

Model	Validity ↑	Uniqueness ↑	Novelty ↑	Internal diversity ↑	FCD ↓
Tay *et al.* [33]	0.904	0.753	0.998	**0.885**	1.794
smiles-gpt (fine-tuned)	0.903	0.663	0.996	0.873	**1.290**
ChemGPT (fine-tuned)	**0.999**	**0.939**	**0.999**	0.882	14.28

3.2 Visualization of the Distribution in Physicochemical Space of Generated Molecules

We visualized the distribution of molecules generated by the original and fine-tuned models, along with COCONUT compounds, using t-distributed stochastic neighbor embedding (t-SNE). We randomly selected 2,000 molecules from the generated ones and embedded them in two dimensions using t-SNE based on 209 physicochemical descriptors for each molecule. For the calculation of the descriptors, we utilized `Descriptors.CalcMolDescriptors` from RDKit. The visualization results are shown in Figs. 2 and 3.

From the smiles-gpt results in Fig. 2, it appears that the overall distribution of the molecules has moved closer to COCONUT through fine-tuning. In contrast, as shown in Fig. 3, ChemGPT still exhibits a different distribution from COCONUT even after fine-tuning.

3.3 Distribution of Scores for Generated Molecules

We calculated the natural product-likeness score (NP score) [9] and the synthetic accessibility score (SA score) [10] for molecules generated by the original model and the model after fine-tuning, as well as for molecules generated in the previous research by Tay *et al.*, and compared their distributions with those of the natural product data. Kernel density estimation was performed on the NP and SA score data for each molecular library, and the results are plotted in Figs. 4 and 5.

The NP score is an index that measures the natural product-likeness of a compound, calculated based on the frequency of occurrence of substructures in natural products. The SA score is an index used to quantitatively assess the synthetic accessibility of a compound, where a lower score indicates a greater ease of synthesis.

smiles-gpt, through fine-tuning, has approached a distribution of both NP scores and SA scores closer to those of COCONUT, whereas ChemGPT continues to generate compounds with a significantly different distribution from COCONUT even after fine-tuning. Furthermore, in comparison to previous research, the fine-tuned smiles-gpt is capable of generating compounds that are closer to those in COCONUT, particularly in terms of SA score.

From the above results, it is evident that fine-tuned smiles-gpt can generate compounds that are more reminiscent of natural products compared to fine-tuned ChemGPT. Although it is difficult to make a definitive statement due to differences in training conditions and model specifics, it is believed that the

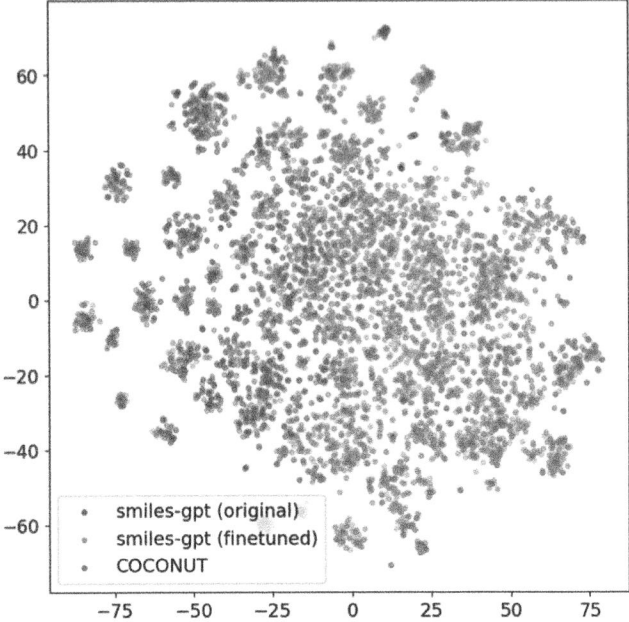

Fig. 2. t-SNE visualization of 2,000 molecules generated by the original and fine-tuned models of smiles-gpt, along with molecules from COCONUT.

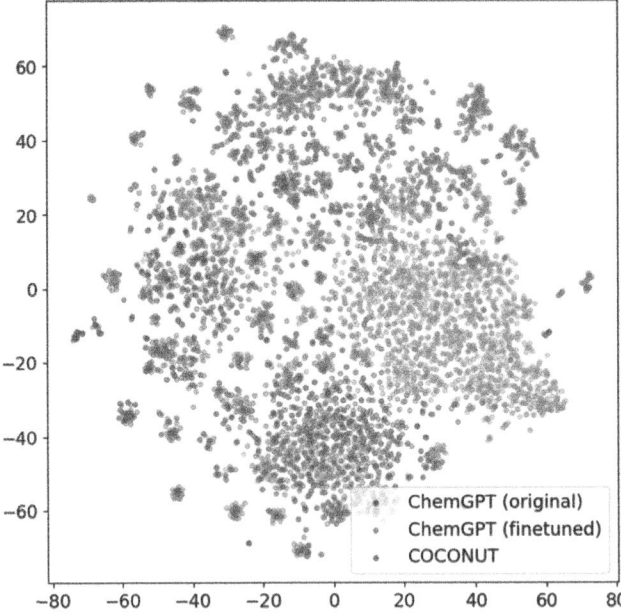

Fig. 3. t-SNE visualization of 2,000 molecules generated by the original and fine-tuned models of ChemGPT, along with molecules from COCONUT.

distinction between SMILES and SELFIES plays a significant role. Although it is advantageous that SELFIES are 100% valid, they appear to be a more verbose and relatively less intuitive molecular representation compared to SMILES.

Comparative studies between SMILES and SELFIES have reported that SMILES-trained models exhibit better performance [13,14]. Although the lower validity of SMILES has been a concern, current language models have become sufficiently adept at learning the syntax of SMILES. Gao *et al.* have pointed out that the advantage of SELFIES being 100% valid is decreasing [13].

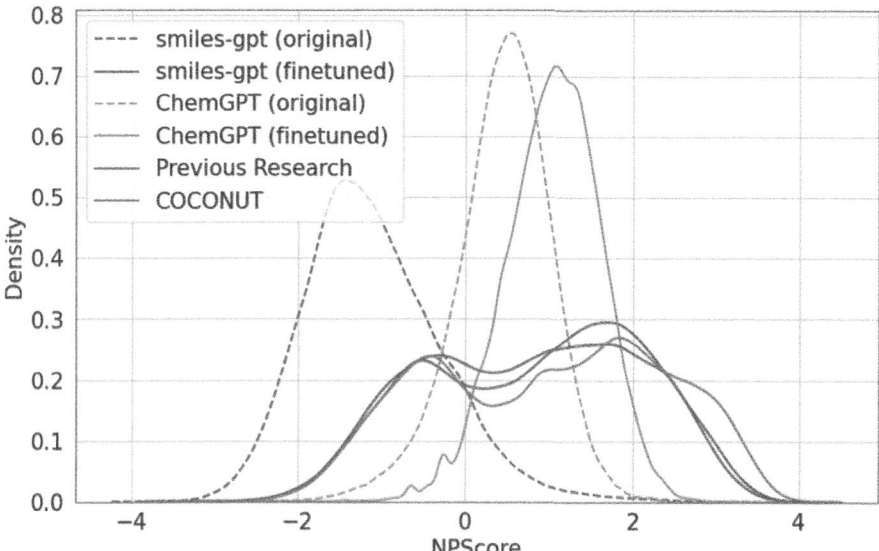

Fig. 4. Kernel density estimation of NP scores for molecules generated by the original and fine-tuned models of smiles-gpt and ChemGPT, compared with molecules generated in the previous research (Tay *et al.* [33]) and natural products from COCONUT.

3.4 Evaluation of Bioactivity Potential by Protein–Ligand Docking

The utility of the generated compound library as potential drug candidates was evaluated through protein–ligand docking calculations with proteins. We evaluated the viability of these compounds for pharmaceutical use from protein–ligand interactions.

For the target protein, the epidermal growth factor receptor (EGFR) was selected. Inhibition of EGFR has been reported to significantly suppress cancer cell proliferation [23], and several EGFR inhibitors have been developed as pharmaceuticals. Gefitinib and erlotinib are among the well-known inhibitor drugs. In this experiment, the crystal structure of EGFR with PDB ID: 2ITY [36] was used, which is the complex structure of EGFR and gefitinib.

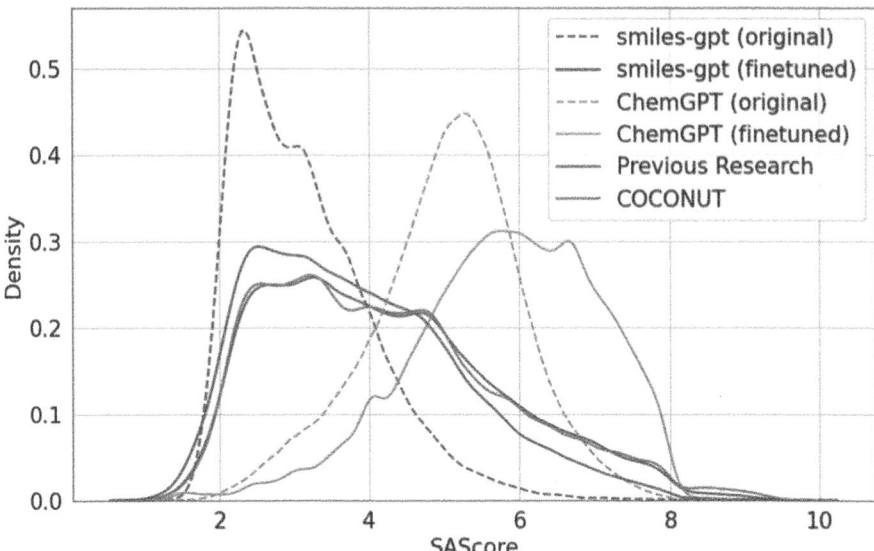

Fig. 5. Kernel density estimation of SA scores for molecules generated by the original and fine-tuned models of smiles-gpt and ChemGPT, compared with molecules generated in the previous research (Tay *et al.* [33]) and natural products from COCONUT.

Initially, 1,000 molecules were randomly selected as ligands from those generated by the fine-tuned smiles-gpt. As indicated in the results above, because the fine-tuned ChemGPT was unable to generate natural product-like compounds, molecules generated by ChemGPT were not used for docking. Subsequently, the ligands were prepared using Schrödinger LigPrep [30], and the generated 12,930 conformers were docked using Schrödinger Glide software version 2020-2 [12].

The distribution of GlideScores for each conformation obtained from the docking is shown in Fig. 6. The GlideScore represents the predicted binding free energy between a protein and a ligand, with lower values indicating stronger binding. Although the GlideScore for gefitinib is -7.02 kcal/mol [24], there are 1,216 conformations with a better score than gefitinib, accounting for 9.8% of all docked conformations. Among these, the lowest GlideScore was -11.51 kcal/mol. This indicates that a significant number of compounds with docking scores that are better than those of existing inhibitors have been generated.

Table 3 presents the top 10 compounds with the best GlideScores of the 1,000 compounds subjected to docking, together with the natural products of the COCONUT database that exhibited the highest similarity to each of these compounds. Although compounds with substructures similar to those of gefitinib were generated, most have relatively complex structures. Furthermore, observing similar natural products reveals that the model has successfully learned to build scaffolds of natural products. Figure 7 shows the docking pose of the compound with the best GlideScore.

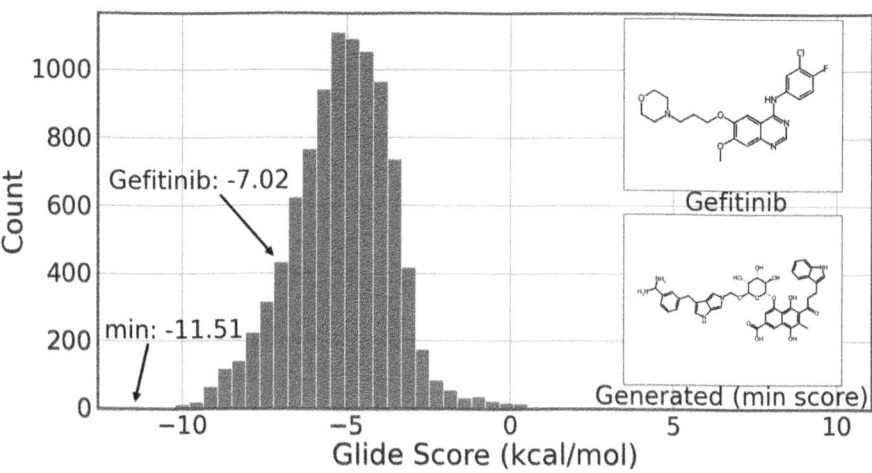

Fig. 6. Distribution of GlideScore for 12,930 docked conformations of 1,000 molecules generated by fine-tuned smiles-gpt.

Furthermore, to verify whether natural product-likeness influences drug-likeness, we calculated the similarity between the natural products and the compounds subjected to docking and investigated the correlation. The Tanimoto index of the ECFP4 fingerprint with a radius of 2 and 2,048 bits was used for similarity measures. For the 1,000 compounds selected for docking, we calculated their mean similarity to all compounds in the COCONUT database and depicted the relationship with the GlideScore in Fig. 8. For compounds with multiple stereoisomers, the one with the minimum GlideScore was chosen. The Pearson correlation coefficient between mean similarity to natural products and GlideScore was $r = -0.313$, indicating a modest correlation. From these results, it can be inferred that compounds with a certain degree of natural product-likeness tend to have better docking scores (although it should be noted that there is a tendency for docking scores to improve as molecular weight increases [29, 37]).

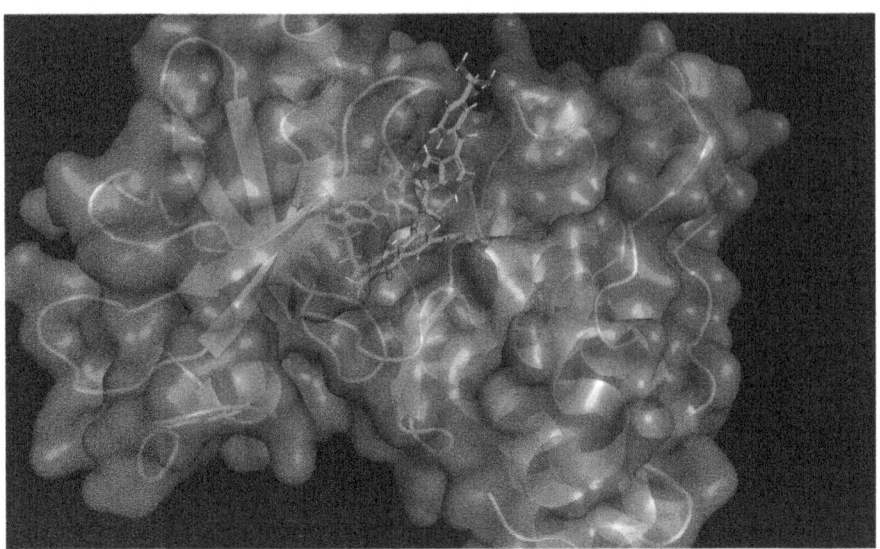

Fig. 7. Docking pose of the compound with the best GlideScore with EGFR.

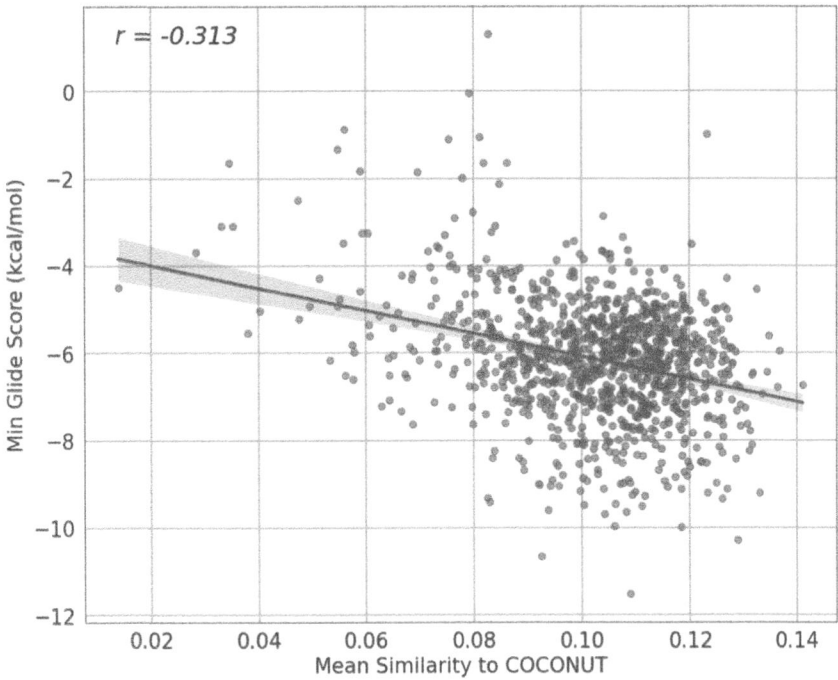

Fig. 8. Relationship between the mean similarity with all compounds in COCONUT and GlideScore for 1,000 molecules generated by fine-tuned smiles-gpt.

Table 3. Structures of the top 10 compounds out of 1,000 compounds, based on GlideScore in the docking experiment, and the natural products with the highest similarity to those compounds

	Structure	Most similar natural product	GlideScore (kcal/mol)
1			−11.51
2			−10.63
3			−10.28
4			−9.99
5			−9.96
6			−9.96
7			−9.96
8			−9.96
9			−9.96
10			−9.96

4 Conclusion

In this research, we fine-tuned a language model pretrained on a natural product dataset to generate natural product-like compounds. We measured various metrics for the molecules generated by the fine-tuned model and demonstrated that they are closer to the distribution of natural products.

In the docking experiments with EGFR, we found that the molecules generated by the fine-tuned smiles-gpt model included viable drug candidates. This illustrates the effectiveness of the language model developed in this research in creating a collection of potential pharmaceutical candidate compounds.

Compared to the previous research by Tay *et al.* [33], we have been able to create a model that generates compounds that are closer to natural products. Furthermore, this study demonstrates the relationship between the similarity of natural products and the potential utility as drug candidates, which distinguishes it from the previous study. Moreover, there is a need to develop methodologies to extract knowledge from functional structures, such as the potential bioactivity of natural products. Visualization studies focusing on substructures [16, 35] may prove to be a valuable tool in this area.

Acknowledgment. This work was financially supported by the Japan Science and Technology Agency FOREST (Grant No. JPMJFR216J), the Japan Society for the Promotion of Science KAKENHI (Grant Nos. JP23H04880 and JP23H04887), and the Japan Agency for Medical Research and Development Basis for Supporting Innovative Drug Discovery and Life Science Research (Grant No. JP23ama121026).

References

1. Adilov, S.: Generative pre-training from molecules. ChemRxiv (10.26434/chemrxiv-2021-5fwjd) (2021)
2. Bilodeau, C., Jin, W., Jaakkola, T., Barzilay, R., Jensen, K.F.: Generative models for molecular discovery: recent advances and challenges. Wiley Interdiscip. Rev. Comput. Mol. Sci. **12**(5) (2022)
3. Bjerrum, E.J.: SMILES enumeration as data augmentation for neural network modeling of molecules. arXiv preprint (arXiv:1703.07076) (2017)
4. Black, S., Gao, L., Wang, P., Leahy, C., Biderman, S.: GPT-Neo: large scale autoregressive language modeling with mesh-tensorflow (2021). https://doi.org/10.5281/zenodo.5297715
5. Chithrananda, S., Grand, G., Ramsundar, B.: ChemBERTa: large-scale self-supervised pretraining for molecular property prediction. arXiv preprint (arXiv:2010.09885) (2020)
6. Cragg, G.M., Newman, D.J.: Natural products: a continuing source of novel drug leads. Biochim. Biophys. Acta **1830**(6), 3670–3695 (2013)
7. Demain, A.L.: Importance of microbial natural products and the need to revitalize their discovery. J. Ind. Microbiol. Biotechnol. **41**(2), 185–201 (2014)
8. Dias, D.A., Urban, S., Roessner, U.: A historical overview of natural products in drug discovery. Metabolites **2**(2), 303–336 (2012)

9. Ertl, P., Roggo, S., Schuffenhauer, A.: Natural product-likeness score and its application for prioritization of compound libraries. J. Chem. Inf. Model. **48**(1), 68–74 (2008)
10. Ertl, P., Schuffenhauer, A.: Estimation of synthetic accessibility score of drug-like molecules based on molecular complexity and fragment contributions. J. Cheminform. **1**(8) (2009)
11. Frey, N.C., et al.: Neural scaling of deep chemical models. Nat. Mach. Intellig. **5**, 1297–1305 (2023)
12. Friesner, R.A., et al.: Glide: a new approach for rapid, accurate docking and scoring. 1. method and assessment of docking accuracy. J. Med. Chem. **47**(7), 1739–1749 (2004)
13. Gao, W., Fu, T., Sun, J., Coley, C.: Sample efficiency matters: a benchmark for practical molecular optimization. Adv. Neural. Inf. Process. Syst. **35**, 21342–21357 (2022)
14. Ghugare, R., Miret, S., Hugessen, A., Phielipp, M., Berseth, G.: Searching for high-value molecules using reinforcement learning and transformers. In: AI4Mat - NeurIPS 2023 Workshop (2023). https://openreview.net/forum?id=O8mZO2ri33
15. Jin, W., Barzilay, D., Jaakkola, T.: Hierarchical generation of molecular graphs using structural motifs. In: Proceedings of the 37th International Conference on Machine Learning, vol. 119, pp. 4839–4848 (2020)
16. Kengkanna, A., Ohue, M.: Enhancing property and activity prediction and interpretation using multiple molecular graph representations with MMGX. Commun. Chem. **7**(1), 74 (2024)
17. Kim, S., et al.: PubChem 2023 update. Nucleic Acids Res. **51**(D1), D1373–D1380 (2023)
18. Krenn, M., Häse, F., Nigam, A., Friederich, P., Aspuru-Guzik, A.: Self-referencing embedded strings (SELFIES): a 100% robust molecular string representation. Mach. Learn. Sci. Technol. **1**(4), 045024 (2020)
19. Landrum, G., et al.: RDKit: open-source cheminformatics. http://www.rdkit.org
20. Li, J.W.H., Vederas, J.C.: Drug discovery and natural products: end of an era or an endless frontier? Science **325**(5937), 161–165 (2009)
21. Loshchilov, I., Hutter, F.: Decoupled weight decay regularization. arXiv preprint (arXiv:1711.05101) (2017)
22. Newman, D.J., Cragg, G.M.: Natural products as sources of new drugs from 1981 to 2014. J. Nat. Prod. **79**(3), 629–661 (2016)
23. Normanno, N., Bianco, C., De Luca, A., Maiello, M.R., Salomon, D.S.: Target-based agents against ErbB receptors and their ligands: a novel approach to cancer treatment. Endocr. Relat. Cancer **10**(1), 1–21 (2003)
24. Ochiai, T., et al.: Variational autoencoder-based chemical latent space for large molecular structures with 3D complexity. Commun. Chem. **6**(1), 249 (2023)
25. Pelaez, F.: The historical delivery of antibiotics from microbial natural products can history repeat? Biochem. Pharmacol. **71**(7), 981–990 (2006)
26. Polykovskiy, D., et al.: Molecular sets (MOSES): a benchmarking platform for molecular generation models. Front. Pharmacol. **11**, 565644 (2020)
27. Preuer, K., Renz, P., Unterthiner, T., Hochreiter, S., Klambauer, G.: Fréchet ChemNet distance: a metric for generative models for molecules in drug discovery. J. Chem. Inf. Model. **58**(9), 1736–1741 (2018)
28. Radford, A., et al.: Language models are unsupervised multitask learners (2019). https://openai.com/research/better-language-models
29. Reynolds, C.H., Tounge, B.A., Bembenek, S.D.: Ligand binding efficiency: trends, physical basis, and implications. J. Med. Chem. **51**(8), 2432–2438 (2008)

30. Schrödinger, LLC: LigPrep (2023)
31. Shen, B.: A new golden age of natural products drug discovery. Cell **163**(6), 1297–1300 (2015)
32. Sorokina, M., Merseburger, P., Rajan, K., Yirik, M.A., Steinbeck, C.: COCONUT online: collection of open natural products database. J. Cheminform. **13**(1), 2 (2021)
33. Tay, D.W.P., Yeo, N.Z.X., Adaikkappan, K., Lim, Y.H., Ang, S.J.: 67 million natural product-like compound database generated via molecular language processing. Sci. Data **10**(1), 296 (2023)
34. Weininger, D.: SMILES, a chemical language and information system. 1. Introduction to methodology and encoding rules. J. Chem. Inf. Comput. Sci. **28**(1), 31–36 (1988)
35. Wu, Z., et al.: Chemistry-intuitive explanation of graph neural networks for molecular property prediction with substructure masking. Nat. Commun. **14**(1), 2585 (2023)
36. Yun, C.H., et al.: Structures of lung cancer-derived EGFR mutants and inhibitor complexes: mechanism of activation and insights into differential inhibitor sensitivity. Cancer Cell **11**(3), 217–227 (2007)
37. Zhu, H., Yang, J., Huang, N.: Assessment of the generalization abilities of machine-learning scoring functions for structure-based virtual screening. J. Chem. Inf. Model. **62**(22), 5485–5502 (2022)

Improved Early–Modern Japanese Printed Character Recognition Rate with Generated Characters

Norie Koiso[1]([envelope]), Yuki Takemoto[2], Yu Ishikawa[3], and Masami Takata[1]

[1] Nara Women's University, Nara, Japan
xan_koiso@cc.nara-wu.ac.jp, takata@ics.nara-wu.ac.jp
[2] College of Information Science and Engineering Ritsumeikan University,
Osaka, Japan
y-tkmt@fc.ritsumei.ac.jp
[3] Kyoto Women's University, Kyoto, Japan
ishikaway@kyoto-wu.ac.jp

Abstract. The National Diet Library's digital collection contains about $400,000$ valuable books from the Meiji period to the early Showa period. The books are stored as image data and have not been converted into text. Therefore, the use of information is limited. There are manual and automatic methods of texting Early–modern Japanese printed book, but manual methods cost a fortune. OCR is used for automation, but Early–modern Japanese printed book's characteristics reduce recognition rates. Therefore, it is necessary to develop a character recognition method specific to Early–modern Japanese printed book. Collecting Early–modern Japanese printed character is also manual, and it is difficult to collect many characters evenly. In this paper, we propose a method to improve Early–modern Japanese printed character recognition accuracy using images generated from modern characters. CycleGAN is used to generate images of modern characters from modern characters. The generated image is incorporated into train data to create a character recognition model. The experiment showed that the recognition rate was improved by using the generated image in train data.

Keywords: Deep Metric Learning · Early-modern Japanese printed character recognition

1 Introduction

The National Diet Library [4] has published various books on the web as the National Diet Library Digital Collection [9]. About 3.5 million of these books exist as double page image data. There are $400,000$ books published from the Meiji period to the early Showa period. In Early–modern Japanese printed book, there are not only books such as novels, but also books in various fields, such as academic materials, in which you can learn about the culture of the time.

© The Author(s), under exclusive license to Springer Nature Switzerland AG 2025
H. R. Arabnia et al. (Eds.): CSCE 2024, CCIS 2256, pp. 167–181, 2025.
https://doi.org/10.1007/978-3-031-85638-9_13

Many of these Early–modern Japanese printed book books are out of print and are valuable books that are not available today. By storing such Early–modern Japanese printed book as image data in digital collections, the possibility of information loss due to theft or damage has been reduced. However, since the storage format is image data and cannot be converted into text, information such as content retrieval and reading out is not utilized. Against this background, a textualization of Early–modern Japanese printed book is required.

There are two ways to text Early–modern Japanese printed book: manually and automatically. When texting is performed manually, there is an advantage that texting can be performed accurately. However, there are disadvantages such as the huge cost of time and labor. Therefore, it is impractical to convert all 400, 000 books into text manually. On the other hand, when automatic texting is performed, the disadvantage of manual texting can be eliminated. But automatic texting also presents challenges. Modern books can be automatically texted using optical character recognition (Optical Character Recognition, OCR). However, it has been reported that the use of OCR for Early–modern Japanese printed book reduces the recognition rate compared to the use for modern books [8]. It is considered that this is due to the fact that Early–modern Japanese printed character, which is included in Early–modern Japanese printed book, does not have a uniform standard and that ink is blurred or snatched due to printing on letterpress. For these reasons, a character recognition method specific to Early–modern Japanese printed book is necessary for automatically texting Early–modern Japanese printed book. Therefore, character recognition methods and models specific to Early–modern Japanese printed book are being developed [6,13].

It is necessary to prepare a large number and many character types of character images in order to realize Early–modern Japanese printed character recognition with high accuracy and corresponding to many character types. However, the current method for collecting character images is manual segmentation, and it is impossible to collect character images in large quantities. There is also a difference in the frequency of characters. In Early–modern Japanese printed book, it has been reported that characters with high frequency tend to cluster, while characters with low frequency tend to cluster very poorly [3]. For these reasons, it is impossible to prepare a large number and evenly distributed text image of Early–modern Japanese printed book. This situation has become a challenge for Early–modern Japanese printed character recognition to improve accuracy and generalize.

In this paper, we aim to improve the accuracy of Early–modern Japanese printed character recognition by compensating for the lack of Early–modern Japanese printed character by character images generated from printed characters. In the proposed method, a character image generated from printed characters and an Early–modern Japanese printed character are combined to form a train data. A character recognition experiment is performed using train data.

2   Related Work

2.1   Early–Modern Japanese Printed Character Image Generation Using CycleGAN

CycleGAN is an image transformation method using GAN(Generative Adversarial Network) [14]. Generally, GANs have two neural networks called Generator and Discriminator. By performing optimization while these two neural networks compete with each other, it is possible to generate highly accurate images. In CycleGAN, the two GANs are combined to capture the relationship between domains, which is the set of unique features of an image for two data sets. Therefore, in CycleGAN, it is possible to learn the features of two kinds of image data sets which are different domains, respectively, and convert an image of one domain into an image having the features of the other domain. Moreover, since GAN is an unsupervised training method, correct answer data that is paired for each image is not required when training CycleGAN. Therefore, in the research on character recognition, generation of handwritten Japanese character image [2] and style conversion [10] have been proposed. It also does not require paired data for learning, making it very suitable for deep learning in areas where data collection is difficult, and many studies have shown its effectiveness [1,12]. Using such a CycleGAN, data expansion of Early–modern Japanese printed character image is performed.

The flow of image generation is shown in Fig. 1. First, CycleGAN is used to train the relationship between Early–modern Japanese printed character and printed characters, and a trained model is created. The data used for training is a 64×64 pixel grayscale text image of $1,200$ characters each Thus, the characteristics of each image and the relationship between domains can be grasped. In addition, it is possible to find how the features of one domain can be converted into the image of the other domain from the features of the captured image and the relationship between the domains. Next, by inputting the printed character into the trained model, an image in which the feature of the printed character is converted into the feature of Early–modern Japanese printed character is generated. Hereafter, Early–modern Japanese printed character is referred to as "character O" and the generated image is referred to as "character M". It can be confirmed that the character M has features such as blurring and raspiness peculiar to the character O while keeping the shape of the inputted printed character. A comparison with the character O also shows that the character M does not completely reproduce a particular character O.

2.2   Early–Modern Japanese Printed Character Recognition Using Deep Metric Learning

Deep metric learning is a method for evaluating the degree of similarity between input data by comparing feature vectors for each input data after learning a neural network for predicting multi–class classification. In deep metric learning, a feature vector extracted by a neural network for predicting multi–class classification is processed after extraction. This allows the neural network that predicts

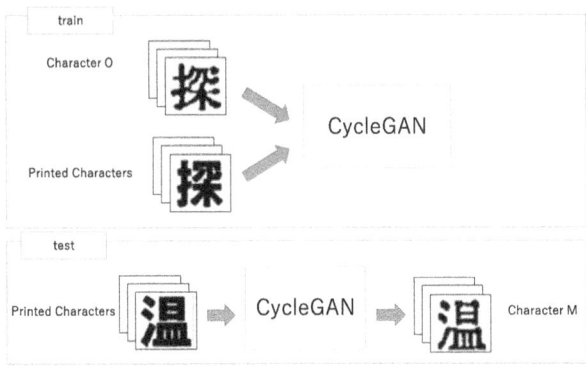

Fig. 1. Flow of image generation

multiclass classification to identify things that could not be linearly separated. In Early–modern Japanese printed character recognition using deep metric learning [13], CNN (Convolutional Neural Network, CNN [7]) is used as a neural network to predict multi–class classification. This is because the accuracy of character O was as high as 95% or more in the previous study [13]. Based on this network, deep metric learning layer is added to the final layer to achieve a more accurate Early–modern Japanese printed character recognition. L2–constrained Softmax [11] is used as deep metric learning layer. L2–constrained Softmax is a constraint added to SoftMax Loss so that the L2 norm of feature extraction is a constant α. As a result, the learning proceeds so that the cosine similarity of the feature vectors becomes large in the case of the same class and small in the case of different classes.

$$\text{minimize} \quad -\frac{1}{M}\sum_{i=1}^{M}\log\frac{e^{W_{y_i}^T f(\mathbf{x}_i)+b_{y_i}}}{\sum_{j=1}^{C}e^{W_j^T f(\mathbf{x}_i)+b_j}} \tag{1}$$
$$\text{subject to} \quad \|f(\mathbf{x}_i)\|_2 = \alpha, \quad \forall i = 1,2,\dots M,$$

This is formulated as follows: (1). x_i is the i–th input data, $f(x_i)$ is the feature vector obtained through the neural network for multi–class classification, M is the mini–batch size, and W_i and b are the weights and biases set in the last layer.

3   Method

In this section, we describe a method to generate a character M with character O characteristics using CycleGAN and utilize it as a character recognition train data. The flow of the proposed method is shown in Fig. 1 and 2. The proposed method is explained in two steps.

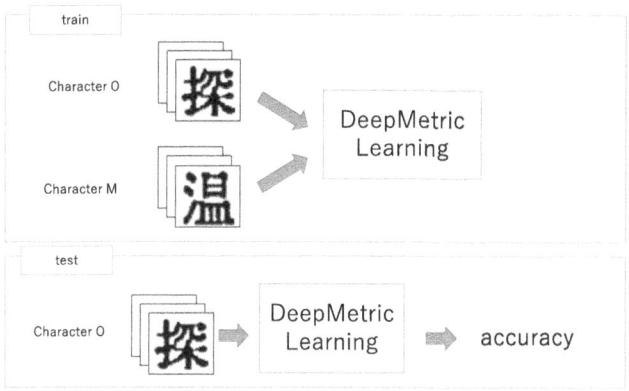

Fig. 2. Flow of character recognition

3.1 Generation of Character Images that Imitate Early–Modern Japanese Printed Characters

The first procedure, the generation of character M images, is described. Figure 1 shows the flow. First, CycleGAN training is described. The data sets used to train CycleGAN are grayscale text images of 64×64 pixels each. Regarding the font used for the image of printed characters, a previous study [5] found that some fonts of printed characters cannot generate character M well, and the shape of the characters is lost. A failure example is shown in Fig. 3. Therefore, the fonts to be used for learning are limited to 41 fonts whose character shapes were preserved in the previous study [5]. Table 1 lists fonts for printed characters. An example of a printed character image and a character O image used for training is shown in Fig. 4. In addition, the type of characters for collecting printing characters in each font shall be 2647 types which character O Image can collect. In the printed character image used for training CycleGAN, $1,200$ images are randomly selected from them. Similarly, $1,200$ character O images are selected at random. Because CycleGAN uses unsupervised training, there is no one–to–one connection between characters across datasets. However, in the image generation as in the existing research, the character types of both character image data sets are common in order to simplify the data set creation. Next, character M image is generated using the trained model of the created CycleGAN. The character types to be generated are $2,647$ types for which character O images exist. An example of a generated character M image is shown in Fig. 5. The font of printed characters to be input to the learned model shall be the same as the font used for training.

3.2 Character Recognition

The second step, character recognition, is described. Figure 2 shows the flow. The model is trained by including character M image generated in the flow of

Fig. 3. Failure example

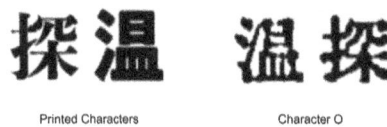

Fig. 4. Example of train data

Fig. 1 in train data. Using the trained model, character O character recognition is performed. The model for character recognition is the same as deep metric learning used in the previous study [6] described in Sect. 2. Figure 6 shows the configuration. There are three convolutional layers, each with a filter count of $(160, 320, 640)$. The filter size shall be $(7 \times 7, 5 \times 5, 3 \times 3)$ per layer. Deep metric learning's training combines character M and character O images into a training dataset. The input image size is a grayscale text image of 64×64 pixels. This data set is input, and a model is trained to recognize characters from each character image. After completion of training, test data is inputted to the learned model to recognize character O image.

4   Experiment

In this section, character recognition experiments are conducted using the generated character M to demonstrate the effectiveness of the proposed method. First, we describe the dataset used for character O recognition using deep metric learning. Next, we compare the results of training by changing the percentage of character M to be included in the train data. The metric for comparison is the recognition rate output from inputting character O into the trained model.

4.1   Dataset

Two types of character O and character M are used in the training dataset. The character O image dataset consists of 6 types of character O. The character

Fig. 5. Generated image example

Table 1. List of fonts for printed characters

A1 Gothic B	New Go U
Arial Unicode MS	Midashigo MB1
BIZ UD Gothic	Kokutai
HGS Gothic E	Shuei Nijimi Kaku Gothic Gold B
HGS Soei presence EB	Shuei Nijimi Kaku Gothic Silver B
HGS Soei Kaku pop	Shuei Nijimi Mincho L
HGS Mincho E	Shuei Karafuto Mincho M
HG Round Gothic M-PRO	Shuei Kaku Gothic Silver B
MigMix	Shuei Round Gothic B
MS Gothic	Shuei Mincho M
UD Digital Kyokasyotai NP-B	New Round Go H
Gothic MB101U	Futo Go B101
Koburina Gothic W6	Chu Gothic BBB
Jun 34	Toppan Bunkyu Gothic DB
Soft Gothic U	Toppan Bunkyu Midashi Mincho EB
Hiragino Kaku Go W9	Migu
Hiragino Kaku Go Orudo W6	Meiryo
Hiragino Kaku Go Orudo W9	Ryumin U
Hiragino Kaku Gothic Std	Ryumin Y20U
Hiragino Round Go W8	Ryumin Y30U
Hiragino Mincho W8	

M image dataset consists of 41 types of character M. In each experiment, the required number of types of character images are randomly extracted from these datasets.

Four types of character recognition experiments will be conducted. In all experiments, the test data shall be one type of character O not used in the train data or validation data. In Experiment 1, 10 different experiments will be conducted. In these experiments, we will check the change in recognition rate due to the change in the ratio of character O to character M in the train data. The data to be used is shown in Table 2. In Experiment 2, eight different experiments will be conducted. In these experiments, we will check the relationship between the number of train data and the recognition rate when there is enough char-

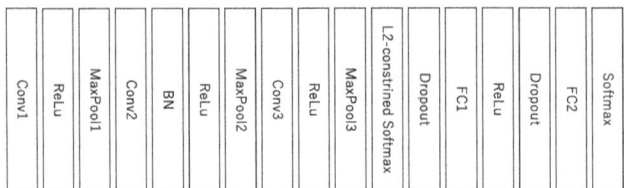

Fig. 6. Deep Metric Learning Structure

acter O. The data used in Experiment 2 are shown in Table 3. In Experiment 3, eight different experiments will be conducted. In these experiments, we will check the relationship between the number of train data and the accuracy of the recognition rate when the number of character O is inadequate. The data used in Experiment 3 are shown in Table 4. In Experiment 4, eight different experiments will be conducted. Among these experiments, we will check the relationship between the number of train data and the accuracy of the recognition rate when character O is not present. The data used in Experiment 4 is shown in Table 5.

4.2   Experiment Result and Discussion

We discuss the results of the experiments. First, the results of Experiment 1 are shown in Fig. 7. In Experiment 1, we checked the change in the accuracy of the recognition rate due to the change in the ratio of character O to character M in the train data. The highest recognition rate is 93.43%, and the highest recognition rate is when the ratio of character M in the train data is 0%. The recognition the accuracy of the recognition rate decreased as the ratio of character M in the train data increased. Therefore, when the train data is 4 pieces per character type, character M is considered to be an obstacle to training. Similarly, even when the validation data is for character M instead of character O, the ratio of character M in the train data decreases as the ratio of character M in the train data rises. However, when comparing the case where the validation data is character O and the case where the validation data is character M within the same ratio, the accuracy of the recognition rate in the case of character M exceeds that in the case of character O in 25%, 50%, and 75% of the cases. Therefore, when the ratio of character M is high, it is more effective to use character M for validation data.

Next, the results of Experiment 2 are shown in Figure 8. In Experiment 2, we checked the relationship between the number of train data and the accuracy of the recognition rate when the character O is sufficiently present in the train data. The highest accuracy of the recognition rate was 97.81%, and the highest recognition rate was achieved when the number of train data was 34 pieces per character type. The highest accuracy of the recognition rate in Experiment 1 was 93.43%, and the accuracy of the recognition rate increased as the number of train data increased. The results of Experiment 2 also show an increase in training data and the accuracy of the recognition rate. Experiment 1 shows that an

Table 2. Dataset used in Experiment 1

Experiment No.	dataset	train data	validation data	test data
Experiment 1–1	character O	4	1	1
	character M	-	-	-
Experiment 1–2	character O	3	1	1
	character M	1	-	-
Experiment 1–3	character O	2	1	1
	character M	2	-	-
Experiment 1–4	character O	1	1	1
	character M	3	-	-
Experiment 1–5	character O	-	1	1
	character M	4	-	-
Experiment 1–6	character O	4	-	1
	character M	-	1	-
Experiment 1–7	character O	3	-	1
	character M	1	1	-
Experiment 1–8	character O	2	-	1
	character M	2	1	-
Experiment 1–9	character O	1	-	1
	character M	3	1	-
Experiment 1–10	character O	-	-	1
	character M	4	1	-

increase in the ratio of character M in the train data hinders training. However, from Experiment 2, it can be said that a large increase in the overall number of train data by utilizing not only character O but also character M is effective in improving the accuracy of the recognition rate. However, when the number of character M in the train data becomes 40, the recognition rate decreases both when the validation data is character O and when the validation data is character M. This is believed to be due to the fact that the ratio of character O in the train data is too low. Therefore, we can see that the number of train data should be watered down below a certain level. Furthermore, a comparison is made for each validation data. In the experiments with 20 or more pieces of character M, the accuracy of the recognition rate when the validation data is character M is higher than the accuracy of the recognition rate when the validation data is character O. Therefore, similar to the results of Experiment 1, the results show that it is more effective to use character M as the validation data when training data that contains a large number of character M.

Next, the results of Experiment 3 are shown in Fig. 9. In Experiment 3, we checked the relationship between the number of train data and the accuracy of the recognition rate when the number of character O in the train data is insuffi-

Table 3. Dataset used in Experiment 2

Experiment No.	dataset	train data	validation data	test data
Experiment 2–1	character O	4	1	1
	character M	10	-	-
Experiment 2–2	character O	4	1	1
	character M	20	-	-
Experiment 2–3	character O	4	1	1
	character M	30	-	-
Experiment 2–4	character O	4	1	1
	character M	40	-	-
Experiment 2–5	character O	4	-	1
	character M	10	1	-
Experiment 2–6	character O	4	-	1
	character M	20	1	-
Experiment 2–7	character O	4	-	1
	character M	30	1	-
Experiment 2–8	character O	4	-	1
	character M	40	1	-

Table 4. Dataset used in Experiment 3

Experiment No.	dataset	train data	validation data	test data
Experiment 3–1	character O	1	1	1
	character M	10	-	-
Experiment 3–2	character O	1	1	1
	character M	20	-	-
Experiment 3–3	character O	1	1	1
	character M	30	-	-
Experiment 3–4	character O	1	1	1
	character M	40	-	-
Experiment 3–5	character O	1	-	1
	character M	10	1	-
Experiment 3–6	character O	1	-	1
	character M	20	1	-
Experiment 3–7	character O	1	-	1
	character M	30	1	-
Experiment 3–8	character O	1	-	1
	character M	40	1	-

Table 5. Dataset used in Experiment 4

Experiment No.	dataset	train data	validation data	test data
Experiment 4–1	character O	1	1	1
	character M	10	-	-
Experiment 4–2	character O	1	1	1
	character M	20	-	-
Experiment 4–3	character O	1	1	1
	character M	30	-	-
Experiment 4–4	character O	1	1	1
	character M	40	-	-
Experiment 4–5	character O	0	-	1
	character M	10	1	-
Experiment 4–6	character O	0	-	1
	character M	20	1	-
Experiment 4–7	character O	0	-	1
	character M	30	1	-
Experiment 4–8	character O	0	-	1
	character M	40	1	-

cient. The highest accuracy of the recognition rate was 94.90%, which is better than that of Experiment 1. Therefore, even when the number of character O in the train data is insufficient, the accuracy of the recognition rate can be maintained by using character M. As in the previous experiments for the validation data, the recognition rate when the validation data is character M is higher than the recognition rate when the validation data is character O. And the difference between the recognition rate when the validation data is the character M and the recognition rate when the validation data is the character O is larger than in Experiment 1 and Experiment 2. Experiment 3 is a dataset with a particularly low ratio of character O in the train data compared to Experiments 1 and 2. Therefore, using character M as the validation data when the ratio of character O in the train data is low contributes to the improvement of the accuracy of the recognition rate.

Finally, the results of Experiment 4 are shown in Fig. 10. In Experiment 4, we checked the relationship between the number of train data and the accuracy of the recognition rate when character O is not present in the train data. The highest accuracy of the recognition rate was 87.99%. Compared to Experiment 1, in which the ratio of character M in the train data was 100%, the accuracy of the recognition rate was improved. Therefore, it can be said that increasing the number of character M is effective in improving the accuracy of the recognition rate. However, compared to the accuracy of the recognition rate in Experiments 2 and 3, the accuracy of the recognition rate in Experiment 4 is lower and

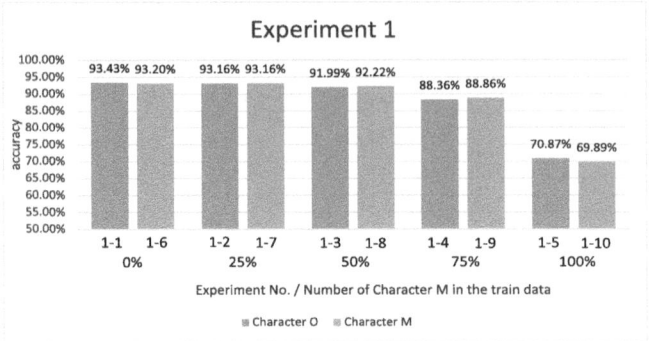

Fig. 7. Experiment1 result

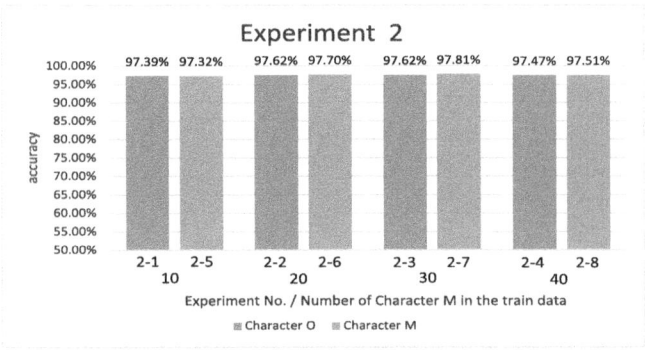

Fig. 8. Experiment2 result

cannot be said to be sufficiently accurate. When the number of characters M in the train data is less than 30, the recognition rate when the validation data is character O is higher than the accuracy of the recognition rate when the validation data is character M. This is due to the fact that character M is not a perfect reproduction of character O. Therefore, it is thought that the learning process is progressing so that the use of character O in the validation data does not depend too much on the characteristics of character M. However, when there are 40 pieces of character M in the train data, the accuracy of the recognition rate is higher when the validation data is character M. This is because the number of pieces of training data has increased. This is thought to be due to the fact that more features can be trained by increasing the number of pieces of train data.

Through Experiments 1 through 4, it was found that by using the character M, the accuracy of the recognition rate is equivalent to the case where there are six copies of the character O per character type, even when there is only one copy of the character O per character type. Currently, there are only 2,647 character types for which six copies per character type can be collected. Thus, the range in which character recognition can be performed while maintaining the

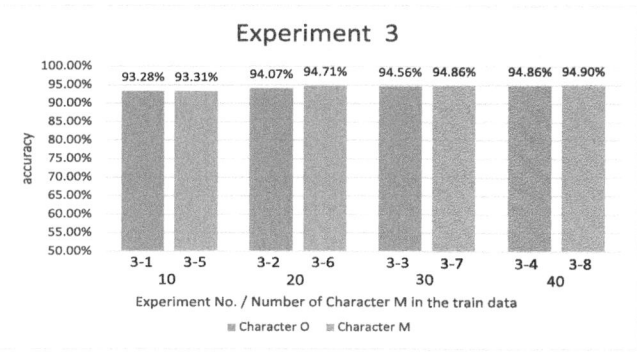

Fig. 9. Experiment3 result

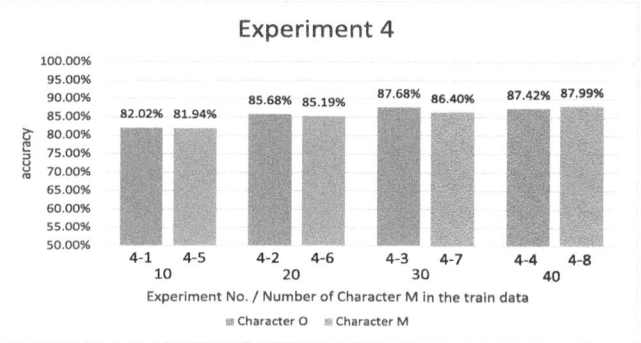

Fig. 10. Experiment4 result

accuracy of the recognition rate is very small. Therefore, it is expected that the range in which only one piece of character O can be collected will be expanded and recognition can be performed for more character types. Even if character O is not present at all in the train data, the accuracy of the recognition rate of the recognition rate is not significantly reduced. Therefore, it is believed that character recognition can be performed using character M even for character types for which character O has not been collected.

5 Conclusion

The proposed method combines images of characters generated from printed characters and character O to create a model for character recognition using train data. The method uses CycleGAN to generate an image of the character M, which is converted from a printed character to the character O. Then, the image of the character M is combined with the image of the character O, which is converted from a printed character to the character M. Next, the character M and character O are combined and trained.

To confirm the effectiveness of the proposed method, four experiments are conducted. Experiment 1 shows that the accuracy decreases as the percentage of character M in the train data increases. In addition, when the proportion of character M in the train data is high, the accuracy of the recognition rate tends to increase when the validation data is character M. Experiment 2 showed that when the character O is sufficiently present in the train data, the number of train data increases and the accuracy of the recognition rate improves. However, if the ratio of character M in the train data is too high, the accuracy of the recognition rate decreases. As in Experiment 1, when the ratio of character M in the train data is high, the recognition rate tends to increase when the validation data is character M. Experiment 3 showed that even when the number of characters O in the train data is insufficient, the accuracy of the recognition rate can be maintained by utilizing the character M. Experiment 4 showed that even when there is no character O in the train data, the accuracy of the recognition rate can be improved by increasing the number of character M. The accuracy of the recognition rate is lower than in Experiment 1, but not significantly so. The validation data also showed that the use of character O in the validation data improves the accuracy of the recognition rate. The four experiments confirmed that the use of character M is effective in improving the accuracy of the recognition rate. It was also shown that the use of character M can improve the accuracy of the recognition rate even when the number of character O in the train data is insufficient.

Disclosure of Interests. The data used in the paper will be available upon request.

References

1. Bao, F., Neumann, M., Vu, N.T.: Cyclegan-based emotion style transfer as data augmentation for speech emotion recognition. In: Interspeech (2019)
2. Chang, B., Zhang, Q., Pan, S., Meng, L.: Generating handwritten chinese characters using cyclegan. In: 2018 IEEE Winter Conference on Applications of Computer Vision (WACV) (2018)
3. Fujita, M., Takemoto, Y., Ishikawa, Y., Takata, M., Joe, K.: Acquisition of low-frequency character types in early-modern Japanese printed books. Technical report, Nara Women's Univercity, Nara Women's Univercity, Shiga Univercity, Nara Women's Univercity, Nara Women's Univercity (2019)
4. Japan: National diet library. http://www.ndl.go.jp. Accessed 5 May 2024
5. Kakuhari, R., Iida, S., Joe, K.: Generation of early-modern Japanese printed book-stule characters using cyclegan and its application to data extension. Technical report, Nara Women's Univercity, Nara Women's Univercity, Nara Women's Univercity (2021)
6. Koiso, N., Takemoto, Y., Iida, S., Ishikawa, Y., Takata, M., Joe, K.: Application of deep metric learning to early-modern Japanese printed character recognition. Adv. Parallel Distrib. Process. Appl. (2022)
7. LeCun, Y., Bottou, L., Bengio, Y., Haffner, P.: Gradient-based learning applied to document recognition. Proc. IEEE **86**(11), 2278–2324 (1998)

8. Library, N.D.: OCR text conversion of digitized materials in 2021. https://lab.ndl. go.jp/data_set/ocr/r3_text. Accessed 5 May 2024
9. Library, N.D.: National diet library digital collections. http://www.dl.ndl.go.jp. Accessed 5 May 2024
10. Narusawa, A., Yanai, K., et al.: Font image conversion by style transition. IPSJ SIG Tech. Rep. (2018)
11. Ranjan, R., Castillo, C.D., Chellappa, R.: L2-constrained softmax loss for discriminative face verification. arXiv preprint arXiv:1703.09507 (2017)
12. Sandfort, V., Yan, K., Pickhardt, P.J., Summers, R.M.: Data augmentation using generative adversarial networks (cyclegan) to improve generalizability in Ct segmentation tasks. Sci. Rep. (2019)
13. Suzuka, Y., Koiso, N., Takemoto, Y., Ishikawa, Y., Takata, M., Joe, K.: Applying CNNs to early-modern Japanese printed character recognition. PDPTA, pp. 189–195 (2019)
14. Zhu, J.Y., Park, T., Isola, P., Efros, A.A.: Unpaired image-to-image translation using cycle-consistent adversarial networks. In: Proceedings of the IEEE International Conference on Computer Vision, pp. 2223–2232 (2017)

Improved Method for Similar Music Recommendation Using Spotify API

Miho Chiyonobu[1] and Masami Takata[2]

[1] Graduate School of Humanities and Sciences, Nara Women's University, Nara, Japan
chiyonobu-miho1611@lics.nara-wu.ac.jp
[2] Research Group of Information and Communication Technology for Life, Nara Women's University, Nara, Japan
takata@ics.nara-wu.ac.jp

Abstract. In this study, we improved a similar music–recommendation method. A similar music recommendation method using the Spotify API was proposed as a music retrieval method. The baseline method computes the Euclidean distance between the audio features obtained from the Spotify API. In this method, the normalization of the obtained audio features and validation of the features used were insufficient. Therefore, in this study, we improved this method by adopting normalization, audio feature selection, and similarity computations based on cosine similarity. It was verified through experiments that the method of normalizing appropriate features by adopting the min–max method and computing similarity using the Euclidean distance was effective.

Keywords: Euclidean distance · cosine similarity · audio feature · Spotify API · normalization

1 Introduction

In recent years, the number of music streaming service users has increased. According to statistics from the Recording Industry Association of Japan, in 2013 the audio record market had sales of $1238 million [1] and the music distribution market had sales of $257 million [2]. In 2022, the audio record market had sales of $838 million [1] and the music distribution market had sales of $700 million [2]. Comparing sales in the music distribution market in 2022 to those in 2013, sales increased by approximately 2.5 times, indicating that the mainstream music market is shifting to the Internet. To further expand the music market, a similar music recommendation method was proposed [3]. A similar music recommendation method that uses Euclidean distance to compute similarity based on multiple audio features obtained from the Spotify API was proposed[1,2]. However, in [3] neither a validation of the combination of audio

---

[1] Spotify, https://open.spotify.com/?.
[2] "Web API", Spotify for Developers, https://developer.spotify.com/documentation/web-api.

© The Author(s), under exclusive license to Springer Nature Switzerland AG 2025
H. R. Arabnia et al. (Eds.): CSCE 2024, CCIS 2256, pp. 182–191, 2025.
https://doi.org/10.1007/978-3-031-85638-9_14

features nor user experiments was conducted. In this study, we improved a similar music–recommendation method. In the improved method, normalization was adopted for the audio features obtained from the Spotify API, an appropriate combination of audio features was determined, and similarity computation was based on cosine similarity. Additionally, a comparison based on a questionnaire survey was conducted.

2   Similar Music Presentation Method

In [3], a similar music presentation method was proposed to support a music search as a search that does not require metadata in the search query.

In [3], 3738 tracks from the Spotify API, a music distribution service, were used. Only music that satisfied the following conditions was used:

- 7 genres.
- Japan marketplace.
- Tracks formatted MP3.

The genres can be obtained using the Spotify API[3]. The target genres were *acoustic, anime, j–dance, j–idol, j–pop, j–rock, and techno.*

Based on audio features obtained using the Spotify API, 9 evaluation indices were defined.

$F1$ danceability
$F2$ acousticness
$F3$ energy
$F4$ instrumentalness
$F5$ liveness
$F6$ loudness_norm
$F7$ speechiness
$F8$ tempo_norm
$F9$ valence

$F1$ describes the suitability of a track for dancing based on a combination of musical elements. The confidence in $F2$ is measured to determine whether the track is acoustic. $F3$ represents a perceptual measure of intensity and activity. $F4$ predicts whether a track contains no vocals. $F5$ detects the presence of an audience member during the recording. $F6$ is the normalized values of *loudness*, in which the overall loudness of the track is in decibels (dB). $F7$ detects the presence of spoken words on a track. $F8$ is the normalized values of *tempo*, in which the overall estimated tempo of a track is in beats per minute (BPM). $F9$ describes the musical positivity conveyed by the track.

---

[3] "Web API", Spotify for Developers, https://developer.spotify.com/documentation/web-api.

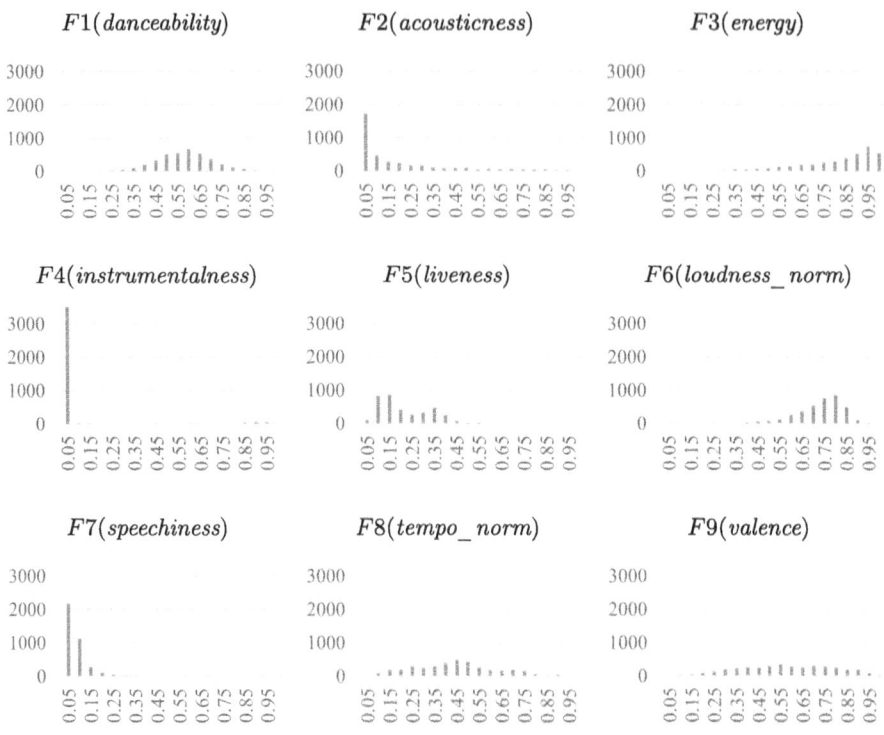

Fig. 1. Distribution for each Fj.

For similarity, $F1$-$F9$ are defined as the vector values of the music, and the distance between the vectors is computed using the Euclidean distance.

$$d(\boldsymbol{X}_o, \boldsymbol{X}_i) = \sqrt{\left(x_{o(F1)} - x_{i(F1)}\right)^2 + \cdots + \left(x_{o(F9)} - x_{i(F9)}\right)^2},$$

where $d(X_o, X_i)$ denote the similarity, X_o and X_i are vectors representing the given music and other music, respectively. Vector X_i is represented by $X_i = (x_{i(F1)}, \cdots, x_{i(F9)})$ where $x_{i(Fj)}$ contains the value of the evaluation index Fj.

3 Preliminary Investigation

3.1 Distribution of Music in the Spotify

In this study, 3738 tracks of music from the music distribution service Spotify were targeted, as in [3]. The evaluation indices Fj for these tracks of music were used to confirm the distribution.

Figure 1 presents a histogram of the distribution for each Fj. In the histogram, the vertical and horizontal axes represent the number of music pieces and the numerical value of Fj, respectively. The horizontal axis has a step width of 0.05. From Fig. 1, it can be confirmed that $F6(loudness\_norm)$ and $F8(tempo\_norm)$ are normalized. $F1(danceability)$ and $F9(valence)$ were close to a normal distribution. We confirmed that $F2(acousticness)$, $F3(energy)$, $F4(instrumentalness)$, $F5(liveness)$, and $F7(speechiness)$ were biased. In particular, $F2(acousticness)$, $F4(instrumentalness)$, and $F7(speechiness)$ contained large amounts of music in their histograms. These evaluation indices were unsuitable for numerical comparisons.

3.2 Questionnaire Survey

Concept. A questionnaire survey was conducted to confirm the effectiveness of similar music–recommendation methods. The survey was conducted online, and questionnaires was performed.

The questionnaire used 10 music obtained using a similar music recommendation method. The user then ranked the 10 pieces of music. The number of respondents was 40.

Results. As a major key, "LOVER" [4] was used.

Table 1. Result of the questionnaire surveys for the major key.

1	2	3	4	5
虹の空	胸キュンライト	決戦スピリット	Fantasista	徹
6	7	8	9	10
gives	サンディ		27 小さな恋のうた	よる☆かぜ

Table 1 presents the result of the questionnaire surveys for the major key. The music titles were written in Japanese. The numbers in lines 1 and 3 of Table 1 shows the rankings. The rankings were colored based on the color circle to provide an intuitive impression of the ranking. $1st$, $4th$, and $7th$–ranked music were assigned red, yellow, and blue, respectively.

Table 2. Color coding of the keys in Table 1

1	2	3	4	5
虹の空	胸キュンライト	決戦スピリット	Fantasista	徹
6	7	8	9	10
gives	サンディ		27 小さな恋のうた	よる☆かぜ

Table 2 presents the result of the color coding of the major key in Tables 1. Orange and blue represent major and minor keys, respectively. From Tables 2, the music in the major key is often the same as the given music. However, it can be confirmed that music in the opposite key is also selected. Therefore, it is believed that users do not judge music similarities based on their keys.

Friedman's Test. Friedman's test [5–7] was performed on the questionnaire results to test the significance of the rankings of several persons. The procedure for computing Friedman's test includes the following steps:

1. The rejection limit $\chi_0{}^2$ is computed based on Eq. (1):

$$\chi_0{}^2 = \frac{12}{mn(n+1)} \sum_{i=1}^{n} R_i{}^2 - 3\,m(n+1) \tag{1}$$

2. Because $\chi_0{}^2$ follows χ^2 distribution with $n-1$ degrees of freedom, compute the upper probability p value from the chi–square distribution table.

Here, R_i^2 indicates the rank sum of music i, where m is the number of respondents to the questionnaire, and n is the number of tracks.

For the major keys, $p < 0.01$ because the number of responses is 40 and $\chi^2 = 84.5$. Hence, this result is significant at the 1% level. Therefore, Friedman's test allows us to treat the rank order of the survey results in ascending order of the rank sum of all responses.

4   Proposed Method

In this study, three improvements were made to increase the accuracy of similar music. The first step was the normalization of each similarity index. Only $F6$ and $F8$ have already been normalized values [3]. The second step was the selection of appropriate indexes to be used in the similarity computation. The third step was the introduction of different similarity formulas.

4.1   Normalization

In the computation of similar music, Euclidean distance was used for each Fj. In the Euclidean distance, when a certain Fj was biased, the difference decreased. Therefore, its influence was small. To avoid this problem, normalization was adopted for each Fj.

Normalization methods have different advantages. In this study, the following 3 normalization methods were used for improvement:

- min–max Method
- Normalization using the log method
- Normalization to round numbers outside the standard deviation 3σ

Min–Max Method. The min-max method was used to scale–transform the minimum value of the data to 0 and the maximum value to 1. The min–max method is susceptible to outliers, which means that the presence of outliers can prevent the data from achieving a normal distribution even after normalization.

Normalization Using the Log Method. In normalization using the log method, value $x_{i(Fj)}$ was first log–transformed. The min–max method was then adopted for the log–transformed values. The log method is effective for approximating a normal distribution for data that follow a lognormal distribution. A log–normal distribution has a characteristic that rises sharply from the left side to the mode and becomes smoother as it moves to the right.

Normalization Using Standard Deviation. In the method with standard deviation σ, the standard deviation of the data was computed and the values outside $\pm 3\sigma$ of the mean μ of the data were rounded. After rounding off the values outside $\mu \pm 3\sigma$, the data were normalized using the min-max method. The amount of data within the range of $\mu \pm 3\sigma$ was approximately 99.7%. Therefore, it is possible to mitigate the effects of outliers by rounding the data outside this range.

4.2   Method of Selecting Evaluation Indicators

The greater the number of evaluation indices adopted for the similarity computation, the more computationally expensive it becomes. Additionally, if the normalization does not follow a normal distribution and the bias is large, it is not appropriate as an evaluation index for use in similar music recommendation methods. In [3], 9 evaluation indices were employed. This section describes the evaluation indices that should be removed. We also discuss whether the audio features obtained from the Spotify API, which are numerical values, should be added.

Evaluation Indicators to be Deleted. From Fig. 1, some evaluation indicators exhibited biased distributions regarding their numerical values. Specifically, $F2(acousticness)$, $F3(energy)$, $F4(instrumentalness)$, $F5(liveness)$, and $F7(speechiness)$ exhibited a greater bias. Highly biased indices have less impact on similarity computation. Therefore, if possible, they should be removed from the evaluation indices adopted for the similarity computation to reduce the computational cost.

Evaluation Indicators to be Added. The similarity–computation method uses audio features that can be numerically expressed among the audio features obtained by the Spotify API. Therefore, all the features that can be expressed numerically should be added to the similarity computation. However, as described in Sect. 4.2, when the number of songs is highly skewed, or if the songs can be set as a selection category, they should not be added.

In the Spotify API, the only other music feature expressed numerically is the *mode*. The *mode* indicates the modality (major or minor) of a track and the type of scale from which its melodic content is derived. The major is represented by 1 and the minor by 0. Hence, all tracks were 0 or 1.

Table 2 implies that the overall ranking was independent of the key but not completely unaffected by the tune. When *mode* was used for similarity computation, the similarity of music in the same key was higher. Basically, the influence of the key is significant. However, this depends on the sensitivity of the user. Therefore, *mode* should not be added to the similarity computation.

4.3 Similarity Computation Using Cosine Similarity Method

A similar music recommendation method uses the Euclidean distance because it considers each Fj as an independent relation. However, it is impossible to prove that there is no relationship between Fj. Therefore, in this section, the similarity computation was performed using cosine similarity. Cosine similarity computes the similarity of the vector orientations. Therefore, the similarity between X_o and X_i is examined using Eq. (2).

$$\cos\left(\boldsymbol{X}_o, \boldsymbol{X}_i\right) = \frac{\sum_{Fj} x_{o(Fj)} x_{i(Fj)}}{\sqrt{\sum_{Fj} x_{o(Fj)}^2} \sqrt{\sum_{Fj} x_{i(Fj)}^2}}. \tag{2}$$

Table 3. Music recommendation with and without the normalization method.

	denormalization	normalization		
		Max-Min	log	3 σ
1	虹の空	虹の空	虹の空	虹の空
2	徹	徹	徹	サンディ
3	胸キュンライト	胸キュンライト	胸キュンライト	徹
4	サンディ	サンディ	サンディ	胸キュンライト
5	KICK BACK	gives	小さな恋のうた	小さな恋のうた
6	gives	よる☆かぜ	gives	gives
7	Fantasista	小さな恋のうた	よる☆かぜ	よる☆かぜ
8	よる☆かぜ	Who I Am	Who I Am	Who I Am
9	27	Clock Strikes	Grab the air	forbidden lover
10	小さな恋のうた	決戦スピリット	Clock Strikes	Grab the air

Table 4. Comparison between using 9 Fj and using 6 Fj.

number of Indicators	denormalization		normalization					
			Max-Min		log		3 σ	
	9	6	9	6	9	6	9	6
1	紅の霜	紅の霜	紅の霜	紅の霜	紅の霜	紅の霜	紅の霜	紅の霜
2	徹	徹	徹	徹	徹	徹	サンディ	徹
3	胸キュンライト	KICK BACK	胸キュンライト	KICK BACK	胸キュンライト	胸キュンライト	徹	サンディ
4	サンディ	胸キュンライト	サンディ	胸キュンライト	サンディ	サンディ	胸キュンライト	胸キュンライト
5	KICK BACK	Fantasista	gives	Fantasista	小さな恋のうた	Fantasista	小さな恋のうた	Fantasista
6	gives	サンディ	よる☆かぜ	サンディ	gives	夜空を翔ける	gives	夜空を翔ける
7	Fantasista	夜空を翔ける	小さな恋のうた	夜空を翔ける	よる☆かぜ	27	よる☆かぜ	小さな恋のうた
8	よる☆かぜ	gives	Who I Am	gives	Who I Am	小さな恋のうた	Who I Am	27
9	27	27	Clock Strikes	27	Grab the air	よる☆かぜ	forbidden lover	gives
10	小さな恋のうた	よる☆かぜ	決戦スピリット	よる☆かぜ	Clock Strikes	gives	Grab the air	よる☆かぜ

Table 5. Euclidean distance and cosine similarity for major key.

	Euclidean distance				Cosine Similarity			
	denormalization	normalization			denormalization	normalization		
		Max-Min	log	3 σ		Max-Min	log	3 σ
1	紅の霜	紅の霜	紅の霜	紅の霜	紅の霜	紅の霜	紅の霜	紅の霜
2	徹	徹	徹	徹	胸キュンライト	胸キュンライト	Pinoccio	胸キュンライト
3	KICK BACK	KICK BACK	胸キュンライト	サンディ	KICK BACK	KICK BACK	Fetish	徹
4	胸キュンライト	胸キュンライト	サンディ	胸キュンライト	THE OVER	決戦スピリット	27	THE OVER
5	Fantasista	Fantasista	Fantasista	徹	徹	THE OVER	ココア	サンディ
6	サンディ	サンディ	夜空を翔ける	夜空を翔ける	決戦スピリット	徹	徹	gives
7	夜空を翔ける	夜空を翔ける	27	小さな恋のうた	gives	ネタンデルタール	僕らが強く。	はじまりの予感
8	gives	gives	小さな恋のうた	27	ネタンデルタール	gives	よる☆かぜ	決戦スピリット
9	27	27	よる☆かぜ	gives	Fantasista	Fantasista	サンディ	小さな恋のうた
10	よる☆かぜ	よる☆かぜ	gives	よる☆かぜ	夏空	夏空	胸キュンライト	ネタンデルター

5   Experiments

To verify the effectiveness of improvements described in Sect. 4, we perform three experiments. In the experiments, 3738 pieces of music were obtained from Spotify. As a major key song, "LOVER" [4] was given.

The first experiment examined the effects of normalization. Therefore, similarity computations were performed for each Fj before and after normalization using the min-max method, log method, and 3σ of the standard deviation. The second experiment examined the evaluation indices that should be used in similarity computations. Specifically, we compared the results obtained using nine evaluation indices with those obtained using six indices. The third experiment compared Euclidean distance and cosine similarity. Similarity computations were performed using six evaluation indices.

Table 3 lists the top 10 music recommendations with and without the normalization method. Here, the coloring is the same as the colored circles in Table 1.

From Table 3, music recommendation with normalization differs from that without normalization in the $8th$ and higher positions. Moreover, different types of music were considered similar, even when using different normalizations. This may be because the normalization improves the bias of each Fj.

Table 4 lists the top 10 music recommendations when $F1$ to $F9$ were used and when six Fj excluding $F2$, $F4$, and $F7$ were used. From Table 4, it can be confirmed that there was less change in the ranking of the music recommendations in both cases. Further, the music included in the questionnaire was more likely to be recommended when six Fj were used for the music in the case of normalization. Hence, $F1(danceability)$, F3($energy$), F5($liveness$), F6($loudness\_norm$), $F8(tempo\_norm)$, and $F9(valence)$ should be used for the similarity computation. In this case, by normalizing each Fj, the ranking became similar to the questionnaire ranking presented in Table 1.

Table 5 lists the results for the major key. The major keys are listed in Table 5 and the music ranked second in the questionnaire was ranked lower only when the log method of cosine similarity was adopted. The music ranked $3rd$ was not recommended by the log method of cosine similarity. The music ranked $4th$ was not recommended for the log method of cosine similarity and 3σ. The music ranked $5th$ was ranked 2nd for Euclidean distance, whereas it was ranked lower for the cosine similarity. The $7th$ and $8th$ ranked music were highly recommended by the log method and 3σ. Based on Table 5, for a given music with a major key, the cosine similarity recommends the top–ranked music in the questionnaire, which is not recommended by Euclidean distance. Furthermore, cosine similarity was valid because the music ranked 5th in the questionnaire was reduced to the appropriate rank. However, when focusing on the relationship with the overall ranking, the Euclidean distance was more similar to the questionnaire results and was considered superior to the cosine similarity.

Thus, it is appropriate to compute the similarity based on the Euclidean distance by adopting normalization using the min-max method. In this case, $F1(danceability)$, $F3(energy)$, $F5(liveness)$, $F6(loudness\_norm)$, $F8(tempo\_norm)$, and $F9(valence)$ were adopted for similarity computation.

6   Conclusion

In this study, we improved a similar music recommendation method using the Spotify API by employing normalization, appropriate Fj selection, and cosine similarity. A questionnaire–based survey was conducted to confirm the effectiveness of these improvements. We compared the rankings obtained from the questionnaire survey with the results obtained through the improvements. The experimental results show that normalization makes the recommended results closer to the perception of the user. For the similarity computation, six types of Fj were sufficient. It is also more appropriate to use the Euclidean distance instead of the cosine similarity.

Acknowledgment. This work was supported by JST SPRING, Grant Number JPMJSP2115.

References

1. Annual Data: Audio,The Recording Industry Association of Japan (RIAJ). https://www.riaj.or.jp/f/e/data/annual/ar_all.html. Accessed 25 Mar 2024
2. Annual Data: Trend of Digital Music Sales: The Recording Industry Association of Japan (RIAJ). https://www.riaj.or.jp/g/e/data/annual/dg_t.html. Accessed 25 Mar 2024
3. Kobayashi, K., Takaku, M.: A visualization method for music retrieval based on similarity, beyond the information technology, vol. 32, no. 2, pp. 287–293 (2022). (in JAPANESE)
4. AAA, "LOVER", Spotify (2015). https://open.spotify.com/track/3TrRiKnSyy2STtLIx5fSiYgo=1&sp_cid=9ccdce859de8c445db5a273618ce43f6&utm_source=embed_player_p&utm_medium=desktop&nd=1&dlsi=96784d3ef06c4489. Accessed 25 Mar 2024
5. Friedman, M.: The use of ranks to avoid the assumption of normality implicit in the analysis of variance. J. Am. Stat. Assoc. **32**(200), 675–701 (1937)
6. Friedman, M.: A correction: the use of ranks to avoid the assumption of normality implicit in the analysis of variance. J. Am. Stat. Assoc. **34**(205), 109 (1939)
7. Friedman, M.: A comparison of alternative tests of significance for the problem of m rankings. Ann. Math. Stat. **11**(1), 86–92 (1937)

Reconfigurable Virtual Accelerator (ReVA) for Large-Scale Acceleration Circuits

Kazuki Yaguchi[1]([✉]), Eriko Maeda[1], Shunya Kawai[1], Daichi Teruya[1], Yasunori Osana[2], Takefumi Miyoshi[3], and Hironori Nakajo[4]

[1] Department of Electrical Engineering and Computer Science, Graduate School of Engineering, Tokyo University of Agriculture and Technology, 2-24-16 Nakacho, Koganei-shi, Tokyo 184-8588, Japan
{s234750v,s244623r}@st.go.tuat.ac.jp
[2] Research and Education Institute for Semiconductors and Informatics, Kumamoto University, 2-39-1 Kurokami, Chuo-ku, Kumamoto 860-8555, Japan
osana@kumamoto-u.ac.jp
[3] WasaLabo, LLC., K-2 Buransyu 6-5-20 Minaminaruse, Machida-shi, Tokyo 194-0045, Japan
miyo@wasa-labo.com
[4] Division of Advanced Information Technology and Computer Science, Institute of Engineering, Tokyo University of Agriculture and Technology, 2-24-16 Nakacho, Koganei-shi, Tokyo 184-8588, Japan
nakajo@cc.tuat.ac.jp

Abstract. In recent years, hardware acceleration in large-scale computing fields such as Artificial Intelligence and High Performance Computing, faces hardware resource shortages. To overcome this problem, we propose Reconfigurable Virtual Accelerator (ReVA), which allows a large-scale acceleration circuit built using multiple FPGAs, processors and memory subsystems, to accelerate application programs.

We have designed and implemented a prototype of Virtual Accelerator (VA) Generator for ReVA to investigate its performance. The VA Generator prototype employs an open-source HLS automated split compilation tool, RapidStream, to automatically generate placed-and-routed virtual accelerators that can be implemented on multiple FPGAs based on HLS dataflow designs. The VA Generator, which places VAs on the appropriate regions of FPGAs, allows large circuits to be performed like a single accelerator using several FPGAs. In addition, RapidStream's parallel compilation technology allows the VA Generator to suppress the increasing compilation time according to the circuit size. Moreover, with our VA Generator prototype we have built and evaluated a VA of a large-scale circuit which cannot be fit in a single FPGA with multiple FPGAs.

Keywords: FPGA · Hardware Acceleration · HLS · Circuit Partitioning

© The Author(s), under exclusive license to Springer Nature Switzerland AG 2025
H. R. Arabnia et al. (Eds.): CSCE 2024, CCIS 2256, pp. 192–206, 2025.
https://doi.org/10.1007/978-3-031-85638-9_15

1   Introduction

Hardware acceleration using field-programmable gate arrays (FPGAs) is commonly utilized in fields that require significant volumes of computations, such as artificial intelligence (AI) and high performance computing (HPC). However, this is affected by the growing scarcity of FPGA resources.

One of the main reasons behind this problem is the rapid development in the AI and HPC fields that, besides leading to remarkable achievements, has increased the demand for fast computation and data-processing in these fields [11].

This trend has been exacerbated by the widespread adoption of high-level synthesis (HLS). Traditionally, digital circuits used in FPGAs are designed at the register transfer level (RTL) using a hardware description language (HDL). However, designing a circuit in HDL is expensive and requires users to have prior knowledge on hardware. This problem is commonly solved by converting programs written in high-level languages (HLLs), such as C, into ones written in HDL using HLS. This enables users to design circuits in HLL, which is easier to debug and design in than HDL, thereby reducing development costs. This allows software programmers with no knowledge of hardware details to design circuits using HLS tools, address the increase in the number of software programmers attempting to use hardware acceleration in personal AI use and development. However, circuits implemented using HLS tend to require more resources than those implemented using HDL directly. This restricts the use of HLS in the implementation of large circuits.

To overcome this problem, we propose Reconfigurable Virtual Accelerator (ReVA) [8], which integrates multiple FPGAs, processors, and memories, and operates them like a single high-speed computer. ReVA constructs and operates hardware accelerators on FPGA clusters to enable large-scale hardware acceleration.

In this study, we propose a VA Generator prototype that supports HLS and circuit distribution for ReVA. It employs an open-source HLS automated split-compilation tool called RapidStream [5]. The circuit-partitioning method and flow of RapidStream are extended by adding new functions to realize the functions of the VA Generator. In particular, the following steps are followed.

1. The input HLS sources are synthesized.
2. The regions on the FPGA cluster are optimized and the circuit is distributed to these regions using integer linear programming (ILP).
3. The distributed circuits for each FPGA are compiled.
4. The placed-and-routed design checkpoint (DCP) files are obtained as output.

In addition, multi-FPGA accelerators are constructed and evaluated for large-scale application programs that do not fit into a single FPGA using the proposed VA Generator prototype.

The reminder of this paper is organized as follows, ReVA is introduced in Sect. 2. ReVA is discussed in comparison with other researches on circuit partitioning and RapidStream is introduced in Sect. 3. The VA Generator prototype is discussed in Sect. 4 and experiments on it are reported in Sect. 5. Finally, the paper is concluded Sect. 6.

2   Reconfigurable Virtual Accelerator (ReVA)

ReVA integrates multiple FPGAs, processors, and memories to accelerate large
software applications. It automatically implements accelerators on multiple
FPGAs, and includes HLS compilation, circuit placement, routing, and execution using accelerators. This enables users to execute their software programs
rapidly by simply inputting them into a ReVA system without knowledge of
hardware acceleration. It is particularly relevant for users who are concerned
about the resource limitations of FPGAs.

2.1   ReVA Structure

ReVA uses a network of interconnected FPGAs, processors and memories. ReVA
operates these devices appropriately using the following functions to achieve
hardware acceleration (Fig. 1).

Sharing Distributed Circuits. In ReVA, acceleration circuits are implemented
on a single FPGA or across multiple FPGAs in a network to utilize additional
hardware resources. Processors in the ReVA system can use the circuits virtually
as a single accelerator, even if they consist of multiple modules across multiple
FPGAs to hide inter-FPGA boundaries. These circuits are called Virtual Accelerators (VAs). The VAs are distributed and shared, thus, this mechanism is
called Distributed Shared Logic (DSL).

Sharing Data with Distributed Shared Memory (DSM). ReVA uses a single virtually shared address space called DSM. The data used in ReVA are stored in
DSM, which is accessible by each processor and VA.

Dynamic Placement of VAs and Data on the DSM. VAs and data on the DSM
can be moved on the DSL and the DSM. ReVA places them at the shortest
physical distance from the processor to achieve the best performance.

Concealment of Connection Forms. ReVA utilizes two APIs (ReVA_APIs) to
conceal the connection type between each pair of devices.

- HC_API (Host Connect API): This conceals the connection between a pro-
  cessor and an FPGA.
- DC_API (Device Connect API): This conceals the connection between two
  FPGAs.

ReVA can use directly and remotely connected devices such as NICs in the
same manner using ReVA_APIs. This makes the accelerator available in clusters
with different configurations.

2.2   ReVA Flow

Figure 2 depicts the acceleration flow of ReVA. Technical terms related to ReVA
used in Fig. 2 are explained below.

- SW-part (software-part)
  The SW-part is executed as a software program by the processors.
- HW-part (hardware-part)
  The HW-part is synthesized into a circuit by HLS and is composed of one or
  more sources that describe hardware accelerators. The sources are written in
  HLS format with optimization directives.

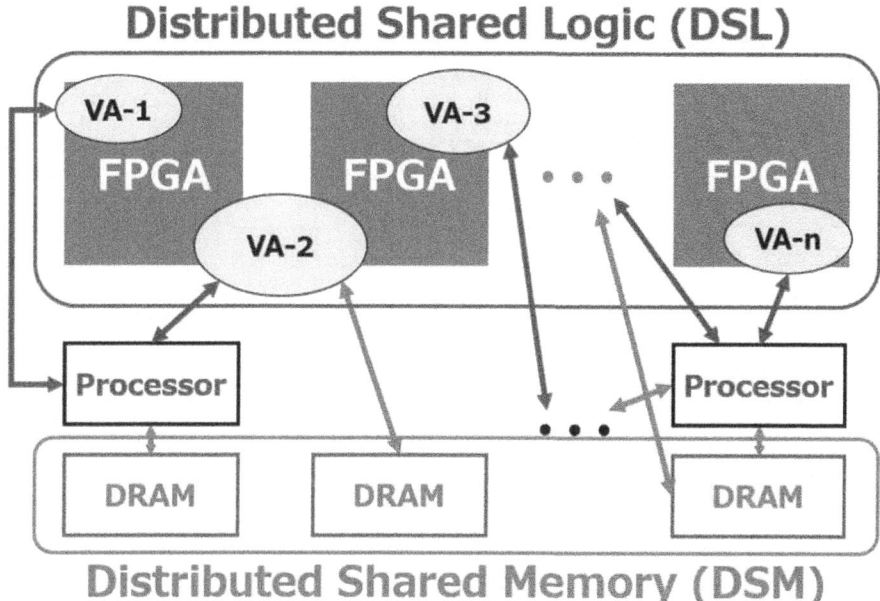

Fig. 1. Structure of ReVA

The main steps of the ReVA acceleration flow are as follows.
Accelerator Implementation Steps (highlighted in blue in the figure):

1. Receiving the input software program.
2. Dividing the software program into SW-part and HW-part.
   In this step, the highly parallel parts of the input program are extracted as
   HW-part, other parts are regarded as SW-part. In addition, ReVA inserts
   optimization directives into the extracted parts.
3. Compiling the HW-part by the VA Generator.
   ReVA inputs the HW-part into the VA Generator, and the accelerator sources
   are converted into VAs. The VA Generator compiles the sources by HLS and
   partitions circuits to implement them on multiple FPGAs as VAs. Finally,
   the VA Generator outputs the VAs sequentially in a placed-and-routed DCP
   file format corresponding to each FPGA.

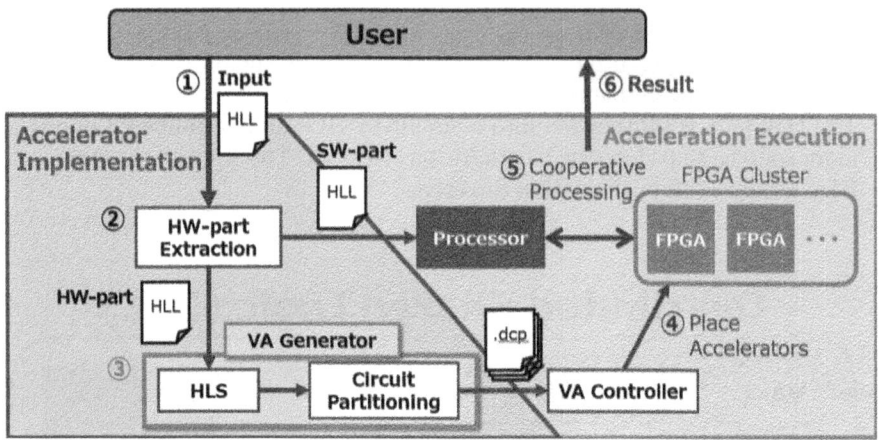

Fig. 2. ReVA acceleration flow

Acceleration Execution Steps (highlighted in green in the figure):

4. Placing VAs on FPGA clusters using the VA Controller.
   The VA Controller manages the placement of VAs by assigning each VA an identifiable ID (VA-ID). The VA Controller monitors FPGA clusters to get each VA's position and free FPGA regions. Subsequently, it adds or moves accelerators to the appropriate regions based on this information.
5. Enabling cooperative processing between processors and VAs.
   In this step, ReVA performs cooperative processing between VAs on FPGAs and the SW-part transmitted to the processor. ReVA executes the SW-part and communicates with the VAs whenever the associated hardware acceleration functions using them are called. For example, Fig. 3 depicts the SW-part pseudo-code using VA_0, whose VA-ID is 0. In this case, ReVA first ensures DSM space and stores the input data for communication between the processor and the VA_0. When the SW-part process has reached the VA_0 function, VA_0 processes the application rapidly and the processor receives the result via HC_API.
6. Returning the execution results to the user.

3   Related Works

3.1   Research on Circuit Partitioning

ReVA constructs a DSL by partitioning circuits and distributing them on multiple FPGAs. In this section, the implementation of circuit partitioning across multiple FPGAs is explained using two circuit-partitioning methods.

Target Feature-Based Circuit-Partitioning Methods. [6,10,12], and [9] present studies on accelerating specific processing tasks by partitioning circuits based on the features of target tasks and implementing them using multiple FPGAs.

The authors utilized deep neural network (DNN) with a layered structure and partitioned it into multiple elements that are computable in parallel [6]. Each element of the partitioned DNN was placed in each FPGA, and the shared data were copied to each FPGA. Processing dependencies between FPGAs were eliminated, enabling the FPGAs to operate in parallel.

```
A_type *a;    // input 1
B_type *b;    // input 2
C_type *c;    // result

// ensure the DSM space for processor-FPGA communication
data_a = dev_shared_malloc(sizeof(A_type) * A_LEN);
data_b = dev_shared_malloc(sizeof(B_type) * B_LEN);
data_c = dev_shared_malloc(sizeof(C_type) * C_LEN);
// transfer data
memcpy(a, data_a);
memcpy(b, data_b);

#pragma parallel
// call VA whose VA-ID is 0 through HC_API
(*HC_API) VA_0(data_a, data_b, data_c);
```

Fig. 3. Illustrative pseudo-code for the SW-part

Circuit-partitioning methods depending on the features of the target processing tasks improve performance with respect to the specific processing tasks, thereby limiting the scope of their application. In contrast, ReVA supports a wide range of processing tasks because of the versatile circuit-partitioning methods used in it. However, circuit-partitioning methods specific to particular processing tasks tend to exhibit better performance improvement compared to more general methods. Therefore, we intend to employ both specialized and common circuit-partitioning methods to improve the performance of the ReVA circuit distribution mechanism in the future.

Highly Versatile Circuit-Partitioning Methods. ForeGraph is a highly versatility circuit-partitioning method [2] that is based on gather-apply-scatter (GAS) model, which abstracts algorithms for various graph processing tasks [3]. ForeGraph is based on the GAS model and allocates an input graph to each FPGA by partitioning it into two levels per-FPGA and per-PE, it reads data from the off-chip memory connected one-to-one to each FPGA and each PE, and executes the process. Thus, ForeGraph can partition and process large graphs efficiently. ForeGraph and ReVA are similar in that they both enable the implementation of large circuits by distributing partitioned circuits using a method that supports a wide range of processing tasks and performs cooperative processing. However, ForeGraph is less flexible in terms of circuit configurations than ReVA, because it does not allow configuration of multiple types of circuits on a single FPGA.

3.2 RapidStream Overview

This section presents an overview of RapidStream employed for the VA Generator prototype.

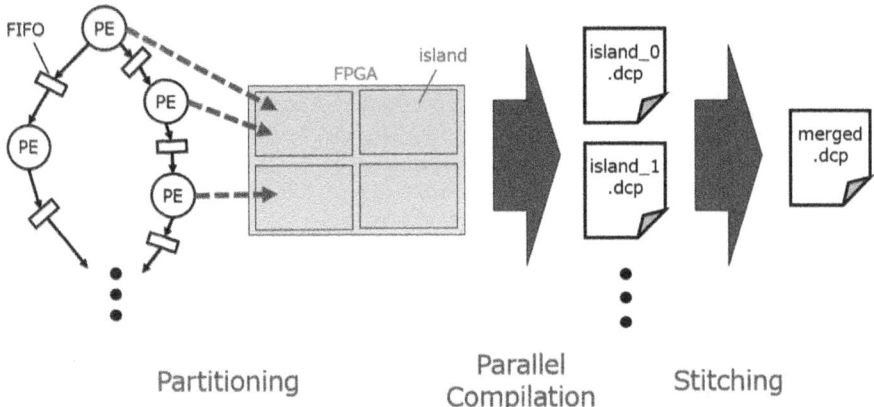

Fig. 4. RapidStream compilation flow

RapidStream is an open-source tool that runs FPGA logic synthesis, placement and routing quickly and automatically using split compilation technology. Figure 4 illustrates the entire RapidStream process. It accepts HLS dataflow designs, consisting of HLS functions that define processing elements (PEs) and first-in-first-outs (FIFOs) connecting them, as input. In RapidStream, the FPGA region is divided into islands that are equal-sized. RapidStream assigns PEs to islands using AutoBridge floorplanning [4] to divide the dataflow design. It then compiles the divided designs in parallel and merges them using RapidWright [7]. Consequently, RapidStream exhibits a reduction in compilation time by a factor of approximately 5–7 and an increase in frequency by a factor of 1.3 compared to the flow of Vivado.

4 VA Generator

As described in Sect. 2.2, the VA Generator executes HLS compilation and partitions circuits to implement VAs.

In this section, we first describe the features of the VA Generator compared to other circuit partitioning tools. Next, we provide the overview of the VA Generator and explain each of its main processes in detail.

4.1   Features of VA Generator

ReVA achieves hardware acceleration using various functions, such as virtualization. To implement these functions, the VA Generator has the following features [13].

Versatile Partitioning Method. ReVA supports not only specific applications, but also diverse applications with different structural circuits, as discussed in Sect. 3.1. In the proposed VA Generator prototype, this specification is satisfied using employing RapidStream, which divides circuits by partitioning corresponding dataflow graphs as described in Sect. 3.2. The RapidStream partitioning method is versatile because the process to be accelerated can be defined as a dataflow graph. Thus, the VA Generator is allowed to partition more types of circuits than previous works.

Use of ReVA_API. As described in Sect. 2.1, ReVA utilizes a dedicated API (ReVA_API) in the circuit on each FPGA for communication between pairs of devices. To implement this function, we reserve the API region in each circuit to place the ReVA_API. Thus, during circuit partitioning, the API region is left empty to enable partitioned circuits to communicate with external devices, e.g. FPGAs containing other partitioned components using ReVA_API.

Strategy for Managing FPGA Regions. ReVA manages VAs and FPGA resources appropriately for the dynamic placement of VAs. To meet this requirement, the VA Generator prototype identifies the FPGA regions for each VA and the boundaries between VAs by explicitly assigning regions to them. The assigned regions are defined as islands, similar to the organization of RapidStream's FPGA fabric, to manage the VAs and FPGA resources in terms of units comprising a single island, e.g. assigning island_X0Y0:X3Y3 of FPGA_0 to VA_0 and island_X0Y0:X3Y7 of FPGA_1 to VA_1. In addition, some islands are reserved as regions for the APIs and others are used for the main part of VAs.

4.2   VA Generator Overview

Figure 5 depicts an outline of the input and output of the VA Generator. The software program (HW-part) serves as the input, the dataflow design consists of PEs and FIFOs similar to that of RapidStream, and the information of FPGA boards in ReVA. The board information describes the FPGA name, available regions provided by the VA Controller, and the connected boards of each FPGA. The VA Generator implements VAs of the HW-part using the optimal resources based on this information. Finally, the VA Generator outputs VAs one at a time, comprising one or more placed-and-routed DCP files corresponding to each FPGA.

The workflow of the VA Generator is illustrated in Fig. 6. First, the VA Generator automatically synthesizes the input software program using the commercial tool Vitis HLS. Then, based on the reports and HDL files generated by HLS, the VA Generator performs three floorplanning steps: region optimization (Sect. 4.3), multi-FPGA floorplanning (Sect. 4.4), solo-FPGA floorplanning (Sect. 4.5). During region optimization, the VA Generator determines appropriate FPGA regions based on the amount of resources required to constructed the VA. During multi-FPGA floorplanning, the VA Generator assigns PEs comprising the circuit to each FPGA, as determined in the previous step. Then, it places them in appropriate positions in the solo-FPGA floorplanning step. These floorplanning processes are repeated with an increasing number of regions until the optimum result is achieved. Finally, the VA Generator inserts ReVA_API into the API islands of the circuit on each FPGA determined during the region optimization step. Then, it compiles the circuits in parallel to implement the VA rapidly and outputs its DCP files.

In following sections, floorplanning processes are described, in which ILP formulation is utilized. In our formulation, we define FPGA regions as Slot composed of one or more islands, such as AutoBridge.

4.3   Region Optimization

The VA Generator determines implementation regions for VAs from available options using ILP formulation.

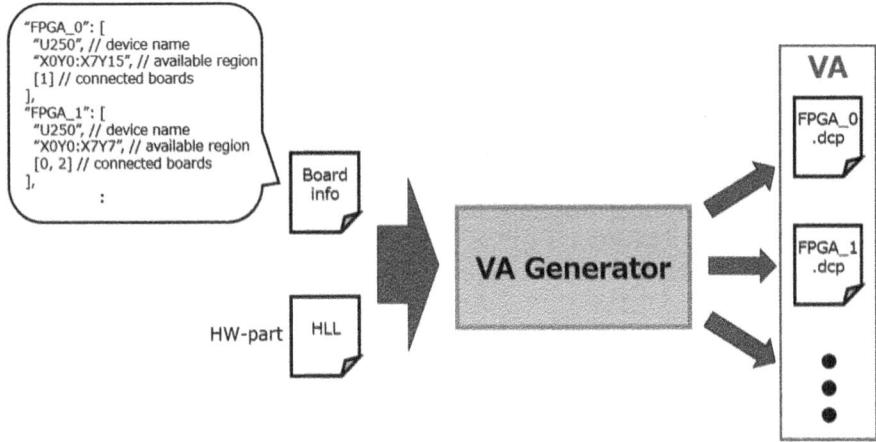

Fig. 5. Input and output of VA Generator

By the mentioned definition, our formulation declares binary decision variables $s_{i,j}$ which represents whether Slot$_j$ on FPGA$_i$ is used for the VA, and a binary variable f_i which represents whether FPGA$_i$ is used. In addition, we impose the following constraints on ILP formulation.

- The total amount of resources of the slots used for a VA should exceed the amount of resources required for the VA.

$s_{i,j}.area$: resources (the number of BRAM, DSP, FF, LUT, URAM) of $Slot_j$ on $FPGA_i$.

$c.area$: resources of a VA

$$\sum_{i,j} s_{i,j} \times s_{i,j}.area > c.area \tag{1}$$

- If $Slot_j$ on $FPGA_i$ is used, $FPGA_i$ must be used.

$$\forall_i f_i \geq s_{i,j} \tag{2}$$

- Only one slot should be used within a single FPGA.

$$\forall_i \sum_j s_{i,j} = 1 \tag{3}$$

- FPGAs used for a VA must be adjacent to each other.
  $route_{i,j}$: represents the existence of a route connecting $FPGA_i$ and $FPGA_j$. This is derived from the input board information.

$$route_{i,j} >= f_i + f_j - 1 \tag{4}$$

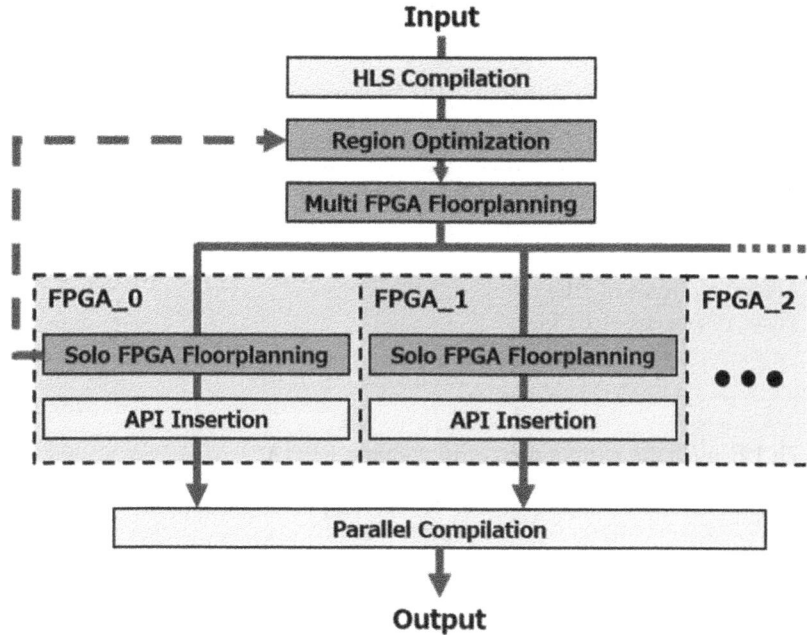

Fig. 6. Workflow of VA Generator

The objective of our formulation is to minimize the number of boards used and the sizes of the slots used, defined in terms of the number of islands, as follows. In this formulation, we prioritize minimization of the number of boards to restrict the overhead of using multiple FPGAs by multiplying the number of boards used with a large factor ($LARGE\_NUM$).

$s_{i,j}.size$: the number of islands contained within $Slot_j$ on $FPGA_i$.

$$minimize LARGE\_NUM \times \sum_i f_i + \sum_{i,j} s_{i,j} \times s_{i,j}.size \tag{5}$$

At the end of this step, the VA Generator reserves islands for ReVA_API based on their suitability for using the required external communication ports within the determined regions to achieve the best performance.

4.4 Multi-FPGA Floorplanning

In this step, the VA Generator assigns the PEs of the input dataflow design to each FPGA with the regions determined in the previous step using ILP. For example, if the entire area of FPGA_0 and the half area of FPGA_1 are extracted, VA Generator targets these areas for floorplanning.

In our formulation, we define the connection between each PE as an edge. We declare binary decision variables $v_{i,j}$ representing whether PE_j is assigned to $FPGA_i$ and e_k representing whether $Edge_k$ connecting PEs involves multiple FPGAs. Moreover, we impose the following constraints of ILP formulation on the floorplan.

- Edges between PEs on different FPGAs must cross the FPGA boundary. If $Edge_n$ connects PE_{n0} and PE_{n1},

$$\forall_i v_{i,n0} \neq v_{i,n1} \leftrightarrow e_n \tag{6}$$

- Resources of an FPGA must exceed the total resources of PEs allocated to it.
  $v_j.area$: resources of PE_j
  $f_i.area$: resources of $FPGA_i$

$$\forall_i \sum_j v_j.area \times v_{i,j} \leq f_i.area \tag{7}$$

- Each PE must be assigned to only a single FPGA.

$$\forall_j \sum_i v_{i,j} = 1 \tag{8}$$

The objective is to minimize the number of edges across the FPGAs and their total width. We give priority to minimization of the number of edges across FPGAs by multiplying the number of edges across FPGAs with a large number ($LARGE\_NUM$).

$e_k.width$: the width of $Edge_k$

$$minimize LARGE\_NUM \times \sum_k e_k + e_k.width \times e_k \tag{9}$$

4.5   Solo-FPGA Floorplanning

In this step, the VA Generator employs AutoBridge floorplanning for each FPGA used and places the PEs assigned to that FPGA on the appropriate islands. This balances the circuit latency within each FPGA, thereby improving its performance.

We virtually place the PEs that lie outside the circuit and communicate with it to employ AutoBridge floorplanning properly. Figure 7 depicts an example of a virtual PE placement. In Fig. 7, blue rectangles represent islands and orange rectangles represent API islands. In this example, PE0 and PE2 are assigned to FPGA0, and PE1 and PE2 are assigned to FPGA1 via multi-FPGA floorplanning. As illustrated in Fig. 7, PE1 and PE3, which communicate with the PEs assigned to FPGA0, are virtually placed on the API island of FPGA0. This process is the same as that for FPGA1. In this manner, the VA Generator places the PEs communicating with external components on islands close to the API island using AutoBridge floorplanning. In this floorplanning formulation, considering the virtually placed PEs, the VA Generator minimizes the total edge cost, which is defined as the product of the edge length and the edge bandwidth to improve the circuit.

$$minimize \sum_k e_k.length \times e_k.width \qquad (10)$$

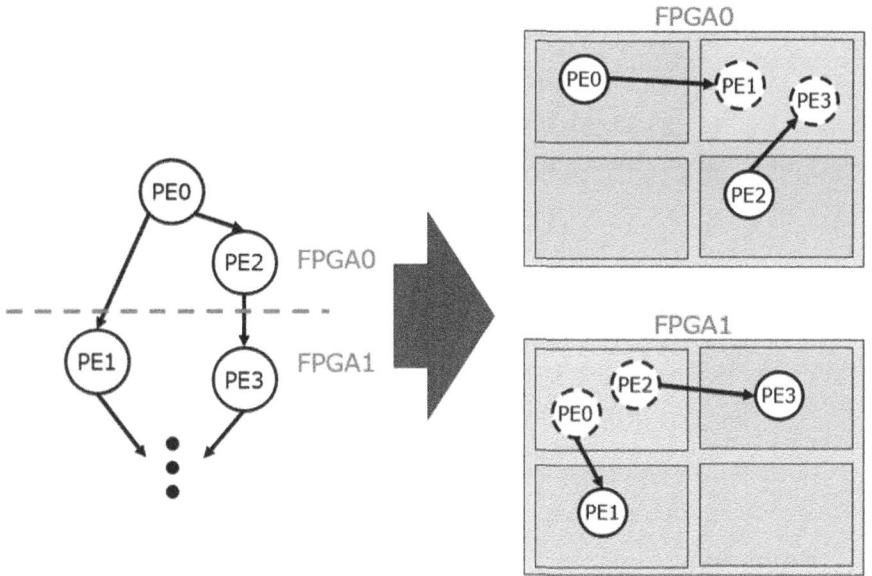

Fig. 7. Example of virtual PE placement in solo-FPGA floorplanning

Table 1. Board information in the experiment

Board_ID	Device name	Available islands	Connected boards
FPGA_0	U250	X0Y0:X3Y7	1
FPGA_1	U250	X0Y0:X3Y7	0

5 Experiments

5.1 Experimental Environment

In our experiments, a Xilinx Alveo U250 with a PCI Express (PCIe) Gen3 interface is targeted. A PC with an Intel core i7-13700F 5.10GHz 16 core processor, 64GB of memory, and Ubuntu 20.04 operating system is used. Vitis HLS 2021.2 is used for HLS compilation. Vivado 2021.2 and RapidWright 2021.2.0 are used to construct the circuits. Although the VA Generator inserts ReVA_APIs into the circuits, as described in Sect. 4.2, ReVA_API is currently still in development. Therefore, in this experiment, PCIe IP blocks [1] is inserted into the circuits instead of ReVA_API.

We have prepared a board information file (Table 1) and Convolutional neural network (CNN) circuits (Table 2) for the experiment, and they are inputted into the VA Generator. Table 1 demonstrates that two interconnected U250 boards are available, which comprise 4×8 islands. Table 2 shows the number of PEs and FIFOs, the utilization rates in HLS reports of CNN circuits.

Table 2. CNN benchmarks

Size	PEs	FIFOs	DSP%	BRAM%	FF%	LUT%
13×14	440	799	59	33	32	50
16×20	740	1373	104	51	69	87

Table 3. Implementation results

Size	Board_ID	Used islands	DSP%	BRAM%	FF%	LUT%
13×14	FPGA_0	X0Y0:X3Y7	59	33	38	36
	FPGA_1	-	-	-	-	-
16×20	FPGA_0	X0Y0:X3Y3	63	30	39	50
	FPGA_1	X0Y0:X3Y7	70	24	41	54

5.2 Evaluation

The results of implementing CNN benchmarks using the VA Generator are listed in Table 3. In Table 3, the region of each FPGA board used for circuits is demonstrated. In addition, resource utilization rates within the regions are presented.

In the experiment of the smallest circuit (13×14), whose demands are met by a single FPGA as illustrated in Table 2, it is constructed on an FPGA. On the other hand, the larger circuit (16×20), that requires slightly more resources than those of a single FPGA, is constructed on regions of one and a half FPGAs.

In these cases, the resource utilization rates in all regions are kept to a maximum of approximately 70%. Therefore, these circuits are expected to achieve stable performance.

In these experiments, circuits are implemented using the VA Generator and their features are demonstrated. However, these circuits have not yet been tested on actual FPGAs, and their exact performances have been unconfirmed. We are currently working on this task, and intend to evaluate them soon, including the overhead of inter-device communication.

6   Conclusion

In this paper, we propose ReVA to overcome hardware resource shortages in acceleration tasks in large-scale computing. To this end, a VA Generator prototype is designed and implemented, which synthesizes software programs via HLS and partitions the circuits to construct them across multiple FPGAs. Circuits are implemented on appropriate regions of several FPGAs based on input HLS sources using the VA Generator. Their performances are expected to be stably high, because the circuits are constructed with balanced utilization of FPGA resources.

In the future works, we intend to build the circuits implemented using the VA Generator on actual FPGAs to evaluate their performances more accurately. Additionally, we intend to improve the VA Generator to support other FPGA devices, enabling its evaluation in conjunction with various devices and connection types.

Acknowledgments. This work is partially supported by JSPS Grant-in-Aid for Scientific Research (C) 24K14874.

References

1. 2024 Advanced Micro Devices Inc.: Ultrascale+ device integrated block for PCI express (PCIE). https://www.xilinx.com/products/intellectual-property/pcie4-ultrascale-plus.html. Accessed 30 Aug 2024
2. Dai, G., Huang, T., Chi, Y., Xu, N., Wang, Y., Yang, H.: Foregraph: exploring large-scale graph processing on multi-FPGA architecture. In: Proceedings of the 2017 ACM/SIGDA International Symposium on Field-Programmable Gate Arrays, pp. 217–226 (2017). https://doi.org/10.1145/3020078.3021739
3. Gonzalez, J.E., Low, Y., Gu, H., Bickson, D., Guestrin, C.: Powergraph: distributed graph-parallel computation on natural graphs. In: 10th USENIX Symposium on Operating Systems Design and Implementation (OSDI 2012), pp. 17–30 (2012)

4. Guo, L., et al.: Autobridge: coupling coarse-grained floorplanning and pipelining for high-frequency HLS design on multi-die FPGAS. In: The 2021 ACM/SIGDA International Symposium on Field-Programmable Gate Arrays, pp. 81–92 (2021). https://doi.org/10.1145/3431920.3439289

5. Guo, L., et al.: Rapidstream: parallel physical implementation of FPGA HLS designs. In: Proceedings of the 2022 ACM/SIGDA International Symposium on Field-Programmable Gate Arrays, pp. 1–12 (2022). https://doi.org/10.1145/3490422.3502361

6. Jiang, W., et al.: Achieving super-linear speedup across multi-FPGA for real-time DNN inference. ACM Trans. Embed. Comput. Syst. (TECS) **18**(5s), 1–23 (2019). https://doi.org/10.1145/3358192

7. Lavin, C., Kaviani, A.: Rapidwright: enabling custom crafted implementations for FPGAS. In: 2018 IEEE 26th Annual International Symposium on Field-Programmable Custom Computing Machines (FCCM), pp. 133–140. IEEE (2018). https://doi.org/10.1109/FCCM.2018.00030

8. Nakajo, H., Oigo, Y., Takeoka, S., Takemoto, M., Miyoshi, T.: Overview of the reconfigurable virtual accelerator reva. IEICE Technical Report, vol. 115, no. 228, pp. 45–50 (2015)

9. Shen, J., Wang, D., Huang, Y., Wen, M., Zhang, C.: Scale-out acceleration for 3D CNN-based lung nodule segmentation on a multi-FPGA system. In: Proceedings of the 56th Annual Design Automation Conference 2019, pp. 1–6 (2019). https://doi.org/10.1145/3316781.3317906

10. Sun, Y., Amano, H.: Fic-RNN: a multi-FPGA acceleration framework for deep recurrent neural networks. IEICE Trans. Inf. Syst. **103**(12), 2457–2462 (2020). https://doi.org/10.1587/transinf.2020PAP0003

11. Thompson, N.C., Greenewald, K.H., Lee, K., Manso, G.F.: The computational limits of deep learning. CoRR abs/2007.05558 (2020). https://arxiv.org/abs/2007.05558

12. Waidyasooriya, H.M., Hariyama, M.: Multi-FPGA accelerator architecture for stencil computation exploiting spacial and temporal scalability. IEEE Access **7**, 53188–53201 (2019). https://doi.org/10.1109/ACCESS.2019.2910824

13. Yaguchi, K., Maeda, E., Teruya, D., Osana, Y., Miyoshi, T., Nakajo, H.: Partitioning and distributing circuit using HLS split compilation tool for reconfigurable virtual accelerator (reva). IEICE Technical Report, vol. 122, no. 354, pp. 7–12 (2023)

Building Simulation Environment of Reconfigurable Virtual Accelerator (ReVA)

Shunya Kawai[1]([✉]), Eriko Maeda[1], Kazuki Yaguchi[1], Yasunori Osana[2], Takefumi Miyoshi[3], and Hironori Nakajo[4]

[1] Tokyo University of Agriculture and Technology, Graduate School of Engineering, Tokyo, Japan
{s244623r,s234750v}@st.go.tuat.ac.jp
[2] Kumamoto University, Research and Education Institute for Semiconductors and Informatics, Kumamoto, Japan
osana@kumamoto-u.ac.jp
[3] WasaLabo, LLC., Tokyo, Japan
miyo@wasa-labo.com
[4] Tokyo University of Agriculture and Technology, Institute of Engineering, Tokyo, Japan
nakajo@cc.tuat.ac.jp

Abstract. In recent years, research in AI and HPC has explored accelerating computations using FPGAs. High-Level Synthesis (HLS) is beneficial for implementing algorithms from these fields onto FPGAs as circuits. However, since the circuits generated by HLS are generally larger than those designed with HDL. Moreover, the operations in these fields tend to increase in number and complexity, and the FPGA resources required are increasing accordingly. Therefore, using FPGAs in practice presents challenges regarding resource restrictions. To address these issues, we are researching Reconfigurable Virtual Accelerator (ReVA), which allows the sharing of resources across multiple FPGAs and enables the implementation of large-scale circuits. ReVA creates and shares virtual accelerators (VAs) using the resources of multiple FPGAs. Processors and VAs in a ReVA share data using distributed shared memory (DSM). Furthermore, the data on the VA and DSM are dynamically arranged so that access from each of the processors used is the shortest. In this paper, we propose and implement ReVA Simulator. ReVA Simulator can reproduce ReVA operation without the need to prepare an actual device with an FPGA, processor and memory connected. Furthermore, we estimated the execution time when utilizing ReVA and conducted evaluations. The evaluation result shows that ReVA simulator achieves FFT reduced by 36% against execution in C.

Keywords: FPGA · Hardware Acceleration · Vivado · Post-Implementation Simulation

This work is partially supported by JSPS Grant-in-Aid for Scientific Research (C) 24K14874.

© The Author(s), under exclusive license to Springer Nature Switzerland AG 2025
H. R. Arabnia et al. (Eds.): CSCE 2024, CCIS 2256, pp. 207–221, 2025.
https://doi.org/10.1007/978-3-031-85638-9_16

1   Introduction

In recent years, scientific researches start utilize artificial intelligence (AI) and high-performance computing (HPC). In these fields with vast computational requirements, research aims to accelerate computations. As one approach, there are efforts to accelerate computations by converting hardware to a portion of the processing using FPGA(Field Programmable Gate Arrays).

1.1   Hardware Acceleration in AI and HPC

In recent years, the fields of AI and HPC have seen an increase in the size of computation and data [6]. Therefore, challenges such as FPGA resource constraints and accelerator complexity arise in hardware acceleration within these fields.

Designers describe the circuits to be implemented on FPGAs using Hardware Description Languages (HDL). Designers must have a deep understanding of hardware and mastery of HDL for HDL-designed circuits to perform efficiently. Therefore, in recent years, there has been a trend toward utilizing High-Level Synthesis (HLS) instead of directly describing circuits in HDL. HLS refers to converting programs written in high-level languages (HLL), such as C, into circuit descriptions. By using HLS, it is possible to reduce costs associated with mastering HDL and acquiring knowledge about hardware. When using HLS to describe circuits, it is possible to generate larger circuits than directly describing them in HDL. Using HLS for hardware acceleration in the fields of AI and HPC, where vast processing is required, makes circuit implementation even more challenging.

Our research lab is researching Reconfigurable Virtual Accelerator (ReVA) to address these issues. ReVA enables efficient implementation of large-scale circuits by combining resources from multiple FPGAs.

2   ReVA

2.1   Overview of ReVA

ReVA is a system that enables multiple computers and FPGAs to function as a single unit. ReVA receives programs written in high-level languages as input. ReVA extracts the parts of the input program that are convertible to hardware and performs conversion to circuit descriptions by using HLS. The hardware-transformed parts, which were shared, are distributed across multiple FPGAs.

Image of Using ReVA. Users of ReVA submit the software program that they want to accelerate to the ReVA system. It performs preparation for acceleration and program execution. Since users only need to submit the software program, they can achieve high-speed execution of software without requirements of hardware knowledge or concerns about resource boundaries of computers and FPGAs.

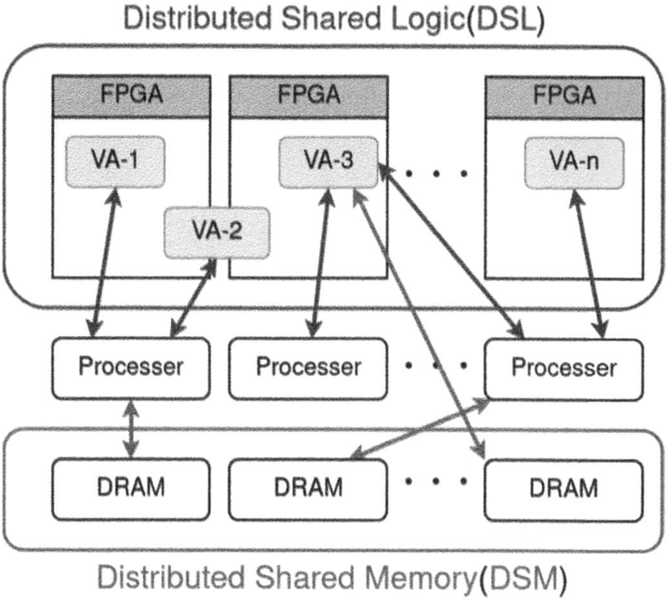

Fig. 1. Conceptual Diagram of ReVA

Function of ReVA. ReVA operates in a network where multiple processors, FPGAs, and memory are connected. Figure 1 describes The overall conceptual diagram of ReVA. Four distinctive features of ReVA are listed below.

Distributed Shared Logic: DSL. The circuits are implemented on a single FPGA or distributed over several FPGAs on a network. Several processors share the implemented circuitry.

Virtual Accelerator: VA. We call Each circuit constructed on the DSL as a virtual accelerator (VA). Each processor can use each VA as a single virtual accelerator.

Distributed Shared Memory: DSM. A virtually shared single address space stores data. Each processor and each VA have access to this address space, facilitating easy data sharing and access.

Dynamic Placement of VAs and Data on DSM. ReVA system places the VAs and data on DSM to maximize performance from the perspective of each accessing processor. In other words, in ReVA, VAs are dynamically placed on the FPGA to minimize physical distance from the core processor. Similarly, data on DSM is dynamically placed in memory to minimize the physical distance of the core processor accessing the data.

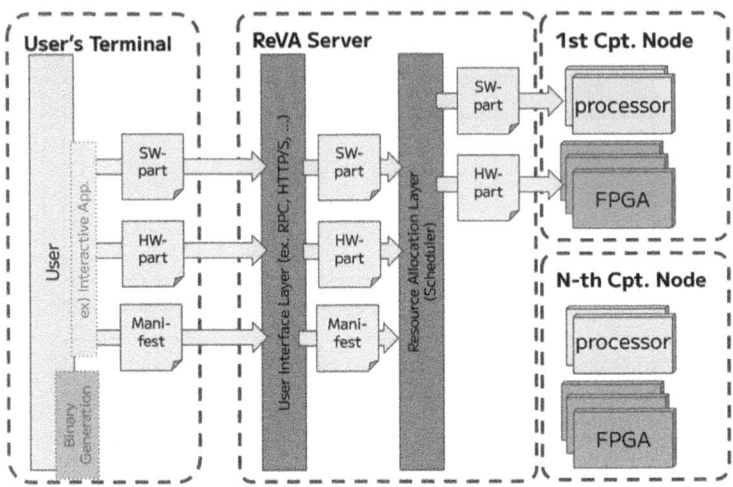

Fig. 2. Diagram of ReVA's Architecture

Architecture of ReVA. Figure 2 is a schematic diagram of the ReVA architecture. The internal architecture of ReVA is composed of three distinct components.

User's Terminal. This mainly refers to the computers through which users access the ReVA system. It converts the user's software program into three binary files: SW-part, HW-part, and Manifest, and sends them to the ReVA server. The software application described below performs this process. The following describes the three binary files generated.

- SW-part(Software part): The part of the software program that is executed as it is.
- HW-part(Hardware part): The parts are to be converted to hardware for higher speeds.
- Manifest: Summary of information required for scheduling when deploying SW-part and HW-part (regions, number of CPU/FPGAs to be used)

ReVA Server. It receives the three binary files from the user terminal. Subsequently, in the scheduler (Resource Allocation Layer), based on the information in the Manifest, the destination computer nodes for the placement of SW-part and HW-part are determined and transmitted.

Computer Node. They are physical connections of multiple processors, FPGAs, and memory, which are present in large numbers within the ReVA system. They receive SW-part and HW-part from the ReVA server. SW-part and HW-part placed on these nodes collaborate to perform processing and return the computation results to the user terminal.

2.2   The Software Application of ReVA

The software application of the ReVA system consists of a UI (User Interface) application and a binary generation application.

UI Application. It is an interactive application that serves as a window for ReVA users. The main functions are as follows.

– Pass input program to binary generation application
– Pass binary files to the ReVA sever
– Receive calculation results

Binary Generation Application. This application converts the input program into three binary files: SW-part, HW-part, and Manifest. The binary generation application consists of following two applications.

Hardware Part Extraction Mechanism. Hardware Part Extraction Mechanism splits the input program into SW-part and HW-part. The main functions are shown as follows.

– Construct SW-part and Manifest
– Convert HW-part to HLS design with optimization directives for HLS

VA Generator. VA Generator is the generic name for HLS and Circuit Partitioning Mechanism. The main functions are as follows.

– HLS:Converts HLS design generated by Hardware Part Extraction Mechanism into circuit description
– Circuit Partitioning Mechanism: Split circuit descriptions and create binary files

2.3   Operation of ReVA

This section describes the process flow when using ReVA. Figure 3 shows the flow of processing in ReVA. There are two main parts to ReVA's processing: implementation of the accelerator and execution of the acceleration. The following sections describe each process.

The Section on Implementing Accelerators. The accelerator implementation section mainly conducts input program partitioning and virtual accelerator (VA) generation.

1. Accepts input programs written in HLL
2. Splits the input program into SW-part and HW-part by HW-part Extraction Mechanism

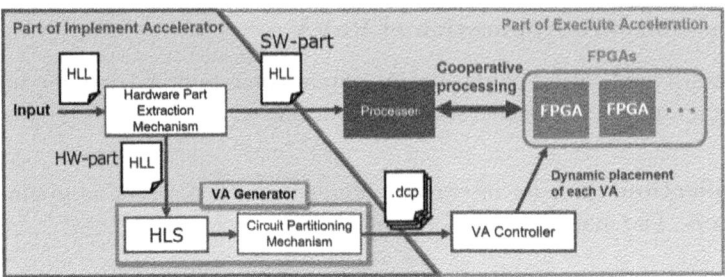

Fig. 3. Process flow of ReVA

3. VA Generator
   (a) Convert each VA belonging to HW-part to circuit description by HLS, and partition the circuit
   (b) Create design checkpoint file (.dcp)
4. Pass SW-part to the processor and the dcp file, which is each VA, to the VA Controller.

The Section Executing on the Acceleration. In the acceleration execution process, the software and hardware work together to perform computations. ReVA simulator proposed in this paper simulates this acceleration execution part. The following outlines the flow of collaborative computation.

1. Start SW-part execution on processor
2. During the execution of SW-part, when the VA calculation results are needed, the VA Controller (described later) dynamically places the VA into the FPGA.
3. Execute calculation at VA and return calculation results to SW-part
4. Restart SW-part execution
5. Repeat step 2 to 4 until completing SW-part execution

VA Controller. The VA Controller is responsible for placement and management of VAs. The VA Controller is always aware of the following.

– VA address: Location of any VA on the FPGA
– Location of unused resources on FPGA

The VA Controller also decides where to place VAs and allocates resources to VAs by extracting only the necessary amount. In addition, VA Controller replaces the HC_API within the ReVA_API described below.

When a SW-part uses a VA, it must first send a request to the VA Controller to obtain the VA address of that VA. After obtaining VA addresses, SW-part can communicate with each VA without going through the VA Controller.

One VA Controller is located at each node and serves as a window for inter-node communication between SW-part and VA across nodes.

3   Related Work

3.1   Research on FPGA Virtualisation

ReVA performs FPGA virtualization and resource sharing using DSL. There are studies on FPGA virtualization as follows.

Comparison of FPGA Virtualisation Methods. [7] is a comparison of FPGA virtualization methods. In this research, various techniques and approaches to FPGA virtualization are analyzed from many aspects, such as flexibility, performance, and security, to classify them into the following categories.

1. Resource level:architecture, I/O virtualisation
    (a) Reconfigurable
    (b) Unreconstructable
2. Node level:virtualisation in a single FPGA
3. Multi-node level:virtualisation in clusters containing two or more FPGAs

In this paper, examples of resource-level include I/O sharing in overlays and multi-tenant systems, examples of node-level include VMM support and runtime systems, and examples of multi-node-level include LEAP (Latency-insensitive Environment for Application Programming) [3], MapReduce, and Catapult.

According to this categorization, FPGA virtualization in ReVA corresponds to the multi-node level. Therefore, LEAP, MapReduce, and Catapult, which are also at the multi-node level, could be relevant references for ReVA research.

FPGA Virtualisation Using Partial Reconfiguration. A similar example to the VA implementation of ReVA exists in the German HZDR study [5]. This study focuses on FPGA utilization to improve the performance of modern data center architectures and proposes virtualization techniques for flexible FPGA utilization in cloud environments. By using a technology called partial reconfiguration, which allows rewriting specific regions of the FPGA, FPGAs are able to be virtualized, enabling the implementation of multiple accelerators on a single FPGA.

In terms of the ability to implement multiple accelerators on a single FPGA, this aspect is similar to a feature of the DSL in ReVA. However, this study does not perform virtualization of multiple FPGAs and differs from the DSL in ReVA.

This proposed method partitions the resources of the FPGA into several blocks before implementing accelerators and passes the required number of blocks during implementation. Therefore, it becomes easy to implement multiple accelerators on a single FPGA and move them within the FPGA. However, if it differs from the size of the implemented circuit to the size of the partitioned block, there may be unused resources. In this regard, in ReVA, partitioning of FPGA resources is not performed in advance. Instead, ReVA dynamically allocates the required resources for each circuit size during implementation. This method allows more flexibility and efficiency for utilization of FPGA resources in accelerator implementation compared to the approach proposed in the study [5].

Overlay. Regarding FPGA virtualization, Sect. 3.1 demonstrated the existence of an architecture called Overlay, which performs resource-level virtualization. Overlay is one of the attempts to enhance the portability of circuits by virtualizing FPGAs. Writing circuit descriptions to an FPGA requires configuration, which involves checking the circuit description, determines the placement of I/O, and generates a bitstream for writing to the FPGA. In conventional methods, bitstream generated by performing configuration to write circuits to an FPGA, could not be used for different types of FPGAs, requiring configuration for each FPGA individually. However, executing configurations can be time-consuming, which is difficult to transplant circuits in the conventional approach. Overlay enables writing to different FPGAs using the same bitstream, significantly reducing configuration time and allowing circuits to have high portability.

There is research that has designed and implemented overlays for data center infrastructure management, allowing for easy management [2]. We believe the high portability of circuits in this study is closely related to the dynamic placement of VAs in ReVA. On the other hand, this method does not consider the placement of multiple circuits on a single FPGA and the virtualization of plural FPGAs as introduced in Sect. 3.1.

LEAP. Regarding the development of applications running on FPGAs, there has been a problem of low design abstraction and long development time compared to application development in software operating systems (OS). In this regard, LEAP [3] focuses on communication in FPGA design and provides an environment where application developers can focus solely on development while maintaining FPGA flexibility. Specifically, LEAP provides an abstract interface to hardware resources, automatic management of those resources, and a mighty system library to support RTL program design. Additionally, LEAP provides an abstraction for memory similar to software.

In this regard, both LEAP and ReVA share commonalities in abstracting communication and memory management between applications on FPGA and processors. However, LEAP does not consider the case where circuits span across multiple FPGAs, which sets it apart from ReVA in this aspect.

3.2   Vivado Simulator

Vivado has a Vivado Simulator that can simulate designed circuits during implementation on an FPGA. Vivado simulator has three simulations: Behavioral Simulation, Post-Synthesis Simulation, and Post-Implementation Simulation [8]. They can all be used to simulate circuits but at different simulation stages.

Before circuit synthesis, we can perform Behavioral simulation. After synthesis, we can perform Post-synthesis simulation. In contrast, Post-Implementation

Simulation executes simulations on designs that have completed implementation. This simulation can verify the design that has completed implementation to meet the logical requirements and function correctly. Therefore, it can perform simulations closer to the state of being implemented on an FPGA than the other two.

The above shows that Post-Implementation Simulation is valuable in ReVA simulators. However, it does not considered the unique behavior of ReVA, which is a calculation in cooperation with software programs. Therefore, in the ReVA simulator, a mechanism is created to allow SW-part and Vivado simulator to exchange input and output, reproducing the collaborative computation between SW-part and HW-part.

4 ReVA Simulator

4.1 Positioning of ReVA Simulator in ReVA

As explained in Sect. 2.3, ReVA Simulator replicates a series of processes starting with calculations in the SW-part and proceeding to execute computations on VAs as needed. Furthermore, We can also utilize ReVA Simulator to aid in the development of ReVA by facilitating tasks such as checking the status of VAs divided by the VA Generator. When using ReVA Simulator, there is no need for physical hardware such as FPGA. ReVA Simulator can execute all operations within software programs and applications. Now, while it is possible to measure the time taken for the computations by using ReVA Simulator, it is unable to calculate the time for tasks such as writing to the FPGA or communication during VA usage.

ReVA Simulator Specifications. This section describes the specifications and operation of the ReVA simulator.

Prepare SW-Part and Design Checkpoint Files. The inputs to the ReVA simulator are SW-part and Design CheckPoint files. For the Design CheckPoint file, first prepare a program in C that describes the process to be accelerated. Next, converting the C program to a circuit description using HLS and perform synthesis and implementation using Vivado. However, It is unable to generate SW-part dynamically because we have not yet determined Hardware Part Extraction Mechanism specification. Therefore, SW-part should be prepared manually.

Obtaining VA Information. ReVA Simulator needs information about the VA's I/O ports and the location where the VA is located on the FPGA to have the VA perform calculations. Therefore, ReVA Simulator needs a function to retrieve this information from the design checkpoint file.

Creating a Test Bench. ReVA Simulator cannot perform Post-Implementation Simulation with a design checkpoint file alone. It is necessary to create a testbench to perform Post-Implementation Simulation. Therefore, ReVA Simulator needs a function to generate a testbench based on input port information and input values.

4.2   ReVA Simulator Operation

ReVA Simulator receives SW-part and Design Checkpoint files(.dcp) as input. There may be more than one design checkpoint file to pass, and we assume SW-part written in C.

Figure 4 shows the process flow of ReVA Simulator. First, it outputs the information of VAs from the received design checkpoint file as input. At this time, the VA-ID allocation, described below, is also carried out. Second, ReVA Simulator executes the cooperative computation between SW-part and HW-part. Execution of SW-part begins, and if SW-part requires computation in the VA during execution, ReVA Simulator performs the simulation of the VA. ReVA Simulator passes the VA-ID and inputs of the VA from SW-part to the function that performs the simulation for the VA. Within this function, ReVA Simulator accesses the necessary files based on the VA-ID and creates a testbench accordingly. Finally, ReVA Simulator executes the Post-Implementation Simulation and returns the results to SW-part. SW-part uses the calculation results in the returned VA and resumes execution. These operations repeat until SW-part finishes executing.

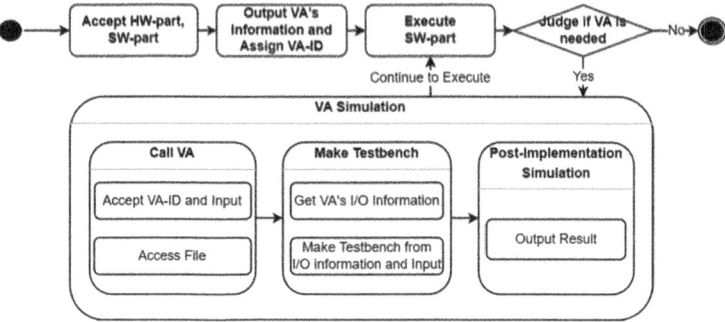

Fig. 4. Flow of operation of ReVA Simulator

4.3   SW-Part in ReVA Simulator

The specifications of Hardware Part Extraction Mechanism in ReVA have not yet been finalized, nor have the specifications of the binary files (SW-part, HW-part, and Manifest) been generated. However, SW-part is essential for ReVA Simulator to work. ReVA Simulator should perform the following two processes for SW-part.

– Creation of files for input delivery to VA
– Running a VA simulation

Creating Files for Input. ReVA Simulator creates a file for input to VA for each VA-ID. VA-ID is an ID assigned to each VA to identify it and is mainly used when SW-part calls a VA. In actual ReVA, SW-part uses the VA-ID to check the location of each VA in the FPGA. However, in addition to identifying each VA, the ReVA simulator also uses it to manage the VA's information and output. ReVA Simulator writes the value passed as VA input from the SW-part to the input file corresponding to that VA.

Running a VA Simulation. ReVA Simulator executes a function that executes VA simulation. The function calls the script file and executes the simulation executable. ReVA Simulator creates a simulation run file for each call to the VA, based on the specification that SW-part calls the VA as necessary. The simulation execution file calls the function that creates the testbench and executes Post-Implementation Simulation. ReVA Simulator obtains the VA output from the output file generated during simulation execution, as described below. ReVA Simulator generates output files for each VA output port.

4.4   Simulation of VA in ReVA Simulators

It can divide the processes performed by ReVA simulator when executing the simulation of a VA as follows.

1. Preparation for simulation runs.
   (a) Allocating VA-ID
   (b) Obtaining information from the VA
2. Reproduction of SW-part and HW-part co-computations
   (a) Creating test benches
   (b) Running Post-Implementation Simulation

Preparation for Simulation Runs. ReVA Simulator needs to retrieve information about the VAs before executing the simulation. ReVA Simulator retrieve VA's information using VA-ID. Using VA-ID allows the management of VA information for each VA individually. Moreover, during simulation execution, it becomes easy to extract only the necessary information.

ReVA Simulator retrieves information about VAs from the design checkpoint files to create test benches. The information to be retrieved includes VA's I/O port information, Pblock constraints [9], and utilization reports. These are obtained on Vivado using Tcl (Tool Command Language). ReVA Simulator generates Utilization reports for each VA-ID and output information regarding I/O ports and Pblock constraints in a CSV file along with the assigned VA-ID. We can use the information gained here not only to build test benches but also to check the condition of the VA. For example, we can use it to check the operation of VA Generator by referring to the information of the divided VAs by VA Generator.

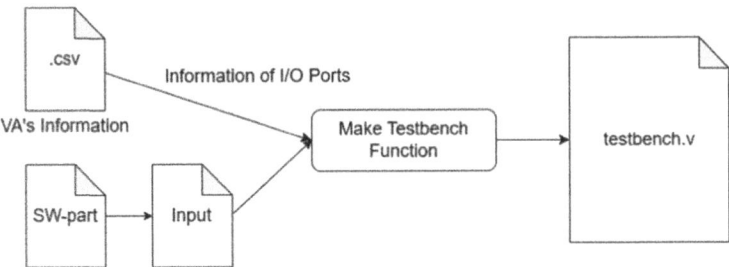

Fig. 5. Testbench creation flow

Creating Test Benches. ReVA simulator requires the creation of test benches to simulate VAs. In addition, in ReVA, it is also conceivable to perform calculations using different inputs of each instance of the VA when using VAs multiple times. ReVA simulator creates a test bench for each VA for each input as needed to accommodate this. As shown in Fig. 5, ReVA Simulator creates test benches accordingly.

The test bench creation function receives I/O port information from the VA's data. Additionally, the test bench receives input from the input file created by the SW-part. ReVA Simulator creates the test bench based on the received information. At this point, this function adds to the testbench with processes to record the accelerator's output and execution time during the simulation of the VA. At this point, this function adds to the testbench with processes to record the accelerator's output and the simulation time of the VA. The output is recorded by exporting the output values to a text file and recording the time-varying changes in input and output values as a VCD file. Additionally, the execution time of the accelerator is recorded as the total number of clock cycles from the start to the end of the simulation of the VA.

Running Post-implementation Simulation. ReVA Simulator executes the Post-Implementation Simulation using Tcl based on the created testbench. As described earlier, the testbench includes processes to record the output of the accelerator and the number of clock cycles. Therefore, ReVA Simulator generates a file containing the recorded results during each execution. After the simulation, ReVA Simulator exports a log file that consolidates the VA-ID, inputs, obtained outputs, and the total clock cycles as execution time. This log file enables the later verification of the accelerator's output concerning the inputs from the SW-part.

5   Evaluation

5.1   Operating Environment and Evaluation Programs

Table 1 shows the operating environment for evaluating ReVA Simulator. As mentioned earlier, the ReVA Simulator does not actually use FPGA hardware.

Therefore, the term "FPGA board" here refers to the FPGA board specified when performing Synthesis and Implementation in Vivado. Hence, the simulation was not conducted using the actual Alveo U50 board [1].

The accelerators used for evaluation are matrix product operation, Fast Fourier Transform (FFT) [4], and convolutional operation. These programs are written in C language. Additionally, The implementation of HLS is using Vitis HLS for these programs and created designs in Vivado.

Table 1. Operating Environment

CPU	Intel Xeon Silver 4210R
Number of physical/logical cores	20/40
Frequency	2.40 GHz
Memory	64 GB
OS	Ubuntu20.04
Tools	Vivado2021.2
	Vitis HLS2021.2
FPGA Board	Xilinx Alveo U50

5.2   Evaluation Results

The results of the experiments conducted in the previous section is shown Table 2. The time measured in C is the average of 10^6 runs of each.

First, from this result, it can be read that the matrix product takes about three times longer to compute than in C as it is. This result is believed to be due to accelerating the computation of a single element of the matrix product. The overall computation time may have increased due to the long time required for the input. Second, from this result, it can be read that the convolutional operation takes about two times longer to compute than in C as it is. This result is thought to be because the computation of one element of the convolution is accelerated as well. However, regarding these results, considering that ReVA allows multiple accelerators to perform the computation simultaneously, it is faster to perform the computation on the accelerators. For example, consider the case of multiple accelerators, one at a time, on multiple FPGAs, with each accelerator performing one element of each operation. In this case, the calculation can be performed with approximately one accelerator for the number of clocks shown in Table 2. Finally, from this result, FFT was confirmed to be about $3 * 10^5$ns faster than execution in C.

Table 2. Comparison of execution times with accelerators and the C language.

	Accelerators		C
	Clocks	Times	
500×500 matrix product	$1.26 * 10^8$	$1.26 * 10^9$ns	$6.42 * 10^8$ns
8192-point FFT	$6.97 * 10^4$	$6.97 * 10^5$ns	$1.08 * 10^6$ns
convolutional operation	$2.97 * 10^6$	$2.97 * 10^7$ns	$1.40 * 10^7$ns

6 Conclusion

We presented the ReVA simulator for verifying the operation of ReVA in cases where there is no physical setup combining FPGAs and so on., towards the realization of ReVA. ReVA Simulator has the following features to reproduce the collaborative computation between SW-part and HW-part in ReVA.

- Allocating VA-ID, Obtaining information from the VA
- Creating test benches
- Running Post-Implementation Simulation

ReVA Simulator presented in this paper enables the estimation of the reduced computation time when using ReVA. As a future outlook, We will extend ReVA simulator to support simulations in cases where VAs are deployed and utilized across multiple FPGAs. In that case, ReVA needs to communicate between FPGAs, we need to extend ReVA simulator to estimate communication delay.

References

1. AMD: Alveo u50 data center accelerator card. https://japan.xilinx.com/products/boards-and-kits/alveo/u50.html. Accessed 31 Jan 2023
2. Bollengier, T., Najem, M., Le Lann, J.C., Lagadec, L.: Overlay architectures for FPGA resource virtualization. In: GDR SOC SIP. Nantes, France (2016). https://hal.archives-ouvertes.fr/hal-01405912
3. Fleming, K., Yang, H.J., Adler, M., Emer, J.: The leap FPGA operating system. In: 2014 24th International Conference on Field Programmable Logic and Applications (FPL), pp. 1–8 (2014). https://doi.org/10.1109/FPL.2014.6927488
4. Kastner, R., Matai, J., Neuendorffer, S.: Parallel Programming for FPGAs. arXiv e-prints (2018)
5. Knodel, O., Genssler, P., Spallek, R.: Virtualizing reconfigurable hardware to provide scalability in cloud architectures. In: CENICS 2017: The Tenth International Conference on Advances in Circuits, Electronics and Micro-electronics, pp. 33–38 (2017)
6. Thompson, N.C., Greenewald, K.H., Lee, K., Manso, G.F.: The Computational Limits of Deep Learning. CoRR (2020). https://arxiv.org/abs/2007.05558
7. Vaishnav, A., Pham, K., Koch, D.: A survey on FPGA virtualization. In: 2018 28th International Conference on Field Programmable Logic and Applications (FPL), pp. 131–1317. IEEE Computer Society, Los Alamitos, CA, USA (2018). https://doi.org/10.1109/FPL.2018.00031. https://doi.ieeecomputersociety.org/10.1109/FPL.2018.00031

8. Xilinx: 63988 - how to run timing simulation using vivado simulator? https://support.xilinx.com/s/article/63988. Accessed 12 Mar 2023
9. Xilinx: Vivado design suite user guide: hierarchical design (UG905). https://docs.xilinx.com/r/2021.2-English/ug905-vivado-hierarchical-design/Pblock-Constraints. Accessed 31 Jan 2023

Vector Register Sharing Mechanism for High Performance Hardware Acceleration

Tomoaki Tanaka[1], Michiya Kato[1], Yasunori Osana[2], Takefumi Miyoshi[3], Jubee Tada[4], Kiyofumi Tanaka[5], and Hironori Nakajo[6(✉)]

[1] Department of Electrical Engineering and Computer Science, Graduate School of Engineering, Tokyo University of Agriculture and Technology, 2-24-16 Nakacho, Koganei-shi, Tokyo 184-8588, Japan
{tomoaki-tanaka,s231841x}@st.go.tuat.ac.jp
[2] Research and Education Institute for Semiconductors and Informatics, Kumamoto University, 2-39-1 Kurokami, Chuo-ku, Kumamoto 860-8555, Japan
osana@kumamoto-u.ac.jp
[3] WasaLabo, LLC., K-2 Buransyu 6-5-20 Minaminaruse, Machida-shi, Tokyo 194-0045, Japan
miyo@wasa-labo.com
[4] Graduate School of Science and Engineering, Yamagata University, 1-4-12 Kojirakawa-machi, Yamagata-shi, Yamagata 990-8560, Japan
jubee@yz.yamagata-u.ac.jp
[5] Japan Advanced Institute of Science and Technology, 1-1 Asahidai, Nomi, Ishikawa 923-1292, Japan
kiyofumi@jaist.ac.jp
[6] Division of Advanced Information Technology Computer Science, Institute of Engineering, Tokyo University of Agriculture and Technology, 2-24-16 Nakacho, Koganei-shi, Tokyo 184-8588, Japan
nakajo@cc.tuat.ac.jp

Abstract. In recent years, demand for data-parallel processing has been growing, and this parallelism often appears in AI processes. One method to accelerate these processes is using DSA, domain-specific architecture. A common data transfer method on DSA is DMA, which is direct memory access. There are several studies on DMA-based accelerators. However, few studies focus on data transfer methods. In this paper, a vector register-sharing mechanism has been proposed as a new data transfer method. Our proposed mechanism is named "SHAVER". In this mechanism, a part of vector registers is directly shared with an accelerator. An open-source RISC-V vector co-processor is used to evaluate the mechanism's potential. It has been implemented on an FPGA and a simulator for the evaluations. The results indicate the possibility of the proposal mechanism to achieve a maximum of 7.13% speedup over DMA transfer.

Keywords: RISC-V · Hardware Acceleration · FPGA · SoC

ⓒ The Author(s), under exclusive license to Springer Nature Switzerland AG 2025
H. R. Arabnia et al. (Eds.): CSCE 2024, CCIS 2256, pp. 222–235, 2025.
https://doi.org/10.1007/978-3-031-85638-9_17

1   Introduction

AI tasks and image processing have been used in many recent applications. A recent AI application has spread in our work and life. Many smartphones use AI technology for face recognition to take a good picture and unlock the device [15,20]. For comfortable engineering, many AI assist applications are released around the world. Many companies have released an AI copilot service that supports us in writing and designing a program. GitHub, Inc. released GitHub Copilot, which assists the programmer and is published as free only for students [11]. AI tasks and processes often contain instructions with data-level parallelism. Processes with data-level parallelism perform the same operation on multiple data, such as matrix multiplication.

One method of speeding up these processes is the implementation of domain specific architecture (DSA). DSA is an architecture specialized for a specific process and is usually used with a main core. The main core offloads specific processes to the DSA to accelerate the processes. An accelerator is often used as the main core's hardware to send the heavy process. For example, Google developed the TPU (Tensor Processing Unit), which many AI developers use today. TPU also uses a technique that offloads some processing to an internal accelerator [13]. With the slowdown of Moore's Law, this type of DSA-based acceleration, other than general-purpose processor acceleration, has gained a high degree of attention in both commercial and academic research.

In addition, recent tasks have tended to use large amounts of data for processing. The recent tasks that use images and videos appear in many applications. The resolution of images and videos, such as WQHD and 4K, is higher than ever. Therefore, it is important to be able to transfer large amounts of data to DSA as quickly as possible to increase the speed of recent applications. However, little research has been involved on data transfer to accelerators.

The current data transfer rate depends on the width of the data bus. The SHAVER, which shares vector registers between the accelerator and processor, is proposed to avoid this dependence and achieve faster communication than now. Figure 1 shows the brief of this mechanism.

This mechanism enables high-speed data transfer to the accelerator because some vector registers are shared without a bus. Modern processors generally have a data cache to reduce overheads when accessing memory. In this case, the data cache accomplishes data transmission to the accelerator by using SHAVER.

In this paper, we implement SHAVER and a Direct Memory Access (DMA) Controller on FPGA using DDR4 memory. We also discuss aspects of the data transfer method through evaluation in simulation and implementation of FPGA.

2   Background and Related Work

2.1   Accelerator

IoT has been spreading worldwide, so there have been demands for digital signal processing and AI processing in embedded systems in recent years. Accelerators are used to achieve faster processing in some embedded systems. Xiaowen

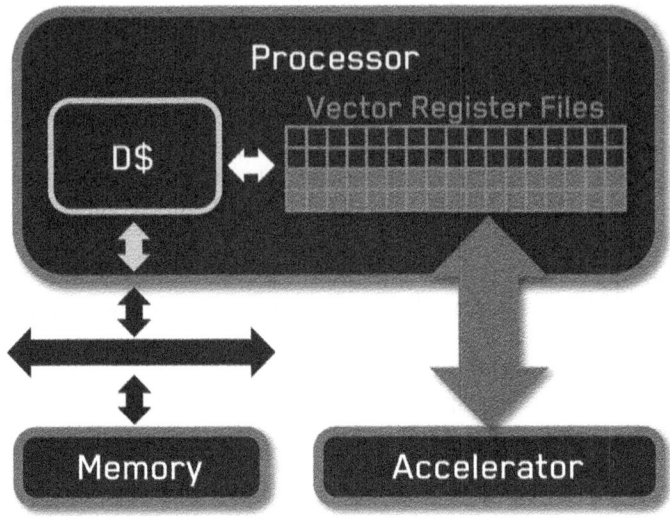

Fig. 1. Data transfer method in this research. (SHAVER: Sharing Vector Registers)

Chen et al. implemented a variable-size Fast Fourier transform (FFT) accelerator in 2018 [9]. FFT is a very common process in the domain of digital signal processing. Commercial devices have been released with the implementation of an FFT accelerator. For example, Sipeed has released the M1 module that implemented FFT accelerator [18]. Many AI domain accelerators have been developed to perform faster AI tasks on edge devices. Kyubaik Choi et al. have developed a low-cost convolutional neural network (CNN) accelerator focused on edge AI using FPGA in 2022 [10]. Commercially, Katsushige Matsubara of Renesas Electronics Corporation et al. have developed a processor that targets applications for autonomous driving systems. CNN accelerator is implemented on this processor [14].

A tightly-coupled accelerator and a loosely-coupled accelerator exist as a type of accelerator. A tightly-coupled accelerator is an accelerator that is connected to a main processor tightly. A loosely coupled accelerator is connected to a bus, not a main processor. Our proposed mechanism and a tightly coupled accelerator are especially alike. Alireza Amirshahi et al. have implemented tightly coupled small-scale systolic arrays (TiC-SATs) in the CPU. The accelerator is connected to general-purpose registers implemented by the CPU [4]. The study focused on recently quantized applications such as quantized neural networks (QNN). However, we have proposed a mechanism to get more performance out of an accelerator that can give and receive big data at once, not only for the acceleration of quantized applications.

This paper uses a simple accelerator for convolution to evaluate our proposed mechanism's performance.

2.2   Direct Memory Access

A commonly used method of transferring data to an accelerator is DMA. This transfer method is used on many devices. For example, ARM has developed DMA-230, a micro DMA controller for Cortex-M series cores, and achieved lower power consumption [6]. The ESP32 series, released by Espressif, is a popular series of microprocessors for IoT because they can use 2.4 GHz Wi-Fi and Bluetooth with no other hardware requirements. They also have a DMA controller [19]. Figure 2 shows the brief flow of DMA transfer. In this data transfer method, the processor first notifies the DMA controller with the address to write and read and the length of data to be transferred. Then, the main processor gives the DMA controller control of the bus connected to the memory and accelerator. The DMA controller is connected to the bus to allow direct communication between the devices to read from and write to. Communication is then performed between both devices. When the communication is completed, the DMA controller returns the bus mastership to the main processor. While the DMA controller has the mastership, the main processor cannot access memory or accelerators. After these flows, this system of peripherals and processors returns to normal operation.

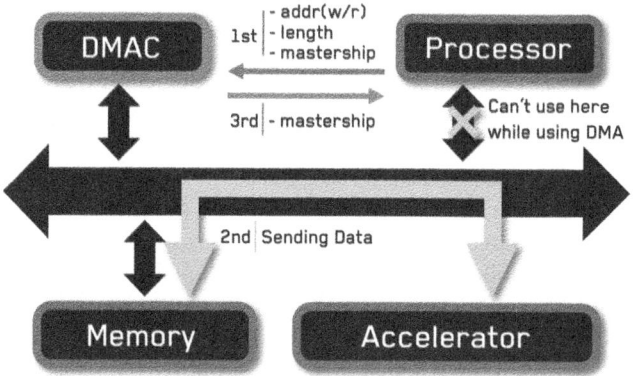

Fig. 2. Direct Memory Access.

Several studies have already been conducted on accelerators using DMA. However, Li Zhao et al. show us some problems with DMA transfer. DMA transfer frees the core from I/O operations. On the other hand, a significant latency occurs on DMA transfer by setup processes [27]. Almost all accelerators require a certain amount of data to maximize performance. In addition, it transfers the data with DMA transfer many times because the size of the data is bigger than the limit of the size of the DMA transfer. Therefore, the setup latency of DMA transfer prevents building a larger accelerator even if an accelerator can be implemented with a bigger size on a chip than now. In other words, DMA transfer cannot achieve the ideal performance of an accelerator.

2.3   RISC-V

RISC-V is an instruction set architecture (ISA) developed at the University of California, Berkeley (UCB) in 2011. The ISA specification is open and public and is provided in a format that anyone can freely access and use, unlike other architectures such as x86 and ARM [5].

RISC-V provides RV32I and RV64I as the basic instruction set. RV32I is a 32-bit basic instruction set, and RV64I is a 64-bit basic instruction set. RV64I is the instruction set that several 64-bit instructions are added to RV32I. These instruction sets contain only the basic instructions for integer operations. Some other instructions are provided as extension instruction sets, such as integer multiplication/division instructions (M extensions), floating-point arithmetic instructions (F extensions, D extensions), compressed instructions(C extensions), and atomic instructions (A extensions). In particular, the combination of the basic instruction set (I), M extension, F extension, D extension, and A extension is also called G extension [5].

2.4   RISC-V Vector Extensions

RISC-V Vector Extension (RVV) is one of the extended instruction sets of RISC-V. The first frozen version of 1.0 of RVV was released in 2021, making this extension a relatively new instruction set [7].

In RVV, there are 32 vector registers, v0 through v31. The length of the vector register (VLEN) is implementation-dependent. The size of the elements to be stored in them (ELEN) can be selected by the user as 8-bit, 16-bit, 32-bit, or 64-bit. ELEN and the length of vector registers can be set by manipulating the designated control status register (CSR).

Various RVV-compatible processors have been developed even before 2021. Matthew Johns et al. have developed a microprocessor that supports RVV version 0.8 in 2020 [12]. Guillem Cabo et al. also developed an ASIC implementation of a vector architecture for RVV version 0.7.1 in 2022, called the DRAC Vector In-Order (DVINO) processor. Several other commercial cores also exist [3]. For example, SiFive released the X280, a core that supports RVV for AI and machine learning at the edge [17].

To evaluate our proposed transfer method, a processor has to be able to be customized by ourselves. So, an open-source RVV core was used in this study.

2.5   RV64GC Processor: CVA6

CVA6 is an in-order processor implementing RV64GC developed by the Swiss Federal Institute of Technology in Zurich (ETH) and the University of Bologna [26]. This processor consists of 6-stages and a cache subsystem. The cache subsystem manages an instruction cache and a data cache.

In addition, the source code of this processor is open source and available on github [1]. It is written in SystemVerilog and has an interface for communicating with Ara, a co-processor supporting RVV. Only vector extension instructions are identified and sent to that interface.

2.6   RVV Co-processor: Ara

Ara is a co-processor implementing RVV, which was developed by ETH and the University of Bologna. Ara works in tandem with CVA6 [16]. An implementation of Ara mounted on CVA6 and a simulation evaluation environment are available on Git Hub. The core was released in Dec. 2019 before the RVV specification was frozen. The first implementation was based on the version 0.5 draft of RVV [8]. After the frozen version 1.0 of RVV was released, Ara started to support its instructions. The brief block diagram of this system is shown in Fig. 3.

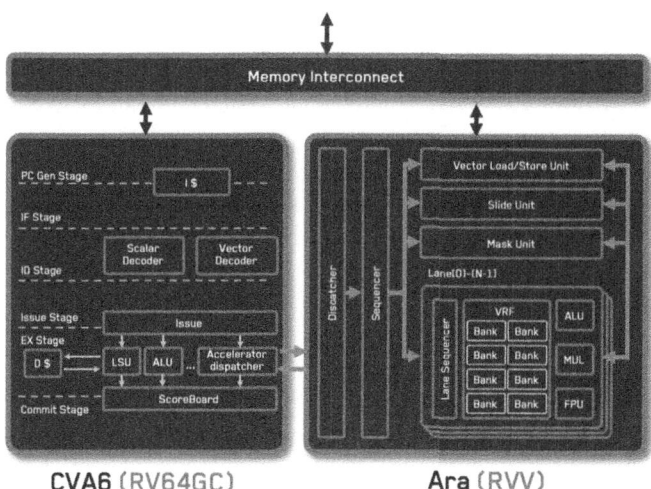

Fig. 3. Brief block diagram of system constructed CVA6 and Ara.

Vector extension instructions are sent from CVA6 to Ara. In Ara, the dispatcher receives instructions and sends the instructions to each lane after the sequencer arbitrates between these instructions, vector load/store unit, and slide unit. When the instruction is finished to execute, the sequencer sends an Ack signal or scalar result to CVA6. Vector processors execute instructions in parallel by distributing processing across lanes. In Ara, the number of lanes is variable and can be changed to 1, 2, 4, 8, or 16. In addition, VLEN can be selected from 128 bits, 256 bits, 512 bits, 1024 bits, 2048 bits, or 4096 bits. The vector register file (VRF) is divided into eight banks per lane. All elements of the vector registers are placed on the banks. The banks are designed to avoid access conflicts by arithmetic units and other units out of the lane. Therefore, all banks can be implemented with a one-port SRAM on a hardware device such as an FPGA because each bank has only one port to read and write.

However, Ara doesn't contain data caches. In this paper, Ara and CVA6 are used for evaluation. When measuring the performance of the SHAVER, the performance with a data cache is estimated from a result on a simulator.

3   Implementation

3.1   CVA6 and Ara on an FPGA

A way to execute a system of CVA6 and Ara on a simulator is published on the GitHub repository [16]. However, there are no publications about implementing this system using the FPGA. So, some modules of CVA6 and Ara have been modified to be implemented on an FPGA. Displaying characters is required to measure the performance of a system executing on an FPGA. So, a serial communication module is implemented as a memory-mapped device. This module allows characters to be displayed through a C function. Moreover, it allows the main memory to be rewritten via a user serial console. Alveo U250 is used for evaluation in this paper [21]. This board has four 16 GB DDR4 memories. In addition, this board includes one of UltraScale+ Devices, so the UltraRAM (URAM) is supported [22]. In our implementation, the main memory is replaced by DDR4 memory from a BRAM to measure the latency of DMA transfer. All banks of vector register files on Ara are implemented with URAM through XPM_MEMORY_SPRAM macro. The macro, available only in Vivado, can generate a single-ported RAM [23].

3.2   DMA Controller

The Ara and CVA6 implementations published on GitHub do not provide a DMA controller. Hence, the DMA controller is implemented independently. An example of C programming for using DMA is shown by Listing 1.1. For startup DMA transfer, some parameters are written before starting the transfer.

Listing 1.1. Example of DMA (memory to an accelerator).

```
1  extern uint8_t dma_len,dma_start;// A register on DMAC
2  extern uint8_t *dma_addr_read;    // A register on DMAC
3  extern uint8_t *dma_addr_write;   // A register on DMAC
4  extern uint8_t *acc;              // Accelerator
5  int main(void){
6    uint8_t source_array[512];
7    ...
8    dma_len = 8*512; // set the transfer data length
9    dma_addr_read  = source_array; // set the source address
10   dma_addr_write = ACC;  // set the destination address
11   // Waiting until finished to set parameters
12   _asm_ volatile("fence");
13   dma_start      = 1; // Start DMA transfer
14   _asm_ volatile("fence"); // Wait until finished to transfer
15   ...
16 }
```

3.3   SHAVER: Sharing Vector Registers

In our proposed mechanism, an accelerator is connected to Ara directly, not through the memory interconnect module in the core. For the connection, some modules are designed to sort the values of the banks. In addition, the signals to control an accelerator are designed to use an accelerator. The brief block diagram of SHAVER is shown in Fig. 4.

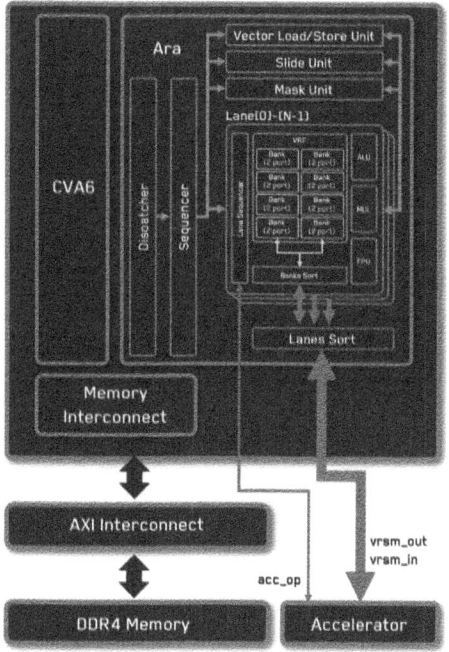

Fig. 4. Implemented SHAVER.

For this mechanism, signals are defined like Table 1. An accelerator usually needs some control signals to execute the task. These three signals are designed for communication between the shared vector registers and an accelerator.

Table 1. Signals for SHAVER.

name	description
acc_op	for controlling an accelerator
vrsm_out	for overwriting the vector registers to write through SHAVER
vrsm_in	for reading the vector registers to read through SHAVER

A bank is designed to be implemented with a single-ported SRAM in Ara. In SHAVER, a bank is accessed from an accelerator, not only Ara modules.

Therefore, all banks should be designed as dual-port SRAM for processes on Ara and an accelerator. Dual-ported SRAMs replace all banks through *XPM_MEMORY_TDPRAM* macro in Vivado [24]. The vector register file on Ara is shuffled to avoid conflicting register accesses. To use correct order values on an accelerator, the modules for sorting values of banks are implemented on a lane and a top module of Ara. Length of *vrsm_out* and *vrsm_in* is variable, but it depends on the VLEN of Ara and the number of vector registers shared with an accelerator. For example, each signal is 16384 bits if VLEN is 4096 bits and four-vector registers are shared.

An example of using SHAVER is shown by Listing 1.2. First, the RVV parameters are set by *vsetvli* instruction. In Listing 1.2, RVV is set according to the value of *size_of_array*. After that, the values are loaded to a vector register from memory with *vle8* instruction. *vle8* is one of the load instructions of RVV. In this program, the loaded values are assigned at v8. For sending the value, *vrsm.send* instruction is defined as a custom instruction. Ara sets *acc_op* as *0b0001* when this instruction is called. *0b0001* shows an acceleration that the main core sends values to an acceleration.

Listing 1.2. Example of SHAVER (memory to an accelerator).

```
 1  int main(void){
 2    uint8_t source_array[512];
 3    uint8_t size_of_array = 512;
 4    ...
 5    // Setting RVV CSRs
 6    _asm_ volatile("vsetvli t0,
 7    // Load from memory to vector register
 8    _asm_ volatile("vle8.v v8, (
 9    // Sending to an accelerator
10    _asm_ volatile("vrsm.send v0, v0, v0");
11    ...
12  }
```

4   Evaluation

4.1   Performance

The convolution task is executed for evaluation. An accelerator is designed for a convolution process. The element length of the accelerator is 8 bits. The size of the window on convolution is 3×3. This accelerator can execute convolution that is constrained by 4096-bit rows.

VLEN is 4096 bits, and the number of lanes on Ara is 4. The width of data on the AXI interface is 128 bits. Ara does not contain data caches. So, when measuring SHAVER's performance, the performance with a data cache is estimated from the evaluation result on a simulator. Systems for measuring performance are implemented on Alveo U250 using Vivado 2021.2 [25]. Evaluation on a simulator executes on Verilator 4.214 [2]. The results of measurement are shown in Fig. 5.

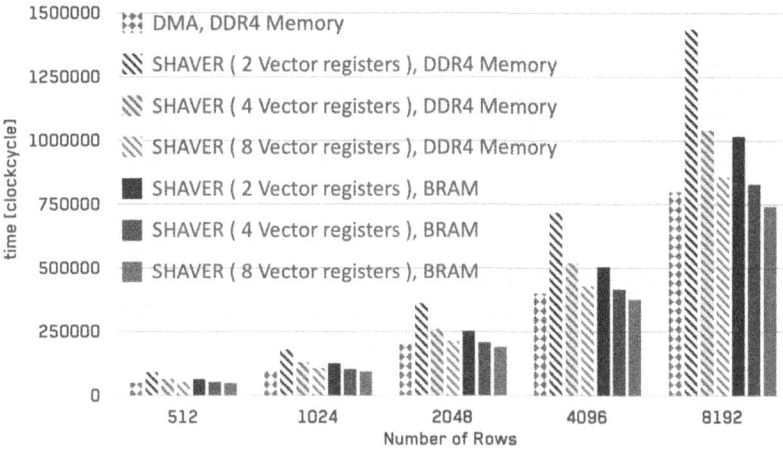

Fig. 5. Result of the performance evaluation.

Comparing the simulation results of SHAVER, when increasing the number of shared registers, the clock cycles for processing are reduced. Similarly, when SHAVER is run on an FPGA, the more registers are shared, the shorter the processing time. When comparing the outcomes of sharing two vector registers with those of sharing eight vector registers, a speedup of approximately 40% is observed. The reason for the 40% speedup is that the number of memory loads remains unchanged despite the number of shares being quadrupled. RVV instructions can load data to two, four, or eight vector registers simultaneously, reducing the memory overhead. These instructions are used differently in the programs of this evaluation, depending on the number of registers to be shared. These instructions allow the vector processor to execute load instructions with less overhead. As a result, up to 40% speedup can be achieved by increasing the number of instructions shared.

For all transfer methods of the evaluation, the number of clock cycles increased when running on the FPGA than on the simulation. The maximum increase is about 16%. Since DDR4 memory is used as the main memory on FPGA, operation on FPGA is slower than simulation. This is a latency-free memory access operation similar to a cache with no misses.

To compare SHAVER utilizing cache with conventional methods such as DMA, we compare the simulation results of the SHAVER with those of DMA running on FPGA using DDR4 memory. This comparison shows that our proposed SHAVER can perform the same process in up to 7.13% fewer clock cycles than DMA.

4.2   Resource Usage and Maximum Operating Frequency

Resource usage and maximum operating frequency of each system are measured by Vivado 2021.2. The results are shown in Table 2.

These results indicate that increasing the number of shared vector registers in SHAVER does not affect the maximum operating frequency. In addition, we found that the resource usage and maximum operating frequency of SHAVER do not change significantly compared to DMA transfers, except for SRAM. SRAM usage increases when the number of shared vector registers is increased. This increase in SRAM usage can be attributed to the increase in SRAM used for operations in the accelerator.

Table 2. Resource Usage and Maximum Operating Frequency on Alveo U250.

Target System	LUT	FF	SRAM	DSP	Frequency [MHz]
DMA	526,036	150,768	258	228	80.972
SHAVER: 1 vector register	445,183	160,125	238	228	80.574
SHAVER: 2 vector registers	447,440	172,425	366	228	81.182
SHAVER: 4 vector registers	457,585	197,021	622	228	80.821
SHAVER: 8 vector registers	462,695	246,039	1134	228	80.919

5   Conclusion

In this paper, SHAVER was proposed as a new data transfer method. This mechanism was implemented using Ara and CVA6. This implementation was run on FPGA and a simulator for evaluation. A DMA for comparison was also implemented and evaluated on Ara and CVA6.

For performance evaluation, we used an accelerator for convolutional operations and measured the number of clock cycles required. The results indicate the potential of SHAVER to achieve a maximum of 7.13% speedup over DMA transfer.

The evaluation of resource usage and maximum operating frequency showed that SRAM utilization increases with the number of shared vector registers, depending on the accelerator's structure. The maximum operating frequency of the system using the SHAVER exhibited a minimal difference in comparison to the system using DMA transfer. Therefore, SHAVER does not significantly affect the maximum operating frequency.

6   Future Work

In the evaluation, we assessed SHAVER on a simulator, assuming no data cache misses. In future work, we plan to enhance the evaluation by incorporating caching into Ara, utilizing DDR4 memory as the main memory, and evaluating the performance of SHAVER. If a data cache is introduced in Ara, unlike the behavior observed in this simulation, penalties due to data cache misses are expected in SHAVER. However, considering temporal and spatial locality, the incurred latency is anticipated to be sufficiently low after excluding the initial miss penalty. Therefore, the performance evaluation results of SHAVER with a data cache in Ara are likely to be inferior compared to the behavior in the simulation, but the magnitude of the difference is expected to be minimal. On the other hand, attaching a cache to the DMA transfer system will invariably involve communication to maintain coherence with the data cache. Consequently, it can be anticipated that the performance evaluation results of the DMA system will also be inferior compared to the results of the current evaluation.

Furthermore, the accelerator used for the evaluation in this paper was exclusively designed for convolutional operations. In future work, we aim to diversify the types of accelerators and assess the performance of SHAVER across various tasks. Specifically, we intend to conduct a comparative evaluation between SHAVER and DMA using real-world applications. This will involve expanding the range of accelerators and exploring the effectiveness of SHAVER in diverse tasks.

Through the evaluation of resource utilization in this paper, it is speculated that the SRAM influenced the increase in resource usage within the accelerator. In other words, the resource utilization of our proposed mechanism depends on the length of the shared vector registers. In the future, it is necessary to discuss the structure of accelerators to remove the dependence.

In addition, we implement SHAVER for ASIC rather than FPGA. Some PDK tools are published as open-source software. In addition, some companies have started inexpensive chip fabrication services. According to them, chip fabrication services have expanded rapidly worldwide, not only in companies. Therefore, we aim to conduct measurements for not only resource utilization and maximum operating frequency on FPGA but also the impact of SHAVER on ASIC designed by an open-source EDA tool in the future. In particular, we anticipate significant differences between FPGA and ASIC in the dual-port SRAM used as the vector register banks. In future investigations, we aim to measure how these differences affect the maximum operating frequency and resource utilization.

Acknowledgments. This work is partially supported by JSPS Grant-in-Aid for Scientific Research (C) 24K14874.

References

1. github | OpenHW Group: cva6 (2023). https://github.com/openhwgroup/cva6. Accessed 22 Dec 2023
2. github | verilator: verilator(tag:v4.214) (2023). https://github.com/verilator/verilator/tree/v4.214. Accessed 22 Dec 2023
3. Abella, J., et al.: An academic RISC-V silicon implementation based on open-source components. In: 2020 XXXV Conference on Design of Circuits and Integrated Systems (DCIS), pp. 1–6 (2020). https://doi.org/10.1109/DCIS51330.2020.9268664

4. Amirshahi, A., Klein, J.A.H., Ansaloni, G., Atienza, D.: Tic-sat: tightly-coupled systolic accelerator for transformers. In: Proceedings of the 28th Asia and South Pacific Design Automation Conference, ASPDAC 2023, pp. 657–663. Association for Computing Machinery, New York (2023). https://doi.org/10.1145/3566097.3567867

5. Waterman, A., Asanovic, K., Hauser, J.: The RISC-V instruction set manual volume II: privileged architecture document version 20211203 (2021). https://github.com/riscv/riscv-isa-manual/releases/download/Priv-v1.12/riscv-privileged-20211203.pdf

6. arm: Primecell micro dma-230 (2023). https://www.arm.com/ja/products/silicon-ip-system/embedded-system-design/dma-230. Accessed 22 Dec 2023

7. Asanovic, K.: Vector extension 1.0, frozen for public review (2021). https://github.com/riscv/riscv-v-spec/releases/tag/v1.0. Accessed 22 Dec 2023

8. Cavalcante, M., Schuiki, F., Zaruba, F., Schaffner, M., Benini, L.: Ara: a 1-GHz+ scalable and energy-efficient RISC-V vector processor with multiprecision floating-point support in 22-nm FD-SOI. IEEE Trans. Very Large Scale Integr. (VLSI) Syst. **28**(2), 530–543 (2020). https://doi.org/10.1109/TVLSI.2019.2950087

9. Chen, X., Lei, Y., Lu, Z., Chen, S.: A variable-size FFT hardware accelerator based on matrix transposition. IEEE Trans. Very Large Scale Integr. (VLSI) Syst. **26**(10), 1953–1966 (2018). https://doi.org/10.1109/TVLSI.2018.2846688

10. Choi, K., Sobelman, G.E.: An efficient CNN accelerator for low-cost edge systems. ACM Trans. Embed. Comput. Syst. **21**(4) (2022). https://doi.org/10.1145/3539224

11. Github, I.: Github copilot · your AI pair programmer (2023). https://github.com/features/copilot. Accessed 22 Dec 2023

12. Johns, M., Kazmierski, T.J.: A minimal RISC-V vector processor for embedded systems. In: 2020 Forum for Specification and Design Languages (FDL), pp. 1–4 (2020). https://doi.org/10.1109/FDL50818.2020.9232940

13. Jouppi, N., et al.: TPU v4: an optically reconfigurable supercomputer for machine learning with hardware support for embeddings. In: Proceedings of the 50th Annual International Symposium on Computer Architecture. ISCA 2023. Association for Computing Machinery, New York (2023). https://doi.org/10.1145/3579371.3589350

14. Matsubara, K., et al.: A 12-nm autonomous driving processor with 60.4 tops, 13.8 TOPS/W CNN executed by task-separated ASIL D control. IEEE J. Solid-State Circuits **57**(1), 115–126 (2022). https://doi.org/10.1109/JSSC.2021.3120191

15. PAPER, X.M.P.W.: 4.14 AI technology (2023). https://trust.mi.com/docs/miui-privacy-white-paper-global/4/14. Accessed 22 Dec 2023

16. Perotti, M., Cavalcante, M., Wistoff, N., Andri, R., Cavigelli, L., Benini, L.: A "new ara" for vector computing: an open source highly efficient RISC-V v 1.0 vector processor design. In: 2022 IEEE 33rd International Conference on Application-specific Systems, Architectures and Processors (ASAP), pp. 43–51 (2022). https://doi.org/10.1109/ASAP54787.2022.00017

17. SiFive, I.: Sifive intelligence x280 (2023). https://www.sifive.com/cores/intelligence-x280. Accessed 22 Dec 2023

18. Sipeed: Sipeed m1/m1w (lichee dan) (2023). https://wiki.sipeed.com/soft/maixpy/en/develop_kit_board/core_module.html. Accessed 22 Dec 2023

19. ESP32 series datasheet | v4.4 (2023). https://www.espressif.com/sites/default/files/documentation/esp32_datasheet_en.pdf. Accessed 22 Dec 2023

20. An on-device deep neural network for face detection (2023). https://machinelearning.apple.com/research/face-detection. Accessed 22 Dec 2023

21. Xilinx: Alveo u250 data center accelerator card (2023). https://www.xilinx.com/products/boards-and-kits/alveo/u250.html. Accessed 22 Dec 2023

22. Xilinx: Ultraram: Breakthrough embedded memory integration on ultrascale+ devices (wp477) (2023). https://docs.xilinx.com/v/u/en-US/wp477-ultraram. Accessed 22 Dec 2023

23. Xilinx: Ultrascale architecture libraries guide (UG974) | xpm_memory_spram (2023).   https://docs.xilinx.com/r/2021.2-English/ug974-vivado-ultrascale-libraries/XPM_MEMORY_SPRAM. Accessed 22 Dec 2023

24. Xilinx: Ultrascale architecture libraries guide (UG974) | xpm_memory_tdpram (2023).   https://docs.xilinx.com/r/2021.2-English/ug974-vivado-ultrascale-libraries/XPM_MEMORY_TDPRAM. Accessed 22 Dec 2023

25. Xilinx: Adaptive computing support/downloads/vivado archive/vivado ml edition - 2021.2 full product installation (2023). https://www.xilinx.com/support/download/index.html/content/xilinx/en/downloadNav/vivado-design-tools/archive.html. Accessed 22 Dec 2023

26. Zaruba, F., Benini, L.: The cost of application-class processing: energy and performance analysis of a linux-ready 1.7-GHz 64-bit RISC-V core in 22-nm FDSOI technology. IEEE Trans. Very Large Scale Integr. (VLSI) Syst. **27**(11), 2629–2640 (2019). https://doi.org/10.1109/TVLSI.2019.2926114

27. Zhao, L., Iyer, R., Makineni, S., Bhuyan, L., Newell, D.: Hardware support for bulk data movement in server platforms. In: 2005 International Conference on Computer Design, pp. 53–60 (2005). https://doi.org/10.1109/ICCD.2005.64

Efficient Compute Resource Sharing of RISC-V Packed-SIMD Using Simultaneous Multi-threading

Shogo Takata[1]([✉])[iD] and Hironori Nakajo[2][iD]

[1] Department of Electrical Engineering and Computer Science, Graduate School
of Engineering, Tokyo University of Agriculture and Technology,
2–24–16 Nakacho, Koganei-shi, Tokyo 184–8588, Japan
s231276x@st.go.tuat.ac.jp
[2] Division of Advanced Information Technology Computer Science,
Institute of Engineering, Tokyo University of Agriculture and Technology,
2–24–16 Nakacho, Koganei-shi, Tokyo 184–8588, Japan
nakajo@cc.tuat.ac.jp

Abstract. AI tasks are gaining popularity in the area of IoT and edge
devices. To run such tasks on devices, QNNs are used because of their
reduced size and ability to be computed with simple integer arithmetic.
There have been many implementations to support such a network format. However, when considering thread-level parallelism to speedup the
program, many often implement a multi-core architecture or clusters
which needs to copy all resources for each core. In this paper, we introduce a new RISC-V Out-of-Order Simultaneous Multi-Threading core
"B4SMT" with RISC-V Packed-SIMD extension for evaluation. We also
show that even a single executor could increase the performance of a
1D median filter by over 100×, and a matrix multiplication by over 30
on more than 16 threads efficiently. Furthermore, we suggest that other
infrequently used executors may be placed as a shared resource efficiently
in an SMT core.

Keywords: SMT · SIMD · RISC-V · Quantization · Edge
computing · Resource efficient

1 Introduction

AI technology has become a significant factor when designing and implementing
Internet-of-Things (IoT) devices. There are applications in fields such as health
[1], industrial [2], agriculture [3], and more. Such devices operate with limited
storage and lack computing power compared to state-of-the-art computers with
GPUs or TPUs where the networks are trained. Quantization techniques are
often used to make neural networks runnable on these devices. When training
a neural network model, floating point 32-bit numbers are commonly used to
calculate variables of weights and biases. Due to the complexity of the hardware

© The Author(s), under exclusive license to Springer Nature Switzerland AG 2025
H. R. Arabnia et al. (Eds.): CSCE 2024, CCIS 2256, pp. 236–250, 2025.
https://doi.org/10.1007/978-3-031-85638-9_18

required to process these numbers, using full-precision floats could be problematic for embedded targets. Quantized neural networks (QNN) are neural networks with weights and biases represented as 16-bit, 8-bit, or even less, which makes the model small in size and easier to compute with fixed-point or integer arithmetic. Studies have shown that such networks can retain a high accuracy and the difference compared to the original network could be neglegible [4–6].

Many architectures and libraries have been introduced to take advantage of QNNs. Arm-based library for QNNs "CMSIS-NN" [7] have been developped by Arm. There are other researches for mobile platform arm devices [8]. PULP-NN [9] is a neural network library focused on inferencing QNNs on RISC-V devices. It supports representation from a byte down to 1-bit integers. An implementation supporting this sub-byte representation is XplupNN [10], which uses a custom multiply and accumulate unit to process byte (8-bits), nibble (4-bits), and crumbs (2-bits). RISC-V extensions, such as vector extensions, provide vector registers with a size of up to 2^{16}-bits and vector instructions to manipulate many data in a single instruction, including instructions helpful for quantized networks such as half-word and byte data. RISC-V Packed-SIMD extension or P-extension extension is a draft specification and uses general-purpose registers as an array of 32-bit, 16-bit, or 8-bit values. It is possible to construct programs that accelerate filters and matrix multiplication using P-extension.

However, when constructing a program using RISC-V P-extension, we found that the usage of the P-extension executor was low during the evaluation. Using this fact, we predict that if we could share a P-extension executor among a multi-threaded core, it could reduce the resource usage and still be performant.

Simultaneous Multi-Threading (SMT) is a technique to implement a multi-threaded core. Its main feature is the ability to execute instructions from multiple threads simultaneously and to share computational resources among threads [11]. It is possible to add an arbitral executor as a computational resource and share it among multiple threads. In contrast to a multi-core system, which needs to duplicate any computational resources to the number of threads, SMT can operate with fewer or more resources as needed. Resources with high demand, such as ALUs, could be increased more than the thread count to distribute the load of multiple threads. On the other hand, if the demand for a resource is low, it is possible to reduce the number of duplications. This paper suggests that a single Packed-SIMD executor can support multiple threads.

The main contributions of this paper are the following:

- We propose a new SMT RISC-V core *"Base for SMT" (B4SMT)*, which is written in Chisel and presents its customizability.
- We integrate the RISC-V P-extension into *B4SMT* and show that the resource usage of the core is less than that of a multi-core processor when increasing the number of threads.
- We run evaluations on *B4SMT* with a single RISC-V P-extension executor to show that the performance is not significantly affected and the efficiency of the entire core stays high.

Both resource and performance efficiency demonstrate that an implementation of even a single RISC-V P-extension executor in an SMT core is beneficial for operating on quantized data, especially on resource-restricted platforms such as IoT and edge devices. Furthermore, we suggest that any executor that has a low usage could be shared in an SMT core in the same manner to reduce resource usage without sacrificing performance.

2   Background

2.1   RISC-V and Packed-SIMD Extension

RISC-V is an open standard Instruction Set Architecture (ISA), and the specification can be found here [12]. The ISA is made of a base instruction set called I, and extension instructions with an address space of 32,64,128-bits each represented as `RV32I`, `RV64I` and `RV128I`. Some of the extensions that are common and relevant to this paper are shown in Table 1. When displaying the implemented extensions of a given core, the Extension names are concatenated. For example, `RV32IMAC` is a 32-bit RISC-V core with multiply-division (M), atomics (A), and compressed-instruction (C) support.

Table 1. Example of RISC-V Extensions and their status and description.

Extension	description	Status
I	Base Integer Instruction Set	Ratified
M	Integer Multiplication and Division	Ratified
A	Atomic Instructions	Ratified
F	Single-Precision Floating-Point	Ratified
D	Double-Precision Floating-Point	Ratified
Zicsr	Control and Status Register Instructions	Ratified
Zifencei	Instruction-Fetch Fence	Ratified
C	Compressed Instructions	Ratified
Zmmul	multiplication subset of the M extension	Ratified
P	Packed SIMD	Draft

RISC-V P-extension or *"Packed-SIMD Extension"* is a draft specification that defines SIMD instruction using general-purpose registers. An example of an instruction is *UCMPLT16* visualized in Fig. 1(a). It performs a comparison in each of the 16-bit values in the operand registers and produces a bitmask. If the target core is 64-bit, then it can perform four comparisons as a single instruction. Another example is *SMALBB* visualized in Fig. 1(b). It can be used to multiply 16-bit values from the operand and then accumulate the result with the destination register. If the target core is 64-bit, then it can perform two multiplications of 16-bit values.

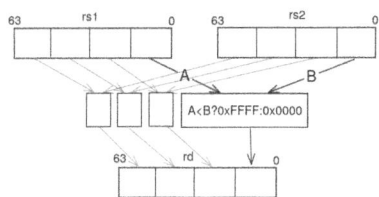
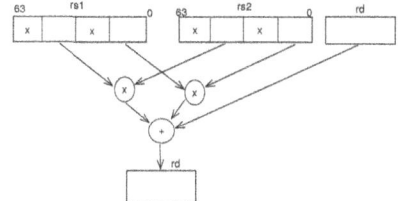

(a) *UCMPLT16* instruction overview. It takes 4 16-bit values on *rs1* and *rs2*, then checks if each value on *rs1* is less than *rs2*, finally stores a bit mask of the result to *rd*. There is an 8-bit variant of this instruction, namely *UCMPLT8*, which does the same operation on 8-bit values. Each of these instructions can process up to 4 or 8 values simultaneously.

(b) *SMALBB* instruction overview. It takes 16-bit values on [15:0] and [47:32] from *rs1* and *rs2*, then multiplies them and accumulates the result to *rd*. There are some variants of this operation, namely *SMALTT*, which uses [31:16] and [63:48] of the registers as input, and *SMALBT*, which uses [15:0] and [47:32] from *rs1* and [31:16] and [63:48] from *rs2* as inputs.

Fig. 1. Sample visualizations of P-Extension instructions

Listing 1.1. Pseudo code for median using *UCMPLT8*. Every loop computes eight elements. `input` is the input array of bytes, `result` is the output array of bytes, `len` is the length of both arrays.

```
1   for (int i = 0; i < len / 8 - 1; i++) {
2       // take two 64-bit values
3       v1 = ((long *)input)[i]
4       vt = ((long *)input)[i+1]
5       // create shifted input values
6       v2 = (v1 >> 8)  | (vt << 56)
7       v3 = (v1 >> 16) | (vt << 48)
8       // compare
9       c1 = ucmplt8(v1, v2)
10      c2 = ucmplt8(v2, v3)
11      c3 = ucmplt8(v3, v1)
12      // create bitmask
13      m1 = ~(c1 ^ c3)
14      m2 = ~(c1 ^ c2)
15      m3 = ~(c2 ^ c3)
16      // apply mask
17      o1 = v1 &m1
18      o2 = v2 &m2
19      o3 = v3 &m3
20      result[i] = o1 | o2 | o3
21  }
```

An example pseudo-code of a 1D median filter is shown in Listing 1.1. Normally, when writing a median filter, it processes one value at a time in a loop. P-extension instruction allows to write the algorithm with SIMD instructions; specifically, *UCMPLT8* is used. This method can process eight values in one loop, which speeds up the process.

2.2   Thread-Level Parallelism and SMT

Thread-level parallelism exploits multiple tasks that can run independently, often implemented with multi-threaded cores or processors. A simple implementation of a multi-thread processor is a multi-core processor. It is made of multiple cores in a single package, and by providing separate tasks to each thread, it can perform operations in parallel. Another method is to implement multi-threading in a single core. There are three ways to achieve this. The first is to implement *Fine-grained multi-threading*, which is implemented by changing the active thread every cycle. The second implementation is *Coarse-grained multi-threading*, which switches the active thread on major stalls such as loading and storing to memory. The third implementation is *Simultaneous multi-threading*, which runs multiple threads simultaneously by sharing computational resources such as the ALU. A visualization of each method is shown in Fig. 2 In our paper we use simultaneous multi-threading to share a P-extension executor.

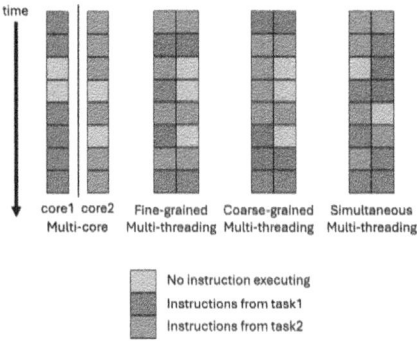

Fig. 2. Comparison of different multi-threading methods. Simultaneous multi-threading is shown as having two executors.

3   Related Work

3.1   Packed-SIMD for AI Accelaration

PULP-NN [9] is a neural network library made for QNN inference on RISC-V cores. It targets byte and sub-byte data types down to 1-bit integers. PULP-NN is used on the PULP RISC-V processor and it can exploit thread-level parallelism using its clusters [13]. XpulpNN [10] is an implementation that uses PULP-NN and adds a custom RISC-V extension with nubble (4-bit) and crumb (2-bit) instructions with a custom Dot-Product Unit.

These works focus on running a QNN faster on a RISC-V core or a cluster of cores. On a cluster, many cores have to be duplicated. We suggest that the cluster's resource usage may be further reduced by using a shared executor.

3.2   Simultaneous Multi-threading and RISC-V

Chichibu RISC-V SMT (CRVS) [14] is an SMT processor based on the previous work of *simply efficient multithreaded processor (SEMP)* [15] both developed at Tokyo University of Agriculture and Technology. The implementation is written in SystemVerilog and uses custom RISC-V extensions to manage threading.

In this paper, we introduce a new RISC-V SMT core *B4SMT*, a successor to the previous cores, and use it as the main processor in our paper. By reimplementing the SMT core in Chisel, we achieve higher flexibility using parameters and easier extendability to add or change modules in the core. Also, we changed the threading behavior to match that of a multi-core processor. Therefore, it is easier to port multi-threading libraries made for multi-core processors.

4   Implementation

4.1   A New SMT Core *B4SMT*

Base for SMT (B4SMT) is our new implementation of RISC-V SMT core written in Chisel [16], an HDL implemented as a DSL on scala language, to evaluate various aspects of an SMT core. It is compatible with `RV64IAC_Zicsr_Zifence_Zmmul`. When building this processor, one of the goals was to make it flexible and extendable. To accomplish this, we built all modules with parameterization in mind, which was made possible by the flexibility of the Scala language and the Chisel framework. It implements AXI to interface with various peripherals on FPGA boards. The source for *B4SMT* could be found here[1].

Because debugging on an SMT processor is quite challenging, we have utilized CSR registers such as *cycle, instret, machine performance-monitoring counter* to hold information about the state of the processor. The full list of performance monitoring registers used and the information it collects is shown in Table 2. By using these registers, it is easy to derive performance characteristics, such as *Cycle per Instruction, P-extension executor utilization*, and *Memory access usage*.

Although many features are working, this core still has issues, and it is still a work in progress. At the time of writing, *B4SMT* does not implement any data-caching. It is not a big issue for simulators since the memory can be configured to respond quickly. On the other hand, implementing the core on an FPGA could lead to slow memory access and overall slow performance. Another issue is the lack of branch prediction. Branch prediction greatly impacts SMT cores since they implement an Out-of-Order execution model. These issues should be fixed in future releases.

---

[1] https://github.com/NakajoLab/B4SMT.

Table 2. B4SMT performance monitoring registers and description. Many registers are implemented as counters.

register	description
cycle	cycles since power on
instret	instructions executed since power on
hpmcounter4	load instructions executed
hpmcounter11	P-extension executor used

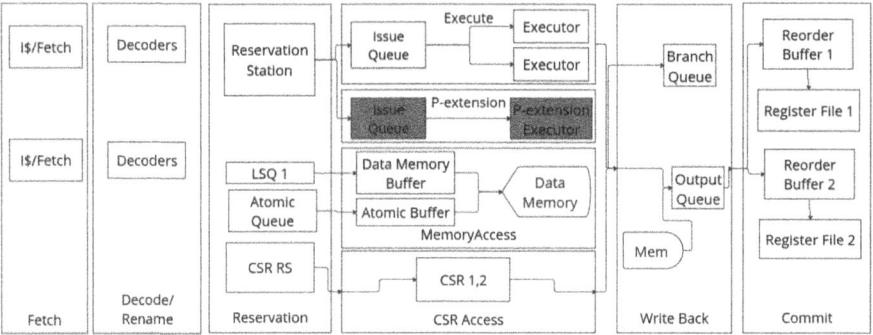

Fig. 3. Pipeline overview of *B4SMT* with P-extension. This is configured with two threads, two executors, and 1 P-extension executor. The components added to support P-extension are highlighted in red. (Color figure online)

4.2 B4SMT with P-Extension

P-extension is added to *B4SMT* for performance evaluation of quantized data processing. The specification we implemented is *RISC-V "P" Extension Proposal Version 0.9.11-draft-20211209* [17]. Since the P-extension is still in a draft state, the instructions or the executor's details may need to change in the future. An overview of the implementation is shown in Fig. 3. Adding the P-extension executor, we modified the decoder and the issue queue logic and added a new executor.

By implementing this executor and the additional modifications, the core is now compatible with RV64IACP_Zicsr_Zifence_Zmmul. The P-extension executor is implemented in Chisel and is available as a standalone executor.

5 Evaluation

5.1 Setup

We evaluate three different properties of this core. Firstly, we show that by increasing the thread count, *B4SMT*'s resource usage's rate of increase is less than that of a multi-core processor. We do this by executing the *B4SMT* chisel program to generate the core's SystemVerilog file with varying parameters of threads and measuring the resource usage after synthesis. Next, we show that when running programs involving the P-extension executor, the usage time of the executor is low. We perform this check by inspecting the CSR register *hpm-counter11*. Finally, we show that when running a program using quantized data, the performance of the core increases along with the thread count. We also calculate its efficiency during evaluation.

Vivado is used to measure resource usage. *B4SMT* cores with the same simple configuration other than thread counts were generated and synthesized. We chose the core count to be 1 to 4 and kept the other configuration on minimum values. We specifically checked the changes in *Slice LUT*, *Slice Registers*, *Block RAM*, *DSPs*.

We use two programs for evaluation, 1D median filter and matrix multiplication, and execute them on a single 16-threaded *B4SMT* core and calculate its speedup. Thread counts less than 16 are measured by disabling one core at a time until it runs out of cores. Speedup will be calculated using the performance compared to the baseline, a program running on a single core without using P-extension. Given the results, we then calculate the efficiency by dividing the individual speedups by thread count and show that even a single P-extension executor could make an efficient core.

After running a program on *B4SMT*, Every thread starts executing from the same address after initialization. To run different tasks on each thread, it has to read the *mhartid* CSR and check its ID. *mhartid* CSR is uniquely hardcoded into the core for each thread. Then depending on the ID, it can change what to run. In our case, the first thread (id = 0) initializes the core and memory; then each thread runs its task. Measurements of the performance during the task are done by reading performance monitoring CSRs. We use the specification provided metrics, such as *cycle* CSR which holds the cycles passed from initialization, and some custom specified metrics, such as *hpmcounter4* CSR which in our case is used to store how many load operations were performed. By taking the difference of the metrics before and after the task, it is possible to calculate the performance. Ideally, every thread should be given a task by a scheduler as provided by an operating system, but since we can only use bare metal programs, we run the same tasks on all threads in the evaluation.

The usage of the P-extension executor per thread could be calculated with Eq. (1) where P_instructions is the number of P-extension instructions executed and instructions is the number of all instructions. By transforming the equation, we get that the usage could be computed by the ratio of P-extension instructions P_instruction_ratio times the instruction per cycle IPC shown in Eq. (2).

Using the fact that the ratio of instruction P_instruction_ratio does not change significantly, we can assume that $\text{Usage}_{\text{per}}$_thread only depends on IPC.

$$\text{Usage}_{\text{per}}\text{\_thread} = \frac{\sum\limits_{m=1}^{n} \text{P\_instructions}_m}{\sum\limits_{m=1}^{n} \text{Cycle}_m} = \frac{\sum\limits_{m=1}^{n} \text{P\_instructions}_m}{\sum\limits_{m=1}^{n} \text{instructions}_m} \cdot \frac{\sum\limits_{m=1}^{n} \text{instructions}_m}{\sum\limits_{m=1}^{n} \text{Cycle}_m} \tag{1}$$

$$= \text{P\_instruction\_ratio} \cdot \text{IPC} \tag{2}$$

Usage of the executor on all threads can be derived by multiplying the thread count as shown in Eq. (3).

$$\text{Usage} = n \times \text{Usage}_{\text{per\_thread}} \tag{3}$$

Furthermore, we can derive the maximum number of threads a given executor can support by taking the inverse of the $\text{Usage}_{\text{per\_thread}}$ as shown in Eq. (5).

$$\text{MaximumThreads} = \frac{1}{\text{P\_instruction\_ratio} \cdot \text{IPC}} \tag{4}$$

$$= \frac{\text{CPI}}{\text{P\_instruction\_ratio}} \tag{5}$$

Speedup indicates how much performance has increased compared to a single-threaded core without P-extension and is calculated using Eq. (7) where Speedup_n is the speedup of a n threaded core, P_m is the performance of the m-th thread, $P_{\text{single\_thread\_without\_p-extension}}$ shows the performance of single-threaded core without using P-extension. We use the fact that the performance could be calculated by taking the inverse of the time taken to execute a task. Cycles are used as a measure of time and are read from the CSR register *cycle*. When calculating the performance, we take the minimum performance among threads to show the worst-case scenario.

$$\textit{Speedup}_n = n \times \frac{\min_{m=1..n}(P_m)}{P_{\text{single\_thread\_without\_p-extension}}} \tag{6}$$

$$= n \times \frac{\textit{Cycles}_{\text{single\_thread\_without\_p-extension}}}{\max_{m=1..n}(\textit{Cycles}_m)} \tag{7}$$

Efficiency indicates how efficiently the SMT core is able to share the resource, which is calculated as Eq. (8) where $P_{\text{single\_thread}}$ shows the performance of single-threaded core with the same configuration. The ideal case is when all the threads use the core at separate times, and hence do not stall any threads. In that case, *Efficiency* = 1 should be achieved.

$$\textit{Efficiency}_n = \frac{\min_{m=1..n}(P_m)}{P_{\text{single\_thread}}} = \frac{\textit{Cycles}_{\text{single\_thread}}}{\max_{m=1..n}(\textit{Cycles}_m)} \tag{8}$$

The specification and parameters for *B4SMT* used for evaluation are shown in Table 3. For the maximum number of threads, we chose a number that both shows a trend of the metrics and finishes in a reasonable time on the evaluation machine. It is possible to configure the core with higher thread counts if needed. To accurately measure the efficiency using the P-extension executor, the other instructions should not be the bottleneck. We have used eight executors and large enough parameters for the load store queue and reorder buffer.

Table 3. B4SMT specification and parameters for evaluation

parameter	value
ISA	RV64IACP_Zmmul_Zifence_Zicsr
P-extension	0.9.11-draft-20211209
Threads	1 to 16
Decoders per thread	2
Executors (ALUs)	8
P-extension executor	1

5.2   Resource Usage Results

We compare the resource usage of a single thread and when the thread count is increased. Figure 4 shows the resource usage of *Slice LUT*, *Slice Registers*, *Block RAM*, *DSPs* when the thread increases from 1 to 4. The multi-core baseline represents the value expected when duplicating the single-threaded core, calculated by multiplying the single-threaded core's resource by the thread count. Looking at *Slice Registers* and *Block RAM*, we notice that the rate of increase is close to the multi-core value. This is expected because some modules need to be duplicated for each thread, such as the Fetch module, Decoder module, Reorder Buffer module, and others, and it is an inherit property of SMT.

While we can see that *Slice LUT* does increase with threads, it is significantly less than the multi-core value and the above two. This is where SMT starts to show its strength, and we can see that it is possible to increase the thread count without a significant resource increase.

Looking at the value of *DSPs*, we can see it levels out at two threads. *DSPs* are used mainly for arithmetic and multiplication, which is used in ALU and P-extension executor. Since there are the same number of executors on all configurations, the leveling out suggests that the increase of threads is not affecting the resource usage of *DSPs*.

These results show that this *B4SMT* with P-extension executor is a resource-efficient core.

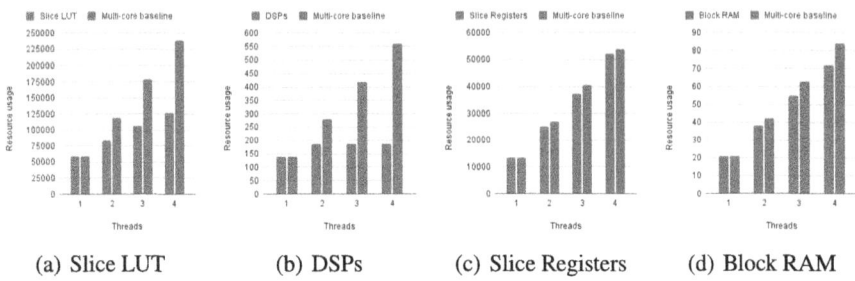

| (a) Slice LUT | (b) DSPs | (c) Slice Registers | (d) Block RAM |

Fig. 4. Resource usage of *B4SMT*. The blue bars represent the resource usage of the core. The red line represents the resource usage of a multi-core processor calculated by multiplying the single-threaded core's resource by the thread count.

5.3   P-Extension Instruction Usages

In this section, we check that the time using the P-extension executor is low. The instruction statistics are shown in Table 4. We show the maximum value of *Cycles* to represent the worst case, during execution, and show the sum of P-extension instructions executed. By comparing the ratio of P-extension instructions executed in a task, the maximum ratio is from the matrix multiply transposed program with 14%. To share an executor with another thread, it has to have a ratio of less than 50%. Thus it is safe to assume that P-extension instructions are infrequent and P-extension executors are a good candidate for sharing.

Table 4. Instruction statistics estimation for each configuration. Cycles are the clock cycles needed to finish the task, and P-extension cycles are the cycles in which the P-extension executor was used. The ratio of P-extension instructions in all instructions is shown in the parentheses. MaximumThreads are estimated values for the maximum number of threads a core can work with one ly a single executor.

Configuration	Max Cycles	Sum of P-extension cycles (ratio)	Max Thread Count
1D median filter (16-bit)	13,084	768 (5.9%)	17.0
1D median filter (8-bit)	6,163	384 (6.2%)	16.0
matrix multiplication	239,287	16,384 (7.0%)	14.6
matrix multiplication transposed	115726	16384 (14%)	7.1

5.4   *Speedup* and *Efficiency* Results

In this section, we analyze the results of running the evaluation programs. The *Speedup* evaluation results of the median filter are shown in Fig. 5(a) and the results for the matrix multiplication are shown in Fig. 5(b). Reading the data we calculated the MaximumThreads for each configuration which is shown in Table 4.

Looking at the speedup results of the baseline in both cases, we can see that it levels out at around 4 threads. This is due to the frequent accesses to memory compared to the P-extension counterparts shown in Table 5. We can see that the P-extension variants perform better in all cases. When looking at the memory access of matrix multiplication, we can see there is a significant difference between non-transposed and transposed. The effects could be seen in the speedup where the non-transposed variant levels out and the transposed variant is increasing. These results show that by using a P-extension executor with *B4SMT*, it speeds up the core on quantized computations.

Table 5. Memory access count on a single thread during evaluation

Program	type	load	store
1D Median filter (16-bit)	baseline	3,387	1,548
	P-extension	830	768
1D Median filter (8-bit)	baseline	3,390	1,553
	P-extension	524	540
Matrix Multiplication (32 × 32 on 16-bit)	baseline	67,480	4,774
	P-extension	42,714	3,839
	P-extension transposed	17,521	2,609

Next, we analyze the *Efficiency*. The results for the median filter and matrix multiplications are shown in Fig. 6(a) and Fig. 6(b) Note that the configuration of *B4SMT* used for evaluation provides 8 normal executors and a single P-extension executor. Looking at the baseline in both cases, we see a quick decline in efficiency. In the median filter, we can see that the efficiency for *byte* size operations does not drop below 90% until 14 threads, and then drops significantly. If we see the P-extension executor usage results shown in Fig. 7, the curve of *p-median 8-bit* is saturating at around 90%. This could be due to more frequent memory access or, conflicting use time of the P-extension executor. For the *half* case, although it is below the *byte* line most of the time, it does not drop significantly anywhere. In matrix multiplication, we can see that the results of P-extension without transposing the input are below the baseline in most cases.

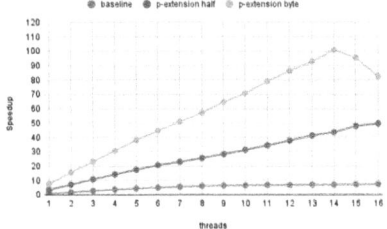

(a) 1D median filter. The *baseline* is a core without P-extension. *p-extension half* and *p-extension byte* both use P-extension instructions and operate on 16-bit,8-bit values respectively.

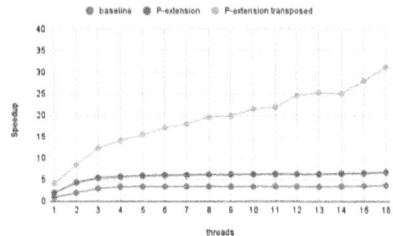

(b) Matrix multiplication on 32 × 32. The *baseline* is a core without P-extension. *P-extension* is a core with P-extension using instructions *SMALBB* and *SMALTT*. *P-extension transposed* is a core with P-extension using data witch is pre-transposed

Fig. 5. Evaluation result of *Speedup*

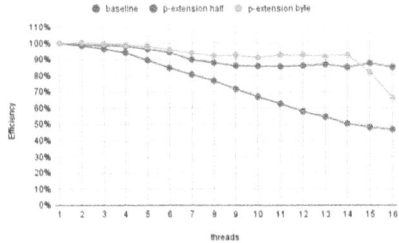

(a) 1D median filter. Note that the baseline is computed with 8 ALUs.

(b) Matrix multiplication on 32 × 32. Note that the baseline is computed with 8 ALUs.

Fig. 6. Evaluation result of *Efficiency*

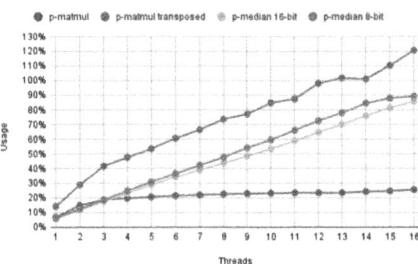

Fig. 7. The total usage of P-extension executor.

By transposing the input, we can see that the efficiency is better, and even with 16 threads, the efficiency is over 40%. When looking at the usage result of the transposed, we can see that after 14 threads it goes higher than 100%. This is due to the tasks not running at the exact same time and being shifted in time.

Hence creates some windows of time when a single thread can keep the executor to itself, thus increasing the usage over 100%.

6   Conclusion

The execution of quantized neural networks is a crucial topic when discussing IoT and edge devices with AI capabilities. However, thread-level parallelism is often implemented as a multi-core processor or a cluster. Results from this paper suggest that simultaneous multi-threading with a shared P-extension executor can be implemented with fewer resources to compute quantized data. We have implemented a new SMT-enabled RISC-V core, "*B4SMT*" to evaluate the performances of shared resources on SMT. Furthermore, we were able to achieve a $100\times$ improvement in performance and showed that it could be done without a significant reduction in efficiency.

In this work, we demonstrated sharing a P-extension executor. Since the method of evaluation is generic among different resources shared in SMT, one may be able to consider different executors or other resources and similarly evaluate them. These results suggest that, depending on the frequency of use, and the performance of the core (IPC) it is possible to increase the thread count without sacrificing performance. An example of such a module could be a matrix multiply unit, FFT unit, or cryptography unit. We believe this opens up a new field of modules and resources to be shared among threads.

Acknowledgment. This work is partially supported by JSPS Grant-in-Aid for Scientific Research (C) 21K11804 and 24K14874.

References

1. Alshehri, F., Muhammad, G.: A comprehensive survey of the internet of things (IoT) and AI-based smart healthcare. IEEE Access **9**, 3660–3678 (2021)
2. Peres, R.S., Jia, X., Lee, J., Sun, K., Colombo, A.W., Barata, J.: Industrial artificial intelligence in industry 4.0 - systematic review, challenges and outlook. IEEE Access **8**, 220121–220139 (2020)
3. Machida, K., et al.: Navigable areas segmentation method for unmanned surface vehicles in paddy fields. In: 2023 IEEE 11th Region 10 Humanitarian Technology Conference (R10-HTC), pp. 1088–1094 (2023)
4. Hubara, I., Courbariaux, M., Soudry, D., El-Yaniv, R., Bengio, Y.: Quantized neural networks: training neural networks with low precision weights and activations. J. Mach. Learn. Res. **18**(187), 1–30 (2018)
5. Jacob, B., et al.: Quantization and training of neural networks for efficient integer-arithmetic-only inference. In: Proceedings of the IEEE Conference on Computer Vision and Pattern Recognition (CVPR) (2018)
6. Zhu, S., Duong, L.H.K., Liu, W.: XOR-net: an efficient computation pipeline for binary neural network inference on edge devices. In: 2020 IEEE 26th International Conference on Parallel and Distributed Systems (ICPADS), pp. 124–131 (2020)

7. Cmsis-nn: Cmsis nn software library. https://arm-software.github.io/CMSIS-NN/latest/index.html

8. Trusov, A., Limonova, E., Slugin, D., Nikolaev, D., Arlazarov, V.V.: Fast implementation of 4-bit convolutional neural networks for mobile devices. In: 2020 25th International Conference on Pattern Recognition (ICPR), pp. 9897–9903 (2021)

9. Garofalo, A., Rusci, M., Conti, F., Rossi, D., Benini, L.: Pulp-NN: a computing library for quantized neural network inference at the edge on RISC-V based parallel ultra low power clusters. In: 2019 26th IEEE International Conference on Electronics, Circuits and Systems (ICECS), pp. 33–36 (2019)

10. Garofalo, A., Tagliavini, G., Conti, F., Rossi, D., Benini, L.: XpulpNN: accelerating quantized neural networks on RISC-V processors through ISA extensions. In: 2020 Design, Automation & Test in Europe Conference & Exhibition (DATE), pp. 186–191 (2020)

11. Tullsen, D.M., Eggers, S.J., Levy, H.M.: Simultaneous multithreading: maximizing on-chip parallelism. In: Proceedings of the 22nd Annual International Symposium on Computer Architecture, ISCA 1995, New York, NY, USA, pp. 392–403. Association for Computing Machinery (1995)

12. Waterman, A., Asanović, K.: The RISC-V instruction set manual, volume I: User-level ISA, document version 20191213. RISC-V Foundation (2019). https://github.com/riscv/riscv-isa-manual/releases/download/Ratified-IMAFDQC/riscv-spec-20191213.pdf

13. Rossi, D., et al.: Energy-efficient near-threshold parallel computing: the PULPv2 cluster. IEEE Micro **37**(5), 20–31 (2017)

14. Tanaka, H., Tanaka, T., Higashi, R., Sekibe, T., Takada, S., Nakajo, H.: Implementation of a RISC-V SMT core in an AI processor. In: Proceedings of the 11th International Symposium on Information and Communication Technology, SoICT 2022, New York, NY, USA, pp. 15–22. Association for Computing Machinery (2022)

15. Tate, I., et al.: A model of implementable SMT processor on FPGA. In: PDPTA, pp. 909–915 (2006)

16. Bachrach, J., et al.: Chisel: constructing hardware in a scala embedded language. In: Proceedings of the 49th Annual Design Automation Conference, DAC 2012, New York, NY, USA, pp. 1216–1225. Association for Computing Machinery (2012)

17. RISC-V. RISC-V "p" extension proposal

Introducing Competitive Mechanism to Differential Evolution for Numerical Optimization

Rui Zhong[1($\boxtimes$)], Yang Cao[1], Enzhi Zhang[1], and Masaharu Munetomo[2]

[1] Graduate School of Information Science and Technology, Hokkaido University, Sapporo, Japan
`{rui.zhong.u5,yang.cao.y4,enzhi.zhang.n6}@elms.hokudai.ac.jp`
[2] Information Initiative Center, Hokkaido University, Sapporo, Japan
`munetomo@iic.hokudai.ac.jp`

Abstract. This paper introduces a novel competitive mechanism into differential evolution (DE), presenting an effective DE variant named competitive DE (CDE). CDE features a simple yet efficient mutation strategy: DE/winner-to-best/1. Essentially, the proposed DE/winner-to-best/1 strategy can be recognized as an intelligent integration of the existing mutation strategies of DE/rand-to-best/1 and DE/cur-to-best/1. The incorporation of DE/winner-to-best/1 and the competitive mechanism provide new avenues for advancing DE techniques. Moreover, in CDE, the scaling factor F and mutation rate Cr are determined by a random number generator following a normal distribution, as suggested by previous research. To investigate the performance of the proposed CDE, comprehensive numerical experiments are conducted on CEC2017 and engineering simulation optimization tasks, with CMA-ES, JADE, and other state-of-the-art optimizers and DE variants employed as competitor algorithms. The experimental results and statistical analyses highlight the promising potential of CDE as an alternative optimizer for addressing diverse optimization challenges.

Keywords: Evolutionary Computation (EC) · Competitive Mechanism · Differential Evolution (DE) · Novel Mutation Strategy · Numerical Optimization

1 Introduction

Differential Evolution (DE) [1] is a potent optimization algorithm categorized within the evolutionary algorithm (EA) family. Unlike conventional mathematical optimization methods that hinge on gradients, DE is a stochastic optimization approach inspired by the principles of natural selection and evolution [2,3]. By iteratively applying crossover, mutation, and selection operations, DE refines the population of candidate solutions for a given problem, progressively steering it towards more optimal solutions [4].

© The Author(s), under exclusive license to Springer Nature Switzerland AG 2025
H. R. Arabnia et al. (Eds.): CSCE 2024, CCIS 2256, pp. 251–263, 2025.
https://doi.org/10.1007/978-3-031-85638-9_19

Due to its simplicity, robustness, and efficiency in addressing complex optimization problems across various domains, DE is particularly adept at handling scenarios where the objective function is non-linear, non-convex, noisy, or lacks derivative information [5]. These exceptional characteristics render DE a versatile tool for addressing real-world optimization challenges encountered in engineering [6], finance [7], machine learning [8], and numerous other fields [9]. Consequently, DE has garnered widespread attention from researchers and scholars. Concurrently, numerous variants of DE have been introduced to tackle diverse optimization tasks. While this paper does not delve into the comprehensive history and evolution of DE, readers keen on exploring this topic further can refer to [10].

This paper introduces a novel competitive mechanism into DE and presents a mutation operator termed DE/winner-to-best/1. By integrating this innovative mutation strategy with the basic DE optimizer, we propose a simple yet efficient variant of DE, termed Competitive DE (CDE). To thoroughly investigate the performance of our proposed CDE, we conduct a comprehensive series of fair comparison experiments on the IEEE CEC2017 benchmark functions. Furthermore, we extend CDE to address real-world engineering simulation optimization problems. Through this straightforward modification, we achieve satisfactory performance across various optimization tasks, even when competing with state-of-the-art DE variants. The experimental results and statistical analyses highlight the efficacy and versatility of CDE in tackling diverse optimization challenges.

The remainder of this paper is organized as follows: Sect. 2 introduces the framework of basic DE and engineering simulation problems. Section 3 introduces our proposed CDE in detail. Section 4 presents numerical experiments and statistical analyses, and the performance analyses are discussed in Sect. 5. Finally, Sect. 6 concludes this paper.

2   Basic DE

We begin the introduction of the basic DE by the definition of optimization problems. Without loss of generality, the minimization problem is mathematically defined by Eq. (1).

$$f(\boldsymbol{x}^*) = \min f(\boldsymbol{x}), s.t. \boldsymbol{x} \in \mathcal{R}^D \tag{1}$$

where $\boldsymbol{x} = \{x_1, x_2, ..., x_D\}$ is a solution vector with D dimensions. Optimization algorithms aim to find optimum $\boldsymbol{x}^*$ with a limited computational budget.

Subsequently, we outline the four primary components of DE: initialization, mutation, crossover, and selection. It's important to note that all explanations are presented within the context of the minimization.

Initialization: The first step of DE implementation is population initialization, which is described in Eq. (2).

$$
X = \begin{bmatrix} \boldsymbol{x}_1 \\ \boldsymbol{x}_2 \\ \boldsymbol{x}_3 \\ \vdots \\ \boldsymbol{x}_N \end{bmatrix} = \begin{bmatrix} x_{11} & x_{12} & \cdots & x_{1D} \\ x_{21} & x_{22} & \cdots & x_{2D} \\ x_{31} & x_{32} & \cdots & x_{3D} \\ \vdots & \vdots & \ddots & \vdots \\ x_{N1} & x_{N2} & \cdots & x_{ND} \end{bmatrix} \tag{2}
$$
$$
x_{ij} = r \cdot (\boldsymbol{ub}_j - \boldsymbol{lb}_j) + \boldsymbol{lb}_j
$$

where $\boldsymbol{x}_i$ denotes the ith individual and x_{ij} represents the value in the jth dimension of the $\boldsymbol{x}_i$. $\boldsymbol{lb}_j$ and $\boldsymbol{ub}_j$ are the lower and the upper bound of the jth dimension, respectively, and r is a random number in $(0, 1)$.

Mutation: When DE enters the main loop, the mutation operation is first activated to construct the mutant vector, and the representative mutation schemes are listed in Eq. (3).

$$
\begin{aligned}
\text{DE/rand/1} &: \boldsymbol{v}_i^t = \boldsymbol{x}_{r1}^t + F \cdot (\boldsymbol{x}_{r2}^t - \boldsymbol{x}_{r3}^t) \\
\text{DE/cur/1} &: \boldsymbol{v}_i^t = \boldsymbol{x}_i^t + F \cdot (\boldsymbol{x}_{r1}^t - \boldsymbol{x}_{r2}^t) \\
\text{DE/best/1} &: \boldsymbol{v}_i^t = \boldsymbol{x}_{best}^t + F \cdot (\boldsymbol{x}_{r1}^t - \boldsymbol{x}_{r2}^t)
\end{aligned} \tag{3}
$$

where $\boldsymbol{x}_{r1}^t$, $\boldsymbol{x}_{r2}^t$, and $\boldsymbol{x}_{r3}^t$ are randomly selected individuals from the population and mutually distinct in the tth iteration, $\boldsymbol{x}_{best}^t$ denotes the best solution found so far, and F is the scaling factor to control the amplification of differential vector.

Crossover: Although many novel crossover strategies such as exponential crossover and blending crossover have been proposed, the most commonly utilized binomial crossover is expressed in Eq. (4).

$$
v_{i,j}^t = \begin{cases} u_{i,j}^t, & if \ r \leq Cr \ or \ j = j_{rand} \\ x_{i,j}^t, & otherwise \end{cases} \tag{4}
$$

Cr represents the crossover rate to control the probability of inherited genes between the mutant vector $\boldsymbol{u}_{i,j}^t$ and the parent individual $\boldsymbol{x}_{i,j}^t$. j_{rand} is a random integer in $\{1, 2, ..., D\}$.

Selection: The selection mechanism in basic DE ensures the survival of elite individuals to the next iteration, as formulated in Eq. (5).

$$
\boldsymbol{x}_i^{t+1} = \begin{cases} \boldsymbol{u}_i^t, & if \ f(\boldsymbol{u}_i^t) \leq f(\boldsymbol{x}_i^t) \\ \boldsymbol{x}_i^t, & otherwise \end{cases} \tag{5}
$$

The one-to-one greedy selection mechanism in DE can survive the elites while maintaining population diversity.

3   Competitive Differential Evolution (CDE)

This section introduced the proposed CDE in detail. Based on the simple yet effective architecture of DE, the main flowchart of CDE is presented in Fig. 1. The novel component in CDE is highlighted in red.

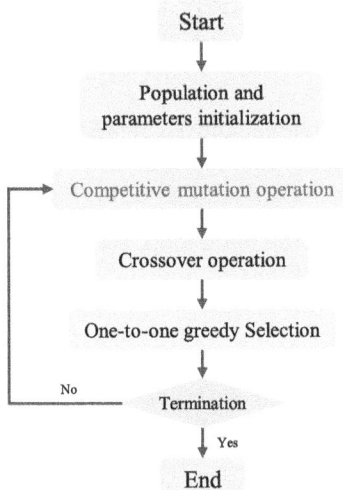

Fig. 1. The flowchart of CDE. (Color figure online)

We introduce the competitive mechanism to CDE and propose a novel DE/winner-to-best/1 mutation operation, as formulated in Eq. (6).

$$
v_i^g = \begin{cases} x_{r1}^g + F_1 \cdot (x_{best}^g - x_{r1}^g) + F_2 \cdot (x_{r2}^g - x_{r3}^g), \ (a) \\ x_i^g + F_1 \cdot (x_{best}^g - x_i^g) + F_2 \cdot (x_{r2}^g - x_{r3}^g), \ (b) \end{cases}
\tag{6}
$$

where F_1 and F_2 are two random values following a normal distribution $N(0.5, 0.3)$ as recommended in [11]. Simply, the proposed DE/winner-to-best/1 strategy randomly selects a competitor individual x_{r1}^g first, and if it has a better fitness value, x_{r1}^g will replace the current individual x_i^g and act as the base vector in the mutation operator to construct the mutant vector v_i^g using the DE/rand-to-best/1 scheme, as expressed in Eq. (6) (a); otherwise, the current individual x_i^g will survive and the DE/cur-to-best/1 mutation scheme in Eq. (6) (b) is activated to construct the mutated vector v_i^g.

The structure of the proposed DE/winner-to-best/1 strategy resembles a fusion of the DE/cur-to-best/1 and DE/rand-to-best/1 strategies. However, incorporating a competitive mechanism enables the automatic selection of the most suitable mutation strategy, ensuring the utilization of superior knowledge to construct the mutated vector. Furthermore, CDE can benefit from the proposed

DE/winner-to-best/1 mutation strategy from (i). Strengthened convergence: By leveraging a superior base vector, the optimization process experiences rapid convergence and contributes to accelerating the approach to optimal solutions. (ii). The prevention of premature optimization: The inclusion of the random differential vector $F_2 \cdot (\boldsymbol{x}_{r2}^g - \boldsymbol{x}_{r3}^g)$ serves to mitigate premature optimization and promote the exploration of diverse search spaces. (iii). Versatile scaling factor: The utilization of a simple yet effective random generator-based scaling factor F_i facilitates the generation of differential vectors with varying scales, thereby enhancing the adaptability and robustness of the mutation strategy.

Furthermore, the conventional constant crossover rate in basic DE is replaced by a random value sampled from a normal distribution $N(0.5, 0.3)$, as recommended in [12]. This simple modification in CDE yields two significant benefits. First, it enhances the balance between exploration and exploitation. By introducing a randomly chosen crossover rate, CDE can explore a broader search space by occasionally performing crossover operations, potentially leading to the discovery of new promising solutions. Simultaneously, it retains the capability to exploit current best solutions by occasionally abstaining from crossover operations. Second, this modification strengthens the robustness of CDE. Introducing randomness into the crossover rate helps prevent the algorithm from becoming trapped in specific regions of the search space, thereby improving its robustness when tackling complex optimization problems.

4   Numerical Experiments

This section introduces the details of the designed numerical experiments to evaluate the performance of CDE. Section 4.1 details the experimental setting, and Sect. 4.2 presents the experimental results and statistical analyses for further discussion.

4.1   Experiment Settings

Benchmark Functions. We conduct comprehensive numerical experiments on CEC2017 benchmark functions and six engineering simulation optimization tasks [13]. The details of engineering problems are presented in the following contexts. These benchmarks are accessed via the OpFuNu library [14] and the ENOPPY library [15] using Python 3.11.

Six engineering simulation models adopted in our numerical experiments include cantilever beam design (CBD), corrugated bulkhead design (CBHD), gear train design (GTD), three-bar truss design (TBTD), tubular column design (TCD), and welded beam design (WBD). In the following mathematical models, $f(x)$ denotes the objective function, and $g_i(x)$ represents the ith constraint function.

Cantilever Beam Design Problem (CBD): CBD aims to minimize the overall mass of the cantilever beam while ensuring it meets the specified bearing capacity requirements. Equation (7) describes the mathematical model and Fig. 2(a) presents a demonstration.

$$\min f(X) = 0.0624(x_1 + x_2 + x_3 + x_4 + x_5)$$

$$\text{s.t. } g(X) = \frac{61}{x_1^3} + \frac{37}{x_2^3} + \frac{19}{x_3^3} + \frac{7}{x_4^3} + \frac{1}{x_5^3} - 1 \le 0 \tag{7}$$

$$\textbf{where } 0.01 \le x_i \le 100, \ i \in \{1, 2, 3, 4, 5\}$$

Corrugated Bulkhead Design (CBHD): CBHD aims to design a bulkhead that can efficiently resist certain forces or loads, in which the design variables are the width x_1, depth x_2, length x_3, and plate thickness x_4. The mathematical model of the CBHD is presented in Eq. (8).

$$\min f(X) = \frac{5.885x_4(x_1 + x_3)}{x_1 + \sqrt{|x_3^2 - x_2^2|}}$$

$$\text{s.t. } g_1(X) = -x_4 x_2 (0.4x_1 + \frac{x_3}{6})$$

$$+ 8.94(x_1 + \sqrt{|x_3^2 - x_2^2|}) \le 0$$

$$g_2(X) = -x_4 x_2^2 (0.2x_1 + \frac{x_3}{12})$$

$$+ 2.2(8.94(x_1 + \sqrt{|x_3^2 - x_2^2|}))^{4/3} \le 0 \tag{8}$$

$$g_3(X) = -x_4 + 0.0156x_1 + 0.15 \le 0$$

$$g_4(X) = -x_4 + 0.0156x_3 + 0.15 \le 0$$

$$g_5(X) = -x_4 + 1.05 \le 0$$

$$g_6(X) = -x_3 + x_2 \le 0$$

$$\textbf{where } 0 \le x_1, x_2, x_3 \le 100$$

$$0 \le x_4 \le 5$$

Gear Train Design Problem (GTD): GTD aims to minimize the gear ratio, defined as the ratio of the output shaft's angular velocity to the input shaft's angular velocity. The design variables include the number of teeth of gears $n_A = x_1$, $n_B = x_2$, $n_C = x_3$, and $n_D = x_4$, as expressed in Eq. (9) and demonstrated in Fig. 2(b).

$$\min f(X) = \left(\frac{1}{6.931} - \frac{x_3 x_2}{x_1 x_4}\right)^2 \tag{9}$$

$$\textbf{where } x_1, x_2, x_3, x_4 \in \{12, 13, 14, ..., 60\}$$

Three-Bar Truss Design Problem (TBTD): The objective of TBTD is to find the optimal configuration of a truss made up of three bars subject to the optimal cross-sectional areas $A_1 = x_1$ and $A_2 = x_2$. The mathematical model and demonstration are presented in Eq. (10) and Fig. 2(c).

$$\min f(X) = (2\sqrt{2}x_1 + x_2) \cdot l$$

$$\text{s.t. } g_1(X) = \frac{\sqrt{2}x_1 + x_2}{\sqrt{2}x_1^2 + 2x_1x_2} P - \sigma \le 0$$

$$g_2(X) = \frac{x_2}{\sqrt{2}x_1^2 + 2x_1x_2} P - \sigma \le 0 \tag{10}$$

$$g_3(X) = \frac{1}{\sqrt{2}x_2 + x_1} P - \sigma \le 0$$

$$l = 100 \text{ cm}, P = 2 \text{ kN/cm}^3, \sigma = 2 \text{ kN/cm}^3$$

$$\text{where } 0 \le x_1, x_2 \le 1$$

Tubular Column Design Problem (TCD): TCD through optimizing two decision variables: the mean diameter of the column $d = x_1$ and the thickness of tube $t = x_2$ to determine the optimum of a tubular column. Equation (11) formulates the model and Fig. 2(d) presents a demonstration.

$$\min f(X) = 9.8x_1x_2 + 2x_1$$

$$\text{s.t. } g_1(X) = \frac{P}{\pi x_1 x_2 \sigma_y} - 1 \le 0$$

$$g_2(X) = \frac{8PL^2}{\pi^3 Ex_1x_2(x_1^2 + x_2^2)} - 1 \le 0 \tag{11}$$

$$\text{where } 2 \le x_1 \le 14$$

$$0.2 \le x_2 \le 8$$

Welded Beam Design (WBD): The objective of WBD is to design a welded beam subjected to the weld thickness $h = x_1$, height $l = x_2$, length $t = x_3$, and bar thickness $b = x_4$, as formulated in Eq. (12) and visualized in Fig. 2(e).

$$\min f(X) = 1.10471x_1^2 + 0.04811x_3x_4(14 + x_2)$$

$$\text{s.t. } g_1(X) = \tau(X) - \tau_{max} \le 0$$

$$g_2(X) = \sigma(X) - \sigma_{max} \le 0$$

$$g_3(X) = \theta(X) - \theta_{max} \le 0$$

$$g_4(X) = x_1 - x_4 \le 0$$

$$g_5(X) = P - P_c(X) \le 0 \tag{12}$$

$$g_6(X) = 0.125 - x_1 \le 0$$

$$g_6(X) = 1.10471x_1^2 + 0.04811x_3x_4(14 + x_2) - 5 \le 0$$

$$\text{where } 0.1 \le x_1, x_4 \le 2$$

$$0.1 \le x_2, x_3 \le 10$$

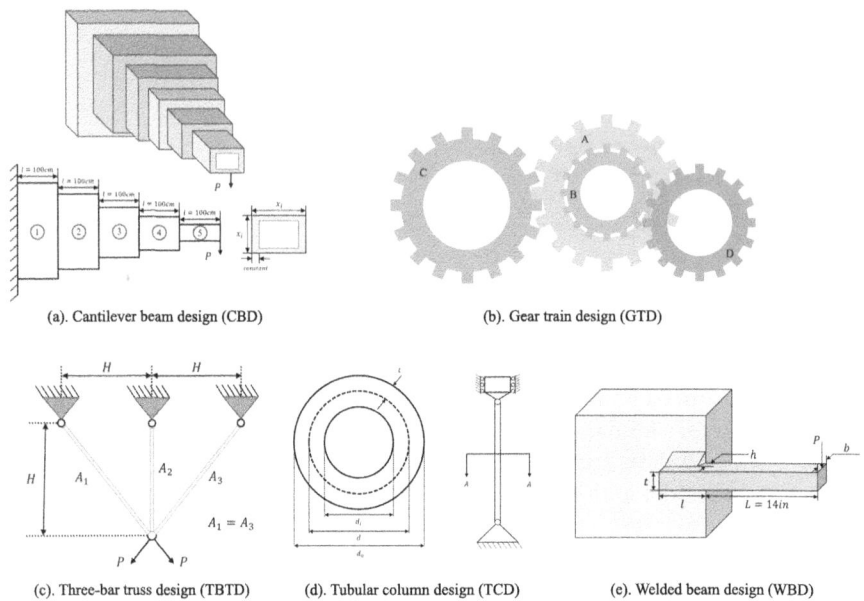

(a). Cantilever beam design (CBD)   (b). Gear train design (GTD)

(c). Three-bar truss design (TBTD)   (d). Tubular column design (TCD)   (e). Welded beam design (WBD)

Fig. 2. The demonstration of engineering simulation tasks.

Competitor Algorithms. We compare CDE with state-of-the-art optimizers and DE variants. The specific algorithms and corresponding parameter settings are listed in Table 1.

Except for L-SHADE and L-SHADE-PWI, the population size for the rest of the algorithms is fixed at 100. The maximum fitness evaluation (FE) for CEC2017 benchmark functions and engineering simulation optimization tasks are set to 500 × D and 10,000, respectively. Each single algorithm is implemented with 30 trial runs to alleviate the effect of randomness. Additionally, the Holm multiple comparison test [20] is employed to determine the significance between every pair of compared algorithms. The symbols +, ≈, and − denote that the proposed CDE is significantly better, has no significant difference, and is significantly worse than the compared algorithm.

4.2   Experimental Results and Statistical Analyses

We summarize the experimental results and statistical analyses on the CEC2017 benchmark functions and engineering simulation optimization tasks in Tables 2 and 3, respectively. The convergence curves on engineering tasks are demonstrated in Fig. 3.

Table 1. The compared optimizers and parameter settings

Method	Parameters	Value
CDE	μ_F and σ_F	0.5 and 0.3
	μ_{Cr} and σ_{Cr}	0.5 and 0.3
DE [1]	scale factor F	0.5
	crossover rate Cr	0.8
	mutation strategy	DE/rand/1/bin
CMA-ES [16]	σ	1.3
SaDE [11]	μ_F and σ_F	0.5 and 0.3
	μ_{Cr} and σ_{Cr}	0.5 and 0.1
JADE [17]	μ_F and μ_{Cr}	0.5 and 0.5
L-SHADE [18]	population size N	$18 \times D$
	μ_F and μ_{Cr}	0.5 and 0.5
L-SHADE-PWI [19]	population size N	$18 \times D$
	N_{min}	4
	μ_F and μ_{Cr}	0.5 and 0.5
GTDE [12]	μ_F and σ_F	0.7 and 0.5
	μ_{Cr} and σ_{Cr}	0.5 and 0.3

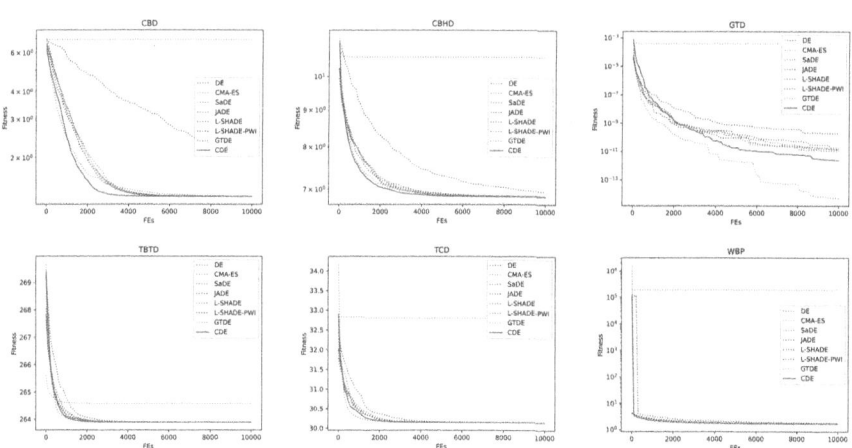

Fig. 3. Convergence curves of eight algorithms on six engineering simulation optimization tasks.

5   Discussion

5.1   Performance Analysis on CEC2017

Since the CEC2017 benchmark suite contains test functions with various characteristics such as unimodal, multimodal, hybrid, and composite, thus the opti-

Table 2. Experimental results and statistical analyses on 30-D CEC2017. f_1: Unimodal function; $f_3 - f_9$: Simple multimodal functions; $f_{10} - f_{19}$: Hybrid functions; $f_{20} - f_{30}$: Composite functions.

Func.		DE	CMA-ES	SaDE	JADE	L-SHADE	L-SHADE-PWI	GTDE	CDE
f_1	mean	5.103e+10 +	3.727e+10 +	6.658e+06 +	2.557e+05 +	2.247e+05 +	2.005e+05 +	4.846e+05 +	**3.935e+03**
	std	4.548e+09	4.131e+09	3.586e+06	1.062e+05	8.170e+04	9.129e+04	7.482e+05	2.858e+03
f_3	mean	2.570e+05 +	8.737e+04 +	1.256e+05 +	1.097e+05 +	7.925e+04 ≈	9.514e+04 +	**5.365e+04** −	6.566e+04
	std	3.839e+04	1.087e+04	1.324e+04	1.553e+04	2.571e+04	2.334e+04	1.578e+04	1.017e+04
f_4	mean	5.598e+03 +	1.040e+04 +	5.155e+02 +	4.971e+02 ≈	5.119e+02 +	5.069e+02 +	5.229e+02 +	**4.947e+02**
	std	1.001e+03	1.669e+03	1.121e+01	9.735e+00	1.317e+01	1.516e+01	5.260e+01	2.754e+01
f_5	mean	9.157e+02 +	8.647e+02 +	7.067e+02 +	6.830e+02 +	6.812e+02 +	6.961e+02 +	**6.188e+02** +	6.793e+02
	std	1.467e+01	2.180e+01	8.716e+00	1.230e+01	8.704e+00	1.070e+01	2.373e+01	2.163e+01
f_6	mean	6.854e+02 +	6.841e+02 +	6.039e+02 +	6.030e+02 +	6.017e+02 +	6.016e+02 +	6.094e+02 +	**6.000e+02**
	std	4.509e+00	6.360e+00	6.699e−01	6.214e−01	2.573e−01	1.715e−01	6.514e+00	6.747e−02
f_7	mean	2.885e+03 +	1.316e+03 +	9.519e+02 +	9.257e+02 +	9.164e+02 ≈	9.245e+02 +	**9.008e+02** −	9.177e+02
	std	1.479e+02	5.799e+01	1.039e+01	1.219e+01	1.091e+01	1.012e+01	4.178e+01	1.398e+01
f_8	mean	1.225e+03 +	1.108e+03 +	1.010e+03 +	9.816e+02 +	9.784e+02 −	9.940e+02 ≈	**9.204e+02** −	9.891e+02
	std	2.398e+01	2.175e+01	1.576e+01	1.171e+01	9.673e+00	1.037e+01	3.005e+01	1.463e+01
f_9	mean	2.034e+04 +	9.916e+03 +	1.080e+03 +	9.334e+02 +	9.227e+02 +	9.204e+02 +	2.833e+03 +	**9.121e+02**
	std	3.367e+03	1.739e+03	3.154e+01	1.779e+01	6.416e+00	7.894e+00	1.252e+03	2.395e+01
f_{10}	mean	8.535e+03 +	8.965e+03 +	8.526e+03 +	7.857e+03 −	7.788e+03 −	8.264e+03 ≈	**6.230e+03** −	8.288e+03
	std	1.251e+02	3.064e+02	2.501e+02	5.205e+02	4.083e+02	4.103e+02	1.218e+03	3.137e+02
f_{11}	mean	5.459e+03 +	7.084e+03 +	1.580e+03 +	1.418e+03 +	1.330e+03 +	1.331e+03 +	1.336e+03 +	**1.211e+03**
	std	9.216e+02	1.281e+03	7.087e+01	1.369e+02	2.471e+01	1.982e+01	7.101e+01	3.607e+01
f_{12}	mean	2.890e+09 +	9.017e+09 +	8.847e+06 +	2.351e+06 +	2.646e+06 +	2.455e+06 +	1.394e+06 +	**3.315e+05**
	std	7.294e+08	1.469e+09	3.007e+06	1.061e+06	9.611e+05	1.091e+06	1.272e+06	2.678e+05
f_{13}	mean	3.517e+08 +	8.504e+09 +	1.856e+06 +	7.919e+05 +	8.107e+05 +	6.539e+05 +	1.891e+05 +	**1.791e+04**
	std	1.550e+08	2.622e+09	1.525e+06	4.738e+05	3.963e+05	3.435e+05	8.023e+05	1.141e+04
f_{14}	mean	1.545e+05 +	3.709e+06 +	4.919e+04 +	5.594e+04 +	9.363e+03 +	1.253e+04 +	**3.568e+03** −	5.788e+03
	std	8.448e+04	3.375e+06	2.024e+04	1.000e+05	3.375e+03	6.404e+03	3.773e+03	4.171e+03
f_{15}	mean	1.099e+07 +	1.057e+08 +	2.662e+05 +	1.879e+05 +	7.902e+04 +	8.338e+04 +	1.527e+04 +	**7.296e+03**
	std	5.523e+06	7.358e+07	2.447e+05	1.815e+05	3.691e+04	2.115e+04	1.292e+04	4.826e+03
f_{16}	mean	4.100e+03 +	6.112e+03 +	3.283e+03 ≈	3.146e+03 ≈	3.137e+03 ≈	3.202e+03 ≈	**2.717e+03** −	3.121e+03
	std	2.520e+02	7.003e+02	2.261e+02	1.656e+02	2.096e+02	1.460e+02	2.888e+02	1.890e+02
f_{17}	mean	2.902e+03 +	3.591e+03 +	2.302e+03 +	2.278e+03 +	2.201e+03 +	2.202e+03 +	2.241e+03 +	**2.071e+03**
	std	1.397e+02	4.381e+02	1.375e+02	1.029e+02	9.999e+01	8.212e+01	1.897e+02	1.211e+02
f_{18}	mean	8.635e+06 +	2.787e+07 +	2.636e+06 +	3.552e+05 −	8.008e+05 ≈	9.985e+05 ≈	**2.694e+05** −	6.445e+05
	std	2.858e+06	1.867e+07	1.543e+06	7.014e+05	3.289e+05	3.210e+05	3.029e+05	2.997e+05
f_{19}	mean	5.534e+07 +	1.479e+08 +	3.885e+05 +	2.783e+05 +	1.231e+05 +	1.098e+05 +	2.082e+04 +	**1.071e+04**
	std	1.531e+07	6.526e+07	1.993e+05	3.473e+05	5.324e+04	4.258e+04	2.342e+04	8.252e+03
f_{20}	mean	2.895e+03 +	2.980e+03 +	2.753e+03 +	2.645e+03 +	2.685e+03 +	2.679e+03 +	**2.422e+03** −	2.574e+03
	std	1.522e+02	1.782e+02	1.530e+02	1.059e+02	9.051e+01	1.390e+02	1.717e+02	1.038e+02
f_{21}	mean	2.703e+03 +	2.702e+03 +	2.497e+03 +	2.482e+03 +	2.477e+03 +	2.480e+03 +	**2.421e+03** −	2.473e+03
	std	1.745e+01	3.178e+01	1.541e+01	1.360e+01	7.071e+00	2.119e+01	2.781e+01	1.477e+01
f_{22}	mean	1.007e+04 +	9.432e+03 +	4.272e+03 +	3.152e+03 +	2.380e+03 +	2.332e+03 +	6.922e+03 +	**2.302e+03**
	std	2.811e+02	6.399e+02	2.839e+03	2.109e+03	1.794e+02	4.572e+01	2.150e+03	4.604e+00
f_{23}	mean	3.048e+03 +	3.864e+03 +	2.850e+03 +	2.845e+03 +	2.835e+03 +	2.836e+03 +	**2.791e+03** ≈	2.800e+03
	std	2.042e+01	1.486e+02	1.184e+01	1.235e+01	1.104e+01	1.078e+01	1.802e+01	3.928e+01
f_{24}	mean	3.168e+03 +	4.123e+03 +	3.021e+03 +	3.014e+03 +	3.003e+03 +	3.002e+03 +	**2.965e+03** −	2.981e+03
	std	1.452e+01	1.231e+02	1.162e+01	1.262e+01	9.793e+00	1.587e+01	3.329e+01	3.151e+01
f_{25}	mean	7.916e+03 +	4.393e+03 +	2.896e+03 ≈	**2.888e+03** ≈	2.889e+03 ≈	2.890e+03 ≈	2.908e+03 +	2.896e+03
	std	7.414e+02	2.358e+02	5.233e+00	1.622e+00	1.329e+00	3.488e+00	2.653e+01	1.487e+01
f_{26}	mean	8.009e+03 +	1.022e+04 +	5.733e+03 +	5.441e+03 +	5.381e+03 +	5.432e+03 +	5.082e+03 +	**4.319e+03**
	std	1.622e+02	4.395e+02	1.563e+02	1.552e+02	1.210e+02	1.653e+02	6.734e+02	9.410e+02
f_{27}	mean	3.319e+03 +	5.137e+03 +	3.237e+03 ≈	**3.227e+03** −	3.229e+03 ≈	3.231e+03 ≈	3.245e+03 ≈	3.234e+03
	std	1.968e+01	3.727e+02	6.785e+00	4.321e+00	3.571e+00	7.636e+00	2.469e+01	1.278e+01
f_{28}	mean	5.625e+03 +	6.320e+03 +	3.273e+03 +	3.243e+03 ≈	3.253e+03 +	3.244e+03 +	3.374e+03 +	**3.235e+03**
	std	7.238e+02	4.928e+02	1.409e+01	2.169e+01	1.408e+01	1.688e+01	2.394e+02	2.565e+01
f_{29}	mean	4.892e+03 +	7.512e+03 +	4.229e+03 +	4.071e+03 +	4.070e+03 +	4.122e+03 +	4.009e+03 +	**3.846e+03**
	std	2.164e+02	6.220e+02	2.283e+02	1.605e+02	1.524e+02	1.161e+02	2.031e+02	1.855e+02
f_{30}	mean	3.759e+07 +	1.003e+09 +	1.192e+06 +	3.945e+05 +	4.913e+05 +	5.271e+05 +	1.283e+05 ≈	**5.083e+04**
	std	1.225e+07	4.249e+08	7.053e+05	2.741e+05	1.892e+05	1.731e+05	2.266e+05	3.913e+04
+/≈/−		29/0/0	29/0/0	26/3/0	20/6/3	18/9/2	20/9/0	14/5/10	−
Avg. rank		7.3	7.5	5.7	3.8	3.2	3.7	2.9	1.9

Table 3. Experimental results and statistical analyses on engineering optimization problems.

Func.		DE	CMA-ES	SaDE	JADE	L-SHADE	L-SHADE-PWI	GTDE	CDE
CBD	mean	2.015e+00 +	6.910e+00 +	1.341e+00 +	1.341e+00 +	1.340e+00 +	1.340e+00 +	1.344e+00 +	**1.340e+00**
	std	2.139e−01	1.248e+00	3.301e−04	3.767e−04	1.935e−04	1.705e−04	2.207e−03	3.705e−05
CBHD	mean	6.949e+00 +	1.064e+01 +	6.845e+00 +	6.847e+00 +	6.844e+00 +	6.844e+00 +	6.850e+00 +	**6.843e+00**
	std	3.671e−02	1.251e+00	1.237e−03	1.529e−03	3.915e−04	5.784e−04	3.810e−03	3.375e−04
GTD	mean	1.838e−10 +	3.924e−04 +	1.087e−11 +	1.805e−11 +	1.373e−11 +	1.200e−11 +	**5.568e−15** −	2.560e−12
	std	2.820e−10	7.737e−04	1.283e−11	3.519e−11	2.412e−11	2.425e−11	1.670e−14	5.844e−12
TBTD	mean	2.639e+02 +	2.646e+02 +	2.639e+02 +	2.639e+02 +	2.639e+02 +	2.639e+02 +	2.639e+02 +	**2.639e+02**
	std	7.558e−06	6.359e−01	7.622e−07	1.574e−06	3.310e−07	4.045e−07	1.063e−04	5.984e−08
TCD	mean	3.015e+01 +	3.281e+01 +	3.015e+01 +	3.015e+01 +	3.015e+01 +	3.015e+01 +	3.015e+01 +	**3.015e+01**
	std	8.503e−05	1.439e+00	2.198e−06	1.019e−05	2.300e−06	2.962e−06	1.013e−04	5.172e−07
WBP	mean	1.761e+00 +	1.932e+05 +	1.696e+00 +	1.692e+00 +	1.690e+00 +	1.689e+00 +	1.712e+00 +	**1.687e+00**
	std	2.811e−02	1.040e+06	9.128e−03	3.993e−03	2.950e−03	2.224e−03	4.087e−02	5.447e−03
+/≈/−		6/0/0	6/0/0	6/0/0	6/0/0	6/0/0	6/0/0	5/0/1	—
Avg. rank		6.7	8.0	4.0	5.0	2.8	2.8	5.5	1.2

mization in these test functions can fully reflect the performance of optimizers and support us in investigating the features of involved algorithms thoroughly.

Initially, f_1 is unimodal functions, and the optimization in these functions allows the performance evaluation in the aspect of the exploitative capacity. The superiority of CDE is apparent in CEC2017 f_1 compared with state-of-the-art optimizers. Therefore, we conclude that CDE has a remarkable exploitation ability and robust performance across various problem domains.

Subsequently, f_3 to f_9 are multimodal functions. These functions contain more than one local optima and evaluate the performance of optimizers in escaping from local optima and global convergence. Through the experimental results and statistical analyses summarized in Table 2, the competitiveness of our proposed CDE is observable. As the state-of-the-art DE variant, GTDE outperforms CDE in some instances such as f_3, f_5, and f_8. However, the excellent performance of CDE cannot be neglected. Overall, CDE best performs in f_4, f_6, and f_9, and the capacities in escaping from local optima and global convergence are experimentally verified through the results.

Finally, the rest of the functions are hybrid and composite. These functions have complex fitness landscapes and multiple optima, which challenges optimizers' ability to balance exploitation and exploration, avoid premature convergence, and achieve global optimization. Upon review of the result summary, it becomes evident that CDE consistently demonstrates superior performance across many test functions within this category, thereby highlighting its efficacy in complex optimization environments.

5.2 Performance Analysis on Engineering Tasks

Engineering simulation optimization tasks serve as real-world challenges in evaluating the performance of optimizers in complex optimization scenarios. This study introduces CDE as a novel approach to engineering optimization tasks. Remarkably, our proposed CDE outperforms all other methods across all instances except for GTD when compared with GTDE, showcasing its superior performance in this domain.

In summary, our proposed CDE is a satisfactory variant of DE in both benchmark and engineering optimization. We owe this success to the integration of the competitive mechanism and the intelligent hyper-parameter adaptation inherited from the previous research [11,12]. These elements collectively empower CDE with outstanding efficiency and effectiveness.

6   Conclusion

This paper proposes a novel competitive DE (CDE) to solve numerical optimization problems. We introduce a competitive mechanism to DE and propose a novel DE/winner-to-best/1 mutation strategy. Moreover, CDE inherits the hyper-parameter adaptation schemes recommended in [11,12]. To assess the performance of CDE, we conduct comprehensive numerical experiments on CEC2017 benchmark functions and engineering simulation optimization problems. The experimental results and statistical analyses confirm the competitiveness of our proposed CDE compared to state-of-the-art EAs and advanced variants of DE, including CMA-ES, JADE, L-SHADE, L-SHADE-PWI, and GTDE.

In conclusion, our proposed CDE exhibits significant potential as a powerful optimizer in real-world scenarios. In future research, we plan to further develop CDE and leverage its capabilities to address complex tasks across various application domains.

Acknowledgement. This work was supported by JSPS KAKENHI Grant Number 21A402 and 24K15098 and JST SPRING Grant Number JPMJSP2119.

References

1. Storn, R., Price, K.: Differential evolution - a simple and efficient heuristic for global optimization over continuous spaces. J. Glob. Optim. **11**, 341–359 (1997)
2. Li, Y., Wang, S., Yang, H., Chen, H., Yang, B.: Enhancing differential evolution algorithm using leader-adjoint populations. Inf. Sci. **622**, 235–268 (2023)
3. Ren, C., Song, Z., Meng, Z.: Differential evolution with fitness-difference based parameter control and hypervolume diversity indicator for numerical optimization. Eng. Appl. Artif. Intell. **133**, 108081 (2024)
4. Yang, Q., Yan, J.Q., Gao, X.D., Xu, D.D., Lu, Z.Y., Zhang, J.: Random neighbor elite guided differential evolution for global numerical optimization. Inf. Sci. **607**, 1408–1438 (2022)
5. Zhong, R., Zhang, E., Munetomo, M.: Cooperative coevolutionary surrogate ensemble-assisted differential evolution with efficient dual differential grouping for large-scale expensive optimization problems. Complex Intell. Syst. 1–21 (2023)
6. Zhang, Y., Li, S., Wang, Y., Yan, Y., Zhao, J., Gao, Z.: Self-adaptive enhanced learning differential evolution with surprisingly efficient decomposition approach for parameter identification of photovoltaic models. Energy Convers. Manage. **308**, 118387 (2024)

7. Xue, Z., Yao, S., Ma, H., Zhang, C., Zhang, K., Chen, Z.: Thermo-economic optimization of an enhanced geothermal system (EGS) based on machine learning and differential evolution algorithms. Fuel **340**, 127569 (2023)
8. Zhong, R., Zhang, E., Munetomo, M.: Cooperative coevolutionary differential evolution with linkage measurement minimization for large-scale optimization problems in noisy environments. Complex Intell. Syst. **9**, 4439–4456 (2023)
9. Zhang, Y.J., Wang, Y.F., Yan, Y.X., Zhao, J., Gao, Z.M.: Self-adaptive hybrid mutation slime mould algorithm: case studies on UAV path planning, engineering problems, photovoltaic models and infinite impulse response. Alex. Eng. J. **98**, 364–389 (2024)
10. Ahmad, M.F., Isa, N.A.M., Lim, W.H., Ang, K.M.: Differential evolution: a recent review based on state-of-the-art works. Alex. Eng. J. **61**(5), 3831–3872 (2022)
11. Qin, A., Suganthan, P.: Self-adaptive differential evolution algorithm for numerical optimization. In: 2005 IEEE Congress on Evolutionary Computation, vol. 2, pp. 1785–1791 (2005)
12. Wang, Z.J., Jian, J.R., Zhan, Z.H., Li, Y., Kwong, S., Zhang, J.: Gene targeting differential evolution: a simple and efficient method for large-scale optimization. IEEE Trans. Evol. Comput. **27**(4), 964–979 (2023)
13. Zhong, R., Yu, J., Zhang, C., Munetomo, M.: SRIME: a strengthened rime with latin hypercube sampling and embedded distance-based selection for engineering optimization problems. Neural Comput. Appl. 1–21 (2024)
14. Nguyen, T.: A framework of optimization functions using numpy (opfunu) for optimization problems (2020)
15. Thieu, N.V.: ENOPPY: a python library for engineering optimization problems (2023)
16. Hansen, N., Ostermeier, A.: Completely derandomized self-adaptation in evolution strategies. Evol. Comput. **9**(2), 159–195 (2001)
17. Zhang, J., Sanderson, A.C.: JADE: adaptive differential evolution with optional external archive. IEEE Trans. Evol. Comput. **13**(5), 945–958 (2009)
18. Tanabe, R., Fukunaga, A.S.: Improving the search performance of shade using linear population size reduction. In: 2014 IEEE Congress on Evolutionary Computation (CEC), pp. 1658–1665 (2014)
19. Piotrowski, A.P.: L-shade optimization algorithms with population-wide inertia. Inf. Sci. **468**, 117–141 (2018)
20. Holm, S.: A simple sequentially rejective multiple test procedure. Scand. J. Stat. **6**(2), 65–70 (1979)

Hyper-heuristic Differential Evolution with Novel Boundary Repair for Numerical Optimization

Rui Zhong[1]([✉]), Jun Yu[2], and Masaharu Munetomo[3]

[1] Graduate School of Information Science and Technology, Hokkaido University, Sapporo, Japan
rui.zhong.u5@elms.hokudai.ac.jp
[2] Institute of Science and Technology, Niigata University, Niigata, Japan
yujun@ie.niigata-u.ac.jp
[3] Information Initiative Center, Hokkaido University, Sapporo, Japan
munetomo@iic.hokudai.ac.jp

Abstract. Inspired by the architecture of the hyper-heuristic (HH) algorithm, we design a mutation operator archive, a crossover operator archive, and a boundary repair operator archive to propose a novel hyper-heuristic differential evolution (HHDE). The mutation operator archive and the crossover operator archive contain multiple representative search operators derived from different versions. A learning-free selection function, which utilizes an unbiased probability approach, is employed to autonomously determine the optimization sequence from these archives. This function serves as the high-level component of the HH framework. Additionally, we focus on the boundary repair operator, an element often overlooked in the design of the evolutionary algorithm (EA). Based on the previous research, our designed boundary repair operator archive introduces two novel boundary repair techniques: optimum inheritance and iterative opposite-based mapping. Comprehensive numerical experiments on 10-D and 20-D CEC2022 benchmark functions and six engineering optimization problems are conducted to assess the efficacy of our proposed HHDE. The performance of HHDE was compared against a range of other state-of-the-art competitor optimizers. The experimental results and statistical analysis confirm the competitiveness and efficiency of HHDE. The source code of HHDE can be found in https://github.com/RuiZhong961230/HHDE.

Keywords: hyper-heuristic (HH) · differential evolution (DE) · boundary repair · numerical optimization

1 Introduction

Since the conventional differential evolution (DE) algorithm was proposed by Storn and Price in 1996 [1], it has emerged as one of the most popular and efficient stochastic optimization techniques in the evolutionary computation (EC)

© The Author(s), under exclusive license to Springer Nature Switzerland AG 2025
H. R. Arabnia et al. (Eds.): CSCE 2024, CCIS 2256, pp. 264–277, 2025.
https://doi.org/10.1007/978-3-031-85638-9_20

community. Thanks to its superior characteristics such as scalability, applicability, robustness, and easy implementation, DE-based optimization techniques have been widely applied in various domains, such as multi-objective optimization [2], large-scale global optimization [3], and other applications [4]. In the meantime, many remarkable variants of DE have been proposed, including JADE [5], success-history based parameter adaptation DE (SHADE) [6], and its variants. The rich history of DE will not be fully reviewed here, as it can be referred to [7].

The conventional DE employs a series of operations including mutation, crossover, and selection strategies to iteratively search for improved solutions. These time-varying search operators collectively form the optimization sequence. This raises an intriguing question: Is it possible to optimize the optimization sequence itself? The response to this query is in the affirmative, aligning with the concept of the hyper-heuristic (HH) framework. In contrast to tailored meta-heuristic algorithms (MAs), which are specifically designed for particular problems, the HH algorithm represents a more generic, "off-the-peg" technique as opposed to "made-to-measure" [8]. As a high-level automatic methodology, the HH algorithm consists of two crucial components: the low-level component and the high-level component. The low-level component represents the inherent attributes of the algorithm, whereas the high-level component functions as the intelligent decision-maker for determining the optimization sequence. While many HH algorithms have been effectively applied to combinatorial optimization problems, only a few have been focused on continuous problems [9].

Additionally, a critical yet frequently overlooked aspect in the design of the evolutionary algorithm (EA) is the boundary repair technique. In the process of constructing the offspring through search operators, there is a probability that the resultant offspring individual may fall outside the feasible search domain. The traditional method to address this issue involves manually setting the value to the search boundary or randomly generating a value within the search domain. However, this simplistic method often fails to make adequate use of the domain knowledge.

In this paper, we address the aforementioned challenges by integrating the HH framework with DE, leading to the development of a novel hyper-heuristic differential evolution (HHDE) algorithm. The design of HHDE encompasses a mutation operator archive, a crossover operator archive, and a boundary repair strategy archive. As a primary approach, the learning-free stochastic function is employed as the high-level component of HHDE. Moreover, the comprehensive numerical experiments conducted using 10-D and 20-D CEC2022 benchmark functions and six popular engineering optimization tasks, have been compared against nine state-of-the-art competitor EAs. These rigorous comparisons further underscore the effectiveness and superior performance of our proposed HHDE.

The remaining paper is organized as follows. Section 2 introduces the related works, Sect. 3 introduces our proposed HHDE in detail, Sect. 4 describes experimental settings and results, we analyze the performance of HHDE in Sect. 5, and finally, Sect. 6 concludes our work.

2   Related Works

2.1   Differential Evolution (DE)

In this section, we briefly introduce the structure of the basic DE algorithm. Without the loss of generality, the minimization problem is considered in this paper, and the objective is to find an optimum, denoted as x^*, that satisfies the following Eq. (1).

$$f(x^*) = \min_{\vec{x} \in \Omega}(f(\vec{x})) \tag{1}$$

where $f(\cdot)$ is the objective function, $\vec{x} = \{x_1, x_2, ..., x_n\}$ is an n-dimensional trial solution, and Ω denotes the search domain.

As one of the population-based EAs, the first step of DE is to initialize the population through Eq. (2)

$$x_{i,j} = LB_j + r \cdot (UB_j - LB_j)$$

$$X = \{\vec{x}_1, \vec{x}_2, ..., \vec{x}_{NP}\} = \begin{bmatrix} x_{11} & x_{12} & \cdots & x_{1D} \\ x_{21} & x_{22} & \cdots & x_{2D} \\ x_{31} & x_{32} & \cdots & x_{3D} \\ \vdots & \vdots & \ddots & \vdots \\ x_{N1} & x_{N2} & \cdots & x_{ND} \end{bmatrix} \tag{2}$$

where UB_j and LB_j are the upper and lower bound of the jth dimension, respectively, NP is the population size, and X represents the population. Considering the simplest DE/rand/1 mutation strategy, the mutated individual v can be constructed using Eq. (3).

$$\vec{v}_i = \vec{x}_{r_1} + F \cdot (\vec{x}_{r_2} - \vec{x}_{r_3}) \tag{3}$$

where F is a scaling factor, $\vec{x}_{r_1}$, $\vec{x}_{r_2}$ and $\vec{x}_{r_3}$ are mutually different individuals which are randomly selected from the population X. Then, the binomial crossover between the trial vector v_i and parent individual x_i is formulated in Eq. (4)

$$\vec{u}_{i,j} = \begin{cases} \vec{v}_{i,j}, & if \ r < Cr \ or \ j = jrand \\ \vec{x}_{i,j}, & otherwise \end{cases} \tag{4}$$

where r is a random number within the range $(0, 1)$, Cr denotes the crossover rate, and $jrand$ is a randomly selected dimension. Finally, the greedy selection strategy, which ensures the survival of better solutions, is expressed in Eq. (5).

$$\vec{x}_i = \begin{cases} \vec{u}_i, & if \ f(\vec{u}_i) < f(\vec{x}_i) \\ \vec{x}_i, & otherwise \end{cases} \tag{5}$$

The DE algorithm iteratively repeats processes involving the mutation operator, the crossover operator, and the selection, until the optimum is found or the computational budget is exhausted.

2.2   Hyper-Heuristic (HH) Framework

The concept of the HH algorithm can be traced to 1960. Represented as an advanced methodology, the HH algorithm focuses on optimizing the sequence of search operators based on existing knowledge—an approach often described as "heuristics to choose heuristics". A representative architecture of the HH algorithm is illustrated in Fig. 1.

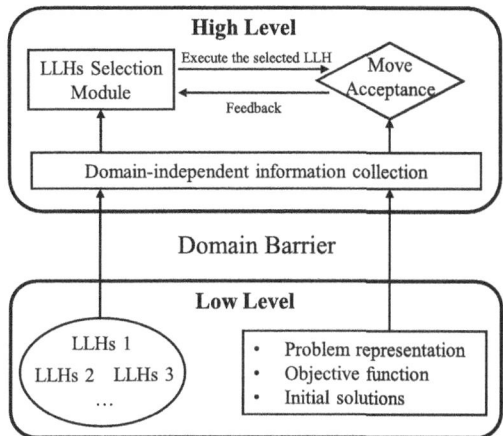

Fig. 1. The representative architecture of the HH algorithm.

A general HH algorithm is composed of two key components: the low-level component and the high-level component. The low-level component contains the problem representation, the objective function(s), initial solutions, and a set of low-level heuristics (LLHs). These elements collectively consist of the intrinsic attributions of the HH algorithm. The high-level component is responsible for managing the LLHs and constructing the sequence of heuristics. It also employs a move acceptance principle to determine whether the generated offspring individual should be accepted or rejected. Additionally, feedback is harnessed as a form of reward to dynamically fine-tune the selection module of the LLHs, enhancing the overall efficiency and adaptability of the algorithm.

3   Our Proposal: HHDE

This section introduces our proposed HHDE in detail. We begin by presenting an overview of HHDE, as illustrated in Fig. 2.

HHDE integrates the basic mutation-crossover-boundary repair-selection skeleton of the conventional DE, while the specific operator for each step is selected from the designated archive. Moreover, we adopt the asynchronous update strategy in HHDE, which denotes that the search process for the next

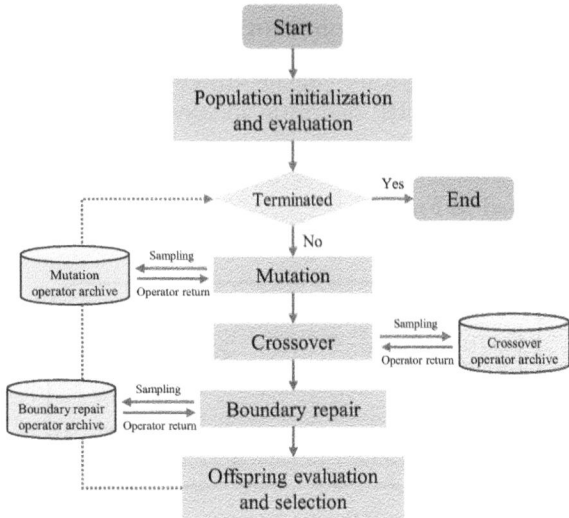

Fig. 2. The flowchart of HHDE.

single individual only commences once the mutation-crossover-boundary repair-selection procedure for the preceding individual is completed. The benefit of this strategy is that, if a better solution is found, this enhanced information can be immediately used in the construction of the offspring for the subsequent individual, which can accelerate the optimization convergence. Next, we will introduce the mutation operator archive, the crossover operator archive, and the novel boundary repair operator archive.

Mutation Operator Archive: The designed mutation operator archive contains five featured operators from different DE versions, which are presented in Eq. (6).

$$
\begin{aligned}
rand/1 &: \vec{v}_i = \vec{x}_{r_1} + F \cdot (\vec{x}_{r_2} - \vec{x}_{r_3}) \\
best/1 &: \vec{v}_i = \vec{x}_{best} + F \cdot (\vec{x}_{r_2} - \vec{x}_{r_3}) \\
cur/1 &: \vec{v}_i = \vec{x}_i + F \cdot (\vec{x}_{r_2} - \vec{x}_{r_3}) \\
cur2best/1 &: \vec{v}_i = \vec{x}_i + F \cdot (\vec{x}_{best} - \vec{x}_i) + F \cdot (\vec{x}_{r_2} - \vec{x}_{r_3}) \\
cur2pbest/1 &: \vec{v}_i = \vec{x}_i + F \cdot (\vec{x}_{pbest} - \vec{x}_i) + F \cdot (\vec{x}_{r_2} - \vec{x}_{r_3})
\end{aligned}
\tag{6}
$$

Here, $\vec{x}_{best}$ denotes the optimum found so far, and $\vec{x}_{pbest}$ indicates the mean of the top-5% solutions as suggested in [5]. To minimize the number of the hyperparameter, we set the scaling factor F as a random number within the range (0, 1) in this study.

Crossover Operator Archive: The crossover operator archive is composed of five crossover operators: binomial crossover with the parent individual and $\vec{x}_{best}$, exponential crossover with the parent individual and $\vec{x}_{best}$, and blending crossover.

The binomial crossover with the parent individual can be found in Eq. (4), and we simply replace the $\vec{x}_{i,j}$ to $\vec{x}_{best,j}$ to realize the binomial crossover with $\vec{x}_{best}$. A visual demonstration of the exponential crossover with the parent individual is provided in Fig. 3.

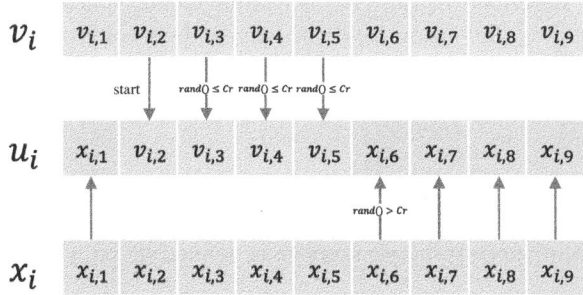

Fig. 3. A 9-dimensional demonstration of the exponential crossover with the parent individual.

First, a random integer generated from $[1,\ n]$ determines the starting point of the crossover. Then, if a dimension-varying random number $rand()$ is smaller than the crossover rate Cr, the offspring individual replicates the corresponding value from the mutated individual $\vec{v}_i$; otherwise, it copies the corresponding value from the parent individual $\vec{x}_i$ and the exponential crossover terminated. Similarly, the parent individual $\vec{x}_i$ can be replaced by the current best solution $\vec{x}_{best}$ to realize the exponential crossover with $\vec{x}_{best}$.

Finally, our designed crossover archive absorbs the blending crossover proposed in [10], which is formulated in Eq. (7)

$$\vec{u}_{i,j} = \begin{cases} b \cdot \vec{x}_{i,j} + (1-b) \cdot \vec{v}_{i,j}, & \text{if } r < Cr \text{ or } j = jrand \\ \vec{x}_{i,j}, & \text{otherwise} \end{cases} \tag{7}$$

b is a blending parameter that controls the proportion of each item derived from the parent individuals, which is randomly selected from $\{0.1, 0.5, 0.9\}$.

Boundary Repair Operator Archive: The phenomenon where a generated offspring individual surpasses the defined search space is prevalent. However, the description of the boundary repair operator is neglected in many pieces of literature. To address this gap, we reviewed many source codes provided by corresponding authors and concluded the two most frequently used principles to implement the boundary repair process in Eq. (8) and Eq. (9)

$$\begin{aligned} & if \ \vec{x}_{i,j} > UB_j \ or \ \vec{x}_{i,j} < LB_j \\ & then \ \vec{x}_{i,j} = LB_j + r \cdot (UB_j - LB_j) \end{aligned} \tag{8}$$

$$\begin{aligned} & if \ \vec{x}_{i,j} > UB_j \ then \ \vec{x}_{i,j} = UB_j \\ & if \ \vec{x}_{i,j} < LB_j \ then \ \vec{x}_{i,j} = LB_j \end{aligned} \tag{9}$$

When the value in a specific dimension falls outside the search space, Eq. (8) adopts the random strategy to guarantee that the newly generated value remains within the domain, while Eq. (9) manually modifies any value exceeding the search space, aligning it with the boundary limits. These two simple principles are involved in our designed boundary repair operator archive. Moreover, another simple strategy described in Eq. (10) is also included, which inherits the value in the corresponding dimension from the current best solution x_{best}.

$$
\begin{aligned}
&if \ \vec{x}_{i,j} > UB_j \ or \ \vec{x}_{i,j} < LB_j \\
&then \ \vec{x}_{i,j} = \vec{x}_{best,j}
\end{aligned}
\tag{10}
$$

Finally, inspired by the opposite-based learning [11], we recognize the potential contribution of this approach to the boundary repair process. The simplest formulation of the opposite-based number is defined in Eq. (11)

$$
\vec{x}'_{i,j} = a + b - \vec{x}_{i,j}
\tag{11}
$$

where a and b are the mapping boundary. We apply this opposite-based mapping operator iteratively until the generated offspring individual is within the search space. Algorithm 1 describes this operator.

Algorithm 1: Iterative opposite-based mapping

Input: Solution individual: $\vec{x}_i$; Search space: LB, UB; Dimension size: n
Output: Corrected solution individual: $\vec{x}_i$
1 **Function** IOBM($\vec{x}_i$, LB, UB, n):
2   **for** $j = 0$ *to* n **do**
3   **while** $\vec{x}_{i,j} > UB_j$ *or* $\vec{x}_{i,j} < LB_j$ **do**
4   **if** $\vec{x}_{i,j} > UB_j$ **then**
5 | $\vec{x}_{i,j} = 2 \cdot UB_j - \vec{x}_{i,j}$
6   **end**
7   **else**
8 | $\vec{x}_{i,j} = 2 \cdot LB_j - \vec{x}_{i,j}$
9   **end**
10   **end**
11   **end**

In summary, the pseudocode of our proposed HHDE is shown in Algorithm 2. Additionally, HHDE samples the mutation operator, crossover operator, and boundary repair operator from their respective archive, employing an unbiased probability approach. The benefit of this simple idea is computationally cheap, as it allows for a diverse range of strategies to be used in the evolutionary process, potentially enhancing the adaptability and robustness of the solution.

Algorithm 2: HHDE

Input: Population size NP; Search space: LB, UB; Dimension size: n;
　　　　Maximum iteration: T
Output: Optimum: x_{best}

1　**Function** IOBM(NP, LB, UB, n, T):
2　　　Generating initial population X by Eq. (2)
3　　　**while** $t = 0$ *and* $t < T$ **do**
4　　　　　**for** $i = 0$ *to* NP **do**
5　　　　　　　Sampling a mutation operator
6　　　　　　　Implementing mutation to x_i
7　　　　　　　Sampling a crossover operator
8　　　　　　　Implementing crossover to x_i
9　　　　　　　Sampling a boundary repair operator
10　　　　　　　Implementing boundary repair to x_i
11　　　　　　　Evaluating and updating the x_{best}
12　　　　　**end**
13　　　**end**
14　　　**return** x_{best}

4　Numerical Experiments

This section introduces our numerical experiments including the settings and results in detail.

4.1　Experiment Settings

Experimental Environments: Our experiments were carried out using Python 3.11 on a Lenovo Legion R9000P device. This device is equipped with an AMD Ryzen 7 5800H processor and 16GB RAM. This well-established environment ensures the integrity and fairness of our numerical experiments conducted in this study.

Benchmark Functions: CEC2022 benchmark functions and six engineering optimization problems are employed to evaluate the performance of our proposed HHDE, which are provided by Opfunu [12] and Enoppy [13] libraries, respectively. Table 1 summarizes the basic information of engineering problems.

Table 1. Summary of eight engineering optimization problems.

Name	Abbr.	Dim.	# of constraints
Cantilever Beam Problem	CBD	5	1
Corrugated Bulkhead Problem	CBHD	4	6
Gear Train Problem	GTD	4	0
Reinforced Concrete Beam Problem	RCB	3	2
Speed Reducer Problem	SRD	7	11
Three Bar Truss Problem	TBTD	2	3

Compared Methods and Parameters: We compare our proposed HHDE with three categories of EAs: (1) Famous DE variants including DE [1], JADE [5], SHADE [6], and LSHADE [14], (2) Latest metaheuristics including Aquila optimization (AO) [15], golden jackal optimization (GJO) [16], Chernobyl disaster optimizer (CDO) [15], and growth optimizer (GO) [17], and (3) State-of-the-art optimizer including CMAES [18]. All competitor algorithms can be sourced from the MEALPY library [19]. The population size of all competitor algorithms except for LSHADE is 100, and the maximum fitness evaluations (FEs) for CEC2022 benchmark functions and engineering problems are 1000 × Dimension and 20,000, respectively. Each algorithm was executed independently 30 times on every single function to ensure statistical robustness. The detailed parameter settings are listed in Table 2.

Table 2. Parameters of competitor algorithms.

EAs	Parameters	Value
DE	Mutation scheme	DE/cur-to-rand/1
	F and Cr	1 and 0.7
CMAES	σ	1.3
JADE	μ_F and μ_{Cr}	0.5 and 0.5
SHADE	μ_F and μ_{Cr}	0.5 and 0.5
LSHADE	μ_F and μ_{Cr}	0.5 and 0.5
	Population size	18 × D
AO	α, θ, and w	0.1, 0.1, and 0.005
GJO	c_1	1.5
CDO	S_α	16,000
	S_β	270,000
	S_γ	300,000
GO	P_1, P_2, and P_3	5, 0.001, and 0.3
HHDE	Crossover rate Cr	0.7

4.2 Experimental Results

This section provides a comprehensive summary of both the experimental and statistical outcomes derived from the analysis of ten EAs. Initially, we obtain the optimal fitness values from 30 trial runs for each EA. Subsequently, we employ the Friedman test to identify the significance of the results. In cases of observed statistical significance, we proceed to employ the Mann-Whitney U test to evaluate the p-value for each pair of algorithms. This is followed by correction using the Holm multiple comparison test to determine statistical significance. Symbols such as +, ≈, and − denote whether our proposed HHDE exhibits statistically better, no significance, or statistically worse performance in comparison to specific competitor algorithms. The best-performed algorithm is denoted in bold.

Results on CEC2022 Benchmark Functions: Table 3 and 4 summarize the experimental and statistical results on 10-D and 20-D CEC2022 benchmark functions. Due to the limitation of space, the convergence curves on the representative functions (i.e. f_1: Unimodal function; f_4: Basic function; f_6: Hybrid function; f_{11}: Composition function) are visualized in Fig. 4.

Table 3. Experimental and statistical results on 10-D CEC2022 benchmark functions. f_1: Unimodal function; $f_2 - f_5$: Basic functions; $f_6 - f_8$: Hybrid functions; $f_9 - f_{12}$: Composition functions; mean and std: the mean and the standard deviation of 30 trial runs.

Func.		DE	CMAES	JADE	SHADE	LSHADE	AO	GJO	CDO	GO	HHDE
f_1	mean	7.14e+03 +	4.22e+02 +	3.09e+02 +	3.02e+02 +	3.03e+02 +	3.46e+03 +	6.47e+02 +	1.35e+04 +	1.19e+03 +	**3.00e+02**
	std	1.73e+03	4.01e+01	5.45e+00	1.37e+00	2.42e+00	1.57e+03	6.25e+02	1.26e+03	2.33e+02	7.67e−11
f_2	mean	4.60e+02 +	4.17e+02 +	4.09e+02 +	4.08e+02 +	4.09e+02 +	6.31e+02 +	4.47e+02 +	8.86e+02 +	4.21e+02 +	**4.06e+02**
	std	1.43e+01	3.04e+00	5.87e−01	1.67e+00	5.91e−01	1.08e+02	1.88e+01	3.58e+01	5.69e+00	1.14e+01
f_3	mean	6.00e+02 +	6.00e+02 +	6.00e+02 +	6.00e+02 +	6.00e+02 +	6.00e+02 +	6.00e+02 +	6.00e+02 +	6.00e+02 +	**6.00e+02**
	std	1.40e−02	6.56e−04	2.79e−07	1.32e−08	1.64e−08	1.19e−01	1.17e−02	3.74e−03	2.62e−03	7.48e−14
f_4	mean	8.01e+02 +	8.01e+02 +	8.01e+02 +	8.01e+02 +	8.01e+02 +	8.01e+02 +	8.00e+02 +	8.01e+02 +	8.01e+02 +	**8.00e+02**
	std	1.96e−01	1.57e−01	1.78e−01	1.78e−01	1.56e−01	2.55e−01	1.53e−01	2.61e−01	1.94e−01	1.42e−01
f_5	mean	9.03e+02 +	9.00e+02 +	9.00e+02 +	**9.00e+02** −	9.00e+02 −	9.02e+02 +	9.00e+02 +	9.04e+02 +	9.01e+02 +	9.00e+02
	std	7.56e−01	6.38e−02	8.08e−04	8.59e−05	1.28e−04	1.21e+00	2.77e−01	7.53e−01	2.01e−01	2.59e−01
f_6	mean	1.00e+05 +	**4.10e+03** ≈	2.78e+04 +	1.93e+04 +	1.81e+04 +	6.14e+06 +	6.16e+04 +	5.63e+08 +	2.57e+05 +	5.91e+03
	std	2.88e+04	6.09e+02	1.25e+04	5.98e+03	5.91e+03	4.83e+06	3.85e+04	4.18e+08	1.45e+05	6.44e+03
f_7	mean	2.07e+03 +	2.08e+03 +	2.04e+03 +	2.04e+03 +	2.04e+03 +	2.29e+03 +	2.12e+03 +	3.84e+03 +	2.06e+03 +	**2.02e+03**
	std	1.02e+01	1.48e+01	5.27e+00	3.87e+00	3.78e+00	1.31e+02	9.19e+01	1.17e+03	9.62e+00	3.00e+00
f_8	mean	2.26e+03 +	2.23e+03 +	2.23e+03 +	2.23e+03 +	2.23e+03 +	1.17e+04 +	3.70e+03 +	2.89e+03 +	2.46e+03 +	**2.22e+03**
	std	1.03e+01	1.94e+00	2.42e+00	4.08e+00	1.58e+00	4.07e+04	6.21e+02	3.72e+02	1.99e+02	6.06e+00
f_9	mean	2.67e+03 +	2.60e+03 +	2.36e+03 ≈	**2.33e+03** ≈	2.34e+03 ≈	2.78e+03 +	2.56e+03 +	3.37e+03 +	2.56e+03 +	2.47e+03
	std	2.67e+01	1.11e+02	1.20e+02	8.99e+01	1.09e+02	7.14e+01	1.93e+02	9.52e+01	1.17e+02	1.80e+02
f_{10}	mean	2.62e+03 ≈	2.61e+03 ≈	2.60e+03 +	**2.60e+03** −	2.60e+03 −	2.73e+03 +	2.66e+03 +	2.80e+03 +	2.61e+03 +	2.65e+03 ≈
	std	5.49e+00	1.07e+00	9.65e−01	6.56e−01	9.85e−01	1.05e+02	7.10e+01	3.14e+01	2.47e+00	6.84e+01
f_{11}	mean	2.66e+03 +	2.74e+03 +	2.60e+03 +	**2.60e+03** −	2.60e+03 −	2.73e+03 +	2.61e+03 +	2.85e+03 +	2.62e+03 +	2.63e+03
	std	1.52e+02	3.01e+02	6.68e−02	1.30e−02	2.82e−02	2.05e+02	1.38e+01	2.70e+01	3.52e+00	1.57e+02
f_{12}	mean	2.87e+03 ≈	2.87e+03 ≈	2.87e+03 +	**2.87e+03** −	2.87e+03 −	2.90e+03 +	2.87e+03 ≈	3.22e+03 +	2.87e+03 ≈	2.87e+03
	std	6.64e−01	5.35e−01	4.22e−01	4.71e−01	5.52e−01	3.46e+01	7.43e+00	1.08e+02	5.96e−01	3.98e+00
+/≈/−:		10/2/0	9/3/0	7/1/4	7/1/4	7/1/4	12/0/0	10/1/1	12/0/0	9/2/1	
Ave. rank:		7.5	5.4	3.6	**2.1**	2.6	8.6	6.3	9.5	6.2	3.0

Results on Engineering Problems: Table 5 summarizes the experimental and statistical findings derived from six engineering problems, and Fig. 5 provides the convergence curves.

5 Discussion

Computational Complexity Analysis: Supposing the population size is N, the dimension size is D, and the maximum iteration is T, the computational complexity of HHDE is methodically analyzed in accordance with its procedural flowchart.

The first process is population initialization, and the computational complexity is $O(N \cdot D)$. Then, HHDE enters the iteration. For a single individual, the computational complexity of the mutation operator sampling can be

Table 4. Experimental and statistical results on 20-D CEC2022 benchmark functions.

Func.		DE	CMAES	JADE	SHADE	LSHADE	AO	GJO	CDO	GO	HHDE
f_1	mean	3.38e+04 +	2.55e+03 +	3.00e+02 +	3.00e+02 +	3.00e+02 +	2.99e+04 +	6.64e+03 +	2.00e+04 +	1.05e+04 +	**3.00e+02**
	std	5.79e+03	4.33e+02	2.34e-01	1.57e-01	2.41e-01	8.78e+03	2.06e+03	1.86e+02	1.69e+03	1.58e-01
f_2	mean	1.05e+03 +	5.10e+02 +	**4.49e+02** −	4.50e+02 +	4.49e+02 −	2.14e+03 +	5.82e+02 +	2.14e+03 +	6.34e+02 +	4.56e+02
	std	1.49e+02	1.54e+01	7.02e-01	4.36e+00	3.73e-03	5.07e+02	4.95e+01	4.48e+01	4.84e+01	1.78e+01
f_3	mean	6.00e+02 +	6.00e+02 +	6.00e+02 ≈	6.00e+02 +	**6.00e+02** −	6.02e+02 +	6.00e+02 +	6.01e+02 +	6.00e+02 +	6.00e+02
	std	5.53e-02	7.24e-03	1.04e-09	8.81e-11	8.05e-11	4.21e-01	7.14e-02	1.06e-02	3.58e-02	1.04e-08
f_4	mean	8.04e+02 +	8.04e+02 +	8.02e+02 +	8.02e+02 +	8.02e+02 +	8.04e+02 +	8.02e+02 +	8.03e+02 +	8.04e+02 +	**8.01e+02**
	std	4.06e-01	3.57e-01	4.69e-01	3.46e-01	3.19e-01	5.72e-01	6.45e-01	5.44e-01	4.49e-01	3.34e-01
f_5	mean	9.16e+02 +	9.03e+02 +	9.00e+02 −	**9.00e+02**	9.00e+02 −	9.12e+02 +	9.02e+02 ≈	9.12e+02 +	9.05e+02 +	9.02e+02
	std	2.30e+00	4.79e-01	3.76e-06	1.65e-06	7.46e-06	2.99e+00	9.23e-01	2.36e+00	9.33e-01	9.68e-01
f_6	mean	2.22e+08 +	5.28e+06 +	**2.36e+04** +	1.33e+06 +	1.31e+06 +	1.65e+09 +	2.76e+07 +	2.43e+09 +	9.09e+07 +	4.77e+04
	std	8.54e+07	2.08e+06	1.34e+04	5.68e+05	6.64e+05	1.31e+09	4.13e+07	4.03e+07	2.27e+07	1.98e+04
f_7	mean	2.82e+03 +	2.29e+03 +	2.08e+03 +	2.07e+03 +	2.08e+03 +	3.34e+03 +	2.26e+03 +	2.63e+03 +	2.53e+03 +	**2.06e+03**
	std	2.06e+02	7.37e+01	2.25e+01	1.13e+01	1.41e+01	6.72e+02	2.31e+02	1.14e+02	1.26e+02	3.62e+01
f_8	mean	1.77e+05 +	2.41e+03 +	2.36e+03 +	2.43e+03 +	2.48e+03 +	1.26e+10 +	7.70e+03 +	1.44e+04 +	7.03e+06 +	**2.30e+03**
	std	3.47e+05	5.48e+01	3.61e+02	2.22e+02	2.80e+02	2.45e+10	3.29e+03	2.02e+04	1.26e+07	7.38e+01
f_9	mean	2.81e+03 +	2.65e+03 +	**2.64e+03**	2.64e+03 +	2.64e+03 −	3.66e+03 +	2.84e+03 +	5.21e+03 +	2.70e+03 +	2.64e+03
	std	4.12e+01	3.92e+00	6.72e-02	3.28e-01	5.50e-01	4.50e+02	9.51e+01	1.48e+02	2.22e+01	3.08e+00
f_{10}	mean	4.02e+03 +	3.14e+03 ≈	2.78e+03 −	2.77e+03 +	**2.77e+03** −	3.75e+03 ≈	3.64e+03 ≈	6.58e+03 +	2.99e+03 ≈	3.11e+03
	std	1.65e+03	9.33e+02	5.01e+01	3.73e+01	8.39e+00	1.46e+03	1.31e+03	1.18e+03	5.72e+02	5.76e+02
f_{11}	mean	2.81e+03 +	2.62e+03 +	2.60e+03 −	2.60e+03 +	**2.60e+03** −	4.38e+03 +	2.65e+03 +	5.60e+03 +	2.66e+03 +	2.60e+03
	std	3.13e+02	3.11e+00	1.87e-03	5.26e-04	7.80e-04	1.51e+03	3.25e+01	1.03e+02	1.34e+01	3.96e+00
f_{12}	mean	2.96e+03 +	2.96e+03 −	**2.94e+03**	2.94e+03 +	2.94e+03 −	3.11e+03 +	3.03e+03 +	3.45e+03 +	2.96e+03 −	2.99e+03
	std	4.04e+00	7.64e+00	8.96e-01	2.43e+00	2.37e+00	7.31e+01	4.12e+01	3.66e+01	9.32e+00	3.43e+01
+/≈/−:		11/0/1	10/1/1	4/1/7	5/0/7	5/0/7	11/1/0	10/2/0	12/0/0	10/1/1	
Ave. rank:		8.2	5.4	**2.2**	2.6	2.7	9.0	5.9	8.8	6.8	3.1

ignored, since the number of mutation operators is a constant. The computational complexity of $rand/1$, $best/1$, $cur/1$, $cur2best/1$, and $cur2pbest/1$ is $O(D)$. Although $cur2pbest/1$ computes the mean of the p-best individuals, this operator increases the practical complexity but does not affect the theoretical analysis. Subsequently, both the crossover operator and the boundary repair operator exhibit computational complexities that are analogous to those of the mutation module. In summary, the total computational complexity of HHDE is expressed in Eq. (12).

$$
\begin{aligned}
& O(N \cdot D + T \cdot (N \cdot D + N \cdot D + N \cdot D)) \\
& = O(N \cdot D + T \cdot (3N \cdot D)) \\
& := O(T \cdot N \cdot D))
\end{aligned}
\tag{12}
$$

Performance Analysis on CEC2022 Benchmark Functions: From the experimental and statistical results presented in Table 3 and 4, our proposed HHDE performs relative competitiveness when compared with other competitor algorithm. Especially in most instances of unimodal, basic, and hybrid functions, HHDE continuously outperforms the famous DE variants and state-of-the-art optimization algorithms. This performance not only underscores the efficiency of HHDE but also empirically validates the effectiveness of our proposed approach.

Moreover, the superior convergence speed of HHDE is evident from convergence curves in Fig. 4. However, the significant inferiority of HHDE can be

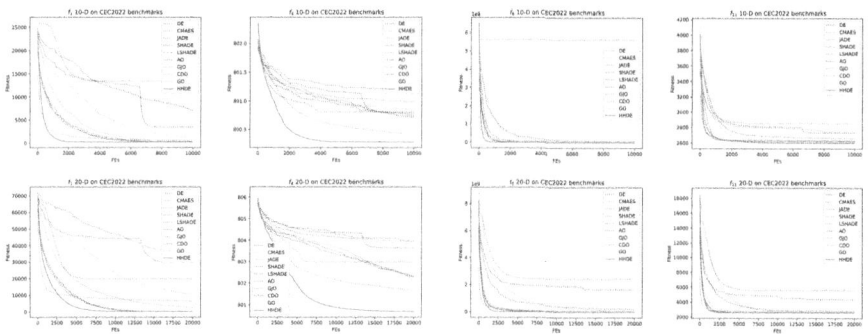

Fig. 4. Convergence curves of ten EAs on representative 10-D and 20-D CEC2022 benchmark functions.

Table 5. Experimental and statistical results on six engineering problems.

Prob.		DE	CMAES	JADE	SHADE	LSHADE	AO	GJO	CDO	GO	HHDE
CBD	mean	1.361e+00 +	1.342e+00 +	1.340e+00 +	1.340e+00 +	1.340e+00 +	1.494e+00 +	1.340e+00 +	1.358e+00 +	1.355e+00 +	**1.340e+00**
	std	6.157e−03	1.283e−03	1.173e−05	8.604e−06	6.160e−06	5.540e−02	3.264e−04	6.720e−03	7.175e−03	2.923e−06
CBHD	mean	6.863e+00 +	6.844e+00 +	6.843e+00 +	6.843e+00 +	6.843e+00 +	9.026e+00 +	7.396e+00 +	**5.923e+00** ≈	6.885e+00 +	6.843e+00
	std	9.405e−03	2.445e−04	1.086e−05	3.729e−07	3.085e−07	1.182e+00	5.028e−01	2.037e+00	1.654e−02	7.358e−05
GTD	mean	2.070e−11 +	1.030e−11 +	1.677e−12 +	1.237e−12 +	8.182e−13 +	3.701e−05 +	7.404e−12 +	2.336e−10 +	6.776e−11 +	**1.605e−32**
	std	4.106e−11	1.465e−11	2.864e−12	1.969e−12	1.189e−12	1.936e−04	9.276e−12	2.907e−10	2.870e−10	8.643e−32
RCB	mean	1.666e+02 +	1.666e+02 +	1.666e+02 +	1.666e+02 +	1.666e+02 +	1.715e+02 +	1.610e+02 ≈	1.610e+02 ≈	1.629e+02 +	**1.605e+02**
	std	6.055e−01	6.055e−01	6.161e−01	6.055e−01	6.055e−01	3.910e+00	1.503e+00	1.725e+00	1.796e+00	1.050e+00
SRD	mean	2.988e+03 +	2.987e+03 +	2.987e+03 +	2.987e+03 +	2.987e+03 +	2.906e+06 +	3.019e+03 +	3.148e+03 +	2.991e+03 +	**2.987e+03**
	std	1.624e+00	4.920e−02	2.325e−05	3.950e−06	3.345e−06	1.967e+06	1.021e+01	3.872e+01	3.977e+00	1.588e−10
TBTD	mean	2.639e+02 ≈	2.639e+02 −	2.639e+02 −	**2.639e+02** −	2.639e+02 −	2.649e+02 +	2.647e+02 +	2.641e+02 +	2.639e+02 ≈	2.639e+02
	std	6.652e−05	1.524e−12	3.799e−12	1.515e−13	2.746e−13	1.411e+00	2.997e+00	1.549e−01	1.684e−03	2.475e−02
+/≈/−:		5/1/0	5/0/1	5/0/1	5/0/1	5/0/1	6/0/0	5/1/0	4/2/0	5/1/0	
Ave. rank:		7.1	5.8	3.6	3.1	3.1	10.0	6.3	6.3	6.6	**2.6**

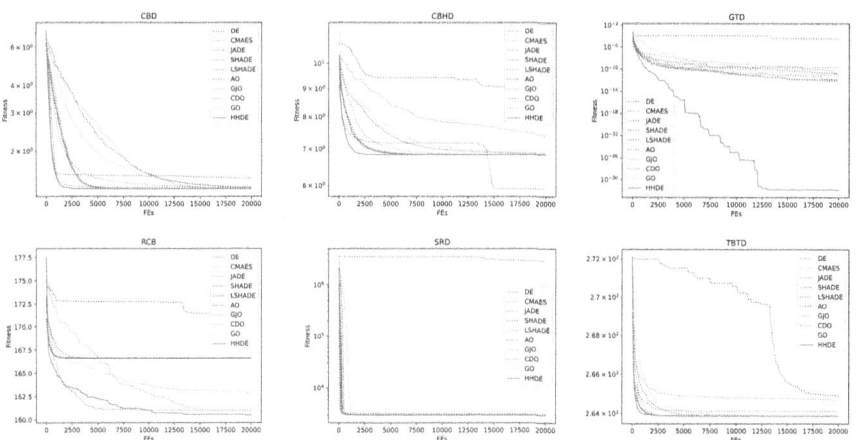

Fig. 5. Convergence curves of ten EAs on six engineering problems.

observed in some instances, specifically in functions f_9, f_{10}, f_{11}, and f_{12}, when compared with algorithms such as JADE, SHADE, and LSHADE. The common feature of these test functions is their composite nature. Therefore, we reasonably infer that HHDE is not good at dealing with composite problems, which is owing to the inner structure of HHDE, possibly.

Performance Analysis on Engineering Problems: Optimizing six engineering tasks provides insights into real-world applications. Through the experimental and statistical results summarized in Table 5, HHDE maintains competitiveness on these tasks, which proves the excellent scalability of HHDE. Furthermore, the poor-performed Chernobyl disaster optimizer (CDO) in CEC2022 benchmark functions achieves the best in the corrugated bulkhead problem (CBHD), and the No Free Lunch Theorem (NFLT) can be applied to explain this phenomenon: NFLT states that for every pair of black-box optimization algorithms, their average performance across all possible problems is identical. If an algorithm excels in a specific category of problems, it must inevitably lag in others. This trade-off is the only means to maintain an equivalent average performance overall. Similarly, we can also utilize this theorem to explain the inferiority of HHDE in composite functions of the CEC2022 suite.

6   Conclusion

In this paper, we propose a hyper-heuristic differential evolution (HHDE) for numerical optimization. Inspired by the architecture of the HH algorithm, our approach involves the creation of distinct archives for mutation operators, crossover operators, and boundary repair operators. As a primary study, the learning-free selection function with unbiased probability is employed to sample the search operator. Moreover, we focus on the boundary repair module, which is usually ignored in the EA description. Based on the previous research on boundary repair, we embed two strategies in our designed boundary repair archive: optimum inheritance and iterative opposite-based mapping. Comprehensive numerical experiments confirm the competitiveness of our proposed HHDE with state-of-the-art optimizers adequately.

In future research, we are committed to the ongoing development and refinement of the proposed HHDE. A promising topic is to intelligently determine the optimization sequence, where machine learning and reinforcement learning techniques may further significantly enhance the performance of the HHDE.

Acknowledgement. This work was supported by JSPS KAKENHI Grant Number 21A402 and 24K15098 and JST SPRING Grant Number JPMJSP2119.

References

1. Storn, R.: On the usage of differential evolution for function optimization. In: Proceedings of North American Fuzzy Information Processing, pp. 519–523 (1996)
2. He, L., Cao, Y., Li, W., Cao, J., Zhong, L.: Optimization of energy-efficient open shop scheduling with an adaptive multi-objective differential evolution algorithm. Appl. Soft Comput. **118**, 108459 (2022)
3. Zhong, R., Zhang, E., Munetomo, M.: Cooperative coevolutionary surrogate ensemble-assisted differential evolution with efficient dual differential grouping for large-scale expensive optimization problems. Complex Intell. Syst. 1–21 (2023)
4. Liu, M., Yao, X., Li, Y.: Hybrid whale optimization algorithm enhanced with lévy flight and differential evolution for job shop scheduling problems. Appl. Soft Comput. **87**, 105954 (2020)
5. Zhang, J., Sanderson, A.C.: Jade: adaptive differential evolution with optional external archive. IEEE Trans. Evol. Comput. **13**(5), 945–958 (2009)
6. Tanabe, R., Fukunaga, A.: Success-history based parameter adaptation for differential evolution. In: 2013 IEEE Congress on Evolutionary Computation, pp. 71–78 (2013)
7. Ahmad, M.F., Isa, N.A.M., Lim, W.H., Ang, K.M.: Differential evolution: a recent review based on state-of-the-art works. Alex. Eng. J. **61**(5), 3831–3872 (2022)
8. Dowsland, K.A.: Off-the-peg or made-to-measure? Timetabling and scheduling with SA and TS. In: Burke, E., Carter, M. (eds.) Practice and Theory of Automated Timetabling II, pp. 37–52. Springer, Heidelberg (1998)
9. Zhong, R., Yu, J., Zhang, C., Munetomo, M.: Surrogate ensemble-assisted hyper-heuristic algorithm for expensive optimization problems. Int. J. Comput. Intell. Syst. **16**, 169 (2023)
10. Ghosh, A., Das, S., Mallipeddi, R., Das, A.K., Dash, S.S.: A modified differential evolution with distance-based selection for continuous optimization in presence of noise. IEEE Access **5**, 26944–26964 (2017)
11. Mahdavi, S., Rahnamayan, S., Deb, K.: Opposition based learning: a literature review. Swarm Evol. Comput. **39**, 1–23 (2018)
12. Thieu, N.V.: Opfunu: an open-source python library for optimization benchmark functions (2020). https://doi.org/10.5281/zenodo.3620960
13. Thieu, N.V.: Enoppy: a python library for engineering optimization problems (2023). https://github.com/thieu1995/enoppy
14. Tanabe, R., Fukunaga, A.S.: Improving the search performance of shade using linear population size reduction. In: 2014 IEEE Congress on Evolutionary Computation (CEC), pp. 1658–1665 (2014)
15. Abualigah, L., Yousri, D., Abd Elaziz, M., Ewees, A.A., Al-qaness, M.A., Gandomi, A.H.: Aquila optimizer: a novel meta-heuristic optimization algorithm. Comput. Ind. Eng. **157**, 107250 (2021)
16. Chopra, N., Mohsin Ansari, M.: Golden jackal optimization: a novel nature-inspired optimizer for engineering applications. Expert Syst. Appl. **198**, 116924 (2022)
17. Zhang, Q., Gao, H., Zhan, Z.H., Li, J., Zhang, H.: Growth optimizer: a powerful metaheuristic algorithm for solving continuous and discrete global optimization problems. Knowl.-Based Syst. **261**, 110206 (2023)
18. Hansen, N., Ostermeier, A.: Completely derandomized self-adaptation in evolution strategies. Evol. Comput. **9**(2), 159–195 (2001)
19. Van Thieu, N., Mirjalili, S.: MEALPY: an open-source library for latest meta-heuristic algorithms in python. J. Syst. Architect. (2023)

Jump Like a Frog: Optimization of Renewable Energy Prediction in Smart Gird Based on Ultra Long Term Network

Xingbang Du$^{(\boxtimes)}$ ID and Enzhi Zhang ID

Hokkaido University, Sapporo, Hokkaido 060-0808, Japan
duxingbang916@gmail.com

Abstract. Renewable energy generation forecasting plays crucial roles in advanced smart grid and sustainable practices. Although many RNN related methods have been utilized to predict power generation time series data, they often struggle to capture very long-term correlations efficiently due to the vanishing gradient issue. To address this challenge, we have introduced the Ultra long term network model that incorporated LSTM, SKIP LSTM and Dense components. This model effectively captures long-term patterns while mitigating the vanishing gradient problem associated with capturing very long term patterns. Our application of this model to renewable power prediction has yielded better performance when compared through metrics like MSE and MAE than previous models such as LSTM, GRU and Simple RNN models in time series analysis within smart grids. The integration of this model holds promise for enhancing the intelligence of renewable energy grids.

Keywords: Renewable energy · Smart grid · LSTM · Optimization · Time series

1 Introduction

Energy sustainability and environmental preservation are global concerns that have attracted increasing attention. The utilization of renewable energy sources, which can be consistently harnessed without depletion, plays a crucial role in mitigating the adverse effects on environmental conservation and promoting the sustainable development of energy resources.

However, renewable energy is heavily influenced by environmental factors and is subject to fluctuation, posing challenges to its stability.

To ensure the stability of the grid, smart grid, also called intelligent grid [1], need to be deployed and applied. Smart gird forms an intelligent electricity networks working with all connected components to deliver stable and sustainable electricity.

It includes management, optimization and control of power systems through information and communication technology. Smart grid-related technologies

© The Author(s), under exclusive license to Springer Nature Switzerland AG 2025
H. R. Arabnia et al. (Eds.): CSCE 2024, CCIS 2256, pp. 278–290, 2025.
https://doi.org/10.1007/978-3-031-85638-9_21

include renewable energy integration, energy management [2] and optimization, energy storage [3], electric vehicle interaction with the grid, data sharing and interactive connection.

In energy management systems, it's necessary to establish a prediction model to forecast unstable renewable energy, and electric load forecasting is also important [4].

In a smart grid, an accurate renewable energy forecasting model plays a critical role in not only predicting the future electricity generation with precision, but also integrating with the real-time complex data of the grid to forecast the supply and demand situation.

The forecasted supply and demand scenarios serve as key inputs to intelligent decision-making systems, assisting in making correct decisions such as procuring energy in advance in the electricity market to prevent potential power outages, activating backup energy sources to ensure stable power supply during peak demand periods, or storing excess energy to minimize waste.

Therefore, a precise renewable energy forecasting model can maximize the efficiency of smart grids, facilitating the transition from fossil fuels to renewable energy sources, while ensuring the stability of grid and city operations.

In recent years, with the advancement in the field of deep learning, LSTM [5], GRU [6] and related models have been increasingly applied to time series forecasting problems. Reference [7] applied GRU to wind power forecasting. Reference [8] applied LSTM to predict the stability of smart grid.

LSTM was also used in wind power short-term prediction in Reference [9]. Reference [10] proposed ConvLSTM and applied it to near-term precipitation forecasting. Reference [11] utilized LSTM to predict hydrological time series data such as flow, precipitation, and evaporation.

Historically, forecasting models developed using deep learning in the energy sector have predominantly targeted the prediction of a singular energy source, such as modeling and forecasting wind energy or solar energy.

However, electricity generation within a specific region may come from a mix of sources, including wind, hydropower, solar, fossil fuels, and nuclear energy. Therefore, to implement these models in smart grid systems within a particular region, it is essential to establish forecasting models for all renewable energy sources in that area, such as wind power combined with hydropower, in order to gradually replace fossil fuels with renewable energy and enhance grid stability.

The forecasting model we have designed focuses on predicting the electricity generation from all renewable energy sources in a given region.

As the variability and patterns of different renewable energy sources differ, we have refined existing models to strike a balance between forecasting accuracy and efficiency, thereby improving the applicability and effectiveness of the model.

2   Methodology

LSTM, GRU and related models such as sample RNN can capture long-term dependencies effectively but often fail to capture extremely long-term correlations due to the vanishing gradient problem. The LSTNet model can effectively capture long term correlations, but its structure is relatively complex and computation cost are high.

So based on upon various existing models, we designed the Ultra-Long-Term network which contains several different components that allow it to jump like a frog to capture super long term correlations in renewable energy data. The structure of the model is shown in Fig. 1.

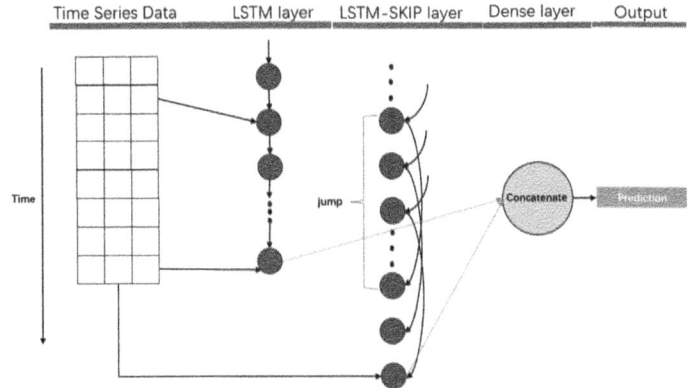

Fig. 1. Ultra-long-term network model. The LSTM component is responsible for extracting long-term patterns while the SKIP-LSTM component utilizes historical periodic data to capture extremely long time patterns. Finally we use the Dense layer to concatenate the outputs of the LSTM and SKIP-LSTM components and output the prediction results.

2.1   LSTM Component

In time series forecasting, the LSTM model with LSTM memory cells can indicate when the network should forget historical information and when to update the memory cells with new input information [12].

Therefore, through the forget gate and input gate in the gate units, LSTM is well equipped to handle the issues of vanishing gradients and exploding gradients. It exhibits greater stability and is more suitable for processing longer time series data.

The calculation of the hidden layer node's state at time t can be represented as follows:

$$i_t = \sigma(W_{xf}x_t + W_{hi}h_{t-1} + W_{ci}c_{t-1} + b_i) \qquad (1)$$

$$f_t = \sigma(W_{xf}x_t + W_{hf}h_{t-1} + W_{cf}c_{t-1} + b_f) \qquad (2)$$

$$c_t = f_tc_{t-1} + i_t tanh(W_{xc}x_t + W_{hc}h_{t-1} + b_c) \qquad (3)$$

$$o_t = \sigma(W_{xo}x_t + W_{ho}h_{t-1} + W_{co}c_t + b_o) \qquad (4)$$

$$h_t = o_t tanh(c_t) \tag{5}$$

In Eqs. (1) to (5), i represent the input gate, f represent the forget gate, c represent cell state while o represent the output gate respectively. And b represent the corresponding bias term, W represents the weight matrix between the gates, σ represents the sigmoid activation function while $tanh$ represents the hyperbolic tangent function.

2.2 LSTM-SKIP Component

The LSTM structure, equipped with memory cells, excels in capturing long term dependencies in data. Nevertheless, the vanishing gradient issue frequently impedes LSTM from capturing exceedingly long term correlations effectively in real-world scenarios.

It is widely acknowledged that the power generation from renewable sources demonstrates a clear cyclic pattern [13].

Hence, besides utilizing the data preceding 16:00 on the current day to forecast the renewable power generation at that specific time, it is apparent that we can also utilize data from the same time on the preceding day or even 2 days prior for predictive purposes.

Therefore in this component, we select multiple non-consecutive points with fixes time intervals as input for prediction, much like a frog jump from one point to another.

We have devised a LSTM-skip component in our model, featuring skip connections. This component enables the model to effectively capture long term patterns and correlations utilizing historical data from the corresponding period, thereby circumventing the vanishing gradient problem and enhancing the prediction model [14].

The calculation of this skip-LSTM component, integrating the jump connection, can be expressed as follows:

$$i_t = \sigma(W_{xf}x_t + W_{hi}h_{t-p} + W_{ci}c_{t-p} + b_i) \tag{6}$$

$$f_t = \sigma(W_{xf}x_t + W_{hf}h_{t-p} + W_{cf}c_{t-p} + b_f) \tag{7}$$

$$c_t = f_t c_{t-p} + i_t tanh(W_{xc}x_t + W_{hc}h_{t-p} + b_c) \tag{8}$$

$$o_t = \sigma(W_{xo}x_t + W_{ho}h_{t-p} + W_{co}c_t + b_o) \tag{9}$$

$$h_t = o_t tanh(c_t) \tag{10}$$

In Eqs. (6) to (10), i represents the input gate, f represents the forget gate, c represents cell state while o represents the output gate respectively. And b represents the corresponding bias term, W represents the weight matrix between the gates, σ represents the sigmoid activation function while $tanh$ represents the hyperbolic tangent function. P represents a specific and applicable time period for real data.

2.3   DENSE Component

We utilize a fully connected layer [15] to merge the output results of the LSTM component and the SKIP-LSTM component. the output of this fully connected layer is as follows:

$$h_t^D = W^L h_t^L + \sum_{i=0}^{p-1} W_i^S h_{t-i}^S + b \qquad (11)$$

In Eq. (11), the input of this fully connected layer consists of two parts: the h_t^L represents the hidden state of the LSTM component at time t, $h_{t-p+1}^S, h_{t-p+2}^S, ..., h_t^S$ are the total of p hidden states from time t-p+1 to t from the SKIP-LSTM layer.

2.4   Renewable Energy Forecasting Model

We establish and train the uni-variate time series prediction model for renewable energy data which consist of fixed time interval observations. In this context, X_{rt} represents the renewable energy data, with t denoting the time point.

To predict renewable power generation, the model utilizes consecutive n time steps of renewable energy data as inputs to predict the power generation at time step t+1. The size of the input layer steps, denoted by n, determines the number of consecutive time steps used for prediction. Therefore, the expressions for the renewable power is as follows:

$$X_{r(t+1)} = f(X_{r(t-n+1)}, ..., X_{r(t-1)}, X_{rt}) \qquad (12)$$

In Eq. (12), $X_{r(t-n+1)}, ..., X_{r(t-1)}$, and X_{rt} represent consecutive n time steps of hydroelectric data, while $X_{r(t+1)}$ is the prediction at time step t+1.

3   Experiment and Result Analysis

In this part we will introduce the data details, parameter settings, data prepossessing steps, as well as the experimental results and analysis.

3.1   Data Preparation

For this experiment, publicly available data from Bonneville Power Administration (BPA) was utilized. BPA, a branch of the U.S. government, oversees electrical operations in the Pacific Northwest region, including Idaho, Oregon, Washington, western Montana and small parts of eastern Montana, California, Nevada, Utah and Wyoming.

In the territory of the Bonneville Power Administration (BPA), a diverse range of energy sources is utilized for electricity generation, encompassing wind power, hydropower, fossil fuel-based generation, and nuclear power. Among these sources, wind power and hydropower fall under the category of renewable energy sources.

Therefore, the renewable power generation data, including wind power and hydroelectric power of the BPA control area from January 1, 2020, to March 31, 2020, was analyzed.

The electricity generation, variability patterns, and forecasting model requirements differ between wind power and hydropower. From Fig. 2 and Fig. 3, several observations can be made:

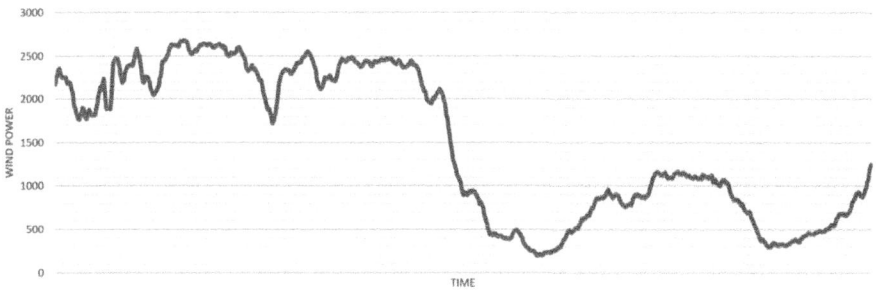

Fig. 2. 3-day wind power generation data

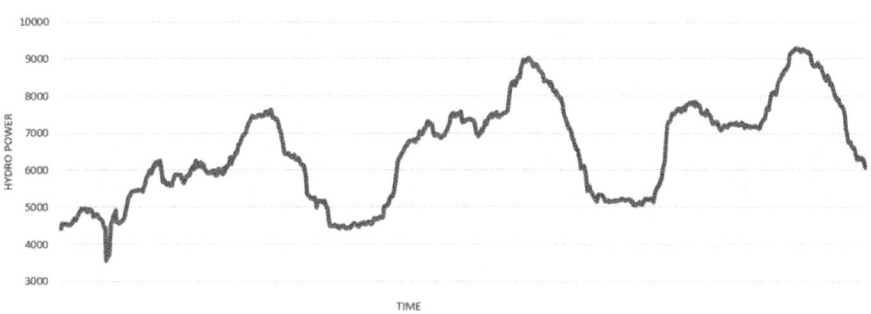

Fig. 3. 3-day hydro power generation data

– Wind power exhibits more frequent and unstable variations compared to hydro power. This is attributed to the presence of a phenomenon known as wind ramp events, where wind speeds sharply increase or decrease within a short period.

  These events significantly impact the stability of wind power generation, and traditional LSTM or GRU models have shown effectiveness in predicting short to medium-term wind power fluctuations.

– Hydropower variations display a high level of regularity, with similar patterns observed daily. Consequently, historical hydropower data from a specific time of day can be utilized to forecast data for the same time period on the following day.
These forecasting and regularity patterns fall into the long-term and extremely-long-term categories, where the LSTNet model demonstrates superior performance due to its suitability for handling data with long-term regularities

When establishing a forecasting model for a combined dataset of wind power and hydropower, utilizing conventional LSTM or GRU models may lead to overlooking the extremely-long-term regularity of hydropower.

On the other hand, employing the LSTNet model may not effectively predict wind power variations and could lead to increased computational expenses due to its complexity.

Therefore, leveraging our designed Ultra-Long-Term network model enables more effective simultaneous forecasting of wind power and hydropower while achieving a balance between forecasting accuracy and computational costs.

The recorded renewable power generation data is the sum of hydroelectric and wind power values and it is captured every five minutes over a three-month period. The dataset, exemplified in Table 1 and depicted in Fig. 4, was sorted chronologically, with the first 80% of the data designated as the training set and the remainder as the test set.

Table 1. 30-min renewable energy data

DateTime	Renewable Energy
2020/01/01 00:00	6591
2020/01/01 00:05	6660
2020/01/01 00:10	6830
2020/01/01 00:15	6861
2020/01/01 00:20	6881
2020/01/01 00:25	6870
2020/01/01 00:30	6833

We select a consecutive sequence of 24 time points as the input datasets, given that each time point is spaced at five-minute intervals. This translates to using a two-hour data window as input for predicting the sub sequence time point's value.

In addition, determining a period P is crucial for the SKIP-LSTM component to introduce data from the dame time point of the prior cycle as input. We have opted for P to represent one day, enabling us to incorporate data from the same time point one day earlier into the SKIP-LSTM component.

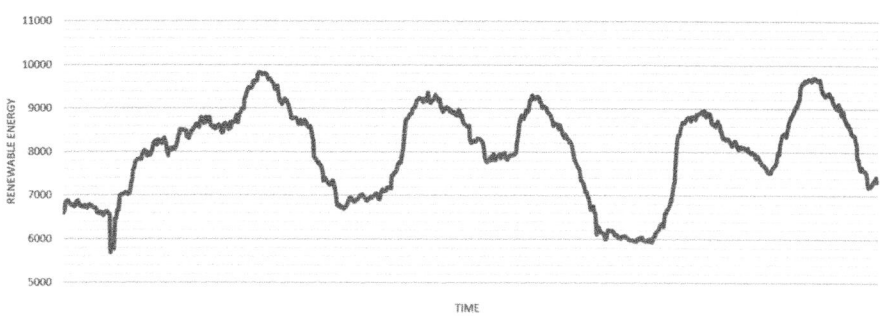

Fig. 4. 3-day renewable power generation data

Prior to training, we normalize the input data to mitigate prediction errors stemming from significant variances in the input data. The normalization range is established as [0,1], with the transformation formula defined as:

$$X^* = \frac{X - min}{max - min} \tag{13}$$

In Eq. (13), max is the maximum value and min is the minimum in the sample data. X is the original data and X* is the normalized data. And we will use inverse normalization to obtain meaningful prediction result data.

3.2 Experiment Environment

The hardware specifications for this experiment are as follows:

– CPU: Intel(R) Xeon(R) Sliver 4214R with a clock speed of 2.40 GHz and 90 GB of memory.
– GPU: 1*RTX 3080Ti with 12 GB of video memory.
– Platform: TensorFlow framework version 2.9.0.
– Programming language: Python 3.8.

3.3 Result and Analysis

We set the experimental parameters as follows and conducted the tests:

– Look back = 24, which means input time steps equals to 24
– Skip = 12, which means period P equals to 1 day, because 24 * 12 * 5 min = 24 h = 1 day
– Training and testing datasets were divided in an 8:2 ratio
– Units = 32
– Activation function: tanh
– Initial learning rate = 0.01
– Minimum learning rate = 0.001

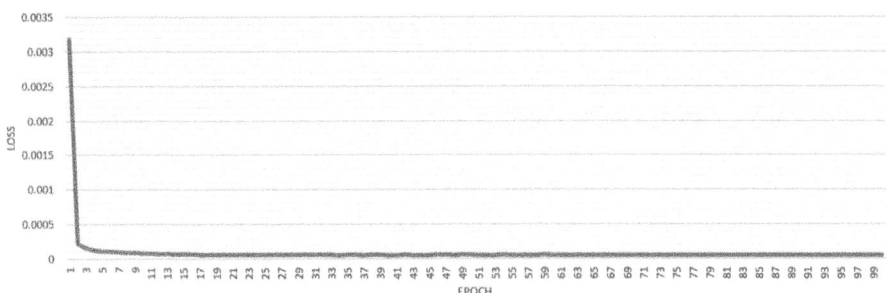

Fig. 5. Loss during 100-epochs training process

- Number of epochs = 100
- Batch size = 32
- Objective function: Mean Squared Error (MSE)

$$MSE = \frac{1}{n} \sum_{t=1}^{n} (Y_t - P_t)^2 \tag{14}$$

In Eq. (14), n represents the number of samples, Y_t denotes the true value, P_t denotes the predicted value.

- We also use Mean Absolute Error (MAE) to evaluate the experimental result

$$MAE = \frac{1}{n} \sum_{t=1}^{n} |Y_t - P_t| \tag{15}$$

In Eq. (15), n represents the number of samples, Y_t denotes the true value, P_t denotes the predicted value.

The loss of renewable power generation forecasting model during the 100-epochs training process are shown in Fig. 5.

The predicted results of renewable power generation prediction is shown in Fig. 6:

We used Mean Squared Error (MSE) and Mean Absolute Error (MAE) to evaluate the experimental results. We can see their formulas in Eqs. 14 and 15. Table 2 compares the experimental results of the Ultra-long-Term network model with other commonly used models (LSTM, GRU and Simple RNN).

The tests were carried out under identical parameters and using the same datasets. ALL predicted values underwent reverse normalization and metric calculation.

The test results indicate that compared to several commonly used models in the past, the Ultra-long-Term network model employed in this study shows enhancements in the MSE and MAE metrics for renewable (wind + hydroelectric) power prediction.

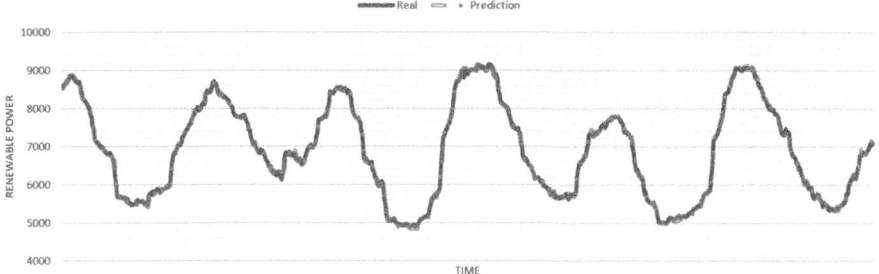

Fig. 6. 3-day Renewable Power Generation Prediction Result

Table 2. Comparison between Ultra-long-Term network model and other commonly used models

Metrics	Ultra-long-term	LSTM	Simple RNN	GRU
MSE	**5384.89**	5712.06	6559.34	5673.76
MAE	**53.55**	53.98	57.69	53.87

3.4   Application In Smart Grid

In a smart grid environment, upon the deployment of the model designed in this paper, it is imperative to integrate it with other models to maximize the efficiency of the smart grid system. In Fig. 7, we illustrate the power load in the BPA territory, from which the following observations are evident:

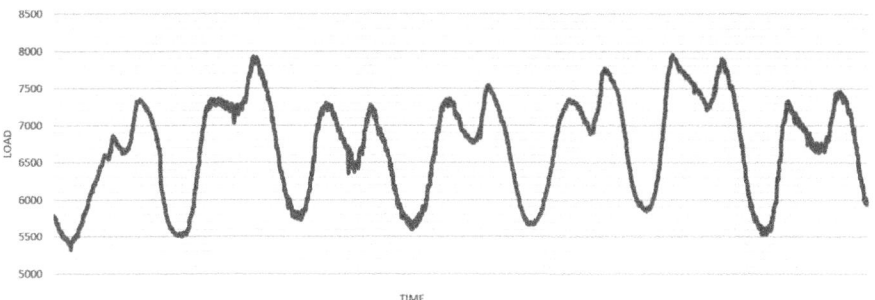

Fig. 7. 7-day Load data

– The power load exhibits continuous fluctuations, necessitating the use of a deep learning-based model for accurate forecasting.
– The variation in power load follows a highly regular pattern, similar to hydropower, enabling the utilization of data from a specific time of day to predict data for the corresponding time on the following day.

This forecasting and regularity fall into the long-term and ultra-long-term categories, where the LSTNet model demonstrates superior performance due to its aptness for handling long-term regular data.

Therefore, by establishing a power load forecasting model based on LSTNet and integrating it with the Ultra-Long-Term network based renewable energy forecasting model proposed in this paper, we can develop a dynamic and real-time renewable energy supply-demand forecasting system, as shown in Fig. 8.

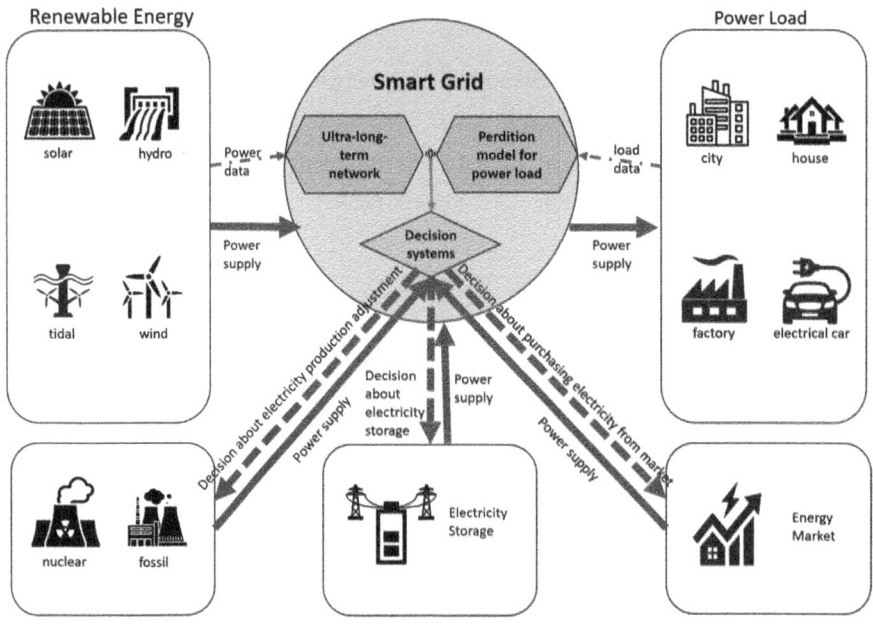

Fig. 8. The operation mechanism of dynamic prediction system and intelligent decision-making system in smart grid

When combined with other smart grid-related systems and technologies, this integrated approach can facilitate continuous and stable power supply, gradual reduction of pollution, and ultimately achieve sustainable development.

4   Conclusion

In this study, we have introduced the Ultra-long-Term network model, integrating components including LSTM, SKIP-LSTM and Dense layers.

This model effectively captures long term patterns in time series data while mitigating the issue of vanishing gradients when capturing extremely long-term patterns.

Our application of this model to renewable power prediction has yielded superior performance compared to previous models such as LSTM, GRU or Simple RNN.

In future research, we plan to combine more renewable energy sources such as solar power. Solar energy is one of the most important renewable energy sources, but it is greatly affected by weather changes and cloud formation. Therefore, the prediction of solar energy requires the design of different deep learning model, covering both time series analysis and image recognition. This is our future research direction, and we will combine models for solar energy and other renewable energy with the model in this paper to ultimately design a compound model that covers all renewable energy sources.

Our goal is to enhance model performance and align with advancements in intelligent grid management and decision-making systems, furthering the transition from fossil/nuclear energy sources to renewable power within the power grid.

References

1. Fang, X., Misra, S., Xue, G., Yang, D.: Smart grid-the new and improved power grid: a survey. IEEE Commun. Surv. Tutor. **14**(4), 944–980 (2011)
2. Gungor, V.C., et al.: Smart grid technologies: communication technologies and standards. IEEE Trans. Ind. Inf. **7**(4), 529–539 (2011)
3. Zame, K.K., Brehm, C.A., Nitica, A.T., Richard, C.L., Schweitzer, G.D., III.: Smart grid and energy storage: policy recommendations. Renew. Sustain. Energy Rev. **82**, 1646–1654 (2018)
4. Hafeez, G., Alimgeer, K.S., Khan, I.: Electric load forecasting based on deep learning and optimized by heuristic algorithm in smart grid. Appl. Energy **269**, 114915 (2020)
5. Hochreiter, S., Schmidhuber, J.: Long short-term memory. Neural Comput. **9**(8), 1735–1780 (1997)
6. Chung, J., Gulcehre, C., Cho, K., Bengio, Y.: Empirical evaluation of gated recurrent neural networks on sequence modeling. arXiv preprint arXiv:1412.3555 (2014)
7. Zheng, J., Chen, X., Yu, K., Gan, L., Wang, Y., Wang, K.: Short-term power load forecasting of residential community based on GRU neural network. In: 2018 International Conference on Power System Technology (POWERCON), pp. 4862–4868. IEEE (2018)
8. Alazab, M., Khan, S., Krishnan, S.S.R., Pham, Q.V., Reddy, M.P.K., Gadekallu, T.R.: A multidirectional LSTM model for predicting the stability of a smart grid. IEEE Access **8**, 85454–85463 (2020)
9. Liu, Y., et al.: Wind power short-term prediction based on LSTM and discrete wavelet transform. Appl. Sci. **9**(6), 1108 (2019)
10. Shi, X., Chen, Z., Wang, H., Yeung, D.Y., Wong, W.K., Woo, W.C.: Convolutional LSTM network: a machine learning approach for precipitation nowcasting. In: Advances in Neural Information Processing Systems, vol. 28 (2015)
11. Sahoo, B.B., Jha, R., Singh, A., Kumar, D.: Long short-term memory (LSTM) recurrent neural network for low-flow hydrological time series forecasting. Acta Geophys. **67**(5), 1471–1481 (2019)

12. Yi, J., Wen, Z., Tao, J., Ni, H., Liu, B.: CTC regularized model adaptation for improving LSTM RNN based multi-accent mandarin speech recognition. J. Signal Process. Syst. **90**, 985–997 (2018)
13. Malhan, P., Mittal, M.: A novel ensemble model for long-term forecasting of wind and hydro power generation. Energy Convers. Manag. **251**, 114983 (2022)
14. Lai, G., Chang, W.C., Yang, Y., Liu, H.: Modeling long-and short-term temporal patterns with deep neural networks. In: The 41st International ACM SIGIR Conference on Research & Development in Information Retrieval, pp. 95–104 (2018)
15. LeCun, Y., Bottou, L., Bengio, Y., Haffner, P.: Gradient-based learning applied to document recognition. Proc. IEEE **86**(11), 2278–2324 (1998)

Vision Transformer-Based Meta Loss Landscape Exploration with Actor-Critic Method

Enzhi Zhang[1(⊠)], Rui Zhong[1], Xingbang Du[1], Mohamed Wahib[2], and Masaharu Munetomo[3]

[1] Graduate School of Information Science and Technology, Hokkaido University, Sapporo, Japan
`enzhi.zhang.n6@elms.hokudai.ac.jp`
[2] RIKEN Center for Computational Science, Kobe, Japan
`mohamed.attia@riken.jp`
[3] Information Initiative Center, Hokkaido University, Sapporo, Japan
`munetomo@iic.hokudai.ac.jp`

Abstract. Detecting and mitigating overfitting in deep neural networks remains a critical challenge in modern machine learning. This paper investigates innovative approaches to address these challenges, particularly focusing on vision transformer-based models. By leveraging meta-learning techniques and reinforcement learning frameworks, we introduce Transformer-based Loss Landscape Exploration (TLLE), which utilizes the validation loss landscape to guide gradient descent optimization. Unlike conventional methods, TLLE employs the Actor-Critic algorithm to learn the mapping from model weights to future values, facilitating efficient sample collection and precise value predictions. Experimental results demonstrate the superior performance of TLLE-enhanced transformer models in image classification and segmentation tasks, showcasing the efficacy of our approach in optimizing deep learning models for image analysis.

Keywords: Loss Landscape · Transformer · Overfitting · Reinforcement Learning · Actor-Critic

1 Introduction

Detecting and mitigating overfitting in deep neural networks stands as a crucial task. Experts have devised various strategies to tackle overfitting while enhancing the training process through careful analysis of training methodologies, particularly observing validation trends during training. These methods encompass a range of techniques such as learning rate scheduling [2,15,26], dropout regularization [31], adversarial training [10,27], data augmentation [30], and the utilization of Adam optimizers [17]. Despite the experts' understanding of the intricate nature of deep models, characterized by their high dimensionality and non-linearity (Shwartz-Ziv et al., 2017), a fundamental question emerges: "Can

© The Author(s), under exclusive license to Springer Nature Switzerland AG 2025
H. R. Arabnia et al. (Eds.): CSCE 2024, CCIS 2256, pp. 291–305, 2025.
https://doi.org/10.1007/978-3-031-85638-9_22

we empower the gradient descent optimizer to minimize validation loss, even when zero training loss suggests learning has halted?"

In tackling this challenge, meta-learning [33] and particularly methods like meta-HPO (Hyper Parameter Optimization) establish a bi-level objective framework. Generally, two main approaches are employed for such bi-level optimization. In the first approach, we focus on optimizing the outer target while letting the controller explore the parameter space. Subsequently, we refine the controller's performance using meta-information derived from the inner optimization process. Although this method, exemplified by techniques like grid search, is straightforward to implement, it incurs significant computational costs due to the intensive inner optimization [7,14]. Alternatively, the second approach involves the direct updating of the outer objective: a meta-gradient-based strategy computes high-order gradients with respect to the hyperparameters or settings [5,25]. However, the impractical computational expense associated with the high-order Hessian matrix, coupled with the serious degradation of the meta-gradient, presents challenges.

This paper leverages the validation loss throughout the gradient descent process to address the computational constraints and performance degradation, particularly concerning vision transformer-based models. Our approach involves treating gradient-based optimization akin to an RL (Reinforcement Learning) task or MDP (Markov Decision Process), akin to prior work by [22,35]. In contrast to [22], where the training loss served as the reward, we consider the validation loss as the reward in our method. Furthermore, compared to [35], we extend our task to encompass transformer-based classification/segmentation and substitute the Deep Q-Learning [28] method with the Actor-Critic algorithm [11,18] to mitigate value prediction variance. To maintain consistency with RL terminology, we dub the gradient action provider "the controller" (trainer) while referring to the model trained on the target dataset for exploring the validation loss landscape as "the worker(s)" (trainee). Evaluation metrics are derived from a distinct test dataset. We named our framework Transformer-based Loss Landscape Exploration (TLLE), and an overview of TLLE is illustrated in Fig. 1.

The main contributions in this paper are listed as follows:

- **Transformer-based Loss Landscape Exploration(TLLE):** In comparison to other meta-learning methods, TLLE applies the Actor-Critic Algorithm to learn the mapping from weights, instead of hyper-parameters, to the future value. As a result, this improves the sample collection speed and makes precise predictions of the future value. Second, a fine-trained Actor avoids calculating the Hessian matrix, making training a large model, like Transformer-based, possible.
- **Higher Performance:** We show that compared with the baseline model, the transformer model using the TLLE method has quality and numerical improvements in both image classification and segmentation, which come from the previous meta-learning process.

In summary, this study explores the application of transformer architectures in the context of image classification and segmentation tasks. Experimental

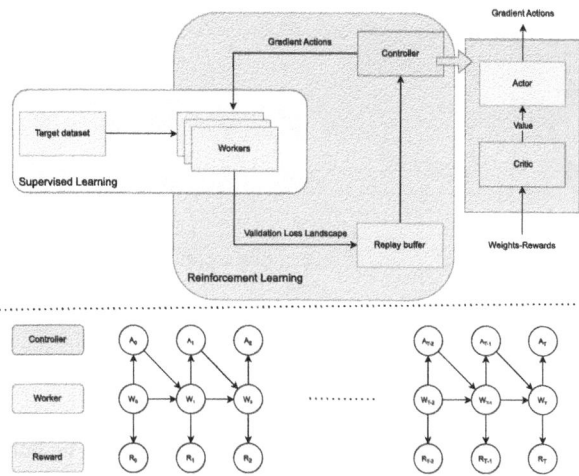

Fig. 1. (Transformer-based Loss Landscape Exploration (TLLE). Top: an overview of how the workers, controller, and replay buffer interact Bottom: an overview of how the controller provides action gradients to update the weights of workers.

evaluations were performed on the proposed model, demonstrating the efficacy of the Actor-Critic algorithm in addressing inherent challenges such as computational complexity and gradient degradation. Serving as an optimizer, the Actor-Critic algorithm effectively learns the dynamics of weight space changes and their corresponding impact on validation loss. Leveraging this acquired knowledge, the algorithm autonomously mitigates validation loss on the dataset, showcasing its utility in optimizing deep learning models for image analysis tasks.

2   Related Work

TLLE utilizes training trajectories sampled from the validation loss landscape to inform subsequent worker training. Prior work by Li et al. [21] visualized loss landscapes of ResNet, elucidating the optimization advantages conferred by skip connections. Other studies have analyzed loss landscape properties such as sharpness [15], smoothness [21], and connectivity [8] to deepen understanding. Some approaches accelerate training or seek generalized solutions via weight ensembling [8,13], or by reducing sharpness-based targets to identify flatness near minima [6,15].

Diverging from prior research, TLLE explores the validation loss landscape instead of the training loss, akin to meta-learning methods [33]. TLLE enhances workers by hyperparameter scheduling, resembling hyperparameter optimization (HPO) or meta-HPO methods [25], particularly reinforcement learning-based solutions [14]. Notably, TLLE treats the weights space as the state space and the gradient space as the action space, aligning with meta-optimizer frameworks [1, 22,24], contrasting with direct outer target updates in meta-gradient methods, prone to performance degradation and high computational costs [33].

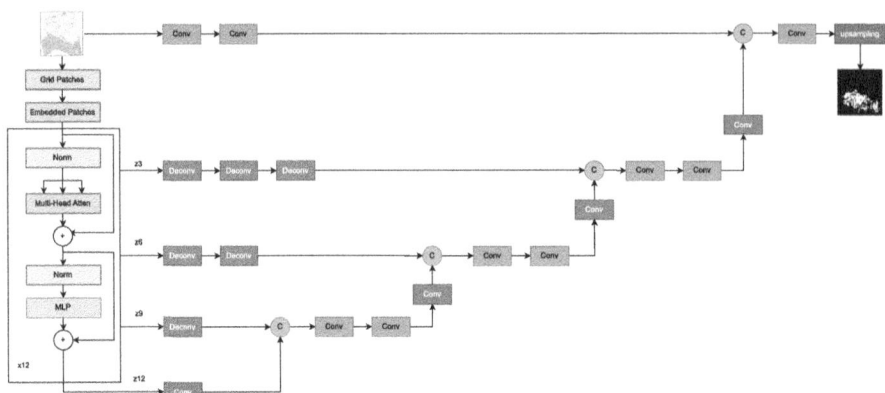

Fig. 2. UNETR model structure for the segmentation work. The encoder is a transformer stack of 12 blocks comprising multi-head self-attention (MSA) and multilayer perceptron (MLP) sublayers. For the decoder, we apply a deconvolutional bottleneck layer to the transformed feature map to increase its resolution by a factor of 2.

Conventional techniques such as decaying the learning rate [26] or Keskar et al.'s linear scaling rule [15] address overfitting and accelerate training. You et al.'s layer-wise learning rate adaptive optimizer (LARS) [34] further advances this. In contrast, TLLE's controller acts as an automated validation loss landscape-aware learning rate scheduler, dynamically adjusting learning rates based on the loss landscape.

Additionally, TLLE draws inspiration from recent Network Architecture Search (NAS) advances [23,29], where reinforcement learning governs high-value network structure generation. In contrast, TLLE treats neural network parameter optimization as a reinforcement learning task, leveraging validation landscape knowledge for subsequent worker training.

3   Methodology

3.1   Vision Transformers and Attention

ViTs [4] comprise an embedding layer, transformer encoder layers, and a classification head. The embedding layer linearly projects the image patches sequence input into a sequence of flattened embeddings. Transformer encoder layers process these embeddings, capturing local and global context through self-attention mechanisms. The attention mechanism in transformers computes attention scores between input tokens, forming the attention matrix. Let $x \in R^{N \times F}$ denote a sequence of N feature vectors of dimensions F. A transformer is a function $T : R^{N \times F} \rightarrow R^{N \times F}$ defined by the composition of L transformer layers $T_1(\cdot), ..., T_L(\cdot)$ as follows,:

$$T_l(x) = f_l(A_l(x) + x). \tag{1}$$

where $A_l(\cdot)$ is the self-attention function. The function $f_l(\cdot)$ transforms each feature independently of the others, and is usually implemented with a small two-layer feedforward network. Formally, the input sequence x is projected by three matrices $W_Q \in R^{F \times D}, W_K \in R^{F \times D}$, and $W_V \in R^{F \times D}$, to corresponding representations Q, K and V. Thus, the attention scores are calculated as follows:

$$Q = xW_Q \tag{2}$$
$$K = xW_K \tag{3}$$
$$V = xW_V \tag{4}$$
$$A_{ij} = \text{Softmax}\left(\frac{(Q_i K_j)^T}{\sqrt{d_k}}\right) \tag{5}$$

where Q_i and K_j are query and key vectors for tokens i and j, and d_k is the dimension of the key vectors. The complexity of the attention matrix is $O(N^2)$, where N is the sequence length. The same is true for the memory requirements because the full attention matrix must be stored to compute the gradients for the weights of the queries, keys, and values.

We further assume that the input is the content of a square image x with a resolution of Z, that is, let $x \in R^{Z \times Z}$, and by assuming that patches arise from the uniform grid patch method of patch size p. Thus the sequence $N = (\frac{Z}{P})^2$. Therefore, the total computation and memory cost of attention scores according to resolution and patch size is $O([\frac{Z}{P}]^4)$. This complexity demonstrates the difficulties of increasing the resolution while decreasing patch size P with the uniform grid patch strategy.

3.2 Actor-Critic Algorithm

In reinforcement learning, the agent interacts with an environment E, and a series of actions reward this interaction. At the state s_t here t means time step, the agent must select a corresponding action a_t from the action space A. For the state of this action (s_t, a_t), the agent will receive a reward r_t, and the reward r_t depends on the reward function $R(s_t, a_t)$. For a certain dataset, we can obtain multiple complete state-action-rewards trajectories denoted as $T = (s_1, a_1, r_1...s_t, a_t, r_t)$, known as Markov Decision Process (MDP), in particular when the number of states and actions is finite. The state transitions are deterministic, and MDP converges to a stable state.

Based on the above definitions, many reinforcement learning algorithms aim to find an agent with the maximum expected reward function in a limited number of iterations. Here, we define the optimal action-value function $Q^*(s, a)$ as follows:

$$Q^*(s, a) = \max_{\pi} E[R_t | s_t, a_t, \pi]$$

where $R_t = \sum_{t'=t}^{T} \gamma^{t'-t} r_{t'}$ is the discounted future rewards from time step t, γ is this discount factor, and π is the policy mapping sequences to actions. It is worth

| | (b) Ground | | (e) |
| (a) Inputs | Truth | (c) Baseline | (d) LR-TLLE | LRRE-TLLE |

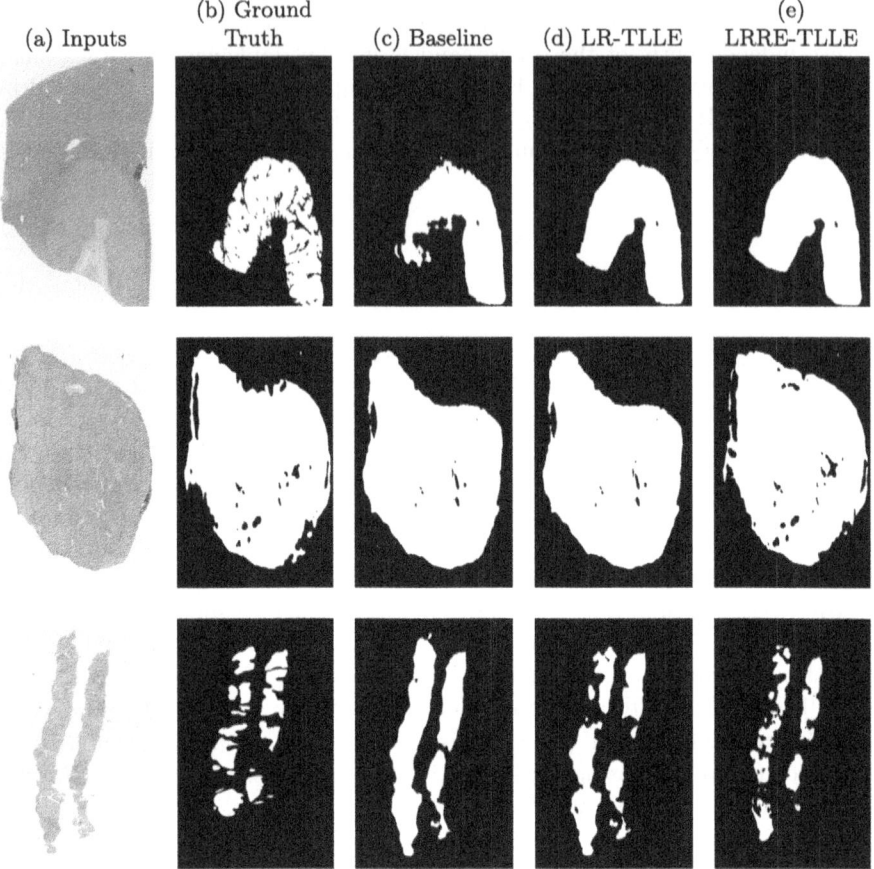

Fig. 3. Quality results among Baseline, LR-TLLE, and LRRE-TLLE.(LR: Learning Rate, RE: Regularization) LRRE-TLLE segmentation has better details when applied on the UNETR model.

mentioning that the optimal action-value function $Q^*(s, a)$ follows the *Bellman Equation* which suggests that if the rewards of each action a are known at state s, then the optimal policy is to select the action a^* with a maximum expected value of $r + \gamma Q^*(a^*, s)$. By using the *Bellman Equation* as the update iteration, $Q_{i+1}(s, a) = E_{s'}[r + \gamma \max_{a'} Q^*(s', a')|s, a]$, then $Q_{i+1} \rightarrow Q^*$ if $i \rightarrow \infty$ [32].

Actor-critic algorithms are policy-based reinforcement learning algorithms combining value-based (critic) and policy-based (actor) methods. The actor proposes actions, while the critic evaluates these actions and provides feedback to the actor. The critic learns the value function $V(s)$, which estimates the expected return from state s, and the actor learns the policy $\pi(a\|s)$, which specifies the probability of taking each action in each state. The advantage function $A(s, a)$ measures how good it is to take an action a in state s compared to the average action chosen under the current policy. It is defined as:

$$A(a, s) = Q_{\theta_\pi}(a, s) - V_{\theta_v}(s) \tag{6}$$

The actor aims to maximize the expected return by adjusting its policy parameters θ_π, while the critic evaluates the actor's actions and updates the value function parameters θ_v. The objective functions of the actor and critic are:

$$L(\theta_\pi) = -E_{s\sim\pi}[A(s, a)\nabla_\theta log\pi(a|s; \theta_\pi)] \tag{7}$$

$$L(\theta_v) = \frac{1}{2}E_s[(r + \gamma V(s') - V(s))^2] \tag{8}$$

3.3   Image Classification and Segmentation

Although the TLLE framework is not restricted to a specific class of supervised learning tasks, here we discuss TLLE in the context of training models for image classification tasks. Consider an image dataset D consisting of input images $x \in R^d$ and the one-shot label $y \in R^K$ where K is the number of classes. We denote the model as $f : R^d \rightarrow R^K$ and parameterize it by the trainable weights θ. For each sample $(x, y) \in D$, the output prediction is given by $\tilde{y} = f(x; \theta)$. Let $l : R^K \times R^K \rightarrow R$ denote a loss function, then the optimization process can be written as:

$$\min_\theta \quad L(x, y) = \frac{1}{N}\sum_n^N l(f(x_i; \theta), y_i) \tag{9}$$

where N is the size of the training dataset D, and the loss L is the training loss. For the classification task, we applied cross-entropy loss l_{bce}, and for the segmentation task, The loss function L is a combination of dice loss L_{dice} and binary cross-entropy loss l_{bce}:

$$L(\hat{y}, y) = w \cdot L_{bce}(\hat{y}, y) + (1 - w) \cdot L_{dice}(\hat{y}, y) \tag{10}$$

$$= -w \cdot \frac{1}{N}\sum_{i=1}^N [y_i \log(\hat{y}_i) + (1 - y_i) \log(1 - \hat{y}_i)] \tag{11}$$

$$+ (1 - w) \cdot (1 - \frac{2\sum_{i=1}^N(\hat{y}_i \cdot y_i) + \epsilon}{\sum_{i=1}^N \hat{y}_i + \sum_{i=1}^N y_i + \epsilon}) \tag{12}$$

where $L(\hat{y}, y)$ represents the combined loss function, composed of a weighted sum of Binary Cross-Entropy (BCE) loss and dice loss. w is the weight parameter controlling the contribution of BCE loss versus the dice loss:, we set it to 0.5 during the experiments. ϵ is a smoothing term, and we keep it to 1.0 during the experiments.

Many useful gradient-based optimization methods can be applied to optimize this objective function Eq. 9. Here, for simplicity, we consider the widely used stochastic gradient descent (SGD) to update the trainable weights θ:

$$\theta \leftarrow \theta - \alpha \nabla_\theta L(x, y; \theta) - \lambda \nabla_\theta ||\theta||_{l_2} \tag{13}$$

where α is the learning rate, λ is the penalty factor of the regularization, ∇_θ is the differentiation operator w.r.t θ.

3.4 Transformer-Based Loss Landscape Exploration with Actor-Critic Algorithm

Based on the above notation, if we replace the state space S with the weights space Θ, the cost function C with validation loss function V, and the action space A with gradient space G, then we could transfer the context of supervised learning to become reinforcement learning. Here we can rewrite the optimal action-value function $Q^*(\theta, g)$ as follows:

$$Q^*(\theta, g; \phi) = \min_\pi E[V_t | \theta_t, g_t, \pi]$$

where ϕ is the trainable weights of Q-network, $V_t = \sum_{t'=t}^{T} \gamma^{t'-t} v_{t'}$ is the discounted future costs, and π is the policy, they are the same notions as before. The loss function of this actor-network is also the same as Eq. 7, and the following loss function update the actor and critic network:

$$L(\theta_\pi) = -E_{\theta \sim \pi}[A(\theta, g)\nabla_\theta log\pi(a|\theta; \theta_\pi)] \tag{14}$$

$$L(\theta_v) = \frac{1}{2}E_\theta[(r + \gamma V(\theta') - V(\theta))^2] \tag{15}$$

Therefore, we applied the above Eq. 14 in the experiment. Here, we first replace the validation loss with the validation accuracy. Then, replace the total gradient space with a set of Action A expanded by a group of learning rates αs or regularization penalty factors λs, where the number of the total actions is $||A|| = ||\alpha|| \times ||\lambda||$. The pair (α, λ) is selected at the beginning of the training step to update the workers.

4 Experiments

4.1 Datasets

Classification. We conducted the classification work on the MNIST, CIFAR-10 and CIFAR-100 dataset. MNIST [3] is a dataset of handwritten digits containing $60,000$ training examples and $10,000$ test examples. CIFAR-10 [19] and CIFAR-100 [20] datasets contain $50,000$ training images and $10,000$ testing images with 10 and 100 classes, respectively. These datasets are commonly used across many classification tasks. When training the workers, we shuffled the training and test dataset. We split the dataset into 20% for the validation set and 80% training set. When training the workers, we also collect the validation metrics and weights to train the controller.

Segmentation. We conducted the segmentation work on the PAIP dataset which [16] is a high-resolution liver cancer pathology (real-world) dataset. The sample resolution size is close to $64K$, far higher than the resolution of conventional image datasets. PAIP includes $2,457$ Whole-Slide Images (WSIs). When needed to use smaller resolutions, we down-scale the images into uniform 512 square images. During the training process, we randomly select 0.7 samples for training, 0.1 samples for validation, and 0.2 samples for testing. All data sets are shuffled and normalized to $[0.0, 1.0]$ when used as model input.

4.2 Models for Classification and Segmentation

Classification. We applied the original ViT defined in [4] for the vision transformer model. Typically, it consists of 12 transformer layers. Each layer incorporates a multi-head self-attention mechanism and a feed-forward neural network. The input image is divided into patches of size 4×4 pixels, which are linearly projected into token embeddings. The model utilizes an embedding dimension of 768 for the tokens. Positional embeddings are added to encode spatial information. Pre-training on large-scale datasets like ImageNet with classification objectives enables ViT to learn meaningful visual representations, contributing to its remarkable performance in computer vision tasks. For ResNet-56, we used the settings reported in [12]. All workers are initialized to the same weights by using the *glorot* initializer [9]. The loss function is *cross entropy* loss and the optimizer is the naive SGD optimizer with a learning rate of 0.1. For the experiments with the Learning Rate Decaying (LRD), it starts at $(50\%, 75\%)$ steps of the total epochs with a factor of 0.1. The batch size is set to be 256 and all the workers are trained for 120 epochs (MLP) and 200 epochs (ResNet-56). For the experiments with Data Augmentation (DA), we process the images as recommended in [12].

Segmentation. Overall, UNETR shown in Fig. 2 uses a contraction-expansion pattern consisting of a bunch of transformers as an encoder. It is connected to the decoder via a skip connection. UNETR's initial application was mainly designed for 3D medical organs and related data. Their work also discussed the impact of patch size on the model: the smaller the patch size, the better the model performance will be. However, limited by memory capacity and computing power, conducting experiments with a small patch size is difficult.

Our approach can be seen as a solution to this problem through data augmentation. However, since our experimental data is not 2D medical image data, we only replaced the 3D convolution and deconvolution blocks in UNETR with the 2D version without additional changes to the model structure. Other than that, we have no other improvements to UNETR.

The encoder is a transformer stack of 12 blocks comprising multi-head self-attention (MSA) and multilayer perceptron (MLP) sublayers. The embedding size $K = 768$, Norm denotes layer normalization, and MLP means two linear layers with GELU activation functions. The MSA sublayer contains n parallel self-attention (SA) heads. The attention matrix (A) is computed by measuring the similarity between two elements in a sequence and their key-value pairs according to 2. After the encoder, UNETR extracts a sequence representation from each transformer block $z_i, [i \in 3, 6, 9, 12]$ and reshapes it to a sequence of patches. Then, similarly to the idea of UNet, we apply a deconvolutional bottleneck layer to the transformed feature map to increase its resolution by a factor of 2. Then, output concat with $z_i, [i \in 3, 6, 9, 12]$ sent to 3×3 convolutional layer and upsampling deconvolution. This process continues until the output size meets the mask size. The final layer is 1×1 convolutional layer to project the class to the channel of mask.

4.3   Training of Actor and Critic Nets

Both actor and critic are mainly a four-layer MLP model with a downsampling layer to reduce input size. For each layer in the controller, the number of units is $[128, 64, 32, ||A||]$ where $\alpha = [0.01, 0.1, 1.0, 2.5, 5.0]$ or $\lambda = [0.0, 1.0, 2.0, 4.0, 8.0]$ for learning rate or penalty factor for the discrete action space. For the continuous action space, $A = [-1e-4, 0.0, 1e-4]$ plus the current factors. Worth mentioning that, to avoid numerically unstable, the range of the continuous factors is limited in $[1e-4, 4.0]$. The activation functions are $[ReLU, ReLU, ReLU, Linear]$. The weights are initialized by *glorot* initializer. The loss function we used is the MSE loss. The optimizer is an SGD optimizer with a learning rate of 0.01 and a batch size of 128.

The ϵ-greedy policy has been applied with an annealing strategy during the iteration. Note that each iteration generates N new samples. To keep the balance between the number of new and old samples, we train the controller with N_n new samples and N_o old samples randomly selected from the replay buffer B.

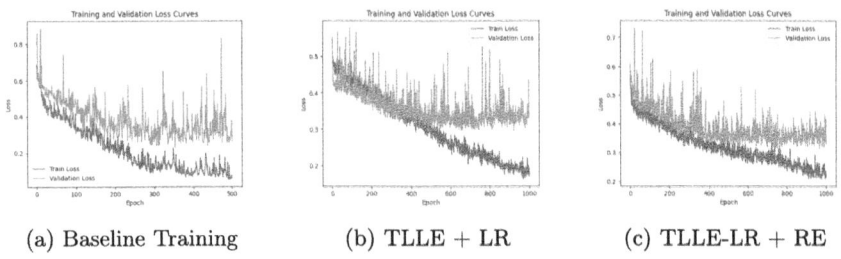

(a) Baseline Training	(b) TLLE + LR	(c) TLLE-LR + RE

Fig. 4. TLLR-LR(Learning Rate) can accelerate the training process by tuning the learning rate. At the same time, TLLR-LRRE(Learning Rate+REgularization) combines the learning rate scheduler and regularization

4.4   Results

Training and Validation Curves of the Workers. We show the training loss and test loss UNETR workers baseline, tuning learning rate, and add penalty factor in Fig. 4. The training curve converges at about 500 or 1000 epoch. Comparing these three figs, TLLR-LR can accelerate the training process by tuning the learning rate. At the same time, TLLR-LRRE combines the learning rate scheduler and regularization by choosing the actions with the max action value; the training could be accelerated or stopped before overfitting by tuning the learning rate or regularization factors. As a result, the TLLR-LRRE can converge to the local minima better and faster. We further show the quantitative differences of TLLE-LR, TLLE-LRRE and baseline in Tab. MNIST and CIFAR-10/100 have been greatly improved $[0.37\%, 0.66\%, 1.63\%]$ in the classification task. On the PAIP dataset, TLLE-LRRE, compared with baseline, improved about $[1.31\%, 1.84\%, 0.79\%]$ evaluated based on dice score for UNETR, UNET, and TransUnet models.

Segmentation Result in Quality. In Fig. 3, we present a comparison between the baseline model without TLLE, the TLLE-RE model with adjusted learning rate (LR), and the TLLE-LRRE variant incorporating both LR adjustment and penalty term RE. It is evident that, compared to the ground truth version, UNETR utilizing the TLLE method exhibits specific errors in image quality, manifesting in discrepancies in both overall pattern and local details. UNETR with TLLE-LR demonstrates enhanced Dice Score, indicative of superior performance, particularly in local details. Moreover, the TLLE-LRRE variant, incorporating the penalty term RE, further mitigates overfitting issues, yielding commendable performance improvements across both global and local image aspects (Table 1).

Table 1. Comparisons using the MNIST, CIFAR-10, and CIFAR-100 datasets with the Baseline (naive training without meta-method). Here, LR-TLLE and LRRE-TLLE mean the action spaces for TLLE are Learning Rate (LR) and REgularization (RE), respectively. LRD = Learning Rate Decay; DA = Data Augmentation

Dataset	Model [Setup]	Baseline	RE-TLLE	LRRE-TLLE
MNIST	ViT	98.16%	98.43%	98.24%
	ViT [LRD]	97.62%	98.85%	98.10%
	ViT [DA+LRD]	98.77%	98.97%	99.17%
CIFAR-10	ViT	52.45%	52.87%	53.52%
	ViT [LRD]	53.45%	54.14%	54.87%
	ViT [DA+LRD]	59.32%	59.80%	61.78%
	ResNet-56	81.71%	82.73%	85.13%
	ResNet-56 [LRD]	83.02%	83.55%	84.72%
	ResNet-56 [DA+LRD]	83.73%	83.78%	84.39%
CIFAR-100	ViT	71.45%	73.21%	74.81%
	ViT [LRD]	72.39%	73.16%	73.33%
	ViT [DA+LRD]	72.43%	73.12%	73.78%
	ResNet-56	60.07%	61.17%	62.72%
	ResNet-56 [LRD]	61.43%	61.88%	63.81%
	ResNet-56 [DA+LRD]	67.06%	68.44%	68.64%

5   Discussions and Improvements

5.1   Comparison to the Meta-HPO Methods

Many Meta-HPO or learning-to-learning methods conduct a bi-level optimization to fit their motivation. Here we refer to the same notation in [25] of the
bi-level objective function:

$$\lambda^* = \arg\min_\lambda L_V(\lambda, \theta^*) \text{ subject to } \theta^* = \arg\min_\theta L_T(\lambda^*, \theta)$$

where L_T is the training loss, θ is the model's weights, L_V is the validation loss,
and λ is the hyperparameters.

The gradient-based method solves the above problem by calculating the hyper
gradient $\frac{\partial L_v}{\partial \lambda}$ directly or indirectly through $\frac{\partial L_v}{\partial \theta} \frac{\partial \theta}{\partial \lambda}$. The direct gradient is easy to
calculate but led to degradation in the prediction accuracy, mainly due to the gra-
dient degradation problem. For the indirect hyper-gradient, the calculation of $\frac{\partial \theta}{\partial \lambda}$
is difficult and needs approximation, for example, [25] applies Implicit Function
Theorem (IFT) and Neumann series for further approximate the inverse Hessian
matrix. However, first, in our proposed method TLLE the action is selected from
the prediction of Q-Net, and the Q-Net is trained online to save the high cost
for the inner optimization. Thus, training such Q-Net avoids the calculation of
both the $\frac{\partial L_v}{\partial \theta}$ and $\frac{\partial \theta}{\partial \lambda}$. The former used the gradient from the validation samples,
and the latter involved an unacceptable calculation. Second, the prediction of
the Q-Net is dependent on the weights, and due to the transferability of weights,
unlike other meta-requires that need to be re-trained on the transfer dataset,
the Q-Net can be reused on the transfer dataset with fine-tuning (Table 2).

Table 2. Improvement in quantities of segmentation for the PAIP dataset against
different baselines.

Dataset	Model [Setup]	Baseline	TLLE-LR	TLLE-RE	Dice Improvement
PAIP	UNTER	74.17	74.83	75.66	1.31%
	UNTER [LRD]	75.88	76.17	77.89	
	UNTER [DA+LRD]	76.32	77.32	78.61	
	UNET	74.98	75.48	76.80	1.84%
	UNET [LRD]	75.23	76.65	77.58	
	UNET [DA+LRD]	76.41	77.85	78.25	
	TransUNet	73.32	74.33	74.65	0.79%
	TransUNet [LRD]	75.72	76.98	77.61	
	TransUNet [DA+LRD]	76.82	77.24	77.63	

5.2   Consistency of the Controller

In the work of Li et al. [23], the validation accuracy estimator s has been shown
to learn the performance of different network structures sampled in the structure

search space. On the other hand, TLLE is using s to learn the discounted validation rewards from weights. In other words, the estimators s of their method can be represented as $s : R^{d_a} \to R$, while in our method the estimator can be represented as $s : R^{d_w} \to R^A$. Here d_a is the dimension of structure space, d_w is the dimension of the weight space, and R^A is the dimension of the actions' space.

Lemma 1. *Let S be a hypothesis class, L_N be the empirical reward, and L be the expected reward. For any $\delta > 0$, with probability at least $1 - \delta$, $\forall s \in S$:*

$$|L_N(s) - L(s)| < \sqrt{\frac{2(d + \ln \frac{2}{\delta})}{N}}$$

where d is Pollard's pseudo-dimension of S, and N is the number of total samples.

Lemma 1 shows us the convergence of the error bound is decided by Pollard's pseudo-dimension d and the number of total samples N. With a fixed d and infinite samples N, the gap between empirical reward and expected reward asymptote is less than a constant. Although using an infinite number of samples is impossible in experiments, this lemma suggests that we can move faster toward the error bound by reducing the input dimension of s and accelerating the training of workers.

6   Conclusion and Future Work

In conclusion, this paper has delved into the crucial task of detecting and mitigating overfitting in deep neural networks, particularly focusing on the challenges posed by vision transformer-based models. Through an exploration of meta-learning and reinforcement learning methodologies, we have introduced the Transformer-based Loss Landscape Exploration (TLLE) framework. TLLE leverages the validation loss landscape to guide gradient descent optimization, employing the Actor-Critic algorithm to learn the mapping from model weights to future values efficiently. Our experimental results have demonstrated the efficacy of TLLE-enhanced transformer models in improving image classification and segmentation tasks. Future research could further refine and extend TLLE to tackle broader challenges in machine learning optimization.

References

1. Antoniou, A., Edwards, H., Storkey, A.: How to train your MAML. arXiv preprint arXiv:1810.09502 (2018)
2. Deng, J., et al.: Imagenet: a large-scale hierarchical image database. In: IEEE Conference on Computer Vision and Pattern Recognition, pp. 248–255. IEEE (2009)
3. Deng, L.: The MNIST database of handwritten digit images for machine learning research. IEEE Signal Process. Mag. **29**(6), 141–142 (2012)

4. Dosovitskiy, A., et al.: An image is worth 16×16 words: transformers for image recognition at scale. arXiv preprint arXiv:2010.11929 (2020)
5. Finn, C., Abbeel, P., Levine, S.: Model-agnostic metalearning for fast adaptation of deep networks. In: International Conference on Machine Learning, pp. 1126–1135. PMLR (2017)
6. Foret, P., et al.: Sharpness-aware minimization for efficiently improving generalization. arXiv preprint arXiv:2010.01412 (2020)
7. Franceschi, L., et al.: Bilevel programming for hyperparameter optimization and meta-learning. In: International Conference on Machine Learning, pp. 1568–1577. PMLR (2018)
8. Garipov, T., et al.: Loss surfaces, mode connectivity, and fast ensembling of DNNs. In: Advances in Neural Information Processing Systems, vol. 31 (2018)
9. Glorot, X., Bengio, Y.: Understanding the difficulty of training deep feedforward neural networks. In: Proceedings of the Thirteenth International Conference on Artificial Intelligence and Statistics. JMLR Workshop and Conference Proceedings, pp. 249–256 (2010)
10. Goodfellow, I.J., Shlens, J., Szegedy, C.: Explaining and harnessing adversarial examples. arXiv preprint arXiv:1412.6572 (2014)
11. Haarnoja, T., et al.: Soft actor-critic algorithms and applications. arXiv preprint arXiv:1812.05905 (2018)
12. He, K., et al.: Deep residual learning for image recognition. In: Proceedings of the IEEE Conference on Computer Vision and Pattern Recognition, pp. 770–778 (2016)
13. Izmailov, P., et al.: Averaging weights leads to wider optima and better generalization. arXiv preprint arXiv:1803.05407 (2018)
14. Jomaa, H.S., Grabocka, J., Schmidt-Thieme, L.: Hyp-RL: hyperparameter optimization by reinforcement learning. In: arXiv preprint arXiv:1906.11527 (2019)
15. Keskar, N.S., et al.: On large-batch training for deep learning: generalization gap and sharp minima. arXiv preprint arXiv:1609.04836 (2016)
16. Kim, Y.J., et al.: PAIP 2019: liver cancer segmentation challenge. Med. Image Anal. **67**, 101854 (2021). https://doi.org/10.1016/j.media.2020.101854. https://www.sciencedirect.com/science/article/pii/S1361841520302188. ISSN 1361-8415
17. Kingma, D.P., Ba, J.: Adam: a method for stochastic optimization. arXiv preprint arXiv:1412.6980 (2014)
18. Konda, V., Tsitsiklis, J.: Actor-critic algorithms. In: Advances in Neural Information Processing Systems, vol. 12 (1999)
19. Krizhevsky, A., Nair, V., Hinton, G.: CIFAR-10 (Canadian Institute for Advanced Research). http://www.cs.toronto.edu/~kriz/cifar.html
20. Krizhevsky, A., Nair, V., Hinton, G.: CIFAR-100 (Canadian Institute for Advanced Research). http://www.cs.toronto.edu/~kriz/cifar.html
21. Li, H., et al.: Visualizing the loss landscape of neural nets. In: Advances in Neural Information Processing Systems, vol. 31 (2018)
22. Li, K., Malik, J.: Learning to optimize. arXiv preprint arXiv:1606.01885 (2016)
23. Li, Y., et al.: Neural architecture search in a proxy validation loss landscape, pp. 5853–5862 (2020)
24. Li, Z., et al.: Meta-SGD: learning to learn quickly for few-shot learning. arXiv preprint arXiv:1707.09835 (2017)
25. Lorraine, J., Vicol, P., Duvenaud, D.: Optimizing millions of hyperparameters by implicit differentiation. In: International Conference on Artificial Intelligence and Statistics, pp. 1540–1552. PMLR (2020)

26. Loshchilov, I., Hutter, F.: SGDR: stochastic gradient descent with warm restarts. arXiv preprint arXiv:1608.03983 (2016)
27. Madry, A., et al.: Towards deep learning models resistant to adversarial attacks. arXiv preprint arXiv:1706.06083 (2017)
28. Mnih, V., et al.: Human-level control through deep reinforcement learning. Nature **518**(7540), 529–533 (2015)
29. Pham, H., et al.: Efficient neural architecture search via parameters sharing. In: International Conference on Machine Learning, pp. 4095–4104. PMLR (2018)
30. Shorten, C., Khoshgoftaar, T.M.: A survey on image data augmentation for deep learning. J. Big Data **6**(1), 1–48 (2019)
31. Srivastava, N., et al.: Dropout: a simple way to prevent neural networks from overfitting. J. Mach. Learn. Res. **15**(1), 1929–1958 (2014)
32. Sutton, R.S., Barto, A.G.: Reinforcement Learning: An Introduction. MIT Press, Cambridge (2018)
33. Vanschoren, J.: Meta-learning: a survey. arXiv preprint arXiv:1810.03548 (2018)
34. You, Y., Gitman, I., Ginsburg, B.: Scaling SGD batch size to 32k for imagenet training. arXiv preprint arXiv:1708.03888, vol. 6, no. 12, p. 6 (2017)
35. Zhang, E., Wahib, M., Munetomo, M.: Learning from the past: regularization by validation. In: 2022 Joint 12th International Conference on Soft Computing and Intelligent Systems and 23rd International Symposium on Advanced Intelligent Systems (SCISISIS), pp. 1–8 (2022). https://doi.org/10.1109/SCISISIS55246.2022. 10002143.

Fast Computation Method for Stopping Condition of Range Restricted GMRES Method

Miho Chiyonobu[1] , Masami Takata[2]([✉]), Kinji Kimura[3],
and Yoshimasa Nakamura[4]

[1] Graduate School of Humanities and Sciences, Nara Women's University, Nara,
Japan
chiyonobu-miho1611@lics.nara-wu.ac.jp
[2] Research Group of Information and Communication Technology for Life, Nara
Women's University, Nara, Japan
takata@ics.nara-wu.ac.jp
[3] Faculty of Engineering, University of Fukui, Fukui, Japan
kkimur@u-fukui.ac.jp
[4] Faculty of Data Science, Osaka Seikei University, Osaka, Japan
nakamura-yo@osaka-seikei.ac.jp

Abstract. In this paper, we propose a method for fast computation
of the stopping condition of the Range Restricted General Minimum
Residual (RRGMRES) method. The RRGMRES method is iterative.
As the number of iterations increases, the matrix size increases. The
stopping condition for the iterations requires a condition number. The
condition number is expressed as the ratio of the largest singular value to
the smallest singular value. The proposed method employs the Cholesky
LR method and inverse iteration. By comparing the experimental results
with the conventional method, the proposed method has been 10 times
faster than the conventional method.

Keywords: Condition number · Singular value decomposition ·
Cholesky LR · inverse iteration

1 Introduction

The numerical approach to solving inverse problems has recently been used not
only in the mathematical sciences, but also in engineering fields such as physics,
chemistry, biology, astronomy, architectural engineering, and civil engineering.
As an inverse problem, there is the problem of computing input values from
observed data. In this problem, a linear system of equations with a large condition number matrix on the left–side is solved. In this case, a small amount of
perturbation in the right–hand side vector becomes noise.

To compute approximate solutions to linear equations with large–scale matrices that have singular values of extremely different scales and many small singular values, the method of least residual iteration is applied. However, when

© The Author(s), under exclusive license to Springer Nature Switzerland AG 2025
H. R. Arabnia et al. (Eds.): CSCE 2024, CCIS 2256, pp. 306–317, 2025.
https://doi.org/10.1007/978-3-031-85638-9_23

the large–scale matrix is an extremely ill–conditioned problem and the deter-
minant of the square matrix is numerically zero, the solution is acutely sensi-
tive to the value of the vector on the right–hand side. The Range Restricted
General Minimum Residual (RRGMRES) method [1] is a technique for solving many of the linear ill–conditioned equations in science and technology. The
RRGMRES method solves the equations by iterative computation. As the number of iterations increases, the computational complexity of the condition number
of the upper triangular matrix required by the RRGMRES method increases.
In this paper, we propose a high–speed method for computing condition number of the upper triangular matrix, which is the bottleneck in the RRGMRES
method. Therefore, the Cholesky LR method and the inverse iteration method
are employed.

2 Iteration Stopping Rule by Condition Number

As an iteration stopping rule, the condition number of an upper triangular matrix
$\tilde{R}'_k$ is discussed. The $\tilde{R}'_k$ will be shown in Sect. 4. The largest and smallest
singular values of matrix X are expressed as $\sigma_{\max}(X)$ and $\sigma_{\min}(X)$, respectively.
The condition number $\kappa\left(\tilde{R}'_k\right)$ of the matrix $\tilde{R}'_k$ is defined as follows:

$$\kappa\left(\tilde{R}'_k\right) = \sigma_{\max}\left(\tilde{R}'_k\right) / \sigma_{\min}\left(\tilde{R}'_k\right).$$

The threshold value of the condition number for the iteration stopping rule
needs to be adjusted according to the right–side vector of the simultaneous
linear equations. Machine learning has been validated for automatic setting of
the threshold [2]. However, the fast computation of the condition number in the
upper triangular matrix $\tilde{R}'_k$ has been unsolved problem. Since machine learning
requires input with no or fewer rounding errors, the approximated method for
the condition number of $\tilde{R}'_k$ is not sufficient.

3 GMRES Method

In this section, we introduce the general minimum residual (GMRES) [3], which
computes the same approximate result x_k by generating an orthonormal basis
of the Krylov subspace $K_k(A, r_0)$.

Let $v_0, v_1, v_2, \cdots$ be the orthonormal system obtained by the Gram–Schmidt
orthogonalization of the Krylov sequence $r_0, Ar_0, A^2 r_0, \cdots$ determined from the
residuals $r_0 = b - Ax_0$ of an appropriate initial vector x_0. For each $k = 1, 2, \cdots$,
$v_0, v_1, \cdots, v_{k-2}$ and v_{k-1} is an orthonormal basis of the Krylov subspace:

$$K_k(A, r_0) = \mathrm{span}\{r_0, Ar_0, A^2 r_0, \cdots, A^{k-1} r_0\}$$

Let $n \times k$ matrix $V_k = [v_0, v_1, \cdots, v_{k-1}]$ be defined by arranging the bases.

$$Av_j \in \mathrm{span}\{v_0, \cdots, v_j, v_{j+1}\} \quad (j = 0, 1, 2, \cdots)$$

Algorithm 1. Arnoldi method

1: Initial vector is set to $r_0 \neq 0$ and $v_0 := r_0/\|r_0\|$;
2: **for** $k := 1, 2, \cdots$ **do**
3:    $w := A v_{k-1}$;
4:    **for** $i := 0$ to $k-1$ **do**
5:       $h_{i,k-1} := v_i^\top w$; $w := w - h_{i,k-1} v_i$
6:    **end for**
7:    $h_{k,k-1} := \| w \|$;
8:    **if** $h_{k,k-1} = 0$ **then**
9:       Terminated
10:   **else**
11:      $v_k := w/h_{k,k-1}$
12:   **end if**
13: **end for**

is satisfied. By using $(k+1) \times k$ Hessenberg matrix $\hat{H}_k$,

$$AV_k = V_{k+1}\hat{H}_k$$

is expressed. Here, in the case of $\hat{H}_k = (h_{ij}^{(k)} | 0 \leq i \leq k, 0 \leq j \leq k-1)$ and $i \geq j+2$, $h_{ij}^{(k)} = 0$. In the case of $k < l$, $h_{ij}^{(k)}$ can be abbreviated as h_{ij} because of $h_{ij}^{(k)} = h_{ij}^{(l)}$.

The orthonormal system $v_0, v_1, v_2, \cdots$ and the coefficient $(h_{ij}^{(k)} | 0 \leq i \leq j+1)$ can computed using the Arnoldi method [4]. Algorithm 1 is the pseudo code.

Residuals are minimized in the affine subspace $x_0 + K_k(A, r_0)$. A vector x_k is identified with $x_0 + K_k(A, r_0)$, which is equivalent to being represented as $x_k = x_0 + V_k y_k$ by a vector $y_k \in R^k$. Since v_0 is a normalized version of r_0, $r_0 = V_{k+1} e_{k+1}$. is satisfied. Here, $e_{k+1} = (\| r_0 \|, 0, \cdots, 0)^\top \in R^{k+1}$. Thus, the norm of the residual $r_k = b - Ax_k$ is

$$\| r_k \| = \| r_0 - AV_k y_k \|$$
$$= \| V_{k+1}(e_{k+1} - \hat{H}_k y_k) \|$$
$$= \| e_{k+1} - \hat{H}_k y_k \| . \tag{1}$$

Here, the last equality is caused by the orthogonality $V_{k+1}^\top V_{k+1} = I_{k+1}$ of the column vectors in V_{k+1}. By Eq. (1), the minimization of the residuals is concluded to be a minimization problem of $\| e_{k+1} - \hat{H}_k y_k \|$ for y_k. Since the matrix $\hat{H}_k$ is in Hessenberg form, the solution y_k of the minimization problem can be obtained by using the Givens transformation. The approximate solution x_k is determined from the y_k as $x_k = x_0 + V_k y_k$. This is called the GMRES method.

Algorithm 2 shows the pseudo code of the GMRES method.

Algorithm 2. GMRES Method

1: Initial vector is set to x_0 and $r_0 := b - Ax_0$
2: **if** $r_0 = 0$ **then**
3:　　Terminated
4: **end if**
5: $v_0 := r_0/\parallel r_0 \parallel$;
6: **for** $k := 1, 2, \cdots$ **do**
7:　　$w := Av_{k-1}$;
8:　　**for** $i := 0$　　to　　$k-1$ **do**
9:　　　　$h_{i,k-1} := v_i^\top w$;　　$w := w - h_{i,k-1}v_i$
10:　　**end for**
11:　　$h_{k,k-1} := \parallel w \parallel$;
12:　　y_k is computed to minimize $\parallel e_{k+1} - \hat{H}_k y_k \parallel$; $x_k := x_0 + V_k y_k$;
13:　　**if** $h_{k,k-1} = 0$ **then**
14:　　　　Terminated
15:　　**else**
16:　　　　$v_k = w/h_{k,k-1}$
17:　　**end if**
18: **end for**

4　Range Restricted GMRES Method

A linear ill–conditioned equation problem (2) with an asymmetric matrix A is introduced.

$$Ax = b, \quad A \in \mathbb{R}^{n \times n}, \quad x, b \in \mathbb{R}^n \tag{2}$$

The kth iteration x_k determined by the RRGMRES with the 1st iteration $x_0 = 0$ can solve the minimization problem min $\parallel Ax - b \parallel$, where $\parallel \cdot \parallel$ represents the Euclidean vector norm and $\mathbb{K}_k(A, Ab)$ is the RANGE RESTRICTED Krylov subspace [1].

$$\mathbb{K}_k(A, Ab) = \text{span}\{Ab, A^2b, ..., A^kb\}. \tag{3}$$

The minimization problem min $\parallel Ax - b \parallel$ can be solved using the Arnoldi method.

　　When the Arnoldi method is adopted in k steps to A with an initial vector $v_1 = b/\parallel b \parallel$, the Arnoldi decomposition is obtained.

$$AV_k = V_{k+1}\bar{H}_k. \tag{4}$$

Since $V_{k+1} = [v_1, v_2, ..., v_k, v_{k+1}] \in \mathbb{R}^{n \times (k+1)}$ has an orthogonal matrix, Krylov subspace is

$$\mathbb{K}_{k+1}(A, b) = \text{span}\{b, Ab, ..., A^kb\}. \tag{5}$$

The Krylov subspace is assumed to be $k + 1$ dimension.

The matrix $\bar{H} \in \mathbb{R}^{(k+1) \times k}$ is an upper Hessenberg matrix. The decomposition of Eq. (3) is the most general basis for the implementation of the standard GMRES method. The QR decomposition is introduced.

$$\bar{H}_k = Q_{k+1}\bar{R}_k. \tag{6}$$

The matrix $Q_{k+1} \in \mathbb{R}^{(k+1) \times (k+1)}$ is an orthogonal upper Hessenberg matrix. Let $\bar{R}_k$ be the leading $k \times k$ upper triangular submatrix of the matrix $\bar{R}_k \in \mathbb{R}^{(k+1) \times k}$, and the last row of the matrix $\bar{R}_k$ is a $\mathbf{0}$–vector. The matrix $W_k \in \mathbb{R}^{m \times k}$ consists of the first k columns of $V_{k+1}Q_{k+1}$. By Eq. (4) and Eq. (6),

$$AV_k = W_k R_k, \tag{7}$$

where the range of W_k is $\mathbb{K}_k(A, Ab)$. Hence, the minimization problem min $\| Ax - b \|$ is expressed

$$
\begin{aligned}
\min_{y \in \mathbb{R}^k} \| AW_k y - b \| &= \min_{y \in \mathbb{R}^k} \| A(AV_k)R_k^{-1}y - b \| \\
&= \min_{y \in \mathbb{R}^k} \| AV_{k+1}\bar{H}_k R_k^{-1}y - b \| \\
&= \min_{y \in \mathbb{R}^k} \| V_{k+2}\bar{H}_{k+1}Q_{k+1}\bar{I}_k y - b \| \\
&= \min_{y \in \mathbb{R}^k} \| \bar{H}_{k+1}Q_{k+1}\bar{I}_k y - e_1 \| b \| \| . \tag{8}
\end{aligned}
$$

Here, $\bar{I}_k \in \mathbb{R}^{(k+1) \times k}$ consists of the first k columns of the $k + 1$ identity matrix and e_1 represents the first axis vector. The last equality follows from $V_{k+2}e_1 = b/ \| b \|$.

Since the matrices $\bar{H}_{k+1}$ and Q_{k+1} are upper Hessenberg matrices, the matrix

$$\tilde{H}_k = \bar{H}_{k+1}Q_{k+1}\bar{I} \in \mathbb{R}^{(k+2) \times k}, \tag{9}$$

vanishes below the sub-subdiagonal. Therefore, QR–decomposition can be computed in only $O(k^2)$ arithmetic floating–point operations.

$$\tilde{H}_k = Q'_{k+2}\tilde{R}'_k. \tag{10}$$

Here, $Q'_{k+2} \in \mathbb{R}^{(k+2) \times (k+2)}$ are orthogonal and $\tilde{R}'_k \in \mathbb{R}^{(k+2) \times k}$ is a leading $k \times k$ upper triangular submatrix whose the last two rows are $\mathbf{0}$–vectors. Hence, the minimization problem min $\| Ax - b \|$ expressed by Eq. (8) can be transformed into

$$
\begin{aligned}
\min_{y \in \mathbb{R}^k} \| AW_k y - b \| &= \min_{y \in \mathbb{R}^k} \| \bar{H}_{k+1}Q_{k+1}\bar{I}_k y - e_1 \| b \| \| \\
&= \min_{y \in \mathbb{R}^k} \| \tilde{H}_k y - e_1 \| b \| \| \\
&= \min_{y \in \mathbb{R}^k} \| Q'_{k+2}\tilde{R}'_k y - e_1 \| b \| \| \\
&= \min_{y \in \mathbb{R}^k} \| \tilde{R}'_k y - (Q'_{k+2})^\top e_1 \| b \| \| . \tag{11}
\end{aligned}
$$

The RRGMRES method stores the matrix V_{k+1} when computing iteration x_k. Therefore, as the number of iterations increases, the storage requirement also increases, and the computation per iteration also increases. Consequently, it is effective to restart the algorithm periodically. If A is a symmetric matrix, the matrix $\tilde{H}_k$ is a pentadiagonal matrix. Then, the above iterative method can be implemented in a short iterative formulation. The number of terms in the iteration formula is bounded independently of the number of iterations. Therefore, the computation and storage requirements of the method can be constrained independently of the number of iterations k.

The computational cost of the kth iteration in the RRGMRES method is shown by Table 1. Here, ℓ is the number of non-zero elements in each row of an n-dimensional sparse matrix. Gram–Schmidt method can compute in parallel. In the case of small iteration number k,

$$O(k^3) < O(nk)$$

However, when the number of iterations increases, it is necessary to speed up the computation since $O(k^3) > O(nk)$. The proposed method adopts the Cholesky decomposition [5], which is known to be a computation method that can maximize the performance of parallel computers.

5   High–Speed Method for Computing Condition Number of Upper Triangular Matrix

5.1   Concept

Let $\tilde{R}'_k$

$$\tilde{R}'_1 = \begin{bmatrix} \alpha_1 \end{bmatrix}, \tilde{R}'_2 = \begin{bmatrix} \tilde{R}'_1 & \beta_2 \\ 0 & \alpha_2 \end{bmatrix}, \cdots, \tilde{R}'_k = \begin{bmatrix} \tilde{R}'_{k-1} & \beta_k \\ 0 & \alpha_k \end{bmatrix},$$

be set to an upper triangular matrix. As the iterations proceed, the computational cost of the condition number computation becomes non–negligible.

An n–dimensional nonsingular matrix is decomposed as

$$A = \begin{pmatrix} X & Y \\ Z & W \end{pmatrix},$$

X: p–dimensional nonsingular matrix,

W: $n - p$–dimensional square matrix.

Table 1. Computational cost

Multiplication of sparse matrix and vectors	$O(n\ell)$
Gram–Schmidt method	$O(nk)$
Upper Hessenberg matrix $\bar{H}_{k+1} \to \tilde{R}'_k$	$O(k^2)$
The condition number in upper triangular matrix $\tilde{R}'_k$	$O(k^3)$

When $T = W - ZX^{-1}Y$ is nonsingular,

$$A^{-1} = \begin{pmatrix} X^{-1} + X^{-1}YT^{-1}ZX^{-1} & -X^{-1}YT^{-1} \\ -T^{-1}ZX^{-1} & T^{-1} \end{pmatrix}.$$

The matrix T is Schur's complement [6]. In the upper triangular matrix $\tilde{R}'_k$, $Z = 0$. Therefore, the inverse of an upper triangular matrix $\tilde{R}'_k$ that expands sequentially is given by

$$\tilde{R}'^{-1}_k = \begin{pmatrix} X^{-1} & -X^{-1}YW^{-1} \\ 0 & W^{-1} \end{pmatrix}$$

$$= \begin{pmatrix} \tilde{R}'^{-1}_{k-1} & -\tilde{R}'^{-1}_{k-1}\beta_k\alpha_k^{-1} \\ 0 & \alpha_k^{-1} \end{pmatrix}.$$

$\tilde{R}'^{-1}_{k-1}$ is computed in the previous iteration. Therefore, it can be computed fast.

n–dimensional matrices X and Y that expand sequentially are decomposed as follows:

$$X = \begin{pmatrix} X_{11} & X_{12} \\ X_{21} & X_{22} \end{pmatrix}, \quad Y = \begin{pmatrix} Y_{11} & Y_{12} \\ Y_{21} & Y_{22} \end{pmatrix},$$

where X_{11} and Y_{11} are p–dimensional square matrices, and X_{22} and Y_{22} are $n - p$–dimensional square matrices. In the multiplication XY can computed as follows:

$$XY = \begin{pmatrix} X_{11}Y_{11} + X_{12}Y_{21} & X_{11}Y_{12} + X_{12}Y_{22} \\ X_{21}Y_{11} + X_{22}Y_{21} & X_{21}Y_{12} + X_{22}Y_{22} \end{pmatrix}. \tag{12}$$

When $X_{11}Y_{11}$ have already be computed and $p = n-1$, Eq. (12) can be computed with high–speed.

To compute the condition number of the upper triangular matrix $\tilde{R}'_k$, the largest and smallest singular values are required. The smallest singular value can be obtained with high–speed and high–accuracy by the inverse iteration method. The largest singular value can be converted to the problem of computing the smallest singular value by using the inverse of the upper triangular matrix $\tilde{R}'_k$. However, the upper triangular matrix $\tilde{R}'_k$ in this study may have clusters of singular values around the largest singular value. Therefore, it is necessary to separate the largest singular values from the clusters. The procedure for this separation is described in Sect. 5.2.

5.2   Separation of the Largest Singular Value in a Cluster

As the iterations proceed, the smallest singular value becomes rapidly smaller and decreases exponentially. Therefore, in the singular value distribution on the inverse of the upper triangular matrix $\tilde{R}'_k$, the ratio of the smallest singular value to the 2nd smallest singular value is sufficiently large. However, the largest singular value of the original matrix, the 2nd largest singular value, and the singular values in the neighborhood are clustered, and the ratio of the largest singular value to the 2nd largest singular value is extremely close to 1. Hence, the largest singular values within a cluster need to be decomposed from the cluster.

Let μ_k be set a lower bound of the smallest singular value of $\left(\tilde{R}'_k\right)^{-1}$, which satisfies that $1/\mu_k$ is extremely close to the largest singular value of $\left(\tilde{R}'_k\right)$. An iteration proceed of the Cholesky LR method is given as

$$
F\left(\tilde{R}'_k\right)^{-1}\left(\tilde{R}'_k\right)^{-\top} F - \mu_k^2 I = LL^\top, \; F = \begin{bmatrix} 0 & & 1 \\ & \cdot^{\cdot^{\cdot}} & \\ 1 & & 0 \end{bmatrix}.
$$

The ratio of the largest singular value to the 2nd largest singular value in the lower triangular matrix L^{-1} satisfying the above equation is sufficiently large. The computational cost of $F\left(\tilde{R}'_k\right)^{-1}\left(\tilde{R}'_k\right)^{-\top} F - \mu_k^2 I$ is $O\left(k^2\right)$. To decompose L and $L^\top$, $O\left(k^3\right)$ is required.

When the lower bound of the smallest singular value of $\left(\tilde{R}'_k\right)^{-1}$ with high–accuracy is given, it is possible to separate it from the cluster using a single iteration of the Cholesky LR method. In practice, however, only the upper bound of the smallest singular value of $\left(\tilde{R}'_k\right)^{-1}$ with high–accuracy is determined. Therefore, we use the properties of the Cholesky LR method to create a lower bound from the upper bound of the smallest singular value. The details of this method are described in Sect. 5.3. Thus, it is possible to separate the largest singular value of the upper triangular matrix from the cluster using two iterations of the Cholesky LR method.

5.3   Shift Value of Cholesky LR Method

Let A be a positive–definite symmetric matrix:

$$
A = \begin{bmatrix} A_{11} & A_{12} & \cdots & A_{1n} \\ A_{21} & A_{22} & \cdots & A_{2n} \\ \vdots & \vdots & \vdots & \vdots \\ A_{n1} & A_{n2} & \cdots & A_{nn} \end{bmatrix}.
$$

A is decomposed into the lower triangular matrix L and its transposed matrix $L^\top$.

$$
A = LL^\top, \quad L = \begin{bmatrix} L_{11} & & & 0 \\ L_{21} & L_{22} & & \\ \vdots & \vdots & \ddots & \\ L_{n1} & L_{n2} & \cdots & L_{nn} \end{bmatrix}.
$$

A single iteration of the Cholesky LR method can compute as follows:

$$A = F \left(\tilde{R}'_k \right)^{-1} \left(\tilde{R}'_k \right)^{-\mathsf{T}} F - \mu^2 I.$$

More precisely,

$$L_{11} = \sqrt{A_{11}}, \quad L_{ii} = \sqrt{A_{ii} - \sum_{k=1}^{i-1} L_{ki}^2},$$

$$L_{ij} = \left(A_{ij} - \sum_{k=1}^{i-1} L_{ki}L_{kj} \right) / L_{ii}, \ (L_{1j} = A_{1k}/L_{11}).$$

If the underlined part is less than or equal to 0, then it fails. To avoid failure, automatic updating of the shift value is performed [5].

1. In the case that the underlined part is 0
   $\mu_k \leftarrow (1 - \varepsilon)\mu_k$, where ε is a machine epsilon.
2. In the case that the underlined part is negative number

$$\mu_k \leftarrow \sqrt{\mu_k^2 + \left(A_{ii} - \sum_{k=1}^{i-1} L_{ki}^2 \right)}$$

A shift value μ_k with high–accuracy must be satisfied following:

$$\mu_k < \sigma_{\min} \left(\tilde{R}'_k \right)^{-1} = \frac{1}{\sigma_{\max} \left(\tilde{R}'_k \right)}.$$

The denominator of the right–hand side equation means the largest singular value of $\tilde{R}'_k$. The upper triangular matrix $\tilde{R}'_k$ is satisfied following:

$$\sigma_{\max} \left(\tilde{R}'_{k-1} \right) \leq \sigma_{\max} \left(\tilde{R}'_k \right) \leq \sigma_{\max} \left(\tilde{R}'_{k+1} \right),$$

and the largest singular value increases with each iteration.

In the proposed method, μ_k is given as follows so that the Cholesky decomposition fails.

$$\mu_k = \frac{1}{\sigma_{\max} \left(\tilde{R}'_{k-1} \right)}.$$

The reason why we adopt this shift amount is that, in the RRGMRES method, the condition $\sigma_{\max} \left(\tilde{R}'_{k-1} \right) \approx \sigma_{\max} \left(\tilde{R}'_k \right)$ is satisfied as the iterations proceed. Failure of the Cholesky decomposition gives us a highly accurate lower bound of the smallest singular value of $\left(\tilde{R}'_k \right)^{-1}$

5.4   Inverse Iteration Method for Computation of the Smallest Singular Value

A high–speed computational method for the condition number of $\tilde{R}'_k$ in an upper triangular matrix employs the inverse iteration method.

The inverse iteration method is a power method for $C = A^{-1}$. Since the power method is a method to compute the eigenvalue of the largest absolute value of C, the inverse iteration method can be used to compute the eigenvalue of the smallest absolute value of A.

The singular values of the $k \times k$ matrix $\tilde{R}'_k$ are $\sigma_{\max} \geq \sigma_2 \cdots \geq \sigma_k$. The distribution of eigenvalues of $A = F \left(\tilde{R}'_k \right)^{-1} \left(\tilde{R}'_k \right)^{-\top} F - \mu_k^2 I$ is as follows:

$$\lambda(A) : \frac{1}{\sigma_{\max}{}^2} - \mu_k{}^2 \leq \frac{1}{\sigma_2{}^2} - \mu_k{}^2 \leq \cdots \leq \frac{1}{\sigma_k{}^2} - \mu_k{}^2$$

$$\lambda(A^{-1}) : \frac{1}{\frac{1}{\sigma_k{}^2} - \mu_k{}^2} \leq \frac{1}{\frac{1}{\sigma_2{}^2} - \mu_k{}^2} \leq \cdots \leq \frac{1}{\frac{1}{\sigma_{\max}{}^2} - \mu_k{}^2}.$$

The largest singular value $\sigma_{\max}$ of the upper triangular matrix $\tilde{R}'_k$, of which dimension size is $k \times k$, is computed below. The power method is performed for $C = A^{-1}$. Let Z be the largest absolute eigenvalue of C.

$$Z = \frac{1}{\frac{1}{\sigma_{\max}{}^2} - \mu_k{}^2}.$$

Z can be computed by using the 2 iterations in the Cholesky LR method and the inverse iteration method. By using Z, the largest singular value $\sigma_{\max}$ of $\tilde{R}'_k$ can be computed:

$$\sigma_{\max} = \frac{1}{\sqrt{\frac{1}{Z} + u_k{}^2}}.$$

Thus, in the power method for $C = A^{-1}$, when x is a vector, it is sufficient to compute $z = A^{-1}x$. Using L, since $A = LL^\top$,

$$z = L^{-\top} L^{-1} x. \tag{13}$$

Equation (13) is equivalent to the following equation.

$$\begin{cases} Ly = x \\ L^\top z = y \end{cases}. \tag{14}$$

Equation (14) can be regarded as a backward substitution in a linear equation. Therefore, since the computation for L^{-1} is not necessary, the computational cost is $O\left(k^2\right)$.

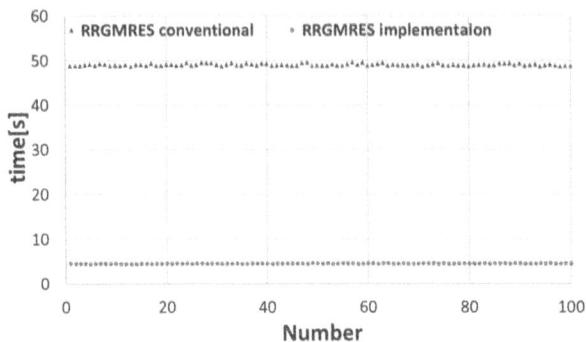

Fig. 1. Total Computation time.

6   Experiment

The experimental environment is shown by Table 2.

100 images of flowers (1000 × 563 pixels) are used in the experiment. The conventional method is used for comparison. The conventional method computes only the singular values using the dqds method. To adopt the dqds method, an upper triangular matrix is transformed into the bi–diagonal matrix using the Householder transformation. The QR method is well known as a method for computing singular values. However, the QR method computes all singular values and singular vectors simultaneously. Therefore, the dqds method is faster for computing singular values only.

Figure 1 shows a comparison of the total computation time for the condition number in the upper triangular matrix between the conventional method and the proposed one using the inverse iterative method. The horizontal axis represents the number of images, and the vertical axis indicates the total computation time of the condition number in the upper triangular matrix. By Fig. 1, the proposed method is more than 10 times faster than the conventional method. The two iterations of the Cholesky LR method have the same computational cost as the conventional method in terms of order. However, the coefficient of the computational cost is small, and the proposed method is compatible with the performance of modern computers. Therefore, it is useful to compute the condition number in the upper triangular matrix using the inverse iteration.

Table 2. Experimental Environment

CPU	Intel Core i3-6100 CPU @ 3.70GHz 2Core
Memory size	16 GB
OS	Rocky Linux 8.7
Compiler	Intel oneapi, FORTRAN
Library	Intel Math Kernel Library

7   Conclusion

The largest singular value of the upper triangular matrix $\tilde{R}'_k$ and its neighboring singular values constitutes a cluster. To separate the cluster, the Cholesky LR method is adopted 2 times. The upper triangular matrix $\tilde{R}'_k$ becomes larger computational cost in terms of the condition number when the number of iterations k is large. To solve the problem, we adopt the inverse iteration method.

By using the proposed method, we have confirmed that the computation is 10 times faster than the conventional method.

Acknowledgment. This work was supported by JST SPRING, Grant Number JPMJSP2115.

References

1. Neuman, A., Reichel, L., Sadok, H.: Algorithms for Range Restricted Iterative methods for linear discrete ill-posed problems. Numer. Algorithms **59**, 325–331 (2012)
2. Chiyonobu, M., et al.: Iterative censoring and highly efficient machine learning with condition number in LSMR method. In: IEEE CPS: 2023 Congress in Computer Science, Computer Engineering & Applied Computing (CSCE), pp. 2190–2197 (2024)
3. Saad, Y., Shultz, M.H.: GMRES: a generalized minimal residual algorithm for solving nonsymmetric linear systems. SIAM J. Sci. Stat. Comput. **7**(3), 856–869 (1986)
4. Arnordi, W.E.: The principle of minimized iterations in the solution of the matrix eigenvalue problem. Q. Appl. Math. **9**, 17–29 (1951)
5. Wilkinson, J.H.: The Algebraic Eigenvalue Problem. Oxford University Press, Oxford (1965)
6. Zhang, F.: The Schur Complement and Its Applications. Springer, Cham (2005). https://doi.org/10.1007/b105056. ISBN 0-387-24271-6

Implementation of the OQDS Method for Principal Component Analysis

Miho Chiyonobu[1]($\boxtimes$)(iD), Masami Takata[2], Kinji Kimura[3],
and Yoshimasa Nakamura[4]

[1] Graduate School of Humanities and Sciences, Nara Women's University, Nara,
Japan
chiyonobu-miho1611@ics.nara-wu.ac.jp
[2] Research Group of Information and Communication Technology for Life, Nara
Women's University, Nara, Japan
takata@ics.nara-wu.ac.jp
[3] Faculty of Engineering, University of Fukui, Fukui, Japan
kkimur@u-fukui.ac.jp
[4] Faculty of Data Science, Osaka Seikei University, Osaka, Japan
nakamura-yo@osaka-seikei.ac.jp

Abstract. In this paper, we propose a method for computing partial singular values and the corresponding singular vectors. PCA (Principal Component Analysis) requires only larger singular values and the corresponding singular vectors. Generally, it is obtained by combining the bisection method and the inverse iteration method. However, there are some input matrices, such as the glued Kimura matrix, for which the inverse iteration method fails. Therefore, the OQDS (Orthogonal QD with Shift) method is adopted in this paper. The OQDS method can compute smaller singular values and the corresponding right singular vectors from a bi-diagonal matrix with high accuracy, in the case that the matrix is not split during the decomposition. However, usually, split occurs. Under split, it is not clear which side of the split the smaller singular values fall on. Therefore, to adopt the OQDS method to the PCA, it is necessary to consider how to deal with split. Thus, in this paper, we propose a new implementation of the OQDS method that is not effected by split. Experiments have confirmed that the method is fast while maintaining reliability.

Keywords: Principal Component Analysis · Singular Value Decomposition · Orthogonal QD with Shift method

1 Introduction

Principal Component Analysis (PCA) [1] is useful in data science. By using the PCA, it is possible to reduce the dimensionality of a given matrix and process multivariate data. To adopt big–data analysis, PCA should be performed with high–speed. The PCA is essentially equivalent to the partial singular value

© The Author(s), under exclusive license to Springer Nature Switzerland AG 2025
H. R. Arabnia et al. (Eds.): CSCE 2024, CCIS 2256, pp. 318–331, 2025.
https://doi.org/10.1007/978-3-031-85638-9_24

decomposition. In the PCA using the statistical computing software R [2], singular value decomposition is performed by the upper bi–diagonal diagonalization and the QR method [3–7] for the upper bi–diagonal matrix. However, in the case of the QR method, all singular values and singular vectors are always computed. Therefore, when the dimension of the matrix is large, the computation time becomes enormous. Hence, for the PCA, a partial singular value decomposition should be adopted. As a partial singular value decomposition, the bisection method and the inverse iteration method [3] are combined. However, the inverse iteration method cannot achieve high accuracy for some matrices, such as the glued Kimura matrix [10]. Therefore, neither singular value decomposition method is appropriate for data analysis.

In this paper, we adopt the OQDS (Orthogonal QD with Shift) method [8] as a partial singular value decomposition. The OQDS method is as reliable as the QR method. The OQDS method is also able to compute singular values with high–accuracy and has high–orthogonality of the right singular vectors. In the OQDS method, splits occur to speed up the process. Split divides a given matrix into two parts. When split doesn't occur, the sorting function of the OQDS method guarantees that the smallest singular values can be obtained in order. However, when a split occurs, the sort function fails to work between the two split matrices. Therefore, we propose an implementation method to enable a partial singular value decomposition without losing the sorting function in the OQDS method. Numerical experiments are evaluated the implementation method in terms of computational speed, accuracy, and orthogonality of left and right singular vectors.

2 Principal Component Analysis

A given information is represented by the matrix $A = (a_{i,j}) \in \mathbb{R}^{m \times n}$. Each row represents one event. This section describes the PCA for the matrix A. By decomposing the matrix A into singular values and the corresponding right singular vectors, it is possible to cluster events according to differences in their features. The given matrix A is normalized. Prepare a matrix M and a matrix S that change the mean of matrix A to 0 and the variance to 1, respectively.

$$M = \begin{bmatrix} \frac{1}{m}(\sum_{i=1}^{m} a_{i,1}) & \cdots & \frac{1}{m}(\sum_{i=1}^{m} a_{i,n}) \\ \frac{1}{m}(\sum_{i=1}^{m} a_{i,1}) & \cdots & \frac{1}{m}(\sum_{i=1}^{m} a_{i,n}) \\ \vdots & \vdots & \vdots \\ \frac{1}{m}(\sum_{i=1}^{m} a_{i,1}) & \cdots & \frac{1}{m}(\sum_{i=1}^{m} a_{i,n}) \end{bmatrix}, \tag{1}$$

$$S = \text{diag.} \left[\frac{1}{\sqrt{\sum_{i=1}^{m}((A-M)_{i,1})^2}} \cdots \frac{1}{\sqrt{\sum_{i=1}^{m}((A-M)_{i,n})^2}} \right]. \tag{2}$$

The normalized matrix $C = (A - M)S$ is obtained. Then, the normalized matrix C is decomposed using a partial singular value decomposition for the PCA. In the PCA, only information on w major components, not all components, is required. In other words, only w larger singular values and the corresponding right singular vectors are required.

A singular value decomposition of C is described. The QR decomposition is performed on C to obtain the upper triangular matrix R. Then, the upper bi–diagonal matrix B is computed by using the Householder transformation [3,6]. By decomposing B, it is possible to obtain the singular value decomposition of C. Since the PCA requires a partial singular value decomposition, only partial singular value decomposition of the matrix B should be needed.

3   Partial Singular Value Decomposition in Larger Order Using the OQDS Method

The details of the OQDS method are described in Sect. 4.

3.1   Singular Value Computation

In the case that splits do not occur, the OQDS method can compute the smaller singular values. PCA requires the larger singular values. Therefore, a given matrix with the larger singular values must be transformed into one with the smaller singular values. The transformation procedure is as follows:

1. Preparation of F' for B.
2. Positive definitization of F'.
3. Modified Cholesky Decomposition.

In step 1), a $2n \times 2n$ symmetric tri–diagonal matrix F' is obtained for an $n \times n$ upper bi–diagonal matrix B. B is shown in Eq. (3).

$$B = \text{bidiag.} \begin{bmatrix} & \beta_1 & \cdots & \beta_{n-1} & \\ \alpha_1 & \cdots & & \cdots & \alpha_n \end{bmatrix}. \tag{3}$$

The eigenvalues and eigenvectors of F are corresponding to the singular values and the singular vectors of B.

$$F = \begin{bmatrix} 0 & \cdots & \cdots & 0 & \alpha_1 & \beta_1 & & O \\ \vdots & & & \vdots & & \ddots & \ddots & \\ \vdots & & & \vdots & & & \ddots & \beta_{n-1} \\ 0 & \cdots & \cdots & 0 & O & & & \alpha_n \\ \alpha_1 & & & O & 0 & \cdots\cdots & 0 \\ \beta_1 & \ddots & & & \vdots & & \vdots \\ & \ddots & \ddots & & \vdots & & \vdots \\ O & & \beta_{n-1} & \alpha_n & 0 & \cdots\cdots & 0 \end{bmatrix}. \tag{4}$$

F' is obtained by a symmetric substitution for F.

$$
F' =
\begin{bmatrix}
0 & \alpha_1 & & & & & & O \\
\alpha_1 & \ddots & \beta_1 & & & & & \\
& \beta_1 & \ddots & \ddots & & & & \\
& & \ddots & \ddots & \ddots & & & \\
& & & \ddots & \ddots & \ddots & & \\
& & & & \ddots & \ddots & \beta_{n-1} & \\
& & & & & \beta_{n-1} & \ddots & \alpha_n \\
O & & & & & & \alpha_n & 0
\end{bmatrix}.
\tag{5}
$$

The singular value $\sigma_1, \cdots, \sigma_n$ of B is the eigenvalue $\pm\sigma_1, \cdots, \pm\sigma_n$ of F'. The left and right singular vectors of B can be computed from the eigenvectors of F'.

In step 2), positive definitization of F' is performed. Let μ be the upper bound for the largest singular value of B. In the case of $\nu = \sqrt{\mu}$,

$$
\nu^2 I - F' =
\begin{bmatrix}
\nu^2 & -\alpha_1 & & & & O \\
-\alpha_1 & \ddots & -\beta_1 & & & \\
& -\beta_1 & \ddots & & \ddots & \\
& & \ddots & \ddots & -\beta_{n-1} & \\
& & & -\beta_{n-1} & \ddots & -\alpha_n \\
O & & & & -\alpha_n & \nu^2
\end{bmatrix},
\tag{6}
$$

is obtained. Here, α_i $(i = 1, \ldots, n)$ and β_i $(i = 1, \ldots, n-1)$ are real number. Since Eq. (6) is a positive definite symmetric matrix, Cholesky decomposition can performed. By using the Cholesky decomposition, the upper bi–diagonal matrix is obtained. The OQDS method can compute the right singular vector of a lower bi–diagonal matrix with high–orthogonality. Therefore, in step 3), from the Eq. (7), we can obtain the $2n \times 2n$ bi–diagonal matrix L.

$$
\nu^2 I - F' = (L)^\top L, \quad L =
\begin{bmatrix}
s_1 & & & \\
t_1 & s_2 & & \\
& \ddots & \ddots & \\
& & t_{2n-1} & s_{2n}
\end{bmatrix}.
\tag{7}
$$

Equation (7) is equivalent to the following recurrence formula:

$$s_{2n} = \nu$$
$$t_{2n-1} = -\frac{\alpha_n}{s_{2n}}$$
$$s_{2n-1} = \sqrt{\nu - t_{2n-1}}\sqrt{\nu + t_{2n-1}}$$
$$t_{2n-2} = -\frac{\beta_{n-1}}{s_{2n-1}}$$
$$s_{2n-2} = \sqrt{\nu - t_{2n-2}}\sqrt{\nu + t_{2n-2}}$$
$$t_{2n-3} = -\frac{\alpha_{n-1}}{s_{2n-2}}$$
$$s_{2n-3} = \sqrt{\nu - t_{2n-3}}\sqrt{\nu + t_{2n-3}}$$
$$t_{2n-4} = -\frac{\beta_{n-2}}{s_{2n-3}}$$
$$s_{2n-4} = \sqrt{\nu - t_{2n-4}}\sqrt{\nu + t_{2n-4}}$$
$$\vdots \qquad\qquad\qquad (8)$$

By $-\nu < t_k < \nu$, $k = 1, \ldots, 2n - 1$, t_k does not diverge to $\pm\infty$. Therefore, it can be satisfied to be a numerically stable recurrence formula. If the singular value of L is $\bar{\sigma}_1 \geq \bar{\sigma}_2 \geq \cdots \geq \bar{\sigma}_{2n-1} \geq \bar{\sigma}_{2n}$, then the singular value of B : $\sigma_1 \geq \sigma_2 \geq \cdots \geq \sigma_{n-1} \geq \sigma_n$ is $\sigma_i = (\nu - \bar{\sigma}_{2n+1-\ell})(\nu + \bar{\sigma}_{2n+1-\ell})$, $\ell = 1, \ldots, n$.

3.2   Singular Vector Computation

This section describes a singular vector computation. Let (ℓ) denote the ℓ component. Also, $\boldsymbol{u}$ and $\boldsymbol{v}$ are the left and right singular vectors of B, respectively. The relationship between the right singular vector X of L and the left and right singular vectors U, V of B is shown as follows:

$$B\boldsymbol{v}_i = \sigma_i \boldsymbol{u}_i \ (i = 1, \ldots, w), \quad B^\top \boldsymbol{u}_i = \sigma_i \boldsymbol{v}_i \ (i = 1, \ldots, w),$$
$$U := [\boldsymbol{u}_1, \cdots, \boldsymbol{u}_w] \in \mathbb{R}^{m \times w}, \quad V := [\boldsymbol{v}_1, \cdots, \boldsymbol{v}_w] \in \mathbb{R}^{n \times w},$$

$$X = \begin{bmatrix} \cdots & \boldsymbol{v}_w(1) & \cdots & \boldsymbol{v}_1(1) \\ \cdots & \boldsymbol{u}_w(1) & \cdots & \boldsymbol{u}_1(1) \\ \cdots & \boldsymbol{v}_w(2) & \cdots & \boldsymbol{v}_1(2) \\ \cdots & \boldsymbol{u}_w(2) & \cdots & \boldsymbol{u}_1(2) \\ \cdots & \vdots & \cdots & \vdots \\ \cdots & \boldsymbol{v}_w(n-1) & \cdots & \boldsymbol{v}_1(n-1) \\ \cdots & \boldsymbol{u}_w(n-1) & \cdots & \boldsymbol{u}_1(n-1) \\ \cdots & \boldsymbol{v}_w(n) & \cdots & \boldsymbol{v}_1(n) \\ \cdots & \boldsymbol{u}_w(n) & \cdots & \boldsymbol{u}_1(n) \end{bmatrix} \qquad (9)$$

The right singular vector of L contains elements of the left and right singular vectors of B. Thus, the left singular vector of L is not necessary.

4   The OQDS Method for Partial Singular Value Decomposition

The OQDS method can compute smaller singular values and the corresponding singular vectors, in the case of no split. The singular values can be computed with high–accuracy in the relative error, and the right singular vector has high–orthogonality. In the proposed implementation, smaller singular values and the corresponding singular vectors are computed, even when splits occur. Let $p = 2n$. In a $n \times n$ upper bi–diagonal matrix B, w smaller singular values and the corresponding singular vectors are computed. The computational cost when no splitting occurs is shown in Table 1.

Table 1. computational complexity.

Bisection method+Inverse iteration method	$O\left(w^2 n\right)$
proposal	$O\left(wn^2\right)$
QR method	$O\left(n^3\right)$

In the proposed implementation method, the dimensions of the matrix L is $p \times p$. Therefore, the computation space for computing the left and right singular vectors by using the right eigenvectors X of the matrix L is two times larger than that of the QR method. However, it is sufficiently faster than that of the QR method. Hence, it is not a weakness for the proposed implementation method to compute the partial singular value decomposition method.

4.1   Acceleration of Convergence

Let $\hat{L}^{(0)} \equiv L$ïïjĹSingular values of LïïjŽ$\bar{\sigma}_1 \geq \bar{\sigma}_2 \geq \cdots \geq \bar{\sigma}_{p-1} \geq \bar{\sigma}_p$ïïjĹ and $\hat{L}^{(i)}$ be the following:

$$\hat{L}^{(i)} = \begin{bmatrix} a_1^{(i)} & & & O \\ b_1^{(i)} & a_2^{(i)} & & \\ & \ddots & \ddots & \\ O & & b_{p-1}^{(i)} & a_p^{(i)} \end{bmatrix}. \tag{10}$$

Here, the shift $r^{(i)}$ can be set any real number satisfying $r^{(i)} \leq \bar{\sigma}_{\min}(\hat{L}^{(i)})$. The closer $r^{(i)}$ is to $\bar{\sigma}_{\min}(\hat{L}^{(i)})$, the faster the convergence is. Also, $\tilde{G}^{(i)}$ is the product of $2p \times 2p$ generalized Givens rotations, $\hat{G}^{(i)}$ is the product of $p \times p$ Givens rotations. To obtain the singular vector, repeat the operation of Eq. (11) with $\tilde{G}^{(i)}$ and $\hat{G}^{(i)}$ until L converges to a diagonal matrix, assuming $z^{(0)} = 0$, $z^{(i+1)} = \sqrt{\left(z^{(i)}\right)^2 + \left(r^{(i)}\right)^2}$.

(LU step) $\tilde{G}^{(i)} \begin{bmatrix} \hat{L}^{(i)} \\ z^{(i)}I \end{bmatrix} = \begin{bmatrix} \hat{B}^{(i)} \\ z^{(i)}I \end{bmatrix}$,

and   (UL step) $\begin{bmatrix} I & O \\ O & \left(\hat{G}^{(i)}\right)^{\top} \end{bmatrix} \begin{bmatrix} \hat{B}^{(i)} \\ z^{(i)}I \end{bmatrix} \hat{G}^{(i)} = \begin{bmatrix} \hat{L}^{(i+1)} \\ z^{(i)}I \end{bmatrix}$. $\quad$ (11)

Equation (11) can be rearranged as following:

$$\left(\hat{G}^{(i)}\right)^{\top} \left(\left(\hat{L}^{(i)}\right)^{\top} \hat{L}^{(i)} - \left(r^{(i)}\right)^2 I\right) \hat{G}^{(i)} = \left(\hat{L}^{(i+1)}\right)^{\top} \hat{L}^{(i+1)}. \quad (12)$$

In the case of $i \to \infty$, L converges as follows.

$$\hat{L}^{(i)} = D = \text{diag.} \left(\sqrt{\bar{\sigma}_1^2 - \sum_{\ell=0}^{i-1} \left(r^{(\ell)}\right)^2}, \cdots, \sqrt{\bar{\sigma}_p^2 - \sum_{\ell=0}^{i-1} \left(r^{(\ell)}\right)^2}\right). \quad (13)$$

By solving the above equations, the singular values can be obtained. The right singular vector can be computed as the product of $\hat{G}^{(i)}$.

To accelerate the convergence of the OQDS method, a lower bound in the smallest singular value is computed by using the Collatz's inequality [11]. A $p \times p$ lower bi–diagonal matrix L is

$$L = \text{bidiag.} \begin{bmatrix} \alpha_1 & \alpha_2 & \cdots & \alpha_p \\ \beta_1 & \cdots & \beta_{p-1} \end{bmatrix}.$$

The all elements in L are positive number. $\hat{L}$ is defined as following:

$$\hat{L} = \text{bidiag.} \begin{bmatrix} \alpha_1 & \alpha_2 & \cdots & \alpha_p \\ -\beta_1 & \cdots & -\beta_{p-1} \end{bmatrix},$$

Since all elements of $\left(\hat{L}\hat{L}^{\top}\right)^{-1}$ are positive number, the lower bound of $\lambda_{\min}\left(LL^{\top}\right)$ is obtained by the Collatz's inequality.

$$\min_{k} \frac{\boldsymbol{v}(k)}{\left(\left(\hat{L}\hat{L}^{\top}\right)^{-1} \boldsymbol{v}\right)(k)} \leq \lambda_{\min}\left(\hat{L}\hat{L}^{\top}\right) = \lambda_{\min}\left(LL^{\top}\right).$$

Here,

$$\boldsymbol{x} = \left(\hat{L}\hat{L}^{\top}\right)^{-1} (1, 1, \cdots, 1)^{\top}, \quad \boldsymbol{v} = \boldsymbol{x} / \max_{k} \boldsymbol{x}(k).$$

$\boldsymbol{v}$ is generated by the inverse iteration method. Since Collatz's theorem satisfies for irreducible nonnegative matrices, the lower bound for the smallest singular value can be obtained high–accuracy, even if the subdiagonal elements β_k $(k = 1, \ldots, p-1)$ of L is 0.

Algorithm 1. LU step in the case of a shift $r^{(i)} = 0$

1: Set $\rho_1^{(i)} = \alpha_1^{(i)}$
2: if $\rho_1^{(i)} \leq \sqrt{\varepsilon} z^{(i)}$ then
3:     Set $\rho_1^{(i)} = 0$
4: end if
5: for $k := 1, 2, \ldots, p - 1$ do
6:     Set $\gamma_k^{(i)} = \sqrt{\left(\rho_k^{(i)}\right)^2 + \left(\beta_k^{(i)}\right)^2}$
7:     if $\gamma_k^{(i)} = 0$ then
8:         Set $\zeta_k^{(i)} = 0, \rho_{k+1}^{(i)} = \alpha_{k+1}^{(i)}$
9:     else
10:         Set $\zeta_k^{(i)} = \left(\beta_k^{(i)}/\gamma_k^{(i)}\right) \alpha_{k+1}^{(i)}$
11:         Set $\rho_{k+1}^{(i)} = \left(\rho_k^{(i)}/\gamma_k^{(i)}\right) \alpha_{k+1}^{(i)}$
12:         if $\rho_{k+1}^{(i)} \leq \sqrt{\varepsilon} z^{(i)}$ then
13:             Set $\rho_{k+1}^{(i)} = 0$
14:         end if
15:     end if
16: end for
17: Set $\gamma_p^{(i)} = \rho_p^{(i)}$

The following techniques can not be adopted when the shift amount $r^{(i)} > 0$. Consequently, when a singular value that can be regarded as 0 in the middle of the iteration is found beforehand by a hypothetical iteration, then, positively, $r^{(i)} = 0$ is assumed. In [9], split is adopted. The LU step with the value $r^{(i)} = 0$ for shift under the condition that the subdiagonal elements of L is not 0 is shown in Algorithm 1. In the step of creating U from L, the elements of U are $\gamma_k^{(i)}$ and $\zeta_k^{(i)}$, respectively. In the case of split, the matrix is split into two separate matrices. If the upper block matrix contains the value of 0 which corresponds to the singular value, the value of 0 can not be moved to the lower block matrix. Therefore, it is not suitable for computing smaller singular values and the corresponding singular vectors in ascending order of $\bar{\sigma}_1 \geq \bar{\sigma}_2 \geq \cdots \geq \bar{\sigma}_{2p-1} \geq \bar{\sigma}_p$.

To overcome this difficulty, our proposal is to redefine the Givens rotation to realize the transfer of the value of 0 between blocks. The definition of the Givens rotation is shown in the following equation.

$$
\begin{bmatrix} I & & \\ & \begin{matrix} \cos\theta & \sin\theta \\ & I & \\ -\sin\theta & \cos\theta \end{matrix} & \\ & & I \end{bmatrix}
\begin{bmatrix} \vdots \\ x \\ \vdots \\ y \\ \vdots \end{bmatrix}
=
\begin{bmatrix} \vdots \\ \sqrt{x^2 + y^2} \\ \vdots \\ 0 \\ \vdots \end{bmatrix},
\quad
\begin{cases} \cos\theta = \dfrac{x}{\sqrt{x^2+y^2}} \\ \sin\theta = \dfrac{y}{\sqrt{x^2+y^2}} \end{cases}
\tag{14}
$$

Algorithm 2. Modified LU step in the case of a shift $r^{(i)} = 0$

1: Set $\rho_1^{(i)} = \alpha_1^{(i)}$
2: **if** $\rho_1^{(i)} \leq \sqrt{\varepsilon} z^{(i)}$ **then**
3:    Set $\rho_1^{(i)} = 0$
4: **end if**
5: **for** $k := 1, 2, \ldots, p - 1$ **do**
6:    Set $\gamma_k^{(i)} = \sqrt{\left(\rho_k^{(i)}\right)^2 + \left(\beta_k^{(i)}\right)^2}$
7:    **if** $\gamma_k^{(i)} = 0$ **then**
8:       Set $\zeta_k^{(i)} = \alpha_{k+1}^{(i)}, \rho_{k+1}^{(i)} = 0$
9:    **else**
10:       Set $\zeta_k^{(i)} = \left(\beta_k^{(i)}/\gamma_k^{(i)}\right)\alpha_{k+1}^{(i)}$
11:       Set $\rho_{k+1}^{(i)} = \left(\rho_k^{(i)}/\gamma_k^{(i)}\right)\alpha_{k+1}^{(i)}$
12:       **if** $\rho_{k+1}^{(i)} \leq \sqrt{\varepsilon} z^{(i)}$ **then**
13:          Set $\rho_{k+1}^{(i)} = 0$
14:       **end if**
15:    **end if**
16: **end for**
17: Set $\gamma_p^{(i)} = \rho_p^{(i)}$

In the case of $x = 0, y = 0$, the conventional definition assumes $\cos\theta = 1, \sin\theta = 0$. On the other hand, in our proposal, $\cos\theta = 0, \sin\theta = 1$. Therefore, the value of 0 can be moved between blocks. The modified LU step is shown in Algorithm 2.

The LU step with the value $r^{(i)} > 0$ for shift under the condition that the subdiagonal elements of L is not 0 is shown in Algorithm 3. In the case of $\alpha_1^{(i)} - r^{(i)} = 0$ or $\left(\rho_k^{(i)}/\gamma_k^{(i)}\right)\alpha_{k+1}^{(i)} - r^{(i)} = 0$ for k iteration in Algorithm 3, $k+1$ iteration is collapsed, since the element of the square root is negative.

Hence, $\alpha_1^{(i)} - r^{(i)} = 0$ or $\left(\rho_k^{(i)}/\gamma_k^{(i)}\right)\alpha_{k+1}^{(i)} - r^{(i)} = 0$ in Algorithm 3 is not acceptable. However, it is not possible to accelerate the computation by shifting the target to the smallest singular value that appears in the middle of the matrix when the recurrence formula moves from the upper left to the lower right of the matrix. Therefore, the following conditions are granted.

1. For $\beta_1^{(i)} = 0$, $\alpha_1^{(i)} - r^{(i)} = 0$ is acceptable.
2. If $\beta_{k+1}^{(i)} = 0$ for $k = 1, \ldots, p - 2$, $\left(\rho_k^{(i)}/\gamma_k^{(i)}\right)\alpha_{k+1}^{(i)} - r^{(i)} = 0$ is acceptable.

It possible to adopt the smallest singular value that exists in the middle of the matrix as the shift amount. With the above implementation method, each block matrix can be treated as a single matrix even when splits occur. The modified LU step with the value $r^{(i)} > 0$ is shown in Algorithm 4.

Algorithm 3. LU step in the case of a shift $r^{(i)} > 0$

Set $temp = \alpha_1^{(i)} - r^{(i)}$
if $temp > 0$ **then**
  Set $\rho_1^{(i)} = \sqrt{temp} \times \sqrt{\alpha_1^{(i)} + r^{(i)}}$
else
  Fail. In the next try, the value of $r^{(i)}$ is changed to a smaller value.
end if
for $k := 1, 2, \ldots, p-1$ **do**
  Set $\gamma_k^{(i)} = \sqrt{\left(\rho_k^{(i)}\right)^2 + \left(\beta_k^{(i)}\right)^2}$
  Set $\zeta_k^{(i)} = \left(\beta_k^{(i)}/\gamma_k^{(i)}\right) \alpha_{k+1}^{(i)}$
  Set $temp = \left(\rho_k^{(i)}/\gamma_k^{(i)}\right) \alpha_{k+1}^{(i)} - r^{(i)}$
  if $temp > 0$ **or** $(k = p-1$ **and** $temp = 0)$ **then**
    Set $\rho_{k+1}^{(i)} = \sqrt{temp} \times \sqrt{\left(\rho_k^{(i)}/\gamma_k^{(i)}\right) \alpha_{k+1}^{(i)} + r^{(i)}}$
  else
    Fail. In the next try, the value of $r^{(i)}$ is changed to a smaller value.
  end if
end for
Set $\gamma_p^{(i)} = \rho_p^{(i)}$

4.2 Guaranteed Smallest Singular Value

When one of the following two conditions described in Eq. (15) and Eq. (16) is satisfied, then it can be confirmed that the smallest singular value is in the lower right corner of L.

$$
\begin{cases}
\beta_{p-1}^{(i)} \le 100\varepsilon \times z^{(i)}, \\
\sqrt{\left(\alpha_p^{(i)}\right)^2 + \left(z^{(i)}\right)^2} = z^{(i)} \text{ is numerically valid.}
\end{cases}
\tag{15}
$$

$$
\begin{cases}
\beta_{p-1}^{(i)} \le 100\varepsilon \times z^{(i)}, \\
\alpha_p^{(i)} \le \text{the lower bound for the smallest singular value} \\
\text{of } p-1 \times p-1 \text{ the leading principal minor in } L
\end{cases}
\tag{16}
$$

Here, ε denotes a computer epsilon.

5 Numerical Experiment

To evaluate the computational speed and accuracy of the OQDS method adopting the proposed implementation method, we have numerical experiments. The input matrix is a bi-diagonal matrix B. The B is obtained by applying the Householder transformation to a square matrix with $[0, 1]$ uniform random elements. Adopting the proposed implementation, we evaluate the computational speed

---

Algorithm 4. Modified LU step in the case of a shift $r^{(i)} > 0$

Set $\beta_p^{(i)} = 0$

Set $temp = \alpha_1^{(i)} - r^{(i)}$

if $temp > 0$ **or** $\left(\beta_1^{(i)} = 0 \ \text{and} \ temp = 0 \right)$ **then**

$\quad$ Set $\rho_1^{(i)} = \sqrt{temp} \times \sqrt{\alpha_1^{(i)} + r^{(i)}}$

else

$\quad$ Fail. In the next try, the value of $r^{(i)}$ is changed to a smaller value.

end if

for $k := 1, 2, \ldots, p - 1$ **do**

$\quad$ Set $\gamma_k^{(i)} = \sqrt{\left(\rho_k^{(i)} \right)^2 + \left(\beta_k^{(i)} \right)^2}$

$\quad$ **if** $\gamma_k^{(i)} = 0$ **then**

$\quad\quad$ Set $\zeta_k^{(i)} = 0$, $\rho_{k+1}^{(i)} = \alpha_{k+1}^{(i)}$

$\quad$ **else**

$\quad\quad$ Set $\zeta_k^{(i)} = \left(\beta_k^{(i)} / \gamma_k^{(i)} \right) \alpha_{k+1}^{(i)}$

$\quad\quad$ Set $temp = \left(\rho_k^{(i)} / \gamma_k^{(i)} \right) \alpha_{k+1}^{(i)} - r^{(i)}$

$\quad\quad$ **if** $temp > 0 \quad$ **or** $\quad \left(\beta_{k+1}^{(i)} = 0 \ \text{and} \ temp = 0 \right)$ **then**

$\quad\quad\quad$ Set $\rho_{k+1}^{(i)} = \sqrt{temp} \times \sqrt{\left(\rho_k^{(i)} / \gamma_k^{(i)} \right) \alpha_{k+1}^{(i)} + r^{(i)}}$

$\quad\quad$ **else**

$\quad\quad\quad$ Fail. In the next try, the value of $r^{(i)}$ is changed to a smaller value.

$\quad\quad$ **end if**

$\quad$ **end if**

end for

Set $\gamma_p^{(i)} = \rho_p^{(i)}$

---

and accuracy of the OQDS method. The dimension of the matrix shall be the following five types: 10000×10000, 15000×15000, 20000×20000, 25000×25000, 30000×30000. The first five singular values of the input matrix are listed in Table 2. Because of the large dimension of the random matrices, the largest singular value is significantly larger than the other singular values. These matrices are the worst for our proposed implementation that convert problems, which are computed sequentially from larger singular values, to problems, which are computed sequentially from smaller singular values.

The evaluation criteria of the experiment are described. Let w be the number of singular values needed for PCA. Let $\sigma_i (i = 1, \ldots, w)$ be the singular value of B, $\Sigma_w = \text{diag.}(\sigma_1, \ldots, \sigma_w)$, U the left singular vector of B of $n \times w$, and V the right singular vector of $n \times w$. The evaluation is performed for the four perspectives shown next.

1. The computation time of the partial singular value decomposition
2. $\|BV - U\Sigma_w\|_F + \|B^\top U - V\Sigma_w\|_F$
3. $\|U^\top U - I\|_F$
4. $\|V^\top V - I\|_F$

Table 2. Input matrices(I)

Dimension	10000	15000	20000	25000	30000
largest	5000.13	7500.05	10000.30	12500.14	15000.27
second	57.71	70.66	81.60	91.19	99.96
third	57.59	70.58	81.55	91.11	99.82
forth	57.57	70.52	81.52	91.08	99.80
fifth	57.52	70.49	81.50	91.01	99.74

Table 3. Experimental environment.

CPU	Intel(R) Xeon(R) Silver 4116 CPU @ 2.10 GHz
OS	Rocky Linux 9.4
Compiler	Intel oneAPI
LIB	Intel Math Kernel Library
Number of cores	8
Memory	192 GB

The experimental environment is shown in Table 3. Table 4 shows the results for $w = 5$. From (1) in the Table 4, the proposed implementation method takes more time to compute than the combined the bisection method and the inverse iterative method. On the other hand, compared to the QR method, the proposed method is by far the fastest. This is consistent with Table 1.

In (2) of the Table 4 shows that in terms of the accuracy of the singular value decomposition, it is computed with almost same accuracy as the QR method. It is also comparable to the combination of the bisection and inverse iteration methods in accuracy.

From (3) and (4) in the Table 4, the orthogonality is inferior to the combination of the bisection and inverse iteration method. On the other hand, it is better than the QR method in term of the orthogonality. Based on the above, the proposed method in this study is one of the effective methods.

Table 4. Result of Experiments

Input size	QR method	Bisection method +Inverse iteration	OQDS method
(1) Computation time(m)			
10000	162.554	0.076	17.737
15000	470.091	0.082	49.943
20000	988.255	0.116	83.726
25000	1751.165	0.144	145.560
30000	2792.195	0.170	237.845
(2) $\|BV - U\Sigma_w\|_F + \|B^\top U - V\Sigma_w\|_F$			
10000	28.291E−12	2.025E−12	14.357E−12
15000	26.574E−12	1.927E−12	20.170E−12
20000	13.597E−12	1.033E−12	20.241E−12
25000	24.332E−12	7.442E−12	27.875E−12
30000	13.028E−12	3.889E−12	26.614E−12
(3) $\|U^\top U - I\|_F$			
10000	81.598E−15	1.063E−15	16.888E−15
15000	95.064E−15	0.859E−15	18.821E−15
20000	87,819E−15	0.416E−15	15.421E−15
25000	357.768E−15	1.512E−15	9.075E−15
30000	80.805E−15	0.927E−15	9.732E−15
(4) $\|V^\top V - I\|_F$			
10000	66.482E−15	0.926E−15	15.682E−15
15000	77.466E−15	1.203E−15	18.519E−15
20000	110.612E−15	0.953E−15	914.656E−15
25000	183.189E−15	1.288E−15	8.641E−15
30000	119.977E−15	0.267E−15	9.671E−15

6   Conclusion

In this paper, we have proposed a new implementation of the OQDS method only for some singular values and singular vectors can be computed. Numerical experiments confirm that the method is faster than the QR method and achieves the same accuracy as the QR method while also meeting the computational goals.

The numerical experiments in this paper were not parallelized. However, since the QR and the combination of the bisection and inverse iteration method are parallelized, parallelization of the proposed method should also be implemented for more precise numerical experiments.

Acknowledgment. This work was supported by JST SPRING, Grant Number JPMJSP2115.

References

1. Abdi, H., Williams, L.J.: Principal component analysis. Wiley Interdiscip. Rev. Comput. Stat. **2**(4), 433–459 (2010)
2. R Homepage. https://cran.r-project.org/. Accessed 25 Mar 2024
3. Demmel, J.: Applied Numerical Linear Algebra. SIAM, Philadelphia (1997)
4. Demmel, J., Kahan, W.: Accurate singular values of bidiagonal matrics. SIAM J. Sci. Sta. Comput **67**, 191–229 (1994)
5. Francis, J.G.F.: The QR transformation a unitary analogue to the LR transformation-part 1. Comput. J. **4**, 265–271 (1961)
6. Golub, G., Kahan, W.: Calculating the singular values and pseudo-inverse of a matrix. SIAM J. Numer. Anal. **2**, 205–224 (1965)
7. Golub, G., Reinsc, C.: Singular value decomposition and least squares solutions. Numer. Math. **14**, 403–420 (1970)
8. von Matt, U.: The orthogonal QD-algorithm. SIAM J. Sci. Comput. **18**, 1163–1186 (1997)
9. Hasegawa, H., Imamura, Y., Ymaada, S., et al.: Eigenvalue and Singular Value Calculations, The Japan Society for Computational Engineering and Science, p. 180 (2019). (in Japanese)
10. Konda, T., Nakamura, Y.: Introduction of double divide and Conquer and the recent progress. In: Proceeding of Algoritmy, pp. 459–466 (2009)
11. Collatz, L.: Einschliessungssatz fuer die charakteristischen Zahlen von Matrizen. Mathemathische Zeitschrift **48**, 221–226 (1942)

Author Index

© The Editor(s) (if applicable) and The Author(s), under exclusive license
to Springer Nature Switzerland AG 2025
H. R. Arabnia et al. (Eds.): CSCE 2024, CCIS 2256, pp. 333–334, 2025.
https://doi.org/10.1007/978-3-031-85638-9

The manufacturer's authorised representative in the EU is Springer
Nature Customer Service Centre GmbH, Europaplatz 3, 69115 Heidelberg,
Germany. If you have any concerns regarding our products, please
contact ProductSafety@springernature.com

Printed and bound by CPI Group (UK) Ltd, Croydon, CR0 4YY

24/04/2026

02096367-0012